RETHINKING HUMAN NATURE

Rethinking Human Nature

A Multidisciplinary Approach

Edited by

Malcolm Jeeves

WILLIAM B. EERDMANS PUBLISHING COMPANY
GRAND RAPIDS, MICHIGAN / CAMBRIDGE, U.K.

© 2011 William B. Eerdmans Publishing Company
All rights reserved

Published 2011 by
Wm. B. Eerdmans Publishing Co.
2140 Oak Industrial Drive N.E., Grand Rapids, Michigan 49505 /
P.O. Box 163, Cambridge CB3 9PU U.K.

Library of Congress Cataloging-in-Publication Data

Rethinking human nature: a multidisciplinary approach / edited
by Malcolm Jeeves.

    p.   cm.
ISBN 978-0-8028-6557-1 (pbk.: alk. paper)
1. Philosophical anthropology. 2. Human beings. 3. Theological anthropology —
Christianity.   I. Jeeves, Malcolm A., 1926-

BD450.R44465   2011
233′.5 — dc22

2010041035

www.eerdmans.com

Contents

CONTRIBUTORS — vii

Introduction — 1
  Malcolm Jeeves

History

How to Be Human: A Historical Approach — 11
  Felipe Fernández-Armesto

Human Persons and Human Brains:
A Historical Perspective within the Christian Tradition — 30
  Fernando Vidal

Philosophical Analyses

Science and the Search for a New Anthropology — 61
  Jürgen Mittelstrass

The Scientific Images and the Global Knowledge
of the Human Being — 70
  Evandro Agazzi

The Peculiarly Human Feature of the Aesthetic Experience:
The Teaching of Kant and the Challenge of Neuroscience — 82
  Franco Chiereghin

CONTENTS

Human Distinctiveness — Clues from Science

The Emergence of Human Distinctiveness:
The Genetic Story   107
Graeme Finlay

Evolution of *Homo sapiens*   149
R. J. Berry

The Emergence of Human Distinctiveness: The Story
from Neuropsychology and Evolutionary Psychology   176
Malcolm Jeeves

The Social Animal   206
David G. Myers

Archaeology and Paleoanthropology

What Is a Human? Archaeological Perspectives
on the Origins of Humanness   227
Alison S. Brooks

Theological Accounts of Human Distinctiveness: The Imago Dei

Humanity—Created, Restored, Transformed, Embodied   271
Joel Green

Imago Dei and Sexual Difference: Toward an Eschatological
Anthropology   295
Janet Martin Soskice

Afterword

On How Complementary Perspectives Produce
Enriched Portraits   309
Malcolm Jeeves

INDEX   328

Contributors

Evandro Agazzi is a Professor of Philosophy at the University of Genoa. His extensive contributions to his field have included studies in philosophy of science, the ethics of science and technology, logic, systems theory, philosophy of language, metaphysics, and philosophical anthropology. He was formerly chair of philosophical anthropology, philosophy of nature, and philosophy of science at the University of Fribourg. Dr. Agazzi is president of the International Academy of Philosophy of Science, has served as the president of the Italian Society of Logic and Philosophy of Science, the Italian Philosophical Society, and the Swiss Society of Logic and Philosophy of Science, and is honorary president of the International Federation of the Philosophical Societies and of the International Institute of Philosophy. Dr. Agazzi is the author of nineteen books, including *Philosophie, Science, Métaphysique* (1987) and *Right, Wrong and Science: The Ethical Dimensions of the Techno-Scientific Enterprise* (Rodopi, 2004).

R. J. Berry, an ecological geneticist, is Professor Emeritus of Genetics at University College London. He is a former president of the Linnean Society, the British Ecological Society, and the European Ecological Federation. He served on the Church of England's General Synod for twenty years and has been president of Christians in Science. His most recent book is *Islands,* published in HarperCollins's New Naturalist series (February 2009). He is the author of a number of books on religious issues, including *God's Book of Works: The Nature and Theology of Nature* (T. & T. Clark International, 2003), the published version of his 1997-88 Gifford Lectures at Glasgow University.

CONTRIBUTORS

Alison Brooks is a Professor of Anthropology at George Washington University and a research associate in anthropology at the Smithsonian Institution. She is widely known for research that supports her argument that the fundamental behavioral repertoire and underlying cognitive abilities characteristic of our species developed gradually in Africa much earlier than once believed. A fellow of the American Academy of Arts and Sciences, Dr. Brooks is former president and a former member of the board of managers of the Anthropological Society of Washington. She is the co-editor of two books: (with Ruth Landman, Linda Bennett, and Phyllis Chock) *Anthropological Careers, Perspectives, Employment and Training* (1981) and (with Eric Delson, Ian Tattersall, and John A. Van Couvering) *Encyclopedia of Human Evolution and Prehistory* (2nd Edition), which was published by Garland Press in 2000. She has written extensively on anthropology for secondary school teachers and students, including the textbook, *People, Places and Change*, which has been published in multiple editions.

Franco Chiereghin, Professor of Theoretical Philosophy at the University of Padua, has devoted his scholarly career to studies of the works of Plato, St. Augustine, Spinoza, and the philosophers associated with German Idealism, as well as the thought of the modern philosophers Friedrich Nietzsche and Martin Heidegger. He directed the translation of Hegel's *Encyclopedia of Philosophical Sciences* into Italian and is the author of eleven books, including *Possibilità e limiti dell'agire umano* (1990); *Il problema della libertà in Kant* (1991); *La "Fenomenologia dello spirito" di Hegel: Introduzione alla lettura* (1994), a work translated into Portuguese; *Dall'antropologia all'etica: All'origine della domanda sull'uomo* (1997); *Tempo e storia: Aristotele, Hegel, Heidegger* (2000); and *L'eco della caverna: Ricerche di filosofia della logica e della mente* (Il Poligrafo, 2004).

Felipe Fernández-Armesto is the Reynolds Professor of History at the University of Notre Dame and a Fellow of the Royal Historical Society, the Society of Antiquaries of London, and the Royal Society of Arts, as well as a Professorial Fellow of Queen Mary College and an associate Fellow of the University of London's Institute for the Study of the Americas. He has been editor or co-editor of fourteen books and two series, the co-author of two books, and the author of twenty others, which have been translated into twenty-five languages. Among the most recent are *Columbus* (1991), *Millennium: A History of the Last Thousand Years* (1995),

Religion (1998), *Truth: A History* (1999), *Civilizations* (2001), *Food: A History* (2001), *Ideas* (2003), *The Americas: A Hemispheric History* (2003), *Humankind: A Brief History* (2004), *Pathfinders: A Global History of Exploration* (2006), *The World: A History* (2006), and *Amerigo: The Man That Gave His Name to America*, published by Random House in 2007.

Graeme Finlay has worked as a cell biologist in the Auckland Cancer Society Research Centre for twenty-five years. Most of his studies were aimed at developing anti-cancer drugs that target DNA to suppress cancer growth. Since 2000, he has been Senior Lecturer in scientific pathology in the Department of Molecular Medicine and Pathology at the University of Auckland. His reading in the area of cancer genetics led to an interest in comparative primate genetics, which has demonstrated the fact of human evolution. Concerned at the widespread misunderstanding of the interaction between Christian theology and evolutionary science, he has sought to increase awareness of the fact of human evolution and the compatibility of these findings with Christian theology. He delivered the termly lecture in science and religion on *Human Genetics and the Image of God*, in the Faraday Institute at Cambridge University in 2006.

Joel B. Green is Professor of New Testament Interpretation and Associate Dean for the Center for Advanced Theological Studies at Fuller Theological Seminary. The author or editor of twenty-eight books, he has published a number of essays on the human person and edited two collections of essays — *What About the Soul? Neuroscience and Christian Anthropology* (2004) and (with Stuart L. Palmer) *In Search of the Soul: Four Views of the Mind-Body Problem* (2005). His most recent book, *Body, Soul, and Human Life: The Nature of Humanity in the Bible*, was published by Paternoster/Baker Academic in 2008.

Malcolm A. Jeeves is a past president of the Royal Society of Edinburgh, Scotland's National Academy of Science and Letters, and Professor Emeritus of Psychology at St. Andrews University. He is a fellow of the Academy of Medical Sciences and the British Psychological Society. For twenty-four years, he served as Foundation Professor of Psychology at St. Andrews and established the university's psychology department. His research has focused on brain mechanisms and neuroplasticity. He formerly taught at Leeds University and was Foundation Professor of

Psychology at Adelaide University in South Australia. He received South Australia's Abbie Medal in Anatomy and the Cairns Medal given by the Society of Neurologists and Neurosurgeons of South Australia. Dr. Jeeves was made a Commander of the British Empire in 1992 by Queen Elizabeth II. He is the author of more than 150 journal papers and book chapters on psychology and neuroscience and author or editor of twelve books, including six related to science and faith. Among his most recent are *Human Nature at the Millennium* (1997), (with R. J. Berry) *Science, Life and Christian Belief* (1998), *From Cells to Souls — and Beyond: Changing Portraits of Human Nature,* a volume of essays he edited for Wm. B. Eerdmans that was published in 2004, and (with Warren Brown) *Neuroscience, Psychology and Religion,* published by the Templeton Foundation Press in 2009.

Jürgen Mittelstrass is a Professor of Philosophy at the University of Konstanz, where he also directs the Center for the Philosophy of Science. He formerly taught at Erlangen University. The recipient of the Leibniz Prize of the German Research Society, the Lorenz Oken Medal of the Society of German Scientists and Physicians, and the Officer's Cross of the Order of Merit of the Federal Republic of Germany, he serves as chairman of the Austrian Science Council. Formerly president of the Academia Europaea and president of the German Philosophical Association, he is a founding member of the German-American Academic Council, as well as a member of the Berlin-Brandenburg Academy of Sciences, the German Academy of Sciences Leopoldina, and the Pontifical Academy of Sciences. The editor of a four-volume encyclopedia of science, he is the co-author of four books, and the author of nineteen others published in German. His *Mind, Brain, Behavior: The Mind-Body Problem and the Philosophy of Psychology* (Walter de Gruyter, 1989), co-authored with Martin Carrier, was published in English in 1991.

David G. Myers is a Hope College social psychologist. His scientific writings have appeared in three dozen periodicals, including *Science,* the *American Scientist,* and the *American Psychologist.* He is also a communicator of psychological science to students and the lay public, through essays and sixteen books, most recently, *A Friendly Letter to Skeptics and Atheists: Musings on Why God Is Good and Faith Isn't Evil* (Jossey-Bass/ Wiley, 2008).

Contributors

Janet Martin Soskice is Professor of Philosophical Theology at Cambridge University and a fellow of Jesus College. She formerly taught at Oxford University and at Heythrop College, London, and is a past president of the Catholic Theological Association of Great Britain and of the Society for the Study of Theology. She is the editor or co-editor of three books, including (with Grant Gillett and K. W. M. Fulford) *Medicine and Moral Reasoning* (1994) and (with Diana Lipton) *Feminism and Theology* (2003), as well as four special issues of *Concilium*. Her widely acclaimed *Metaphor and Religious Language* (1985) has been published in three subsequent paperback editions and translated into Japanese. Dr. Soskice's latest books are *The Kindness of God: Metaphor, Gender and Religious Language* (2007) and *The Sisters of Sinai: How Two Lady Adventurers Discovered the Hidden Gospels*, published by Chatto in London and Knopf in New York in 2009. A volume she edited (with William Stoeger, David Burrell, and Carlo Cogliati), *Creation and the God of Abraham*, was published in 2010 by Cambridge University Press.

Fernando Vidal is a senior research scholar at the Max Planck Institute for the History of Science in Berlin. He formerly taught at the University of Geneva and the University of New Hampshire. The recipient of a Guggenheim Fellowship and the Prix Latsis Universitaire of the Latsis International Foundation, he is the editor of an online edition of the early writings of Jean Piaget and two books on the Swiss philosopher and developmental theorist, *Piaget Before Piaget* (1994) and *Piaget Neuchâtelois* (1996). Other books include (with Lorraine Daston) *The Moral Authority of Nature* (2004) and *Les sciences de l'âme: XVIe-XVIIIe siècle* (2006).

Introduction

Malcolm Jeeves

It is almost thirty years since neuroscientist Nobel laureate David Hubel declared that "fundamental changes in our view of the human brain cannot but have profound effects on our view of ourselves and the world."[1] Around the same time, writing on human nature, Harvard sociobiologist Edward Wilson noted that "we have come to the crucial stage in the history of biology when religion itself is subject to the explanations of the natural sciences." He argued that "socio-biology can account for the very origin of mythology by the principle of natural selection acting on the genetically evolving material structure of the human brain." The implications of all this according to Wilson are that, "If this interpretation is correct, the final decisive edge enjoyed by scientific naturalism will come from its capacity to explain traditional religion, its chief competitor, as a wholly material phenomenon. Theology is not likely to survive as an independent intellectual discipline. But religion itself will endure for a long time as a vital force in society."[2]

This theme was taken up by high-profile science writer John Horgan in 2003, when he wrote about "what is arguably the major cultural question of our times: Can the humanistic and even religious view of human nature be reconciled with science?"[3] In 2004, Francis Crick had no doubt that "in the fullness of time educated people will

---

1. David H. Hubel, "The Brain," *Scientific American,* September 1979, pp. 45-53.

2. E. O. Wilson, *On Human Nature* (Cambridge, MA: Harvard University Press, 1978), p. 192.

3. John Horgan, "Modern Philosophy at Its Best," a review of Owen J. Flanagan's *The Problem of the Soul: Two Visions of Mind and How to Reconcile Them* (2002) for Amazon.com., July 24, 2002.

believe there is no soul independent of the body, and hence no life after death."⁴

Acknowledging the urgency of the issues raised by these and other scientists, a multidisciplinary working group met in the spring of 2006 at the Pontifical Academy of Sciences to discuss the question: "What is our real knowledge about the human being?" The symposium was sponsored by the John Templeton Foundation under the aegis of its Humble Approach Initiative and in partnership with the Academy. While the group assembled at the Vatican represented many different fields of inquiry, there were gaps to be filled if a balanced and well-rounded treatment of the topic of human nature was to be achieved. I have selected from among the presentations made there and added contributions from other scientists, as well as from a biblical scholar interested in the topic but not present at the Rome meeting. As one might expect from a group of specialists from diverse disciplines, there is a corresponding variation in the demands made on the nonspecialist reader in terms of familiarity with specialized knowledge and vocabulary. In one instance, the chapter by Graeme Finlay, we have provided Appendices to further clarify some of the technical details to which he refers in his essay.

The book begins with an essential Historical Perspective. In the opening chapter, Felipe Fernández-Armesto gives depth and breadth to what follows, warning of the dangers of knee-jerk reactions from the past. He also poses questions for philosophers, theologians, and biblical scholars, especially with respect to attempts to define human uniqueness. Similar questions arise for the scientists, and with a fresh urgency, such as the enduring puzzle of why, with the similarities between brain structures and genetic coding of humans and nonhuman primates, there are such massive differences between them in terms of their achievements in, for example, the realms of science, mathematics, art, music, literature, and religion. Fernando Vidal sets out the principal features of the relevant historical background and the context within the Christian tradition against which one must consider more recent views of person and brain. Bearing in mind the current very high profile being given to brain research in understanding the human per-

---

4. Francis Crick quoted in Margaret Wertheim, "Scientists at Work: Francis Crick and Christof Koch; After the Double Helix: Unraveling the Mysteries of the State of Being," *The New York Times*, April 13, 2004.

son, he helpfully reminds us that the notion of "brainhood" is not new, and he traces out its recent emergence into such a dominant position. He makes the important claim that study of the historical development of the anthropology of the "cerebral" subject and of the "cerebralization" of personhood likely resulted from seventeenth-century transformations in the philosophies of matter and of personal identity. He also emphasizes the key importance of the Resurrection, from the early centuries of Christianity to present-day speculations, and how it raises questions about human identity. As he puts it, "Resurrection discussions serve as a historical magnifying glass."

The second main section of the book provides essential philosophical analyses of some of the issues raised later. The three contributors to this section — Jürgen Mittelstrass, Evandro Agazzi, and Franco Chiereghin — alert the reader, with numerous examples, to the importance of maintaining what might be called "semantic hygiene." Mittelstrass reminds us that there have always been two different approaches to answering the question, What is man? — the scientific and the philosophical — and that both approaches are necessary in seeking a fuller understanding of the human condition. Agazzi takes up this theme and poses three basic questions: What is man? What is the world? What is the position of man in the world? In a key section, he emphasizes the need to remember the difference between "telling the truth and telling all the truth." Finally, in this section Chiereghin takes up a specific issue which he describes as "the peculiarly human feature of aesthetic experience," and in so doing, he immediately raises questions in readers' minds about how he knows that aesthetic experience is a peculiarly human feature. He builds extremely useful bridges with some of the contemporary neuroscientific work on brain mechanisms and aesthetic experiences.

The section headed "Human Distinctiveness — Clues from Science" includes contributions from Graeme Finlay, a cell biologist and geneticist; Sam Berry, an evolutionary biologist; my own chapter as a neuropsychologist; and David Myers, a social psychologist, writing on the importance of the social dimension to human life and distinctiveness.

Finlay's chapter helps the reader understand how our genes provide the substrate for all that we are. He opens up the question that was uppermost in the minds of some of those who sequenced the human genome of our closest relative, the chimpanzee: What makes humans unique? He is, however, no doctrinaire reductionist. He writes that while "the unique potential of the human brain must be specified by the human genome, ... the realization of the brain's potential is not genetically determined." It is not true that "genes make minds any more than the viola or a piccolo makes a sonata." Finlay reminds us of the need to distinguish between the use of words within science and the use of the same words, but with different meanings, in nonscientific contexts. Thus while scientists study the randomness of genetic processes, some see this as being totally incompatible with the idea of purpose. But chance events in the statistical sense of being probabilistic do not necessarily imply that the process is, therefore, the outcome of chance in the metaphysical sense of being unplanned. For example, even the exquisitely integrated system of cellular biochemistry arises from random molecular movements. Biological systems make use of randomness as a vital component of how they operate. Genetic mechanisms that operate during sexual reproduction represent institutionalized randomness. Randomness, in fact, is an aspect of design. Thus Finlay leaves us in no doubt but that our genes provide the substrate for what we are, and our environments, physical and social, determine the potential for what we may become.

It would, however, be all too easy to be so dazzled by the evidence from genetics when it is used to identify powerful markers of phylogenetic relationships, and of how they point to our links with primate ancestors who lived millions of years ago, that we forget that the idea that human beings share a common ancestor with other animals was around long before the advent of modern science. Sam Berry's chapter provides a succinct and illuminating account of the development of ideas about the possible links we have with other animals. The motivation of some of the distinguished scientists who fought against the idea of evolution gives a clue to the role of deeply held nonscientific views about human nature such as the status of the human soul.

My chapter focuses primarily on psychology's links with evolutionary biology and with neuroscience, since it is in these two areas that science most naturally raises questions about wider issues concerning human nature, questions such as whether and in what way humans may be cognitively unique as compared with their nonhuman primate cousins, and whether research underlining the intimate links between mind and brain call into question some revered and long-held views about the supposed separate existence of an immaterial and immortal soul attached in some way to the physical body. Evolutionary psychology refers to the study of the evolution of behavior and of the mind using principles of natural selection. The presumption is that natural selection has favored genes that underlay both behavioral tendencies and information-processing systems that solved problems faced by our ancestors, thus contributing to their survival and the spread of their genes. This naturally leads back to the philosophers who have long agonized over questions of what makes us human. Is there a difference in kind or merely a difference in degree between ourselves and other animals? It also affords an opportunity to reexamine some of the traditional views of what, from a theological standpoint, we mean when we say that we are made in the image of God.

Humans are not solitary animals. They live in groups — as emphasized in the current focus in much research in evolutionary and neuropsychology. While group processes in natural selection are noted in the article by Sam Berry, the theme is developed, underlined, and exemplified many times by David Myers in his chapter.

The next main section is on archaeology and paleoanthropology. Here Alison Brooks takes us back to a central theme of this book, namely, to find an answer to the question "What do we mean by human?" She reminds us that the discovery of hundreds of fossil human remains has enabled scientists to develop biological and morphological criteria for inclusion in the human lineage. In order to study the evolution of human behavior, we must turn to the fossil and archaeological records. By focusing on three particular expressions of behavioral capabilities — technological innovation, long-distance exchange, and symbolic behavior — Brooks traces out the beginnings of an answer to the question of when we became fully human. She believes that the appearance of humanness is a gradual process and not a sudden event, pointing out that "the more we know the harder it is to draw a line between human and nonhuman or prehuman."

The next main section gives theological accounts of human distinctiveness and of the imago dei. Joel Green, well informed about neuroscience as well as biblical and theological issues, underlines the congruence between the portraits of the human person emerging from evolutionary psychology and the neurosciences and the theological witness of Scripture. He makes clear his assumptions: that he doesn't look to fit theological claims into any gaps left by the natural sciences; that he does not regard theological statements as trumping or superseding statements made from science. At the same time, he recognizes that theological affirmations about the human person cannot ignore the findings of science. With these assumptions made clear, Green sets out the primary contours of a biblical anthropology. He deals specifically with the way that Scripture describes the creation of humanity "in the image of God," noting how the opening chapters of Genesis underline, on the one hand, the continuity of humanity with all other animals and the rest of creation, and, on the other hand, the difference between humanity and other animals. He discusses how the sense in which humanity is made in the image of God stands out in two key aspects.

Janet Soskice takes up the study of the imago dei by putting it under the microscope of trends in contemporary thinking and, in particular, the current focus on gender differences. Soskice makes the necessary distinction between Christian anthropology and secular anthropology. Having made clear her presuppositions, Soskice addresses the puzzling question of "What can it mean that God created man (*H'adam*, the Hebrew male collective) in his own image, male and female?" Noting that Genesis 1 suggests that sexual difference has something to tell us, not just about human beings, but about God in whose image they are made, male and female, she poses "the unresolved question — where, why, and how does sexual difference make a difference?" She asks the further important question: Does insisting that, "Christologically speaking, men and women cannot be different" mean that "sexual difference is then without theological importance?"

In a concluding chapter, I attempt to pull things together and identify the essential features of the emerging portraits of humankind. This must be read very much as a "work in progress," such is the speed of advance in the relevant sciences as they continue to reveal fascinating and illuminating new glimpses into our complex human nature. The ancient biblical texts, and the wisdom they embody, form a major contribution in this book. The book of God's word is reexamined in light of what we are discovering from the continuing study of the book of God's works. Exhaustive accounts of our complex humanity are emerging at different levels of investigation, from the micro to the macro. At the same time, we recognize that no single exhaustive account can claim to be the only and exclusive account. Thus the aim remains, as Evandro Agazzi urged us to remember, not only to "tell the truth" but to "tell all the truth." With our shared theistic presuppositions, we find that an awe-inspiring and complex set of portraits of humankind are offered by our various sciences, complemented by theological portraits, reminding us that we are indeed "fearfully and wonderfully made" (Ps. 139:14).

HISTORY

How to Be Human: A Historical Approach

Felipe Fernández-Armesto

My wife — I sometimes fear — thinks I am a beast. My students may stare at me as if I were an alien. Usually, however, my fellow-humans have little difficulty in recognizing me as one of themselves. I find it easy to return what, for the present, I take as a compliment.

However unalike we look, and however great the chasms of culture that separate us, humans form a community of recognition, from which no member of the species need be excluded. This experience of acceptance is now so common that it is hard to believe that in historic terms it is a rare and recent innovation. For most people, in most societies, for most of the past, the limits of humankind were narrow. Humans did not normally recognize each other as such; and the idea of a moral community coterminous with our species would have seemed unconvincing or even unintelligible. Typically, members of one human group acknowledged no kinship with others. They felt, indeed, closer to some nonhuman animals, with whom they shared their lives or mythic ancestries, than to fellow-humans from elsewhere. Most languages had no word for "human" apart from whatever term designated the group. The outsider would be called by some other name, usually roughly translatable as "beast" or "demon" or "monster." Monsters proliferate in lore and legend not because people are imaginative but rather the very opposite: a failure of imagination is responsible, for humans have generally found it hard to conceive of strangers in the same terms as themselves.[1] This is surprising, since one might

---

1. C. Lévi-Strauss, *The Elementary Structures of Kinship* (Boston: Beacon Press, 1969), p. 46; this does not of course mean that the stranger is necessarily unwelcome: on the

expect mutual recognition by creatures of a single species to be innate, crafted by evolution to facilitate the selection of mates and the identification of rivals. In humans' case, however, the evidence suggests that this is not so, or, if there is a human recognition-instinct, that culture has occluded it.

So how did we get our present, relatively generous and inclusive notion of humankind? How did our moral community become species-specific? And are the stories of how these outcomes happened really over, or could we take them further and include more beings in our definition of humankind? Further or alternatively, could we stretch our moral community to reincorporate nonhumans?

I propose to approach answers to these questions by sketching briefly the historic outline of two stories: first, of the expansion of our notion of humankind, and second, of the exclusion of nonhuman animals from our moral community. I shall then look at the progress and consequences of some current and recent scientific or scholarly developments, which, I believe, make it impossible to hold the present line around our moral community. These developments have occurred principally in five fields: genetics, robotics, human rights theory, paleoanthropology, and primatology. Other contributors, in the pages that follow, deal with the implications of genetics and paleoanthropology. I shall concentrate on the lessons of primatology, which are perhaps the most challenging and potentially subversive. Between them, the developments I have in mind raise or reinforce a major dilemma for moral philosophy — what we might call the Peter Singer dilemma: How, in the light of present knowledge, can we continue to justify a species-based moral community? I hope to end by suggesting a new solution, or at least a new response.

The story of the expansion of the notion of humankind can be summarized readily. It is hardly surprising that most human groups have been introspective, because inward-looking communities of recognition were characteristic of the long phase of cultural divergence that occupied most of history, from our ancestors' first migrations out of east Africa something like a hundred thousand years ago. Cultures isolated by mutual incomprehension were unlikely to develop inclusive

---

contrary, many cultures privilege strangers; for comprehensive bibliography, see F. Fernández-Armesto, "The Stranger-Effect in Early Modern Asia," *Itinerario* 24, no. 2 (2000): 80-103.

notions. But the dominant trend of global history for perhaps the last ten thousand years has been a form of reconvergence, in which, with increasing intensity, the peoples of the world have reestablished mutual contact. It is not surprising that humans' ability to enfold one another in mutual recognition has grown meanwhile and in consequence.

Documented first in the thought of Indian, Greek, Chinese, and southwest Asian sages of the first millennium BCE, the idea of a common human identity, transcending barriers of culture and differences of appearance, appealed to universalist empires and universalist religions and philosophies in the same period.[2] Familiarity can breed respect as well as contempt, and the growing range of cultural exchange helped to break down barriers to mutual recognition between formerly sundered peoples. Monsters, however, continued to lurk beyond the frontier of each successive encounter. A capacious category, between what was acknowledged as human and what was known to be beastly, was always available, to which to relegate embodiments of alterity. The elder Pliny's famous list, which influenced ethnographers and cartographers in Europe throughout the Middle Ages, shows how broad in his day was the category of the subhuman or parahuman or, as Pliny himself called them, "simulacra" of humankind. "Where people who live far beyond the sea are concerned," he argued reasonably,

> I have no doubt that some facts will appear monstrous and, indeed, incredible to many. For who could ever believe in the existence of black people, before he actually saw them? Indeed is there anything that does not seem marvellous, when first we hear about it? How many things are judged impossible, until they are judged to be facts?[3]

A long list of monsters followed these wise remarks, including the Arimaspi, each with one eye in his or her forehead; the Nasamones, all of whom were hermaphrodites; the creatures Megasthenes described, whose eight-toed feet were turned backward; the dog-headed Cynocephali; the single-footed Sciapods; the Troglodytes with "no necks and with eyes in their shoulders"; the hairy, barking Choromandae; the

---

2. For an outline, see F. Fernández-Armesto, *So You Think You're Human? A Brief History of the Concept of Humankind* (Oxford: Oxford University Press, 2004).

3. *Natural History*, VII.7:6, ed. L. Janus et al., vol. 2, ed. C. Mayhoff (Leipzig, 1885), p. 2 (punctuation modified).

mouthless Astomi who took nourishment by inhaling; tailed men; and men who could enfold themselves in their enormous ears. Pliny also endorsed belief in various races of giants and anthropophagi. "Nature," Pliny concluded, "in her ingenuity, has created all these marvels in the human race, with others of a similar nature, as so many amusements to herself, though they appear miraculous to us."

Tradition hallowed distortion. Medieval travel books were hardly complete without what readers, writers, and publishers called *mirabilia* — prodigies, monsters, enchantments, fabulous people and places, freaks of climate and topography. The *similitudines hominis* clung to the rungs of the ladder of creation in medieval Europe. Hairy wodehouses were among artists' favorite subjects.[4] In the printed version of Columbus's first report, the writer expressed surprise that he had found no monsters in his islands. Cannibal cynocephali illustrated early editions of the voyages of Vespucci. "Anthropophagi and men whose heads do grow beneath their shoulders" confronted Othello.

More than titillation was at stake. Monsters bore the deforming weight of ideological controversy. Some authors, influenced in the West by Christian universalism and in the East by Confucianism and Buddhism, doubted whether the chain of being really had any links in it between beasts and men. St. Augustine denied the existence of monstrosities: it is only, he argued, our warped perceptions of beauty that make us deny the perfection of beings unlike ourselves. Yet despite the skepticism of this revered authority, monsters clawed their way back into medieval geographies, ethnographies, and bestiaries. Their numbers actually grew from the twelfth century onward, partly as a result of the rediscovery of classical texts in which monsters were enumerated. You can still see them, streaming toward the embrace of Christ, in the tympanum of the monastery church of Vézelay. More than their existence, their meaning was at issue. According to a principle of late medieval psychology, laid down in the thirteenth century by Albertus Magnus, perfect reason could only dwell in a perfect body. So monstrosity was a sign of subhumanity.[5]

    4. R. Bernheimer, *Wild Men in the Middle Ages* (London: Cambridge University Press, 1970); T. Husband, *The Wild Man: Medieval Myth and Symbolism* (New York: Metropolitan Museum of Art, 1980).

    5. H. W. Janson, *Apes and Ape Lore in the Middle Ages and Renaissance* (London: Warburg Institute, 1952), pp. 94-99; M. Hodgen, *Early Anthropology in the Sixteenth and Seventeenth Centuries* (Princeton: Princeton University Press, 1971), pp. 154-246.

Each new encounter provoked predictable questions. Were the Mongols, the Canary Islanders, black people, Native Americans, "Hottentots," pygmies, and Australian aboriginals beasts or humans? These questions were all ultimately settled in favor of inclusive conclusions — sometimes by papal fiat but usually by the relentless accumulation of evidence. Gradually, the *similitudines hominis* vanished, as explorers searched for them in vain. Little by little, therefore, monsters have disappeared from categories of scientific classification.[6]

Nowadays, there are few communities left who persist in classifying themselves apart from other humans. Cases of people who withhold recognition from some of their neighbors — such as the Lembu of the Ituri region, who according to press reports justified their cannibalization of pygmies during recent troubles in Congo by explaining that pygmies were not humans — are mercifully rare.

It has been harder, however, to eliminate claims that people deemed meet for exploitation, servitude, or extermination are human, but not "fully" so. Ironically, but perhaps unsurprisingly, *Untermenschen* multiplied as monsters disappeared: subspecies incapable of evolutionary success, inferior "races," quasi-children, instances of phylogenetic arrest. These were common ways of characterizing black people, for example, in the nineteenth-century West.[7] A veritable anthropological industry was dedicated to classifying "negroes" as closer to gorillas than to true humans.[8] Even Darwin, though resolutely opposed to slavery, thought it a matter of indifference whether "races" were best regarded as "subspecies" or potential species.[9] The racists who dominated the Anthropological Society of London in Darwin's day rejected the theory of evolution because they wanted to confine blacks to a separate and inferior creation.[10]

6. Fernández-Armesto, *So You Think You're Human?* pp. 65-71.

7. H. E. Augstein, ed., *Race: The Origins of an Idea, 1760-1850* (St. Augustine's Press, 1996); M. Banton, *Racial Theories* (Cambridge: Cambridge University Press, 1987); N. L. Stepan, *The Idea of Race in Science* (London: Macmillan, 1982); C. Bolt, *Victorian Attitudes to Race* (London: Routledge & Kegan Paul, 1971); L. Kuper, ed., *Race, Science and Society* (London: Allen & Unwin, 1975); G. W. Stocking, ed., *Race, Culture and Evolution: Essays in the History of Anthropology* (New York: The Free Press, 1968); M. D. Biddiss, *Father of Racist Ideology: Social and Political Thought of Count Gobineau* (New York: Weybright & Talley, 1970).

8. C. Blanckaert, "Les Vicissitudes de l'angle faciale et les débuts de la craniométrie," *Revue de synthèse*, 4th s. (1987): 417-53.

9. *The Descent of Man* (1874), ch. 7, p. 929.

10. A. Desmond and J. Moore, *Darwin* (London: Michael Joseph, 1991), pp. 521, 535, 673.

Louis Agassiz devoted much time and effort to an attempt to prove that black and white people were of different species on the alleged grounds that miscegenation led to sterility.[11] A trend in criminology, meanwhile, claimed that crime was the result of "degeneracy" into a subcategory of diminished humanhood.[12]

In the long run, however, none of these beliefs withstood scientific scrutiny. Gradually, by describing a unified human species, science has compelled defenders of categories of imperfect humanhood to discard them, despite painful and sometimes bloody rearguard actions. At the same time, equality has become a universal shibboleth: no differences between people — according to the current consensus — are big enough to justify moral discrimination. That there are no degrees of humanness is, in the present state of knowledge, admissible as a fact: every human is equally human. Therefore, no scale of humankind, arrayed in presumed order of value or of approach to perfection, can justify the extermination or exploitation of some people by others. If, for the moment, we leave aside theoretical questions concerning whether extinct hominid species should be classed as human or nonhuman, or whether some of them are better assigned to an intermediate category — a sort of revival of the notion of the *similitudo hominis* or perhaps of the *Untermensch* — only two exceptions remain: there is no consensus on the status of the unborn and the vegetatively moribund. Such individuals can hardly be classified outside humankind — for to what other species could they possibly belong? — but some parties insist on classifying them as not fully human in the sense of lacking "personhood" or some other supposed qualification for admission to the human moral community.

Meanwhile, taxonomy has reflected the progress of the concept of humankind. We have a name — *Homo sapiens* — for the species to which humans, and only humans, belong. Lively philosophical and biological debate in recent years has left few thinkers who remain confident that the boundaries we draw between species correspond to "essential" differences, and loose language confuses the issue by sometimes extending the term "human" to other species that are classifiable in (or that

---

11. N. Stepan, *Picturing Tropical Nature* (Ithaca, NY: Cornell University Press, 2001), pp. 85-86.

12. D. Pick, *Faces of Degeneration: A European Disorder* (Oxford: Oxford University Press, 2001).

How to Be Human

are candidates for inclusion in) the same genus.[13] But we do now at least have a means of measuring whether a creature belongs to the species or not: we can define humans as falling within a certain range of DNA. This is not necessarily a good criterion for defining a moral community — any more than some other physical characteristic, such as pigmentation, or the length of one's nose, would be. At least, however, it serves to resolve any quibbles — such as those of which, say, Bushmen or pygmies were formerly victims — from ever arising again.

So, with some limitations, the story of what we might call the human frontier, where cultures interact, has been one of the progressive extension of people's power of mutual recognition. On the other hand, the story of what we might call the animal frontier, where humans confront other creatures, has been the opposite: a tale of progressive pruning of the moral community, from which nonhuman animals have, until now, been ever more aggressively excluded. I take it as beyond question that most societies, in the past, admitted nonhuman creatures on terms similar to those extended to humans. There are three main pieces of evidence: first, the ubiquity of totemism; second, the wide occurrence of zoomorphic deities; and third, the archaeological evidence of burial practices in which animals are honored. I think in particular of Europe's biggest Mesolithic graveyard, at Skateholm, where the hunters' dogs lie in graves of their own alongside those of their human companions, often with signs of honor equal to or greater than those of the humans.[14] This was a society that rewarded hunters in proportion to their prowess, not with preference for one species over another. Vestiges of the moral equivalence of different species were still discernible in Europe in the Middle Ages and early modern times. The cults of dogs as

---

13. E. Mayr, *Animal Species and Evolution* (Cambridge, MA: Harvard University Press, 1963); *Towards a New Philosophy of Biology: Observations of an Evolutionist* (Cambridge, MA: Belknap Press, 1988); D. Hull, "A Matter of Individuality," *Philosophy of Science* 45 (1978): 335-60; *Science as a Process: An Evolutionary Account of the Social and Conceptual Development of Science* (Chicago: University of Chicago Press, 1988); M. Ereshefsky, *The Poverty of the Linnaean Hierarchy: A Philosophical Study of Biological Taxonomy* (Cambridge: Cambridge University Press, 2001); for the opposing point of view, cf. R. Wilson, ed., *Species: New Interdisciplinary Studies* (Cambridge, MA: MIT Press, 1999).

14. L. Larsson, "Big Dog and Poor Man: Mortuary Practices in Mesolithic Societies in Southern Sweden," in T. B. Larsson and H. Lundmark, eds., *Approaches to Swedish Prehistory: A Spectrum of Problems and Perspectives in Contemporary Research* (Oxford: Oxford University Press, 1989), pp. 211-23.

saints showed this, as did the practice of putting animals, including rats and locusts, on trial for their imputed misdemeanors.

Yet, matching the emergence of an inclusive concept of humankind, an exclusive attitude to nonhuman creatures was formulated by sages of the first millennium BCE. Broadly speaking, in China, India, and southwest Asia, learned opinion coincided roughly with the notion familiar in the West from Aristotle's formulation. Humans are classifiable apart from other animals because of unique moral or mental qualities, which qualify them for privilege or responsibility — "lordship" in some formulations, "stewardship" in others — over the rest of the animal kingdom.[15] But this consensus was never firmly established. It begged too many questions about the precise nature of supposed human uniqueness, the consistency of the evidence for it, and the justifiability of the moral conclusions that ensued.[16] When, for example, a Daoist master of the third century CE enthused about heaven's partiality for humankind on the grounds that grain, fish, and flesh were available for people to eat, a disarmingly candid child remarked that one might as well say that heaven had favored wolves and tigers by providing them with men to eat. The suspicion that "man is not the only intelligent creature in the universe" and that "the human mind is the same as that of plants and trees, birds and beasts," kept recurring to Chinese thinkers.[17] Convictions that humans are special arise easily enough in human minds; they rarely prove robust in the face of searching comparisons between us and other animals.

The most instructive cases are those of the nonhuman creatures who most obviously resemble humans: the apes we call "great," and some other primates reminiscent of humans in body or behavior.[18] In cultures where they are familiar, these creatures have always been treated as kin: sometimes as humans in a state of arrested development, or as moral exemplars of the virtues of "natural" humanity, or as

---

15. Fernandez-Armesto, *So You Think You're Human?* pp. 44-48.
16. Fernandez-Armesto, *So You Think You're Human?* pp. 48-54.
17. J. Needham, *Science and Civilisation in China* (Cambridge: Cambridge University Press, 1956 — in progress), pp. ii, 17, 56, 374, 575; D. Boddie, *Chinese Thought, Society, and Science: The Intellectual and Social Background of Science and Technology in Pre-modern China* (Honolulu: University of Hawaii Press, 1991), pp. 310-27.
18. The subject is covered in Janson, *Apes and Ape Lore*; R. Corbey and B. Theunissen, eds., *Ape, Man, Apeman: Changing Views since 1600* (Leiden: Brill, 1993); Fernández-Armesto, *So You Think You're Human?* pp. 9-54.

superior beings separated from humans only by their closeness to divinity.[19] In what we now think of as the West, however, knowledge of nonhuman primates was exiguous until the seventeenth century. The "great" apes were virtually unknown — tentatively regarded, on the whole, as degenerate humans. When encounters began, apes were the subjects of the same question as — say — blacks and Native Americans: Were they human? In a typical equivocation, in the early years of the seventeenth century, Andrew Battel, author of the first eye-witness accounts of an encounter with chimpanzees in English, thought them "in all proportion like a man" but "with no more understanding than a beast."[20] Richard Jobson, a keen-eyed merchant in the Gambia a few years later, had no doubt that baboons were humans, whose ancestors had opted rationally for a "natural" way of life and who had lost all the refinements and vices of civilization.[21] In 1641 the famous physician, Nicolaes Tulp, whose anatomy lesson Rembrandt painted, likened what he called an "orang-outang" — an ape he observed in the menagerie of the Stadhouder in The Hague — to the satyrs of classical myth and the hairy homines silvestri or wodehouses of medieval legend.[22] He was clearly aware that *orangutan* (to use the spelling now generally favored) meant "man of the woods" in Malay.

In London in 1698 Edward Tyson resolved to settle the question of the ape's status by performing an anatomization, using a specimen recently arrived on a ship from Africa. He called it variously an "orang-outang" or "pygmy." From his description, however, it was neither, in terms we should use today, but rather a chimpanzee or bonobo. He found it to be seemingly "the nexus of the animal and the rational" — not human but not classifiable with mere brutes, either, and speculated that it might be the original of medieval *similitudines hominis*. Most readers, however, concluded that it was really a kind of human. An en-

---

19. P. J. Asquith, "Of Monkeys and Men: Cultural Views in Japan and the West," in Corbey and Theunissen, pp. 309-26; E. Ohnuki-Tierney, *The Monkey as Mirror: Symbolic Transformations in Japanese History and Ritual* (Princeton: Princeton University Press, 1987); R. van Gulick, *The Gibbon in China: An Essay in Chinese Animal Lore* (Leiden: Brill, 1967).

20. S. Purchas, *Hakluytus Posthumus or Purchas His Pilgrimes,* 4 vols. (London, 1625), pp. ii, 977.

21. S. P. Gamble and P. E. H. Hair, eds., *The Discovery of River Gambra by Richard Jobson* (London: The Hakluyt Society, 1999), p. 120.

22. *Observationes Medicae* (Amsterdam, 1641), pp. 274-79.

graving that accompanied the printed version of Tyson's results encouraged this view: it displayed the creature walking upright with the aid of a stick, which was a standard symbol of tool-use.[23] Breydenbach in the late fifteenth century had shown a baboon with a walking stick, and Sebastian Cabot in 1544 had depicted pygmies with the same object in order to demonstrate their humanity.

Eighteenth-century savants remained uncertain. Linnaeus compromised by classifying apes in the same genus as *Homo sapiens* but not in the same species, though he confessed in private to a secret wish to go further: "If I had called a man an ape, or an ape a man, I should have fallen under the ban of all churchmen. Perhaps as a naturalist I ought to have done so." Maupertuis assumed apes were humans and hoped for "some conversation with those philosophers." In Zaccaria Seriman's deliciously satirical travel fantasy of 1749, the hero fulfills that very wish, becoming a minister of the realm in the land of the apes.[24] Rousseau regarded what he called "gorillas" (but presumably, he really was thinking of orangutans) as the survivors of a presocial phase of human history.[25] Meanwhile, however, clerical prejudice and scientific skepticism alike worked to apes' disadvantage. The last and most notorious defender of their humanity was James Burnett, Lord Monboddo. His aim was political: to argue that the state was a contrivance, that men had no "instinct" to form states, and that Aristotle's claim that "man is by nature a social and political animal" was wrong. Monboddo believed that language was an essential prerequisite of polities; so he sought to prove that language was not natural (unlike the "inarticulate cries" he ascribed to early humans) but a product of what we should now call culture. The basis of his argument was philosophical: language is an idea and ideas are not instinctive, but derived from experience or inspiration. But to support his idea he scoured the world for speechless humans. The humanity of the language-less orangutan was part of his proof.[26] In work he began to publish in 1773, he argued

23. E. Tyson, *Orang-outang, sive Homo Silvestris, or, the Anatomy of a Pygmie* [1699], ed. A. Montagu (London: Dawsons of Pall Mall, 1966).

24. *Viajes de Enrique Wanton a las tierras incognitas australes y al país de los monos*, 4 vols. (Madrid, 1781-85).

25. *Discours sur l'origine et les fondements del'inégalité humaine* (1755); T. Ellingson, *The Myth of the Noble Savage* (Berkeley: University of California Press, 2001).

26. R. Wokler, "Enlightening Apes: Eighteenth-Century Speculation and Current Experiments on Linguistic Competence," in Corbey and Theunissen, pp. 87-100.

that orangutans used tools, recognized human music, and could be taught to play the flute.[27] In satirical tribute to Monboddo's views, Thomas Love Peacock — the funniest of England's many great comic novelists — wrote *Melincourt,* published in 1818. The hero is an orangutan. His name, "Sir Oran Haut-ton," plays on the conceit of the ape-as-flautist, while also hinting at the creature's potential politesse. Because Sir Oran had every rational faculty except speech, he acquired a reputation as "a profound but cautious thinker," which led to his election as a member of parliament and his elevation to a baronetcy.

Yet almost as soon as scientific belief in the continuity of ape and human kinds was severed and dispersed in ridicule, Darwin restored it. The orangutan again played a big part. Darwin read Monboddo and was probably influenced by him. Like much of the rest of London society in his day, he was enchanted with Jenny, the resident orangutan at London Zoo, and impressed with her resemblance to a human, especially when she was attired in the pretty dress she wore for presentation to Queen Victoria. Conversely, viewing the Fuegian he met on the voyage of the *Beagle,* "one can hardly," Darwin wrote, "make oneself believe they are fellow creatures." Whereas the elegant orangutan was humanlike, the "foul, snuffling" Fuegians, "who do not appear to boast of human reason," resembled beasts.[28] The fact Linnaeus acknowledged in private but suppressed in public was irresistible: humans were apes.

Darwin's insistence on the closeness, in evolutionary terms, of the descent of humans and apes was not, perhaps, the most important or even the most original of his insights. But it certainly had an impact. The huge weight of the data he assembled in *The Descent of Man* helped to focus attention on apes as exemplars, from whom we can learn about ourselves, and prompted a revolution in human self-perceptions. One way of measuring the extent of this revolution is in art, which is always the mirror of science. In the eighteenth century, painters of singeries exploited the amusement-value of apes who aped humans. Teniers, Watteau, Chardin, and Goya could decorate walls with self-mocking depictions of apes as artists, without seriously undermining

---

27. A. Barnard, "Monboddo's Orang Outang and the Definition of Man," in Corbey and Theunissen, pp. 71-86.

28. C. R. Darwin, *Voyage of the Beagle* (New York: New American Library, 1972), pp. 183-86; *Works,* vol. 1, ed. N. Barlow (New York: W. W. Norton, 1986), pp. 109-10.

convictions of human superiority. There are still painters of singeries today. One of the most accomplished is Rose-Marie Trockel, whose portraits of pensive apes — extruding crude or kitsch aesthetic ideas, dreaming human dreams, practicing baffled self-awareness — are provocative satires on human imperfections, in which we seem to see ourselves portrayed.[29] For us, these images are more searching and more self-revelatory than their eighteenth-century precursors, because we know that we are apes. And our own dreams of self-elevation above other apes seem to be going awry.

In the last thirty or forty years, primatology has been an astonishingly revealing science, revising informed views of human nature.[30] Anyone old enough to remember chimpanzees' tea parties can document the outlines of the change from his or her own experience. These occasions, in which chimps reduced tea-tables to chaos with slapstick abandon, to the delight of paying onlookers, were a daily form of entertainment in zoos around the world in the 1950s. They no longer happen, because they would affront the dignity of chimpanzees.

The chimps' tea party was funny — or so humans thought then — because we were convinced of our own uniqueness. Only humans, we supposed, had culture; therefore chimps could not understand or participate in our food-rites and table-manners. Their antics at tea were mistaken for proof of our superiority. Now the joke is on us, because primatologists have proved by hundreds of instances that chimps do have culture: indeed, many nonhuman species live in societies differentiated from one another not by adaptations to different environments, but by collective practices learned and transmitted across the generations; not by mere behavior but by socially developed conduct. Chimp cultures actually include food-distribution rites, just as ours include tea parties.

---

29. E. Friis et al., eds., *100 Masterpieces: Statens Museum for Kunst* (Copenhagen, 1997), pp. 220-21.

30. As well as those cited in other notes, excellent general accounts, which enable readers to follow changes in human perceptions and evaluations of apes and other primates, are A. Desmond, *The Ape's Reflection* (New York: The Dial Press, 1979); J. Goodall and D. Peterson, *Visions of Caliban: On Chimpanzees and People* (Boston: Houghton Mifflin, 1993); A. Kuper, *The Chosen Primate: Human Nature and Cultural Diversity* (Cambridge, MA: Harvard University Press, 1994); F. de Waal, *The Ape and the Sushi Master: Cultural Reflections of a Primatologist* (New York: Basic Books, 2001); R. C. Corbey, *The Metaphysics of Apes: Negotiating the Animal-Human Boundary* (Cambridge: Cambridge University Press, 2005).

Nor is it just in possessing culture that apes resemble humans: the forms and features of their cultures are also like ours. Chimps and bonobos, for instance, practice politics (including subterfuge and deception),[31] play games, and make war and peace.[32] They develop rituals (including those associated with friendship and courtship) and have been observed apparently responding to rain, or the imminence of rain, by joining in rhythmic stamping. If observed by an anthropologist among some remote people, this so-called "rain dance" would surely be classed as a ritual, associated with a sense of transcendence, and labeled as "religion."[33] Even orangutans, who were formerly thought to be the least social of great apes because of their solitary tastes, evince cultural divergence.[34] Baboons, as well as great apes, have varieties of cultural practice, especially in connection with mating, that defy environmental or behaviorist explanations.[35]

Everything formerly thought uniquely human turns out to be shared — at least, in small measure — with other apes. Tool use and manufacture were among the first criteria of humanhood that had to be modified in the light of primatological research, when Jane Goodall and many successors accumulated a wide range of instances.[36] Louis

---

31. F. de Waal, *Chimpanzee Politics: Power and Sex among Apes* (Baltimore: Johns Hopkins University Press, 1982).

32. F. de Waal, *Peacemaking among Primates* (Cambridge, MA: Harvard University Press, 1989); *Good Natured: The Origins of Right and Wrong in Humans and Other Animals* (Cambridge, MA: Harvard University Press, 1996).

33. W. C. McGrew, *Chimpanzee Material Culture: Implications for Human Evolution* (Cambridge: Cambridge University Press, 1992); R. W. Wrangham et al., *Chimpanzee Cultures* (Cambridge, MA: Harvard University Press, 1994); A. Whiten et al., "Cultures in Chimpanzees," *Nature* 399 (1999): 682-85.

34. C. P. Van Schaick et al., "Orangutan Cultures and the Evolution of Material Culture," *Science* 299 (2003): 102-5.

35. H. Kummer, R. Sapolski, and S. C. Strum, *Almost Human: A Journey into the World of Baboons* (New York: Random House, 1987).

36. J. Goodall, *The Chimpanzees of Gombe: Patterns of Behavior* (Cambridge, MA: Belknap Press, 1986); N. Toth et al., "Pan the Tool-Maker: Investigations into the Stone Tool-Making and Tool-Using Capabilities of a Bonobo (Pan Paniscus)," *Journal of Archaeological Sciences* 20 (1993): 81-91; K. D. Schick et al., "Continuing Investigations into the Stone Tool-Making and Tool-Using Capabilities of a Bonobo (Pan Paniscus)," *Journal of Archaeological Sciences* 26 (1993): 821-32; C. Boesch et al., "Is Nut-Cracking in Wild Chimpanzees a Cultural Behaviour?" *Journal of Human Evolution* 26 (1994): 325-28; F. Joulian, "Le Casse-noix du chimpanzé: lectures anthropologiques d'un objet simien," in A. and J. Cros and F. Joulian, eds., *La Nature est-elle naturelle? Histoire, épistémologie et applications*

Leakey exaggerated only a little when he responded, "Now we must redefine tool, or redefine man, or accept chimpanzees as human."[37] Ape responses to mirror-images demonstrated self-awareness.[38] The language abilities chimpanzees and bonobos display include the ability to coin words and to apply rudimentary syntax in the sense of appreciating the difference between subject and predicate. Apes skilled in human language use it to communicate with each other and can teach terms to each other and to human pupils.[39] The repertoire of emotions seems identical in all great apes, including humans. It is possible to argue that apes have art, not only because they imitate human arts, especially painting (albeit with inscrutable intentions),[40] but also because they sometimes adorn themselves: Frans de Waal has recorded observations of female chimpanzees wearing dead rats or cockroaches as headgear with all the apparent self-consciousness of a lady in an Ascot hat.

Of course, none of these findings undermine the validity of distinguishing humans from apes: they mean, however, that the distinction is narrower and less readily labeled "essential" or "fundamental" than was formerly thought. In respect of every similarity that can be enumerated, enormous differences remain: but they are differences of degree, not necessarily of quality. Humans remain unique, but their uniqueness no longer appears to be itself of a unique kind, for every species is unique in its own ways. Many biologists now classify humans

---

récentes du concept de culture (Paris, 1998), pp. 115-37; R. W. Byrne, "Social and Technical Forms of Primate Intelligence," in F. de Waal, ed., *Tree of Origin: What Primate Behavior Can Tell Us About Human Social Evolution* (Cambridge, MA: Harvard University Press, 2001); J. Call and N. Mulcahy in *Science,* May 19, 2006.

37. J. Goodall, "Learning from the Chimpanzees: A Message Humans Can Understand," *Science* 282 (December 18, 1998): 2184-85.

38. G. G. Gallup, "A Mirror for the Mind of Man, or Will the Chimpanzee Create an Identity Crisis for Homo Sapiens?" *Journal of Human Evolution* 6 (1997): 301-13; A. Kitchen, D. Denton, and L. Brent, "Self-recognition and Abstraction Abilities in the Common Chimpanzee Studied with Distorting Mirrors," *Proceedings of the National Academy of Sciences* 93 (1996): 7405-8.

39. S. Savage-Rumbaugh, S. G. Shanker, and T. J. Taylor, *Apes, Language and the Human Mind* (New York: Oxford University Press, 1998); B. J. King, *The Information Continuum: Evolution of Social Information Transfer in Monkeys, Apes and Hominids* (Santa Fe: SAR Press, 1994); K. R. Gibson and T. Ingold, eds., *Tools, Language and Cognition in Human Evolution* (Cambridge: Cambridge University Press, 1993).

40. D. Morris, *The Biology of Art: A Study in the Picture-Making of the Great Apes and Its Relationship to Human Art* (London: Methuen, 1962).

and apes in the same genus — though divided over whether humans should be regarded as pongids or apes as hominids.[41]

The challenges of primatology are similar to those of other sciences. Genetics makes possible, in theory, the engineering of creatures such as Dr. Moreau dreamed of: hybrids with human and nonhuman DNA. At what point would the balance tilt and make such a creature human? Robotics — allowing for all the problems of mind-brain dualism explored elsewhere in this volume — if the agenda of artificial intelligence research were ever fulfilled, would produce machines genuinely indistinguishable, in intellect and emotions, from a human interlocutor: in practice, therefore, humans would treat such a machine as human. Above all, paleoanthropology, as is clear from other contributions to this book, has confronted us with evidence that *Homo sapiens* has been matched in the fossil record by many other species with similar tool-kits, cultures, imaginations, sensibilities, and emotional lives.[42] If we are willing to admit that a Neanderthal or *Homo floresiensis* is human, and that we should wish to extend human rights to such a creature if one were still alive today, we are not committing ourselves to a practical course of action, since these species are extinct. But we are making a potentially revolutionary admission: we are envisaging ourselves as part of a moral community open to more than one species.

To judge from the huge sympathy — a kind of romantic, collective nostalgia — the public in the West today evinces for hominid remains, it is inevitable that humankind will be defined in the future as including many hominid and hominin species. Some of these do not even form part of the line of descent of *Homo sapiens*. Neanderthals are a case in point. Modern museum reconstructions contrast vividly with the low-browed, prognathous, and violent-looking individuals typical of

---

41. J. Diamond, *The Third Chimpanzee: The Evolution and Future of the Human Animal* (New York: Harper Perennial, 1992); M. Goodman et al., "Toward a Phylogenetic Classification of Primates Based on DNA Evidence Complemented by Fossil Evidence," *Molecular Phylogenetics and Evolution* 9 (1998): 585-98; E. E. Watson, S. Eastael, and D. Penny, "Homo Genus: A Review of the Classification of Humans and the Great Apes," in P. V. Tobias et al., eds., *Humanity from African Naissance to Coming Millennia: Colloquia in Human Biology and Palaeoanthropology* (Florence: Firenze University Press, 2001), pp. 317-28; D. E. Wildman et al., "Implications of Natural Selection in Shaping 99.4% Nonsynonymous DNA Identity between Humans and Chimpanzees: Enlarging Genus Homo," *Proceedings of the National Academy of Sciences* 100 (2003): 7181-88.

42. M. Cartmill, "Human Uniqueness and Theoretical Content in Paleoanthropology," *International Journal of Primatology* 11 (1990): 173-91.

older displays. Today's waxworks Neanderthals look like us, reflecting the lengthening record of archaeological finds that establish admirable features, including ritual life, concern for the afterlife, and care of the sick and elderly, as Neanderthal traits or practices. *Homo floresiensis* is an even more startling case — classified in the genus *Homo*, with little learned opposition, on the strength of a humanlike tool-kit — despite dwarfish dimensions and a brain smaller than a chimpanzee's. Perhaps because of these singularities, the public took *floresiensis*, whom the press dubbed a "hobbit," to heart. Both Neanderthals and *floresiensis* are recent specimens, the former extinct only some 40,000 years ago, the latter surviving perhaps as recently as 13,000 years ago, but people generally seem increasingly willing to extend the limits of humankind ever farther back into the past. The dwellers in the cave of Atapuerca, whose cave mouth was sealed three hundred thousand years ago, have evoked much fellow-feeling, thanks in part to José Luis Arsuaga's moving books about them.[43] One of the most extraordinary publicity phenomena of modern times has been the success of the three-million-year-old east-African biped known as "Lucy." She resembled humans too little even to be classed as part of the genus *Homo*, yet public identification with her is profound, dramatically witnessed by a recent BBC television program about her, which climaxed in a scene of the presenter, Lord Winston, carrying her body reverently for reburial with human honors.

Of course we might dismiss, as academic or even semantic, the question of where the limits of humankind should be set, were it not for human rights. The development of human rights theory in recent times makes urgent the question of who is and who is not entitled to such rights. It is literally a matter of life and death, since the right to life is the basis of all others. If human rights are genuinely human and genuinely rights, then all humans must have them, whereas non-humans have no automatic entitlement to them. Human rights therefore make our moral community explicitly species-specific and proof (though not absolutely so) against intrusions from other species. Yet ironically, in the very period of the ascent of human rights to almost universal status in the laws of the world, paleoanthropology, primatology, genetics, and robotics have combined to make the coher-

---

43. *El collar del neanderthal* (1999); *El enigma del esfinge* (2001); *El mundo de Atapuerca* (2004).

ence of the concept of human rights questionable and to suggest that our moral community may be permeable by other creatures, or (theoretically) by formerly extant creatures now extinct, or even by hybrids or machines.

The evidence is accumulating that more and more governments, and the people they represent, are in revulsion from the notion of a species-specific moral community. In particular, the conviction that humans share a moral community with other great apes and, indeed, other primates is growing day by day. New Zealand, Britain, Spain, and Norway are now among nations that have encoded ape rights, as well as more extensive human rights, in their legislation. Peter Singer's argument that sentient apes are more deserving of respect than vegetative humans for their lives and the integrity of their persons is hard to answer without what Singer calls "speciesism" — making scientifically unverifiable claims for human uniqueness, or appealing to religious dogma as a basis for a moral distinction between human and other lives.[44] Yet Singer's conclusions have two terrible defects. First, they are morally repugnant, offensive to most people's sense of moral consistency: they mean exempting apes from experimentation while practicing on human beings, and respecting the lives of apes while putting old, sick people to death. Second, they contain a fatal logic that makes them impractical. If apes were admitted to a moral community shared with humans on grounds of their similarity to humans, then other creatures would have to be admitted on the grounds of their similarity to apes, and so on until the whole of creation were encompassed and we should be morally self-disqualified from eating or exploiting any species. All creatures are part of a single continuum and, if the theory of evolution is correct, have common ancestors. As Bertrand Russell once said, there is no logical conclusion "short of votes for oysters."[45]

One way of responding might be to insist that it is premature to raise the question of the rights of other species while human rights are still imperfectly in place. Rather than discarding the myth of human uniqueness, we should first try to live up to it. As the anthropologist Justin Stagl has pointed out, if there is a uniquely human trait, it is perhaps our "utopian potential," our vocation to transcend our fail-

---

44. P. Cavaliere and P. Singer, eds., *The Great Ape Project: Equality beyond Humanity* (London: Fourth Estate, 1993).

45. B. Russell, *History of Western Philosophy* (London: Allen & Unwin, 1946), p. 433.

ures and defects, "to strive to attain superhuman goals and avoid the inhuman."[46]

An alternative and perhaps more satisfying strategy would, I suggest, be to re-express the nature of our moral community as based not on commonality of species but on the power of recognition. Our willingness to embrace, in a single community of rights, everyone now classed as human is itself an act of recognition.

An obvious objection to recognition as a criterion of admission to a moral community is that it is subjective. A community of Nazis, for instance, would presumably withhold recognition from Jews, gypsies, and gays. They could not, however, escape inclusion in a single community, unless one insisted that recognition be mutual. As a matter of fact, practitioners of abortion or euthanizers of the moribund do not acknowledge common membership in a community of rights with humans unable to recognize other humans; but they do form a community with fellow-humans of large sympathies, so that their moral communities overlap. Communities are conceivable in which individuals or groups are included in spite of themselves, or in the absence of mutual commitment. The fierce Jívaro of the forests of Ecuador, for instance, or other self-isolated groups may declare themselves at war with the rest of humankind; but that does not stop others from recognizing them as fellows and enfolding them in love. An individual incapable of reciprocating recognition does not cease to enjoy the benefits of implicitly mutual obligations of care during a spell of sleep or unconsciousness.

Mutuality is therefore not necessary to the formation of a moral community, although it obviously cements it. A striking example of the power of mutual recognition is that it can create communities of more than one species. Most people treat domestic pets as "part of the family." Their dogs reciprocate by seeing human household-members as companions in the pack. Some apes are as aware as their human counterparts of the resemblances primatologists have revealed. Lucy, the chimpanzee who "grew up human" in Maurice Temerlin's home, was typical in including chimpanzees in the pile labeled "human" when asked to sort photographs into categories.[47] Wolves suckle human

46. J. Stagl, "Anthropological Universality: On the Validity of Generalisations about Human Nature," in N. Roughley, ed., *Being Humans: Anthropological Universality and Particularity in Transdisciplinary Perspectives* (Berlin: Walter de Gruyter, 2000), pp. 25-46.

47. M. Temerlin, *Lucy, Growing Up Human: A Chimpanzee Daughter in a Psychotherapist's Family* (Palo Alto, CA: Science and Behavior Books, 1976).

young. It is clearly not necessary to be human to be part of a community of mutual recognition in which humans are included. *A fortiori*, we can admit nonhumans to our moral community without running the risk of having to embrace the whole of creation, or having to exclude any humans.

Recognition — of which mutual recognition is a sufficient but not necessary form — is a better criterion than either species or sentience as the basis for constructing moral communities. It is elastic, without being infinitely so. It enables us to continue the long tradition of expanding our moral community, without committing us to the invidious future that Peter Singer's argument implies.

Whatever happens, if the future is consistent with the past, the limits of our moral community will continue to fluctuate and on the whole to grow. As these pages have shown, the concept of humankind has never been fixed. It has a *Begriffsgeschichte* — a story of change, like every other concept. It is changing now and will continue to change in the future. Partly, this is because humankind, too, is unexempt from evolution; if our progeny survive long enough, they will mutate. If we can ask of the past, "When did our ancestors become human?" it is pertinent ask of the future, "When will our descendants cease to be human?" This is the sort of question it is never too early to ask — the sort of question Zen masters love, because although they may be unanswerable, or intractably formulated, they teach us enlightenment about ourselves.

Human Persons and Human Brains: A Historical Perspective within the Christian Tradition

Fernando Vidal

In his speech of November 21, 2005, to the Pontifical Academies of Sciences and Social Sciences, Pope Benedict XVI recalled that, for Christianity, human beings are part of nature, but also transcend it by virtue of their being free subjects with moral and spiritual values; he also observed that "according to God's intention, the person cannot be separated from the physical, psychological and spiritual dimensions of human nature."[1] Indeed, Christianity asserts the irreducibility of human personhood to one of its dimensions. Being a person, *a fortiori*, cannot be identified with having any one bodily organ — not even the organ whose "emergent properties" may be said to include what is otherwise called *soul* or *personality*, *psychological* or *spiritual life*. From the standpoint of the Church's *magisterium*, these assertions derive from "God's intention" about human nature. From a historical perspective, however, "divine intention" and "human nature" are best approached through their changing definitions and uses. Of course, there are some very basic phenomenological facts, such as our erect posture or the position of our eyes, that help determine our being-in-the-world. Humans walk on two legs; that much is universal. Walking itself, however, is a gradually acquired skill, and there is no such thing as a "natural" way of walking.[2] In any case, "human nature" is irreducible to anatomical

---

1. Joseph Ratzinger (Benedict XVI), "Discorso del Santo Padre Benedetto XVI ai membri delle Pontificie Accademie delle Scienze e delle Scienze Sociali" (2005) www.vatican.va/holy_father/benedict_xvi/speeches/2005/november/documents/hf_ben_xvi_spe_20051121_academies_it.html.

2. Timothy Ingold, "Against Human Nature," in Malcolm Jeeves, ed., *Human Nature* (Edinburgh: The Royal Society of Edinburgh, 2006), p. 123.

features. Beyond that, like the notion of "nature" itself, it tends to be named but not defined and is, in practice, characterized by a vast range of contents and an extraordinary polysemy that radically problematize its usage.[3]

Awareness of the problem is not new. In 1686, the chemist and natural philosopher Robert Boyle, a founding member of the Royal Society of London, argued that the notion of nature should have no place in natural philosophy.[4] Nature, he observed, commonly plays the role of God's vicar, of an "intelligent overseer" appointed "to regulate, assist, and control the motions" of the different parts of the universe. Such reification (the word is obviously not Boyle's) detracts from the honor due to the Creator, and "defrauds the true God" by diverting acts of veneration and gratitude to "the imaginary being" called *nature*. When God gave the laws of matter and motion, and endowed things with particular properties and powers, he set a course that neither needs nor allows for interventions other than his own. This view of the universe seemed to Boyle more consistent with religion than the one that took nature as God's "lieutenant" or "viceregent."

For Boyle, the notion of nature was as prejudicial to science as it was to religion; accounting for phenomena by an appeal to it precluded the search and formulation of precise "physical reasons." The word and its cognates should be therefore discarded and replaced. Thus, "nature" as *natura naturans* can be substituted by "God." Insofar as the word designates "that on whose account a thing is what it is," it can be replaced by "essence." The idea of nature as that which belongs by birth to a living creature may be expressed by saying that the creature under consideration was born so or is so by temperament. As for the notion of nature as internal principle of local motion, it could be couched in terms of a body moving in a certain way or direction spontaneously or as the result of determinate causes. In other cases, the word "nature" can be abandoned in favor of "the established order, or the settled course of things." "Nature" as the name for the powers belonging to a living body designates that body's constitution, temperament or mechanism, condition, structure, or texture; when applied to "greater portions of the world," it is better to use such expressions as "system of the universe." To the ex-

---

3. See Jeeves, *Human Nature,* for a contemporary instance.
4. Robert Boyle, *A Free Enquiry into the Vulgarly Received Notion of Nature,* ed. Edward B. Davis and Michael Hunter (Cambridge: Cambridge University Press, 1996).

tent that "nature" designates *natura naturata,* the universe itself, it can be advantageously replaced by "phenomena of the universe" or "of the world." Finally, Boyle explained, regarding nature as "goddess" or "semideity," the best "is not to employ it in that sense at all."

As a critique of "nature," Boyle's manifesto was unsuccessful. Historian of ideas Arthur Lovejoy found sixty-six meanings of the term, some in literary and philosophical works, others in ethics, politics, and religion.[5] In *Human Universals,* Donald Brown offered a list of about 300 items — from *abstraction, baby talk,* and *belief in the supernatural* to *distinguishing right and wrong, aggressiveness of males, poetic lines demarcated by pauses, promise, semantic category of giving, sexual attraction, sucking wounds, tools,* and *worldview.*[6] How could such a heterogeneous and questionable collection of features define "human nature"? As anthropologist Timothy Ingold has pointed out, whatever attribute one chooses as a defining universal feature of humanity, there is likely to be some creature born of man and woman who does not have it, and some creature of nonhuman ancestry who possesses it.[7] Probably the main function of the notion of "nature" (including "human nature") is, as in the case of papal pronouncements, to serve as a foundation of moral norms, as a means to support one's claims for what humans ought to be and do.[8]

The moral authority of nature derives from conceptions of what the entities to which it applies essentially are; this requires determining which organs, functions, or features they must have in order to be what they are. As far as "person" is concerned, the debate about exactly which attributes or capacities are necessary and sufficient for being one is undecidable. This is obviously so even beyond humanity and materiality: human beings who lack the relevant attributes would not be persons; inversely, machines, immaterial substances, or nonhuman beings that have them should count as persons, and this implies that human corporeal features cannot be considered as signs of personhood. What, then, is the relationship between personhood and corporeality?

---

5. Arthur O. Lovejoy, "Nature as an Aesthetic Norm," in *Essays in the History of Ideas* (Baltimore: Johns Hopkins University Press, 1948). See also John Torrance, ed., *The Concept of Nature* (Oxford: Clarendon Press, 1992), and Raymond Williams, "Nature," in *Keywords: A Vocabulary of Culture and Society* (New York: Oxford University Press, 1983).

6. Donald E. Brown, *Human Universals* (New York: McGraw-Hill, 1991).

7. Ingold, "Against Human Nature," p. 127.

8. Lorraine Daston and Fernando Vidal, eds., *The Moral Authority of Nature* (Chicago: University of Chicago Press, 2004).

In the Christian Aristotelian frameworks that dominated Western thought until the seventeenth century, the soul was, in Aristotle's terms (*De Anima,* 412a20), the "form" or "first actuality of a natural body which potentially has life." The analogy of eye and sight explained its connection to the body. As the philosopher put it, if the eye was an "animal" or living organism, sight would be its soul, so that if soul left it, it would no longer be an eye. In such a perspective, the soul was responsible for the basic functions of living beings (plants, animals, and humans). In the thirteenth century, the Christian church put a canonical end to controversies about the rational soul by decreeing that the soul ought to be considered a unitary substance, and that the rational soul was "by itself and essentially" the "form" of the body. In the sixth century Boethius had defined a person as "an individual substance of a rational nature" *(naturae rationabilis individua substantia);* in the thirteenth, Thomas Aquinas took up that definition, but emphasized that such a substance must be *completissima.* The separate soul, as merely a part of the human being (the "form"), could therefore not be a person; persons, in turn, are not reducible to their souls.[9]

In scholastic thought, the unity of soul and body was therefore not accidental, but belonged to the human person's essence. When the Aristotelianisms disintegrated, the soul ceased to be responsible for the nutritive, vegetative, and sensitive functions, and, as in the philosophy of René Descartes, became equal to mind. Cartesian philosophy incorporated earlier ideas about the union of soul and body, and thus about the person; at the same time, it broke, at least at the explicit level, with scholastic discussions about the "persons" of the Trinity and other technical theologico-metaphysical problems. True, in his *Meditations on First Philosophy,* Descartes developed the fiction of a bodiless self. Such fiction was part of a strategy of systematic doubt (ultimately aimed at proving the existence of God and the immortality of the soul) that led the philosopher to affirm that the only thing we can be certain of is the existence of myself as mind, *res cogitans* or "thinking thing," independent of any material substance. Yet, in his psychology (e.g., *The Passions of the Soul*), and in the *Meditations* as well, he treated humans as a substantial unity of body and soul, and to that extent remained perfectly con-

---

9. On the philosophical history of the concept of person, see "Person," in Joachim Ritter and Karlfried Gründer, eds., *Historisches Wörterbuch der Philosophie* (Basel: Schwabe, 1971-2004), vol. 7.

sistent with Christian anthropology. For him, this unity, or the person as an entity *qui a ensemble un corps et une pensée* (letter to Princess Elizabeth, June 28, 1643), were "primitive notions" that one can represent to oneself through one's immediate experience.

At the end of the seventeenth century, Lockean philosophy reduced substance to an idea we postulate as the substrate of things; this reduction extended to a redefinition of the concept of person. In the second edition of his *Essay Concerning Human Understanding*, John Locke defined the person as "a thinking intelligent Being, that has reason and reflection, and can consider it self as it self, the same thinking thing in different times and places; which it does only by that consciousness, which is inseparable from thinking..."; and he added, "For, since consciousness... is what makes every one to be what he calls self, ... in this alone consists personal Identity, i.e. the sameness of a rational Being: and as far as this consciousness can be extended backwards to any past action or thought, so far reaches the identity of that person" (book 2, ch. 27, § 9). In this view, arguably Locke's most radical philosophical innovation, personal identity, in the sense of both temporal continuity and self-same sameness, depends on memory and consciousness; it thus becomes purely psychological, and distinct from bodily identity or, indeed, from any substance whatsoever. Locke claimed, for example, that if my little finger is cut off my hand, and my consciousness is located in the little finger, then "it is evident the little finger would be the person, the same person; and self then would have nothing to do with the rest of the body" (§ 17). The equation of personal identity with self-consciousness deprives the person of its substantial unity with a body.

As with Aquinas, it is not that Locke went unquestioned; critics have responded to him since the seventeenth century, pointing out problems with the memory criterion, arguing that personal identity should be connected to some form of physical continuity, or defending other attributes and dimensions (such as free will, interpersonal relations, or social and historical situatedness) as identity criteria. Nevertheless, his philosophy of personal identity has framed all subsequent discussion of the topic, and illustrates some of its most important issues and distinctions.[10] On the one hand, it encompasses the difference

---

10. See, for example, Stéphane Ferret, *Le philosophe et son scalpel: Le problème de l'identité personnelle* (The Philosopher and His Scalpel: The Problem of Personal Identity) (Paris:

between synchronic and diachronic identity, between the defining properties of a person (here, chiefly self-consciousness) and that which ensures the person's persistence or continuity in time (here, chiefly memory). Both are connected and, rather than different types of identity, they characterize situations in which questions about identity and diversity arise. On the other hand, Locke's psychological outlook differs both from the much less popular somatic approach (according to which personal identity has no relation to psychological properties) and from substantialist theories that require the person to be tied to some material or immaterial substance, as well as from theories that consider other properties and continuities as essential to personhood. Nevertheless, most positions agree that, whatever else it might be, a person is a conscious, thinking, or rational being.

Most important for our topic, Locke asserted that consciousness may be "attached" to any substance whatsoever, without that making any difference for personal identity. To the extent that they are concerned with materiality, however, subsequent discussions have tended to consider physical attributes as pertinent to the extent that they are inherently connected to the relevant functional properties. In the case of human beings, the brain has emerged as precisely that. Thus, as conclusion to a presentation of philosophical views about personal identity, Stéphane Ferret offered the following formula: "Person P is identical with person P* if and only if P and P* have one and the same functional brain."[11] He thus summarized a theory about the conditions of personhood and personal identity that has become dominant since the second half of the twentieth century: the brain is the only part of the body that we need, and that has to be ours, in order for each of us to be ourselves.

I have proposed to call the human being depicted here a "cerebral subject," and to characterize him or her by the property of "brainhood" — of *being*, rather than simply *having*, a brain. The conception of man epitomized by Ferret is not a purely theoretical entity, but one of the chief anthropological figures of contemporary society and culture, and

---

Minuit, 1993); Harold Noonan, *Personal Identity* (London: Routledge, 1991); Eric T. Olson, "Personal Identity," in *Stanford Encyclopedia of Philosophy*, http://plato.stanford.edu/entries/identity-personal, 2002; John Perry, ed., *Personal Identity* (Berkeley: University of California Press, 1975).

11. Ferret, *Le philosophe et son scalpel*, p. 79.

one that has momentous practical consequences, while it is also expected to solve ancient problems about human nature, monism, and dualism. In particular, many neuroscientists seem convinced that the distinction between brain and mind, or between the neurological and the psychological/psychiatric is a prejudicial vestige of old metaphysical and religious beliefs, and that their discipline unquestionably proves that the mental is nothing more than the cerebral.

The goal of this chapter is to place the ideology of the cerebral subject in a historical perspective, and to suggest that its emergence derives less from the neuroscientific resolution of issues of monism and dualism commonly attributed to the supposedly Cartesian heritage of Western rationality, than from discussions about the relationship of body and self specific to the Christian tradition. Neuroscientists and neurophilosophers may believe that "neuroscientific anthropology" has irreversibly demolished the Christian view of human beings;[12] historically, however, brainhood is better understood as a way of coming to terms with the Christian principle that the human person "is not someone who has a body but whose existence is corporeal."[13] Although there are significant Platonic currents in the history of Christian thought, the understanding of Christianity as a dualistic philosophy is anachronistically colored by Descartes' "dualism." As already pointed out, in his psychology (if not in his metaphysics), Descartes treated humans as a substantial unity of body and soul, and to that extent remained perfectly consistent with Christian anthropology.

The doctrine of the resurrection of the flesh, on which the second part of this chapter will focus, is a major consequence of such anthropology. It proclaims that while human beings are not reducible to their bodies, there is no such thing as a disembodied person. The doctrine stirred debates not only about the possibility and mechanisms of the resurrection, but also about the parts of the body that resurrected persons must have to be the same as while alive. In other words, what parts of the body do we need in order to be ourselves? The ideology of the cerebral subject gives a straightforward answer: if the brain of A were transplanted into the body of B, then the new entity would be A with

---

12. Thomas Metzinger, "[Neuroethik] Unterwegs zu einem neuen Menschenbild" (On the Way Towards a New Image of Man), *Gehirn & Geist* 11 (2005): 50-54, p. 54.

13. Antoine Vergote, "The Body as Understood in Contemporary Thought and Biblical Categories," *Philosophy Today* 35 (1991): 93-105, p. 96.

the body of B; I am where my brain is. "This simple fact," commented leading neuroscientist Michael Gazzaniga, "makes it clear that you are your brain."[14] Yet the fact is simple, and the ontological inference legitimate, only if one has accepted the anthropology of brainhood. As part of humanity's most profound explorations of personal identity, the debates about the resurrection of the body in the Christian tradition constitute an essential cultural context for understanding how the idea that "we are our brains" became so seemingly obvious and natural. As a centuries-long self-reflective thought experiment, those debates have defined and elaborated such questions as "What is a human being?" and "What is the relation of self and body?"

I. The Emergence of Brainhood

Rather than a consequence of advances in knowledge of the brain, the "cerebralization" of personhood seems to have resulted mainly from seventeenth-century transformations in the philosophies of matter and personal identity, which themselves developed as part of the breakdown of the Aristotelian frameworks that long dominated Western thought. According to Locke, as we have seen, personal identity consists in a continuity of consciousness; the person is the result of a subjective process, independently of moral qualities or interpersonal and social circumstances. "For whatever Substance there is," Locke explained, "however framed, without consciousness there is no Person" (*An Essay Concerning Human Understanding*, book 2, ch. 27). It was only natural that the brain, to the extent it was believed to be *somehow* the seat of consciousness, became the only organ essential to the self.

A succinct early formulation of the substantialist-brain theory can be found in the writings of the Swiss naturalist and philosopher Charles Bonnet. In his *Analytical Essay on the Faculties of the Soul*, Bonnet wrote that "[i]f a Huron's soul could have inherited Montesquieu's brain, Montesquieu would still create."[15] The soul and the body could be those of a "savage," provided the brain was the philosopher's own. Bonnet's statement displays one of the possible forms that Christian anthropology could adopt in a post-Cartesian environment. The role he and other

---

14. Michael S. Gazzaniga, *The Ethical Brain* (New York: Dana Press, 2005), p. 31.
15. Charles Bonnet, *Essai analytique sur les facultés de l'âme*, 1760, § 771.

eighteenth-century psychologists attributed to the nerves and the brain derived largely from their supposed functions: nerves operated as the intermediaries between the body and the soul, and the brain contained the organ where body and soul interacted.[16] For Bonnet and other Enlightenment psychologists, the "neurologization" of the science of the soul was consistent with the Christian notion of the person as a composite of body and soul, and could even lend it support.

One feature makes Bonnet's statement about Montesquieu and the Huron look modern: the substantial link for the constitution of personhood is that between soul and *brain*, rather than soul and body. As in Ferret's formula, the body relevant for personal identity is reduced to the brain. At the same time, the fact that the union defining the human person is that between the brain and the *soul*, dates Bonnet's remark to its century — without, however, diminishing the ontological centrality of the brain.

The later development of the neurosciences reinforced such centrality. As self no longer appeared dependent on soul, the connection of brain to self and personhood was confirmed and refined. Cerebral localization, differentiation of function, and the correlation of function and structure became in the nineteenth century basic neuroscientific principles. The rise of the cerebral subject ideology at the time was also embodied in the belief that the characteristic traits of geniuses, criminals, and the mentally ill were inscribed in their brains. Such localizationism paralleled the elaboration of physiognomic, cranial, and bodily typologies, and the measurement of differences in brain weight and size in the early days of physical and racial anthropology.[17]

---

16. Fernando Vidal, *Les Sciences de l'âme, XVIe-XVIIIe siècle* (Paris: Champion, 2006).

17. This is not the place to give details on the history of brain research, a topic on which there is excellent work: see, for example, Mary A. B. Brazier, *A History of Neurophysiology in the Nineteenth Century* (New York: Raven Press, 1988); Edwin Clarke and C. D. O'Malley, *The Human Brain and Spinal Cord* (Berkeley: University of California Press, 1968); Edwin Clarke and L. S. Jacyna, *Nineteenth-Century Origins of Neuroscientific Concepts* (Berkeley: University of California Press, 1987); Pietro Corsi, ed., *The Enchanted Loom: Chapters in the History of Neuroscience* (New York: Oxford University Press, 1991); Stanley Finger, *Origins of Neuroscience: A History of Explorations into Brain Function* (New York: Oxford University Press, 1994); Michael Hagner, *Homo cerebralis. Der Wandel vom Seelenorgan zum Gehirn* (Homo Cerebralis: The Transformation of the Organ of the Soul into the Brain) (Berlin: Berlin Verlag, 1997); Michael Hagner, *Geniale Gehirne. Zur Geschichte der Elitenhirnforschung* (Genius's Brains: The History of Elite Brain Research) (Berlin: Wallstein, 2004); Michael Hagner, *"Der Geist bei der Arbeit." Untersuchungen zur*

In the twentieth century, clinical and experimental methods provided ever more detailed data about the cerebral control of behavior and mental life. Some areas of brain research gained considerable media presence, and became paradigms of what the brain sciences could teach about human personhood. The works of Wilder Penfield and Roger Sperry are among those that had most public impact before the spread of brain imaging and the notion of brain plasticity. Penfield knew that before an epileptic seizure, patients experience an "aura." By provoking the aura through electrical stimulation of the brain, he was able to determine the source of the seizure, and identify the tissue to be removed. By stimulating the human cortex, Penfield mapped the cortical areas responsible for motor and somatosensory functions. His findings are represented in a widely reproduced "homunculus" whose features, drawn proportionally to the associated brain areas, include comically large fingers and lips.[18]

Sperry, a neuroscientist, is famous for his work on split-brain and the ensuing discoveries on complementary hemispheric specialization.[19] A surgical treatment of epilepsy consisted of separating a patient's hemispheres by cutting the corpus callosum (commissurotomy). This resulted in the patient's having two functionally different brains. A typical post-operatory finding was that patients shown an image in the left visual field could not name or say anything about what they saw, because the image had arrived only on the right side of the brain, and speech is generally controlled by areas on the left. Yet they could grasp the corresponding object with the left hand, which is controlled by the right side of the brain. The same happens with touch, smell, or sound stimulation. Starting with these observations, split-brain became a major neuroscientific topic, gave support to the modular model of brain

---

Hirnforschung (Göttingen: Wallstein, 2006); Anne Harrington, *Mind, Medicine, and the Double Brain: A Study in Nineteenth-Century Thought* (Princeton: Princeton University Press, 1987); Robert M. Young, *Mind, Brain, and Adaptation in the Nineteenth Century: Cerebral Localization and Its Biological Context from Gall to Ferrier* (New York: Oxford University Press, 1990).

18. Wilder Penfield and Theodore Rasmussen, *The Cerebral Cortex of Man: A Clinical Study of Localization of Function* (New York: Macmillan, 1950).

19. For this work, Sperry shared in 1981 the Nobel Prize in Physiology or Medicine; see, for example, Roger W. Sperry, "The Great Cerebral Commissure," *Scientific American* 210 (1964): 42-52; Roger W. Sperry, "Some Effects of Disconnecting the Cerebral Hemispheres" (Nobel Lecture), *Science* 217(4566) (1982): 1223-26.

organization, and inspired studies reaching into the areas of consciousness and brain plasticity, as well as philosophical discussions of the implications of commissurotomy for personal identity.[20]

Starting in the 1960s, while the neurosciences established themselves as an autonomous research field, philosophers of the analytic tradition, such as the American philosopher Sidney Shoemaker in *Self-Knowledge and Self-Identity* and later the British thinker Derek Parfit in *Reasons and Persons*, revived Locke's use of thought experiments (e.g., consciousness located in the little finger) as a conceptual tool for thinking personal identity. Now, however, the puzzle-cases concerned various brain experiments: bisection (and the subsequent question of whether two persons can share a single body), grafting of X's brain into Y's brainless body, or transplantation of each hemisphere into a new body.[21] The most widely discussed instance is Harvard philosopher Hilary Putnam's later "brains in a vat," a common theme in 1950s-70s brain movies, and in Putnam's version, a variation of the Cartesian demon that fools you into believing that you have a body and that there is an external world. While you sleep, your brain is removed, placed in a vat, and hooked to a computer that sends the kinds of signals that usually informed your brain. When you wake up, everything looks the same as usual, except that you are in fact no more than a brain in a vat. In the first chapter of *Reason, Truth, and History*, Putnam argued that if you were in such a situation, you could not think you were a brain in a vat. Although his goal was to discuss skepticism rather than personal identity, it is significant that the choice of a brain fiction seemed so natural, as if investigating self-knowledge necessarily implied equating personhood and brainhood. Neurophilosophy, a predominantly eliminative-materialist philosophy of mind, is not primarily about personhood either, but does treat humans as cerebral subjects.

Since the 1980s, the usages and media presence of brain imaging have played a determining role in the diffusion of brainhood as a biosocial norm. Computerized axial tomography (CAT or CT scan-

---

20. Roland Puccetti, "Brain Bisection and Personal Identity," *British Journal for the Philosophy of Science* 24 (1973): 339-55.

21. See, for example, Derek Parfit, "Personal Identity," *The Philosophical Review* 80 (1971): 3-27; Roland Puccetti, "Brain Transplantation and Personal Identity," *Analysis* 29 (1969): 65-77; Puccetti, "Brain Bisection and Personal Identity"; David Wiggins, *Identity and Spatio-Temporal Continuity* (Oxford: Basil Blackwell, 1967).

ning) has been in use since the early 1970s. It employs computers to generate three-dimensional static pictures on the basis of two-dimensional X-rays of "slices" (Gr. *tomos*) of an organ. The development of single photon or positron emitters that stay in the bloodstream or bind to receptors in the brain led to the functional imaging techniques SPECT and PET, single photon emission computed tomography and positron emission tomography. These procedures allow the mapping of blood flow in the brain, and thus the visualization of localized brain activity during cognitive tasks. The discovery that MRI (magnetic resonance imaging) also records blood-flow changes measured by PET opened the way to functional MRI (fMRI), since the 1990s the dominant brain-mapping technique.

Brain imaging has had an enormous impact outside the strictly neuroscientific and medical domains. Judy Illes, a neuroethics pioneer, described the phenomenal expansion of fMRI-based research during the 1990s, and showed that the dramatic decrease in studies of sensory and motor functions correlated inversely with the growth of studies on cognition, attitudes, moral and social judgment, and religious experience.[22] This vast production can be divided into various thematic areas — altruism, empathy, decision making, cooperation, and competition; judging faces and races; lying and deception; meditation and religious experience — and includes such titles as "The Neural Correlates of Maternal and Romantic Love" or "Brain Activation Associated with Evaluative Processes of Guilt and Embarrassment"; "Differential Response in the Human Amygdala to Racial Outgroup vs. Ingroup Face Stimuli" or "Brain Responses to the Acquired Moral Status of Faces"; "A Replication Study of the Neural Correlates of Deception" or "Brain Activity during Simulated Deception"; "Religiosity Is Associated with Hippocampal but not Amygdala Volume in Patients with Refractory Epilepsy" or "Neural Correlates of a Mystical Experience in Carmelite Nuns."

These mostly inconclusive studies have often clustered into imaging-driven new "neuro" fields whose common purpose is to reform the human sciences on the basis of knowledge about the brain. Neuroesthetics, neuroeconomics, neuropsychoanalysis, neurotheology, neuroeducation, and others all emerged during the 1990s, the "Decade of the Brain." As evidenced by the article titles quoted above, these fields

---

22. Judy Illes, M. Kirschen, and J. D. Gabrieli, "From Neuroimaging to Neuroethics," *Nature Neuroscience* 6 (2003): 205.

proceed by looking for "neural correlates." Although the meaning of these correlates is generally unclear, it is claimed that the "neuro" areas redefine "our sense of selfhood and brain-body relations,"[23] or lead "to bold new findings and claims about behavior in health and disease."[24] Yet these findings and claims boil down to the assertion that the neurosciences have replaced "older notions of the soul or mind-body dualism with the doctrine that mind . . . is the brain's exclusive output."[25] The assertion is questionable because brain reductionism did not derive from brain research, but, inversely, predated, inspired, and sustained it. Moreover, as Thomas Nagel pointed out in his classic "What Is It Like to Be a Bat?" the apparent clarity of the verb *is* in the physicalist assumption of most neuroscience — namely, that mental states *are* brain states — remains deceptive as long as neither empirical data nor a theoretical framework justify and make sense of the postulated equation.[26]

The rise of neuroethics, perhaps the most rapidly growing star of the "neuro" constellation, suggests why brainhood has become so compelling. The field deals with the ethical, social, and legal challenges that arise in neuroscience; specifically, most of it concerns the ethics and uses of fMRI studies of the sort mentioned above. There is no doubt that the challenges of the neurosciences are considerable for practice in many areas, from medicine to law, from advertisement to education, and that it is important to ponder them. Nevertheless, it also seems accurate to say that "neuro-ethical anxieties have become part of the very problem they seek to address," and that, implicitly, neuroethics sometimes makes the case for those who live on the futuristic and revolutionary rhetoric of the neurosciences, "be they researchers in search of grants, corporations in search of investment or popular science writers who thrive on sensationalism to sell their products."[27]

---

23. Paul Root Wolpe, "The Neuroscience Revolution," *Hastings Center Report* (July-August 2002): 8.

24. Judy Illes and Eric Racine, "Imaging or Imagining? A Neuroethics Challenge Informed by Genetics," *The American Journal of Bioethics* 5 (2005): 5-18, p. 6.

25. F. E. Lepore, "Dissecting Genius: Einstein's Brain and the Search for the Neural Basis of Intellect," *Cerebrum* 3 (2001) [no page numbers are given in the version available through www.dana.org].

26. Thomas Nagel, "What Is It Like to Be a Bat?" *The Philosophical Review* 83 (1974): 435-50.

27. Ilina Singh and Nikolas Rose, "Neuro-forum: An Introduction," *BioSocieties*

The "Decade of the Brain" saw brain images flood the public domain. In addition to sustaining the legitimacy of the "neuro" areas, this phenomenon has affected how we understand the person-brain relation. In *Picturing Personhood: Brain Scans and Biomedical Identity*, anthropologist of science Joseph Dumit examined how the media presents such images as if they were depictions of human types and realistic portraits of the self, resulting in cerebral typologies and corresponding human kinds, such as normal, healthy, depressed, or handicapped.[28] On the positive side, brain images help destigmatize mental illnesses by visually showing that they are no more than conditions of the brain. One of the consequences of this has been "neurodiversity," a value that "neurotypicals" are asked to respect (see, for example, www.neurodiversity.com).

These developments toward turning humans into cerebral subjects may be connected to a large-scale process of somatization of the self, to the "wider mutation" in personhood that sociologists Carlos Novas and Nikolas Rose, of the BIOS Centre at the London School of Economics, have called "somatic individuality."[29] The psyche, they write, "is becoming flattened out and mapped onto the corporeal space of the brain itself. Such technological developments as neurochemistry . . . and brain scanning . . . appear to establish direct and 'superficial' empirical and observable relations between the physiological and the ethical: between the brain and all that makes a human person."[30] Such analysis, whether or not one agrees with it entirely, points to the recent contexts of the cerebral subject.

The life sciences have generated various notions of the self. Immunology, for example, has been defined as the science of self-nonself discrimination, and genetics has inspired various forms of organic essentialism. Yet, as bioethicist Alex Mauron has noted, "if one compares 'genome-based' and 'brain-based' explanations of Self and behav-

---

1 (2006): 97-102, p. 100; on the rhetoric of brain research, see, for example, Michael Hagner and Cornelius Borck, "Mindful Practices: On the Neurosciences in the Twentieth Century," *Science in Context* 14 (2001): 507-10.

28. Joseph Dumit, *Picturing Personhood: Brain Scans and Biomedical Identity* (Princeton: Princeton University Press, 2004).

29. Carlos Novas and Nikolas Rose, "Genetic Risk and the Birth of the Somatic Individual," *Economy and Society* 29 (2000): 485-513, p. 487.

30. Novas and Rose, "Genetic Risk and the Birth of the Somatic Individual," p. 508.

31. Alex Mauron, "Renovating the House of Being: Genomes, Souls, and Selves," *Annals of the New York Academy of Sciences* 1001 (2003): 240-52, p. 240.

ior, it turns out that neural aspects of human nature are more directly relevant. Many philosophical and ethical questions traditionally raised about genetics and genomics acquire more relevance and urgency when re-examined in the context of neuroscience."[31] To the extent that self and personhood are defined primarily in terms of psychological functions, they remain more directly connected to brain than to genes. "We used to think our fate was in the stars. Now," claims DNA structure co-discoverer John W. Watson, "we know, in large measure, our fate is in our genes."[32] Although the cerebral subject coexists, and sometimes converges, with the genetic one in the landscape of anthropological figures of our culture, Watson's hubristic assertion may have been superseded in the public mind by neuroscientists' similar claims.

Brainhood, of course, has its critics. While it seems to define the spontaneous position of most neuroscientists (even of those who, like Antonio Damasio, are celebrated for apparently bringing a more phenomenological approach into the brain sciences), it has been criticized mainly from the viewpoint of the human sciences through their efforts to understand allegedly natural phenomena ("we are our brains") in historical and social contexts. Among philosophers, I will only mention Kathleen Wilkes, who takes the brain into account as a condition for "real people," but rejects as theoretically irrelevant the brain-related thought experiments that are commonly used for thinking about personal identity.[33]

Although brain fictions (mainly about preservation and transplantation) play an important role as vehicles for the cerebral subject ideology, brainhood is above all a matter of real human consequence. Emblematic of this is the issue of brain death. The brain-death criterion, widely used since the late 1960s, replaces the arrest of cardiac and pulmonary functions as signs of death, and relies on the permanent cessation of signs of central nervous system activity. There are, however, partisans of cardiopulmonary criteria, as well as varieties of brain death (whole-brain, higher-brain, brainstem). Higher-brain criteria assume that such functions as consciousness, memory, and reasoning define us as human persons. Do they therefore imply that anencephalic babies, persons in a permanent vegetative state, or advanced Alzheimer

32. Quoted in Leon Jaroff, "The Gene Hunt," *Time,* March 20, 1989, p. 67.
33. Kathleen V. Wilkes, *Real People: Personal Identity Without Thought Experiments* (Oxford: Clarendon Press, 1988).

patients can be treated as if they were dead (as *persons*), or at least that they can be allowed to die? If that were the case, then, as announced by Robert Veatch, professor of medical ethics at Georgetown University, the whole-brain definition of death may be abandoned, and brain-death criteria reduced to the "irreversible cessation of the capacity for consciousness."[34]

The controversy over brain death ultimately concerns the definition of "human person," and, more specifically, the question of defining the parts of our bodies that must be irreversibly damaged, and the functions that must be destroyed, in order for us to conclude that we are in the presence of an organism that, though alive, is no longer a *person*. Some authors, such as Robert Blank in an analysis of "how the new neuroscience will change our lives and our politics," wonder if it is legitimate to distinguish between life as a strictly organic function, and *human* life "as an integrated set of social, intellectual, and communicative dimensions."[35] What weight should these dimensions have in deciding to terminate life? Should locked-in syndrome patients be allowed to decide that they wish to be killed? Would such a patient be the same person if the preserved parts of his or her brain could be transplanted into another body?

Discussions about brain death potentially raise the issue of "brain life." The problem of conferring personhood status on a human embryo is a prime example of how transitory moral judgments might be in biomedicine, how they evolve hand in hand with research and applications, and how they constantly challenge ideas about human nature.[36] If a brain state marks the end of a person's life, should not a brain state indicate its beginning?[37] Markers, however, shift from fourteen days (formation of the primitive streak), to twenty-three weeks, when the fetus becomes viable; moreover, such boundaries have been broken down by the fact that somatic cell nuclear transplant ("cloning") and research on stem cells take place within the fourteen-day pe-

---

34. Robert M. Veatch, "The Impending Collapse of the Whole-Brain Definition of Death," *Hastings Center Report* 23 (1993): 18-24.

35. Robert H. Blank, *Brain Policy: How the New Neuroscience Will Change Our Lives and Our Politics* (Washington, DC: Georgetown University Press, 1999), p. 36.

36. Gareth Jones, "The Human Embryo: Its Ambiguous Nature," in Jeeves, *Human Nature*.

37. Hans-Martin Sass, "Brain Life and Brain Death: A Proposal for a Normative Agreement," *Journal of Medicine and Philosophy* 14 (1989): 45-59.

riod. If there is such a thing as "human nature," then these questions must certainly concern its very definition.

II. Personhood and the Resurrection of the Body

The previous section sketched some aspects of the emergence of the cerebral subject as a modern view of personhood. The brainhood perspective combines various intuitions about what a person is and how personal continuity is obtained; its durable appeal results from its combining the psychological properties said to define personhood, and the physical substance (the brain) said to sustain those properties. These intuitions can be made problematic. For example, if each hemisphere contained exactly the same information and exerted exactly the same functions, and if each were transplanted into a different body, then there would be two entities with the same personal identity, and yet the original person would not be preserved. (Mainly from such a thought experiment, Parfit concludes that psychological "connectedness," rather than personal identity, is what matters.)

As suggested above, brainhood and the cerebral subject have become a major anthropological figure of contemporary culture, and one that implies a theory about the relationship of self and body. The belief that "we are our brains" (or, more generally, that we may be reducible to one part of our body) contradicts the kind of full corporality Christianity attributes to the human person. That is why, as a fundamental expression of Christian anthropology, the doctrine of the resurrection of the body can be examined as an exploration of personal identity. This is not to say that debates about the resurrection doctrine *were* or could be retrospectively *read as* debates about personal identity; rather, they can be seen as a main context of gestation and elaboration of the very notion of personal identity in Western thought.[38]

The place of the human body in Christian anthropology derives from the mystery of the Incarnation. Although there are reasons to see Christianity as inimical to the body, the church has always condemned

---

38. Caroline Walker Bynum, *The Resurrection of the Body in Western Christianity, 200-1336* (New York: Columbia University Press, 1995a); Caroline Walker Bynum, "Why All the Fuss About the Body? A Medievalist's Perspective," *Critical Inquiry* 22 (1995): 1-33; Fernando Vidal, "Brains, Bodies, Selves, and Science: Anthropologies of Identity and the Resurrection of the Body," *Critical Inquiry* 28 (2002): 930-74.

the denigration of matter and the human body.[39] As historian of early Christianity Peter Brown demonstrated, such practices as permanent sexual renunciation can be understood as a means to live the body as the "temple of the Holy Spirit" (1 Cor. 6:15), and to prepare it to be like the body of the risen Christ.[40] The doctrine of the resurrection of the body is integral to the belief that our existence as persons is intrinsically corporeal, and that there is no such a thing as a disembodied human.

The position that became official in the early centuries of Christianity is that both the bodily and the psychological identity of resurrected individuals will be the same as that of the persons they were while alive. This doctrine generated questions about how decayed bodies will become whole again, or how to reconcile the properties of the "glorious" and "spiritual" resurrected body Paul announces in 1 Corinthians 15 with the old ones of the terrestrial body. They entailed asking, for example: If all our flesh has to be restored to resurrected bodies, what happens with the matter we lose and replace throughout our lives? If I am eaten by a cannibal who assimilates my flesh to his own, where does the assimilated flesh end up, in the cannibal's resurrected body, or in mine? Since Christ declared that "there shall not an hair of your head perish" (Luke 21:18), the doctrine requires that resurrected bodies remain materially identical to the corresponding terrestrial bodies. All this naturally raised classical puzzles about the diachronic identity of things that change over time — be they the water of a river where we bathe twice, Theseus's ship (about which, according to Plutarch, philosophers argued whether it remained the same through successive reparations), or our own bodies. These questions rehearsed the ontological quandaries of personal identity in yet another way, since they resulted from the principle that for each of us to be ourselves, we need to have our own bodies.

This principle was challenged in the context of the seventeenth-century Scientific Revolution, which saw a relative disincarnation of personhood, the psychologization of personal identity, and the increasing focalization on the brain of the body relevant for personal identity. The corpuscular philosophy (espoused, for example, by Robert Boyle

---

39. Frank Bottomley, *Attitudes to the Body in Western Christendom* (London: Lepus Books, 1979).
40. Peter Brown, *The Body and Society: Men, Women, and Sexual Renunciation in Early Christianity* (New York: Columbia University Press, 1988).

and Isaac Newton, as well as by John Locke) explained the phenomena of nature by the motion, figure, rest, and position of interchangeable particles of matter. Differences among physical bodies did not derive from the essential nature of their substance, but from the mechanical properties of the composing particles. As Boyle and others noted, corpuscularianism implied that resurrected bodies no longer had to include exactly the same matter as the corresponding terrestrial bodies. In "Some Physico-Theological Considerations about the Possibility of the Resurrection," he argued that since no one particular portion of matter determines personal identity, the sameness of the terrestrial and the resurrected individual is not to be judged by material criteria. The soul, he believed, "shall be again united, not to an ethereal, or the like fluid matter, but to such a substance as may, with tolerable propriety of speech, ... be called a human body."[41] Material continuity thus lost its importance as a constitutive element of personal identity; and this, as Locke realized, applied not only to resurrected persons, but to the very definition of personhood.

We have already seen that Locke separated substance and personal identity, and made the latter dependent on a continuity of memory and consciousness. The theory had consequences for the resurrection doctrine. In the *Essay* (II.27, § 15), Locke asserted that, in the perspective of his philosophy, it had become possible, "without any difficulty, to conceive the same person at the resurrection, though in a body not exactly in make or parts the same which he had here." As he wrote in a letter, "I being fully perswaded of the resurrection and that we shall have bodies fitted to that state it is indifferent to me whether any one concludes that they shall be the same or not."[42] Reactions to the consequences of Locke's theory for the resurrection doctrine were among the earliest. For example, in *The Resurrection of the (Same) Body Asserted* (1694), the English divine Humphrey Hody acknowledged that sameness of body did not depend on the sameness of every particle. In order

---

41. Robert Boyle [1675], "Some Physico-Theological Considerations about the Possibility of the Resurrection," in *The Works of the Honourable Robert Boyle,* 2nd ed. (1772), vol. 4 (Hildesheim: Olms, 1966), p. 201.

42. John Locke to D. Whitby, January 17, 1698/99, quoted in Maria-Cristina Pitassi, "Une résurrection pour quel corps et pour quelle humanité? La réponse lockienne entre philosophie, exégèse et théologie" (Resurrection: For Which Body and Which Humanity? The Lockean Answer Between Philosophy, Exegesis and Theology), *Rivista di storia della filosofia* 1 (1998): 45-61, p. 61.

to preserve the Christian doctrine of the resurrection, he nevertheless insisted on the corporality of personhood, and explained that three bodies animated by the same soul would be three different persons.

Locke's descendants would not agree, yet did not get rid of the material body. Enlightenment psychologists localized in the brain the mental powers necessary for identity. Resurrection discussions serve again as a historical magnifying glass. In his *Essai de psychologie,* Bonnet defended himself against the accusation that he made the soul too dependent on the body by reminding his readers "that man, by his very nature, is a composite being," made up of a spiritual and a corporeal substance, and explaining that the doctrine of the resurrection of the body is the "immediate consequence" of that principle. "Far from repulsing the deist philosopher," he wrote, "such a clearly revealed dogma should, on the contrary, appear to him as a presumption favorable to the truth of religion, since it is so perfectly consistent with what we most certainly know about the nature of our being."[43] Bonnet and others went on to speculate that our brains enclose a tiny indestructible particle that combines the qualities of a brain and seat of the soul with those of an embryological germ.[44] On Judgment Day, they imagined, the particle will develop and restore each individual's original personality, as well as a body that, though materially different from the original, would still be the person's own because it will grow from a germ that belongs to the person. In this hypothesis, the union of soul and brain makes the individual whole again.

By the end of the eighteenth century, the psychological problem of personal identity had pushed aside the issue of the numerical sameness of bodies. Subsequently, in popular and nontheological academic culture, traditional Christian eschatology was largely replaced by the fashion of spiritualism, reincarnation, and various systems about the persistence of personality after death.[45] Some nineteenth- and twentieth-century authors still explored the relations between the resurrection of the flesh and scientific models and data, updating the germ theory, or imagining that DNA and raw materials would be

---

43. Charles Bonnet, *Essai de psychologie* [1755] (Hildesheim: Olms, 1978), footnote 43.

44. Vidal, "Brains, Bodies, Selves, and Science."

45. Louis-Vincent Thomas, "L'eschatologie: Permanence et mutation" (Eschatology: Continuity and Mutation), in L.-V. Thomas et al., *Réincarnation, immortalité, résurrection* (Brussels: Publications des Facultés Universitaires Saint-Louis, 1988).

enough for the resurrection of the body. Mostly, however, the resurrected will be cerebral subjects.

If, following Locke, only a conscious personality is necessary for a fair Last Judgment, then resurrection might be limited to brains, or even to some brain structures. As German neuroscientist Detlef Bernhard Linke asked, if only part of the brain is necessary to be a person, shall we need it whole to enjoy the beatific vision?[46] The fraction that contains the information necessary for defining our self might be enough. Such information could be stored in a machine. Hence the argument of physicist Frank J. Tipler in *The Physics of Immortality: Modern Cosmology, God, and the Resurrection of the Dead*, published in 1994, that the resurrected *I* need be nothing other than the computer equivalent of my brain. Even a Dominican theologian, considering that there seems to be no absolute obstacle to producing humans who live perpetually, could write that "[s]ince we now know we are essentially our brains, our ultimate problem is to remake our brains and keep them ever-living and ever self-improving."[47]

Concluding Remarks

Since nineteenth-century phrenologists palpated head bumps to identify individual aptitudes, the hope of being able to read the mind and the self through brain recordings has persisted, updated by new technologies (EEGs in the 1930s to 1950s), and given a formidable boost by late twentieth-century brain visualization techniques that revived cerebral localizationism.[48] The disputed use of brain scans in the law courts, the debates about neurological enhancers and prosthetics, the rise of neuropharmacology, and the drive (encouraged by the pharmaceutical and health-insurance industries) of biological psychiatry to question all but the most behavior-oriented psychotherapies are some instances of

---

46. Detlef Bernhard Linke, "Gehirn, Seele und Auferstehung," *Evangelische Theologie* 50 (1999): 128-35.
47. Benedict Ashley, *Theologies of the Body: Humanist and Christian* (Boston: The Pope John Center, 1995), p. 6.
48. Cornelius Borck, *Hirnströme. Eine Kulturgeschichte der Elektroenzephalographie* (Brain Currents: A Cultural History of Encephalography) (Göttingen: Wallstein, 2005); William R. Uttal, *The New Phrenology: The Limits of Localizing Cognitive Processes in the Brain* (Cambridge, MA: MIT Press, 2001).

how the brain functions as a projection surface of aspirations and anxieties, as the object and vehicle of conflicting interests, as an icon of the self — in short, as a social actor all the more powerful in that it is said to be the most complex natural entity in the universe, and, therefore, one of the least known. In a long-term historical perspective, however, the preeminence of brainhood may be related to how it has assimilated two fundamental features of the Christian view of man.

In a story by Roald Dahl, a man called William agrees to survive his body's death as a detached brain. Before the brain extraction operation takes place, he asks his doctor to maintain the optic nerve and one eye attached to "him" so that he can still read the newspaper. William thus keeps on living as a brain in a vat, with an eyeball attached to it. Yet, for neither William nor the surgeon was the eye necessary for William's persistence as exactly the same person he was before being, so to speak, survived by his own brain.[49] This fantasy corresponds to some real people's hopes and decisions: the latest fashion in the quest of immortality through "cryonics" consists of keeping the brain and getting rid of the rest of the body (see, for example, the site of the Alcor Life Extension Foundation, www.alcor.org). "Neuropreservation" is partly driven by its lower cost compared to full body preservation, but also by the conviction that we are our brains.

As both fictions and reality suggest, the culture of brainhood implies a paradox. On the one hand, the brain appears as the material organ par excellence, as the only part of our physical bodies that is necessary for each of us to be ourselves. I am not my body; I am *in* the body that contains my brain. The recent fashion of what might be called "neuroascesis" — practices of cerebral self-discipline aimed at acting on the brain to enhance its performance — treats the brain as a muscle, and brain-building as the royal road to shaping the person. The titles of the books that market this new panacea are eloquent signs of what is at stake in contemporary neurocultures: *Keep Your Brain Alive: 83 Neurobic Exercises to Help Prevent Memory Loss and Increase Mental Fitness; Smart for Life: How to Improve Your Brain Power at Any Age; Build Your Brain Power: The Latest Techniques to Preserve, Restore, and Improve Your Brain's Potential; Brain Power: A Neurosurgeon's Complete Program to Maintain and Enhance Brain Fitness Throughout Your Life; Brain Fitness (Anti-*

---

49. Roald Dahl, "William and Mary," in Dahl, *Tales of the Unexpected* (Harmondsworth: Penguin Books, 1960).

Aging Strategies for Achieving Super Mind Power); Brain Gym for Business: Instant Brain Boosters for On-the-Job Success; or *Cross-Train Your Brain: A Mental Fitness Program for Maximizing Creativity and Achieving Success.*

At the same time, cryogenic companies' advertising and scores of fictions in philosophy, literature, and film locate immortality in the continuance of one's brain. Immortality is ensured through brain preservation under low temperatures, or thanks to successive transplantations of your brain into a younger body, and even into your clone. Contrary to one of the main concerns of industrialized societies, brains never age in this imagined world. The brain has thus incorporated the qualities of the soul, not only as seat of the self, but also, and most important, as the immaterial substance par excellence. Another dimension of the same paradox manifests itself in the relationship of psychology and brain science. As Gary Hatfield convincingly shows, contrary to usual claims and intuitions, neuroscience limits itself to providing an additional source of data about function and brain localization, while research on structure is guided by theories and knowledge about function.[50] That is why even neuropreservation clients, or the cerebral subject ideologists who proclaim "we are our brains," are unlikely to accept the full implications of the ontology of brainhood.

We have seen that, at the end of the seventeenth century, an English divine expressed his objections to Locke's theory of personal identity with the assertion that three bodies animated by the same soul would be three different persons. Two centuries later, Parfit updated the thought experiment: assuming the brain hemispheres to be totally equivalent, if each hemisphere of person A's brain were transplanted into bodies X and Y, then there would be two entities (Ax and Ay) with the same memories and personalities, yet the original person would no longer exist. In the former case, three living human bodies suffice to make up three persons; in the latter, sharing a brain gives Ax and Ay the properties that would make them be the same person. (Actually, Parfit uses the notion of "descendant selves" to argue that Ax and Ay share a past self without *being* the same self, and that, in such a perspective, the word "I" would be used "to imply the greatest degree of psychological connectedness."[51])

---

50. Gary Hatfield, "The Brain's 'New' Science: Psychology, Neurophysiology, and Constraint," *Philosophy of Science* 67 (2000): 388-403.

51. Derek Parfit, "Personal Identity," *The Philosophical Review* 80 (1971): 3-27, 25.

Irrespective of argumentative details, both fictions ask whether different bodies sharing a substance originally located in one body and assumed to be decisive for personal identity constitute one or several persons. The seventeenth-century answer adheres to the Christian view of man as a composite of soul and body; the reason why one soul in three bodies makes up three persons is not that persons are reducible to bodies, but that the rational soul alone, with all its attendant properties and faculties but separate from a body, does not define a person. The twentieth-century answer replaces the soul by the brain; and by emphasizing the "psychological connectedness" that depends on brain function, it reduces to the brain the body relevant for personhood. The comparison of the two thought experiments thus brings forth the differences and continuities between brainhood and traditional Christian anthropology. To the extent that self-awareness as the only constitutive property of the "modern self" resides in the brain, brainhood may rank as the anthropological figure of modernity.[52] By the same token, the brain as it functions in the ideology of the cerebral subject is also a vestige of the Christian tradition, a problematic remnant of the idea that a person cannot *be* without a body.

References

Andreasen, Nancy C. 2001. *Brave New Brain: Conquering Mental Illness in the Era of the Genome.* New York: Oxford University Press.
Ashley, Benedict. 1985. *Theologies of the Body: Humanist and Christian.* Boston: The Pope John Center, 1995.
Blank, Robert H. 1999. *Brain Policy: How the New Neuroscience Will Change Our Lives and Our Politics.* Washington, DC: Georgetown University Press.
Bonnet, Charles. 1755. *Essai de psychologie.* Hildesheim: Olms, 1978.
Borck, Cornelius. 2005. *Hirnströme. Eine Kulturgeschichte der Elektroenzephalographie* (Brain Currents: A Cultural History of Encephalography). Göttingen: Wallstein.
Bottomley, Frank. 1979. *Attitudes to the Body in Western Christendom.* London: Lepus Books.

---

52. For the history of the "modern self," see Charles Taylor, *Sources of the Self: The Making of the Modern Identity* (Cambridge, MA: Harvard University Press, 1989); Fernando Vidal, "Brainhood, Anthropology of Modernity," *History of the Human Sciences* 22 (2009): 5-36.

Boyle, Robert. 1675. "Some Physico-Theological Considerations about the Possibility of the Resurrection," in *The Works of the Honourable Robert Boyle*, 2nd ed. (1772), vol. 4. Hildesheim: Olms, 1966.

Boyle, Robert. 1686. *A Free Enquiry into the Vulgarly Received Notion of Nature*. Edited by Edward B. Davis and Michael Hunter. Cambridge: Cambridge University Press, 1996.

Brazier, Mary A. B. 1988. *A History of Neurophysiology in the Nineteenth Century*. New York: Raven Press.

Brown, Donald E. 1991. *Human Universals*. New York: McGraw-Hill.

Brown, Peter. 1988. *The Body and Society: Men, Women, and Sexual Renunciation in Earlier Christianity*. New York: Columbia University Press.

Bynum, Caroline Walker. 1995a. *The Resurrection of the Body in Western Christianity, 200-1336*. New York: Columbia University Press.

Bynum, Caroline Walker. 1995b. "Why All the Fuss About the Body? A Medievalist's Perspective," *Critical Inquiry* 22: 1-33.

Clarke, Edwin, and L. S. Jacyna. 1987. *Nineteenth-Century Origins of Neuroscientific Concepts*. Berkeley: University of California Press.

Clarke, Edwin, and C. D. O'Malley. 1968. *The Human Brain and Spinal Cord*. Berkeley: University of California Press.

Corsi, Pietro, ed. 1991. *The Enchanted Loom: Chapters in the History of Neuroscience*. New York: Oxford University Press.

Dahl, Roald. 1960. "William and Mary," in Dahl, *Tales of the Unexpected*. Harmondsworth: Penguin Books.

Daston, Lorraine, and Fernando Vidal, eds. 2004. *The Moral Authority of Nature*. Chicago: University of Chicago Press.

Dumit, Joseph. 2004. *Picturing Personhood: Brain Scans and Biomedical Identity*. Princeton: Princeton University Press.

Ferret, Stéphane. 1993. *Le philosophe et son scalpel: Le problème de l'identité personnelle* (The Philosopher and His Scalpel: The Problem of Personal Identity). Paris: Minuit.

Finger, Stanley. 1994. *Origins of Neuroscience: A History of Explorations into Brain Function*. New York: Oxford University Press.

Gazzaniga, Michael S. 2005. *The Ethical Brain*. New York: Dana Press.

Hagner, Michael. 1997. *Homo cerebralis. Der Wandel vom Seelenorgan zum Gehirn* (Homo Cerebralis: The Transformation of the Organ of the Soul into the Brain). Berlin: Berlin Verlag.

Hagner, Michael. 2004. *Geniale Gehirne. Zur Geschichte der Elitenhirnforschung* (Genius's Brains: The History of Elite Brain Research). Berlin: Wallstein.

Hagner, Michael. 2006. *"Der Geist bei der Arbeit." Untersuchungen zur Hirnforschung*. Göttingen: Wallstein.

Hagner, Michael, and Cornelius Borck. 2001. "Mindful Practices: On the Neurosciences in the Twentieth Century," *Science in Context* 14: 507-10.

Harrington, Anne. 1987. *Mind, Medicine, and the Double Brain: A Study in Nineteenth-Century Thought.* Princeton: Princeton University Press.

Harrington, Anne. 1991. "Beyond Phrenology: Localization Theory in the Modern Era," in Corsi, 1991.

Hatfield, Gary. 2000. "The Brain's 'New' Science: Psychology, Neurophysiology, and Constraint," *Philosophy of Science* 67: S388-S403.

Illes, Judy, M. Kirschen, and J. D. Gabrieli. 2003. "From Neuroimaging to Neuroethics," *Nature Neuroscience* 6 (2003): 205.

Illes, Judy, and Eric Racine. 2005. "Imaging or Imagining? A Neuroethics Challenge Informed by Genetics," *The American Journal of Bioethics* 5: 5-18.

Ingold, Timothy. 2006. "Against Human Nature," in Jeeves, 2006.

Jaroff, Leon. 1989. "The Gene Hunt," *Time*, March 20, pp. 62-67.

Jeeves, Malcolm, ed. 2006. *Human Nature.* Edinburgh: The Royal Society of Edinburgh.

Jones, Gareth. 2006. "The Human Embryo: Its Ambiguous Nature," in Jeeves, 2006.

Lepore, F. E. 2001. "Dissecting Genius: Einstein's Brain and the Search for the Neural Basis of Intellect," *Cerebrum* 3 [no page numbers in the version available through www.dana.org].

Linke, Detlef Bernhard. 1999. "Gehirn, Seele und Auferstehung," *Evangelische Theologie* 50: 128-35.

Lovejoy, Arthur O. 1935. "Nature as an Aesthetic Norm," in *Essays in the History of Ideas.* Baltimore: Johns Hopkins University Press, 1948.

Mauron, Alex. 2003. "Renovating the House of Being. Genomes, Souls, and Selves," *Annals of the New York Academy of Sciences* 1001: 240-52.

Metzinger, Thomas. 2005. "[Neuroethik.] Unterwegs zu einem neuen Menschenbild" (On the Way Towards a New Image of Man), *Gehirn & Geist* 11: 50-54.

Nagel, Thomas. 1974. "What Is It Like to Be a Bat?" *The Philosophical Review* 83: 435-50.

Noonan, Harold. 1991. *Personal Identity.* London: Routledge.

Novas, Carlos, and Nikolas Rose. 2000. "Genetic Risk and the Birth of the Somatic Individual," *Economy and Society* 29: 485-513.

Olson, Eric T. 2002. "Personal Identity," in *Stanford Encyclopedia of Philosophy,* http://plato.stanford.edu/entries/identity-personal.

Parfit, Derek. 1971. "Personal Identity," *The Philosophical Review* 80: 3-27.

Penfield, Wilder, and Theodore Rasmussen. 1950. *The Cerebral Cortex of Man: A Clinical Study of Localization of Function.* New York: Macmillan.

Perry, John, ed. 1975. *Personal Identity.* Berkeley: University of California Press.

Pitassi, Maria-Cristina. 1998. "Une résurrection pour quel corps et pour quelle humanité? La réponse lockienne entre philosophie, exégèse et théologie" (Resurrection: For Which Body and Which Humanity? The Lockean An-

swer Between Philosophy, Exegesis and Theology), *Rivista di storia della filosofia* 1: 45-61.
Puccetti, Roland. 1969. "Brain Transplantation and Personal Identity," *Analysis* 29: 65-77.
Puccetti, Roland. 1973. "Brain Bisection and Personal Identity," *British Journal for the Philosophy of Science* 24: 339-55.
Ratzinger, Joseph (Benedict XVI). 2005. "Discorso del Santo Padre Benedetto XVI ai membri delle Pontificie Accademie delle Scienze e delle Scienze Sociali," www.vatican.va/holy_father/benedict_xvi/speeches/2005/november/documents/hf_ben_xvi_spe_20051121_academies_it.html.
Ritter, Joachim, and Karlfried Gründer, eds. 1971-2004. *Historisches Wörterbuch der Philosophie*. Basel: Schwabe.
Sass, Hans-Martin. 1989. "Brain Life and Brain Death: A Proposal for a Normative Agreement," *Journal of Medicine and Philosophy* 14: 45-59.
Singh, Ilina, and Nikolas Rose. 2006. "Neuro-forum: An Introduction," *BioSocieties* 1: 97-102.
Sperry, Roger W. 1964. "The Great Cerebral Commissure," *Scientific American* 210: 42-52.
Sperry, Roger W. 1982. "Some Effects of Disconnecting the Cerebral Hemispheres" (Nobel Lecture), *Science* 217 (4566): 1223-26.
Taylor, Charles. 1989. *Sources of the Self: The Making of the Modern Identity*. Cambridge, MA: Harvard University Press.
Thomas, Louis-Vincent. 1988. "L'eschatologie: Permanence et mutation" (Eschatology: Continuity and Mutation). In L.-V. Thomas et al., *Réincarnation, immortalité, résurrection*. Brussels: Publications des Facultés Universitaires Saint-Louis.
Torrance, John, ed. 1992. *The Concept of Nature*. Oxford: Clarendon Press.
Veatch, Robert M. 1993. "The Impending Collapse of the Whole-Brain Definition of Death," *Hastings Center Report* 23: 18-24.
Uttal, William R. 2001. *The New Phrenology: The Limits of Localizing Cognitive Processes in the Brain*. Cambridge, MA: MIT Press.
Vergote, Antoine. 1979. "The Body as Understood in Contemporary Thought and Biblical Categories," *Philosophy Today* 35 (1991): 93-105.
Vidal, Fernando. 2002. "Brains, Bodies, Selves, and Science: Anthropologies of Identity and the Resurrection of the Body," *Critical Inquiry* 28: 930-74.
Vidal, Fernando. 2006. *Les Sciences de l'âme, XVIe-XVIIIe siècle*. Paris: Champion.
Vidal, Fernando. 2009. "Brainhood, Anthropology of Modernity," *History of the Human Sciences* 22: 5-36.
Wiggins, David. 1967. *Identity and Spatio-Temporal Continuity*. Oxford: Basil Blackwell.
Wilkes, Kathleen V. 1988. *Real People: Personal Identity Without Thought Experiments*. Oxford: Clarendon Press.

Williams, Raymond. 1983. "Nature," in *Keywords: A Vocabulary of Culture and Society*. New York: Oxford University Press, revised edition.
Wolpe, Paul Root. 2002. "The Neuroscience Revolution," *Hastings Center Report* (July-August): 8.
Young, Robert M. 1990. *Mind, Brain, and Adaptation in the Nineteenth Century: Cerebral Localization and Its Biological Context from Gall to Ferrier*. New York: Oxford University Press.

PHILOSOPHICAL ANALYSES

Science and the Search for a New Anthropology

Jürgen Mittelstrass

I

There have always been two different approaches in determining what a human being, what "man" is: a scientific approach and a philosophical one (in a broad sense, including religious and humanistic approaches). Thus, since antiquity, in the European tradition, a distinction has been made between the biological and the cultural nature of man: between what is natural to him in a physical and biological sense, and what pertains to him culturally, what is his "cultural essence." This, however, does not mean that both "essences," the physical and the cultural, fall asunder, and that therefore man disintegrates into two "essences."

In fact, man is a natural being, who can live only as a cultural being and can find his purpose only as such. *Descriptively*, within the context of biological systematics, mankind is a subspecies of the species *Homo sapiens*, namely, *Homo sapiens sapiens*, and is the only recent member of the genus *Homo*. But this definition includes only the empirico-physical side of man, not that which makes up the essence of humanity *ascriptively*, namely, its form of self-description and (not conclusively established) self-determination. This latter was described classically as the *animal rationale*, a being endowed with and determined by reason, or as a being lying between animal and God. Newer philosophical anthropologies (after

---

First published in M. Sánchez Sorondo, ed., *What Is Our Real Knowledge about the Human Being?* (Vatican City: Pontifical Academy of Sciences, 2007), pp. 101-9.

JÜRGEN MITTELSTRASS

Friedrich Nietzsche) capture this notion in the concept of a *"nicht festgestelltes,"* that is, a not-yet-determined being (both biologically and culturally). One makes a category mistake, if one interprets our actions and thoughts as the products of natural processes whereby even the act of interpreting becomes part of nature, a "natural fact." But we fall into a new form of naiveté if we oppose this interpretation with a claim that scientifically discovered facts have no influence, or at least ought to have no influence, on the self-determination of man. Thus it is a matter of adopting a scientifically informed and philosophically considered position, one that is beyond mere *biologism* and *culturalism,* in other words, one that is beyond an absolute distinction between biological and cultural explanations, and that refers to both the lives we lead and the laws we obey. Such a position should reduce man to neither (pure) nature, nor to the (absolute) spirit he aspires to be.

2

Modern philosophical anthropology mirrors this situation. It takes its point of departure from two opposing conceptions: that attributed to Max Scheler and that of Helmut Plessner.[1] According to Scheler, philosophical anthropology is nothing but the quintessence of philosophy itself. According to Plessner it follows the methodology and achievements of the empirical sciences of man in the form of an "integrative" discipline. Scheler hearkens back to traditional determinations of man as *animal rationale;* Plessner embraces the orientation of biological, medical, psychological, and, in the extended sense, social-scientific research, and he does this with the conceptual goal of a structural theory of man. Common to both thinkers in the characterization of man is the concept of *world-openness,* which includes the aspect of the openness of human development.

1. For a more detailed analysis of what follows, see J. Mittelstrass, "Philosophy or the Search for Anthropological Constants," in *Understanding Human Development: Lifespan Psychology in Exchange with Other Disciplines,* ed. U. Staudinger and U. Lindenberger (Dordrecht: Kluwer Academic Publishers, 2003), pp. 483-94, and "The Anthropocentric Revolution and Our Common Future," in *New Pharmacological Approaches to Reproductive Health and Healthy Ageing,* ed. W.-K. Raff et al., Symposium on the Occasion of the 80th Birthday of Professor Egon Diczfalusy (Berlin/Heidelberg/New York: Springer, 2001) (*Ernst Schering Research Foundation. Workshop Supplement* 8), pp. 57-67.

Science and the Search for a New Anthropology

According to Scheler, "man" is the "X that can behave in a world-open manner to an unlimited extent."[2] According to Plessner, "man" is characterized by an "eccentric positionality,"[3] whereby his eccentric existence, that possesses no fixed center, is described as the unity of mediated immediacy and natural artificiality. Accordingly, Plessner formulates three *fundamental laws of philosophical anthropology:* (1) the law of natural artificiality, (2) the law of mediated immediacy, and (3) the law of the utopian standpoint.[4] Similarly, Arnold Gehlen states the thesis that man is by nature a cultural being,[5] whereby his cultural achievements are seen as compensation for organs, and "man" is defined as a creature of lack *(Mängelwesen).*[6] For Nietzsche, as mentioned before, "man" is the not-yet-determined animal,[7] and science is seen as the expression of human endeavor "to determine himself."[8] Furthermore, one of the reasons for the difficulty of saying what man is lies in the fact that man is the (only) creature that possesses a reflective relationship with itself. Man, as Heidegger says, is the creature "which in its being, relates understandingly to its being."[9] This opens up a broad horizon of possible self-interpretations of man, and to this extent a broad horizon for an answer to the question, what a human being, what man is. The only thing that is clear is what, with regard to the essential openness of man, can be called the *anthropologically basic condition.*

This openness affects all phases of human development, from both an ontogenetic and a phylogenetic point of view. There is no "natural"

2. M. Scheler, *Die Stellung des Menschen im Kosmos* (Darmstadt: Otto Reichl, 1927), p. 49.

3. H. Plessner, *Die Stufen des Organischen und der Mensch: Einleitung in die philosophische Anthropologie* (Berlin and Leipzig: Walter de Gruyter, 1928), pp. 362ff.

4. Plessner, *Die Stufen des Organischen und der Mensch,* pp. 309-46. See K. Lorenz, *Einführung in die philosophische Anthropologie* (Darmstadt: Wissenschaftliche Buchgesellschaft, 1990), pp. 102f.

5. A. Gehlen, *Anthropologische Forschung: Zur Selbstbegegnung und Selbstentdeckung des Menschen* (Reinbek: Rowohlt Verlag, 1961), p. 78.

6. A. Gehlen, *Der Mensch: Seine Natur und seine Stellung in der Welt* [1940], 9th ed. (Wiesbaden: Akademische Verlagsgesellschaft Athenaion, 1972), p. 37.

7. F. Nietzsche, *Jenseits von Gut und Böse* [1886], in F. Nietzsche, *Werke: Kritische Gesamtausgabe,* ed. G. Colli and M. Montinari, vol. VI/2 (Berlin: Walter de Gruyter, 1968), p. 79.

8. F. Nietzsche, *Nachgelassene Fragmente Frühjahr 1881 bis Sommer 1882,* in *Werke,* vol. V/2 (1973), p. 533.

9. M. Heidegger, *Sein und Zeit* [1927], 14th ed. (Tübingen: Max Niemeyer, 1977), pp. 52f.

fate in the becoming of man, as an individual or as a species, that might be definitely determined by biological laws, even though of course the "schema" of this development is prescribed by certain biological regularities. Thus, there is no adulthood before childhood, no reverse ageing, no Achilles who is young until he dies. In psychological terminology: the architecture of human ontogeny is incomplete,[10] and not merely in earlier stages, but throughout a lifetime.

It is especially in the opposed but complementary concepts, *nature*, or causal relation, and *culture*, or institutional relation, that in this context (in the framework of human ethology) make clear the different, but in the anthropological context, indelibly reciprocal approaches to analysis. "Causal and intentional regularities constitute strictly distinct ranges of objects that must be studied by the disciplines of natural science and cultural science with different scientific methods. Causal regularities are constrained by initial conditions. Intentional regularities are determined by goal representations which, due to their social mediation, normally do not become conscious. The disputed question of whether, and to what extent sociocultural behavior is naturally and biologically determined or vice versa, is actually a dispute about whether or not some empirically observed behavior is to be taken as 'natural' (belonging to nature) or as 'cultural' (belonging to culture)."[11]

From this, it is also clear what kinds of tensions are involved in all forms of philosophical anthropology. These, correctly, all see themselves (inside and outside philosophy) as fundamental, but in an integrative sense (similar to Plessner's approach) that takes the knowledge of man acquired by other (empirical) disciplines into account. Thus, even within philosophy science has its day.

3

Today we are promised great gains above all from the developments of the "new biology," for example, in medicine. But there are great risks as

---

10. P. B. Baltes, "On the Incomplete Architecture of Human Ontogeny: Selection, Optimization, and Compensation as Foundation of Developmental Theory," *American Psychologist* 52 (1997): 366-80.

11. Lorenz, *Einführung in die philosophische Anthropologie*, p. 23.

well; for instance, in the thoughtless or irresponsible application of bioengineering. This is nothing fundamentally new. Discoveries and inventions that point to the future have throughout human history come saddled with dangers and risks of abuse of a new and usually unimagined order. What may be new in the case of modern biology is that developments in biological knowledge now appear to place man in the unique position of being able to change his own nature, and that this development has ethical consequences. Man intervenes ever more powerfully in evolution, even his own, and he changes the measures by which he previously described and shaped his fate, the human condition itself.

We have known since Darwin that man, not only from the point of view of philosophy and culture, but also biologically, has no fixed essence. Even though this understanding is imperceptible to the individual and only recognizable to science over great periods of time, nevertheless, he is subject to fundamental changes. That man can intervene in these changes himself has only become clear in the light of the new biology — an ability to deliberately change his own genetic constitution and that of his progeny. In fact, the *conditio humana* itself is changing: in the sense that now even man's biological foundations are at his disposal. This creates a completely new and consequential situation in the domain of ethics.

There are various consequences that have been drawn from this situation. One is the call for a *bioethics code,* an applied ethics that deals specifically with biological states of affairs. Such a code would prescribe watchfulness and particular measures in certain fields as well as certain applications that could be formulated as rules for an ethics of responsibility. Such rules if applied to developments in genetic technology might include a careful checking for possible undesirable results and also a rule of caution, permitting choice of the option that offers the greatest security of prognosis and the least expected harm. However, the debate over the ethical problems of biology extends far beyond bioethics into the direction of *environmental ethics,* which attempts to change the foundations of ethics itself.

The point of departure of such a concept of ethics is often an argument about *going against nature.* According to this position, genetic engineering and interventions in human reproductive processes do something that is the business of nature alone; they intervene in a regulatory manner in a self-regulating nature. Gene transfer may cross species boundaries, and thus infringe on the "identity of species"[12] and disturb the (relative) stability of ecological balances.[13] In arguments of this kind, we find biological uncertainty — what is then the "identity of species"? — coupled with ethical unclarity — what does ethics have to say about the order of species, that is, about biological classifications, or even about nature as a whole, however that is imagined? Those who think (and write) this way are confusing the empirical (biological states of affairs) with the domain of the normative, and they commit the naturalistic fallacy, that is, they infer what ought to be from what is; they derive norms from facts.

This is precisely the case in the well-known arguments of Hans Jonas. He declares the natural to be the highest norm and views any intervention into these natural processes as an offense against "naturally" given norms. For Jonas, the technology of cloning is in "contradiction to the dominant strategy of nature"[14] and thus cannot be justified. The natural — here in the form of a natural reproduction — consequently appears as something not to be interfered with and as something that pursues its own goals with strategic means, and by these means makes itself the highest normative authority. As a matter of fact, the attempt is made repeatedly to construct an ecological ethics on the basis of an inference from facts to norms (which usually reveals a concealed naturalism) and to then oppose this new ethics in the form of *physiocentrism* to the *anthropocentrism* that has long dominated ethics and that is now (in many aspects erroneously) declared to have been a basic error. For the anthropocentric position — in questions both of ethics and of nature — man is the point of departure of all arguments, and nature has no intrinsic moral value. For the physiocentric position, nature is characterized by its own (absolute) intrinsic value, which at the same time implies duties of man toward nature. To be more precise, we can distinguish between *pathocentrism* (all sensible creatures have a moral value), *biocentrism* (all living creatures have a moral value), and *radical physiocentrism*, which, as just mentioned, makes all of nature the bearer of moral value. Common to all these variants is that values,

---

12. G. Altner, *Naturvergessenheit: Grundlagen einer umfassenden Bioethik* (Darmstadt: Wissenschaftliche Buchgesellschaft, 1991), p. 214.

13. Altner, *Naturvergessenheit*, p. 217.

14. H. Jonas, "Laßt uns einen Menschen klonieren: Von der Eugenik zur Gentechnologie," in H. Jonas, *Technik, Medizin und Ethik: Zur Praxis des Prinzips Verantwortung* (Frankfurt: Insel-Verlag, 1985), p. 179.

which in fact are always the result of valuations, are declared to be a part of nature itself.

The expansion of a bioethics (a sub-area of applied ethics) to biological ethics, in the form of or against the background of physiocentrism, is thus based on a misunderstanding. This expansion not only makes ethics dependent on a particular view of the world, but also leads by its naturalistic premises to a new (ethical) *biologism*. Biology is expected to be an advisor and also a legislator in ethical affairs. And this in turn involves both a philosophical and a biological misunderstanding, since the new biology teaches us how permeable the boundaries are between the natural and the artificial, that is, those processes determined by man. The appeal to nature in ethical questions, which made sense in archaic cultures, no longer makes sense here.

One more point: the notion that moral conduct as a particular form of social behavior is itself the product of evolution or can be given an evolutionary explanation leads one astray if it is understood in an absolute sense as a foundation of ethics. Whereas in the first case of a biological ethics, natural relations are to be taken as the standard of ethics, in the second case, ethics would be a product of these relations, and thus our ethical deficits would not be due to the failings of reason, but to an evolution that was unfinished and unable to cope adequately with man. An *evolutionary ethics* would in this sense be a convenient excuse for tasks unaccomplished in man's dealing with himself, and with nature. However, nature gives no ethical lessons, neither in the form of physiocentrism nor in the form of evolutionary ethics. Nature only reminds us when harm is caused — think of environmental problems — of the unfinished tasks of rational ethics.

4

Here it is appropriate to remind ourselves of Immanuel Kant's concept of a rational ethics that is both *normative* (not evolutionary or biologistic) and *universal* (not particular or relativistic), that is, the principles of which are universalistic. According to Kant, this concept does not derive its validity from nature or from the values of certain (particular) cultures, but rather from a general will that is best expressed in the so-called end-formula of the categorical imperative: "Act in such a way that you always treat humanity, whether in your own person or in the person of any other, never simply as a means, but always at the same time as an end!"[15] Only the "rational" being exists as "an end in itself."[16] This is why for Kant only rational beings have "dignity." The concept of a universal ethics, like the underlying idea of *universal reason,* is often said to be typically "European," determined by the ideas of Christianity and the Enlightenment, and therefore, at least if seen from the outside, to be particular, that is, not universal. Yet this is a misunderstanding. After all, its expressions of a corresponding ethical universality are, for instance, the concept of human rights and in connection with them, the concept of human dignity.

In other words, as in Kant, anthropological arguments are linked to ethical arguments — and to scientific arguments so far as Kant distinguishes between two worlds, the natural world constituted by natural laws (which is also phenomenal), and the moral world constituted by (universal) reason (which is also noumenal). Man is a citizen of both worlds, and this is why, as I said before, he cannot be reduced either to (pure) nature or to the (absolute) spirit that he aspires to be.

5

In an unpublished manuscript "On truth and lie in an extra-moral sense," Nietzsche made the following comment: "What does Man actually know about himself? . . . Doesn't nature conceal almost everything from him, even concerning his body, in order . . . to drive him and enclose him within a proud and magical consciousness! She [nature] threw away the key."[17] Although this remark is hardly up-to-date from a biological point of view, it remains quite current from the anthropological one. The human condition is still characterized by a need for self-determination. And for this very reason we should not be looking for a lost key. There is no such key. Self-determination is not just the fate of the individual, but is also the fate of humanity itself; it belongs to the essence of humanity. When one overlooks this, for instance,

---

15. I. Kant, *Grundlegung zur Metaphysik der Sitten* B 66f. (*Groundwork of the Metaphysics of Morals,* ed. H. J. Paton [New York: Harper & Row, 1964], p. 96).

16. Kant, *Grundlegung zur Metaphysik,* B 65.

17. F. Nietzsche, "Über Wahrheit und Lüge im außermoralischen Sinne," in *Werke,* vol. III/2 (1973), p. 371.

Science and the Search for a New Anthropology

when we search for *the* biological or *the* philosophical answer, we are threatened on the one hand by biologism (man is only a biological species) and on the other by ideological dogmatism (man is lost in his own ideologies). So, even in the face of a steadily growing body of biological knowledge and a biological nature that is increasingly at our disposal, it is still essential that man take (reasonable) control of his own ascriptions, of his self-definition, and of his designs.

This means, again, that he must determine a measure for himself: that he must strive against the threat both of scientism and of ideology. For man has always tried to draw an image of his future perfection — as individual apotheosis or as social utopia — and has repeatedly turned from this icon in horror, or in boredom. This shows that the human condition in which we describe our particular essence is in a sense not to be optimized. Such an optimization threatens to dissolve our condition precisely because this condition is the essence of humanity. What would remain would be either gods or machines, and neither of these share in what makes us human — our warmth, our odor, our happiness, and our pain.

This does not mean that we ought not work to change our essence, to alter that human condition that defines the space between the available and the unavailable, between happiness and pain, between god and beast. On the contrary, this is precisely our task — one that is served by both ethics and science, not in separate worlds but in a single one. For not only science learns when ethics learns, in that it measures its own actions against ethical standards; ethics also learns when science does, in that it takes account of scientific states of affairs, as in the biological-empirical essence of humanity.

The Scientific Images and the Global Knowledge of the Human Being

Evandro Agazzi

Knowing What Man Is

Know yourself was considered already in antiquity as the imperative in which the core of wisdom was concentrated, and the force of this imperative was stressed by its being attributed to Apollo's oracle (hence to a divine source), so that a correct answer to the question implicit in this imperative ("Who am I?") was considered the solution to the problem of finding one's happiness. That of attaining an adequate knowledge of oneself is a task of paramount importance, since it coincides, in the last analysis, with the problem of finding a sense and a value for one's life, and this is certainly the most radical and essential problem for every conscious being. Unfortunately, many humans do not have the necessary time and existential conditions for devoting adequate reflection to this capital issue, but no *conscious* life (i.e., no genuinely human life) can develop without some kind of awareness of this problem, simply because no human being can escape being confronted with the totality of his whole experience (i.e., his own life taken in all its multi-faceted dimensions), in which he is personally involved and has to find out the best way of spending life.

Is this an easy or a difficult task? At first it seems easy, since in the case of self-knowledge we do not need to "cross the gap" between the subject and the object of knowledge, which is often seen as an obstacle in the effort to ascertain "how things are." Nevertheless we quickly become convinced that in the effort to know ourselves we do not really enjoy a significant privilege with respect to knowledge of the so-called "external world": we do not know, for instance, how the internal structure and functioning of our bodies are organized, how our emotions can drive our conduct, how we can retain memories of past experience, and so on. Of all these aspects of our reality we do not have an immediate knowledge, and this is why humans have tried from time immemorial to obtain such knowledge by suitable means, or by resorting to reliable sources and authorities. This is true, in particular, not only regarding "matters of fact" such as those we have just mentioned, but also (and even more significantly) regarding those "ultimate questions" that regard the sense and value of life taken globally, and imply a correct understanding of "what man is," of "what the world is," and "what the position of man in the world is," besides the question of whether this world exhausts the reality in which human life can find its sense and value. For many centuries humans have resorted to religion and philosophy as sources for the solution of the "ultimate questions," simply because these were considered the most reliable sources of knowledge in general, and because of the methods they used: *divine revelation* and *metaphysical speculation*.

The New Intellectual Authority: Modern Natural Science

The situation changed at the beginning of "modernity," when a new source of knowledge, equipped with its peculiar methods, appeared in Western culture: natural science, understood in the new "modern" sense of this concept. This "new science" (the adjective "new" explicitly appears in the title of Galileo's most scientifically relevant work) was initially well aware of its limited and delimited scope, that is: (i) the object of inquiry was only the "local motion" of material bodies; (ii) the aim of "grasping the essence" of things was considered a desperate enterprise (the "what is?" was not the kind of question to be asked in this science); (iii) only strictly empirical evidence (phenomena) must be considered as reliable knowledge, from which only prudent generalizations can be tentatively admitted; (iv) moreover, among the properties of material bodies only a few will be investigated, those that are expressible as mathematical magnitudes; (v) the combination of empirical evidence with mathematical calculations is the backbone of the experimental method, thanks to which it is possible (and mandatory) to submit to test any scientific assertion that is not empirically supported; (vi) in particular this mathematization and experimental testing are possible because artificial instruments are designed for making observations and measurements.

The new natural science attained, in the course of just one century, such an impressive harvest of knowledge that even philosophers gradually became convinced that this progress was obtained not "in spite of," but "in virtue of" the above-mentioned limitations. While thinkers like Descartes, Spinoza, and other "rationalists" maintained that sound knowledge in any field can be acquired by a generalized adoption of the mathematical method of reasoning, other thinkers, and paradigmatically Kant, theorized that genuine knowledge in general is possible only by respecting the conditions fulfilled by modern natural science (i.e., application of mathematical conceptualization to empirical phenomena). This science was, at that time, a mechanics whose tacit ontological elements were matter and motion. Therefore it was implicitly admitted that genuine knowledge could be attained only in the domain of material things. Philosophers were aware of this situation and, though a minority were already embracing a materialistic metaphysics, the majority were still adhering to the general conception that had been characteristic of Western philosophy and, in particular, admitted a spiritual and transcendent dimension of reality of which God was the supreme being and in which humans participated, in that their nature included the possession of a spiritual immortal soul. The most typical representative of this "spiritualistic" trend was Descartes, whose philosophy was very welcome in his time, especially for having found a plausible solution to the problem of recognizing the full value of the new mechanistic natural science and at the same time the no-less-genuine value of metaphysical speculation. This solution consisted in the famous dualism according to which reality is split into two separate substances (*res cogitans* or spirit, and *res extensa* or matter); and while the study of material entities was entirely and exclusively attributed to the competence of the natural sciences, the study of spiritual entities was entirely and exclusively attributed to the competence of metaphysics, religion, and theology.

Cartesian Dualism

Since the said partition reflected itself also in the consideration of man, the consequence was that the human body (which is a material substance) can and must be studied through the natural sciences and is exclusively endowed with material properties, while the human spirit is immaterial, is endowed with properties that cannot be investigated by natural science, but can and must be studied and recognized with the tools of metaphysical knowledge (which, in particular, justified the traditional perspectives of the Christian religion).

Despite its *prima facie* plausibility, this compromise solution was rather fragile, especially in its interpretation of man. The ontological separateness of the two substances implied the impossibility that the one could act upon the other or have any kind of causal influence on it, and this made it impossible, for example, to explain the sensory knowledge by which we form intellectual immaterial images of the external world, or, inversely, to explain how an immaterial act of volition can produce motions of the material body. These and similar difficulties were actually the consequence of having artificially imagined something that is contrary to the most immediate content of our existential experience, that is, the *unity* of this experience, in which we do not distinguish soul and body, and in which, in any case, any human being apprehends himself as *one* and not as *two*. This is also reflected in our use of language: when I say "this is *my* hand" I do not mean that this hand is my "property," but that it is "part of" myself (at variance with the sense of a sentence like "this is *my* car," which means the possession of something different from myself).

This is why a tendency toward the overcoming of this dualism was tacitly at work in the history of Western philosophy, and it can be seen as the program of eliminating one of the two poles by "reducing" it to the other: materialism pursued the proposal of reducing the whole of reality (in particular of man) to matter, by showing that the alleged spiritual characteristics are either the product of complex material structures or simply intellectual inventions; spiritualism attempted to prove the opposite thesis, that is, that matter is simply an initial, still-unconscious stage in the development of spirit. One could say that such opposite trends were not new, after all, but we must consider what powerful support the materialistic perspective received by the development of the new natural science. This development not only showed that in the domain of matter a great and uncontroversial amount of new knowledge had been actually achieved, but that the validity of this knowledge could also be proved concretely, that is, through the construction of a great array of new artifacts: *machines*.

The Fascination of Machines

The significance of machines in the development of Western culture is often recognized in the sense that they offered to humans the capability of magnifying the practical power of operation and production, paving the way to the industrial revolution. This is true, but even more significant is that modern machines are to a large extent the "application" of knowledge acquired in the natural sciences, so that we know how they will function and why they will function in a given manner *before* their concrete realization (they are invented or projected, not discovered). In this sense they seriously represent a tangible empirical confirmation of the scientific theories that were used in their design and play a genuine intellectual role. Moreover, in a machine nothing remains mysterious or secret: scientific knowledge completely *explains* its structure and functioning. Therefore, if of a certain object of study we are able to propose a "model" in the form of a certain kind of machine, we have the impression of having completely understood and explained this object. We can call this the *epistemological purport* of the machine, which explains the fruitfulness of adopting machines for the modeling of different processes. But this feature very easily drew with itself an *ontological reduction:* if a certain domain X of investigation becomes intelligible by using models derived from a given natural science N, it seems obvious that its properties are reducible to properties of the objects treated by that science, and if N is concerned with material objects, its competence seems to become extended also over X (i.e., the properties of X are "in the last analysis" also material).

This actually happened in the interpretation of the human being. Descartes was one of the first to present an articulated picture of the human organism as a complex mechanical machine, but he explicitly intended that this picture concerned exclusively the human body (including also several functions that we qualify as psychic and are common to many animals). In his view the spirit (that is, the sphere of our conscious activities and in particular self-consciousness) remains out of reach of this mechanical investigation and explanation, and taking the intellectual evidence of the *cogito* as starting point, metaphysical reflection can lead us to prove the existence of God, free will, the immortality of soul, and the other fundamental metaphysical doctrines of the tradition. Other thinkers, however, who subscribed to a materialistic philosophy, did not follow this Cartesian distinction: in his famous work *L'homme machine,* La Mettrie made the effort to show that the whole of human capabilities can be expressed and explained in terms of mechanical procedures taking place in the body, while the alleged spiritual realities in man and outside of man are simply inventions of persons wanting to dominate people by exploiting their general ignorance and their fear of death. This trend never stopped in the following centuries: after mechanics, other sciences attained a leading position in the domain of natural sciences, and they easily suggested various forms of "machines" (chemical, thermodynamic, electrodynamic, cybernetic, and so on) for the modeling of the human being, a modeling that was taken in a reductionist sense by all those who were inspired by a preconceived materialist metaphysics. The novelty that has emerged more recently is that such machines (which formerly had the status of *conceptual* constructions very similar to the hypothetical constructions of scientific theories) can now be *concretely* realized and, in certain cases, can actually perform some functions and operations of which humans (according to traditional views) are capable thanks to their intelligence. This is taken by several scholars as evidence that no spiritual intelligence is needed in order to account for these functions. The reasons why this conclusion is not justified cannot be discussed in this paper.

The Elimination of Finality

The elimination of spirit was not the only reason for dissatisfaction with the materialistic interpretation of reality based on the new natural sciences. An additional reason was that the methodological framework of these sciences explicitly excluded the consideration of *final causes*. Natural science could not dispense with the concept of cause or with causal explanation, but reduced it to the meaning of *efficient cause* (i.e., of something that "produces" an event), which was introduced under the seemingly nonmetaphysical notion of *force*. Force, which produces the *change* of motion (not motion itself, which is as primary as matter), acts on material bodies *from the outside* (and not from the inside, as the ancient formal and final causes were thought to act), and the result of physical actions is fully determined by the initial conditions and the applied forces, but does not conform to any design or pursue any goal. Therefore the suppression of finality and freedom were inexorably included in the worldview based solely on the new natural sciences, and such an elimination (besides posing serious problems in the conceptual and theoretical construction of the life sciences) jeopardized the possibility of giving a sense and a value to any reality whatsoever, and cut the roots of morality. Once again the way for avoiding this conclusion was seen by several philosophers in the adoption of a dualistic perspective. Since it was impossible to deny that natural science had acquired a tremendous amount of knowledge by its methodological restrictions, it seemed legitimate to claim that this approach was pertinent precisely in the domain of nature, but not in other domains. The most interesting example of this special form of dualism is that of Kant, who maintains that deterministic efficient causality is necessarily present in our knowledge of nature, because this knowledge regards only *phenomena* that are organized deterministically by our own intellectual categories. But beside the world of phenomena (the only world we really *know*) there is also the world of *noumena*, of "things in themselves," which we cannot know in a proper sense, but can think of without contradiction. In this world freedom and finality are thinkable and can exist, and we can even come to affirm their existence (without precisely knowing in what they consist and how they act) if we have other sources of information. For Kant this source is the interior experience of morality, which induces us to distinguish a *Homo phenomenon* (a phenomenal man) deterministically included in nature and a *Homo noumenon* (a noumenal man) endowed with free will, inviolable dignity, an end in itself and immortal. In short, we could say that with Kant the following dualistic compromise seemed attained: science had full competence on natural phenomena, while philosophy had competence on man. The scientific discourse had a cognitive status in a full sense, while the philosophical discourse had a less cogent cognitive status; its certitudes were rather "moral certitudes," sharing to a certain extent the characteristics of a faith.

The Irruption of the "Human Sciences"

But this renewed version of dualism could not last long. In the second half of the nineteenth century a new kind of sciences emerged whose domain of inquiry was precisely man (for this reason they are called in certain languages "human sciences," though this expression is not common in English). While the inclusion of the study of man in the field of biology (significantly developed in the nineteenth century, especially after the birth of Darwin's evolutionary theory and of physical anthropology) was essentially a development of the perspective according to which the "body" of man is a proper object of study in the natural sciences, these new sciences presented themselves as investigations of what has traditionally been considered the domain of the human "spirit," that is, the individual human mind (which became the object of "scientific psychology") and the collective product of minds, that is, human culture (which became the object of sociology and various historical and social sciences). It is not really important, here, that the "scientificity" of such new disciplines was advocated by certain authors in virtue of an alleged reducibility of their discourse to that of the natural sciences, by others in the name of a methodological affinity with these sciences, and by others on the contrary, by vindicating a specificity of contents, aims, and methods with respect to the natural sciences. What is important is the fact that, according to a view inaugurated by *positivism,* which became very influential and still dominates among cultivated people, the creation of these sciences completed the maturation of a historical process in which science replaced philosophy everywhere and has been recognized as the only genuine form of knowledge, and the only means for a rational solution to human problems. This attitude is also commonly called scientism.

At first sight this situation has the advantage of having finally overcome dualism and its difficulties, especially regarding the interpretation of man. But it is easy to see that this is not really the case. First, the majority of scientism's partisans openly or tacitly subscribe to a materialistic worldview, so that the alleged elimination of dualism simply amounts to the old reductionist metaphysics. Second, the real shortcomings of dualism consisted in the fact that this perspective was unable to account for the *unity* of reality, and in particular of the reality of man, a unity in which the two dimensions have to interact, to become "joined," so that the unity of experience present to every human being can be accounted for. Now, when the different sciences offer us their different *images* of reality (i.e., of *whatever* reality, including man), we are confronted not just with two, but with a great multiplicity of images, so that the situation is not that of a reduction but of a multiplication of the difficulties already present in dualism. Indeed, contrary to a naïve first impression, two different sciences do not differ because they investigate two different domains of "things," but because they investigate all things *from a delimited and specific point of view*. We can express this basic fact in different ways: from a *logico-linguistic* point of view we can say that every science adopts its specific predicates and constructs its technical vocabulary; from a *methodological* point of view we can say that every science provides the methods for establishing the meaning of its predicates and the immediate truth of its statements (criteria of *referentiality*); from an *ontological* point of view we can say that all this depends on the fact that every science does not investigate any reality *as a whole* but only a delimited number of attributes (properties and relations) of reality. These different ways of describing the situation amount to a unique fact: it is totally illusory to speak of *the scientific image* of reality globally understood no less than of any particular reality. This not so much owing to the fact that science is in a continual process of evolution and modification (such that it would be impossible to say *what is* this alleged scientific image), but especially because *there is not a single scientific image,* even taken at a given historical moment: there are the physical image, the chemical image, the biological image, the psychological image, the sociological image, and so on; and it is obvious that, given a certain "thing," only a limited number of these different images can be applied to it (e.g., it would be meaningless to give the chemical image of a mathematical theorem or of a dream, or the psychological image of a stone). In short, it is an untenable claim to maintain (as Wilfrid Sellars once affirmed) that the progress of our knowledge consists in continually replacing the *manifest image* of the world by the *scientific image,* because the first is intrinsically wrong and only the second is true. Actually there is a sense according to which the manifest image and the different scientific images of the same reality may be "true," but this sense must be carefully indicated.

Telling the Truth and Telling All the Truth

What has been said does not intend to underestimate the cognitive value of the scientific images. Quite the contrary, every scientific image is *partial,* not only because it does not capture "the whole of reality," but also "the whole of any single reality," and this partiality is the price paid for a great advantage: *objectivity.* Indeed, it is the fact of having decided to limit attention to a few attributes of reality, of having denoted them in its language through technically well-defined predicates, of having established standardized operational procedures for testing statements containing these predicates, that has permitted natural scientists first, and other scientists later, to mutually control and test their empirical discoveries and theoretical constructions, attaining in such a way a considerable level of intersubjective agreement and an increased knowledge *regarding those delimited aspects of reality* they intended to investigate. But this is tantamount to saying that the partial scientific images obtained in this way are *true*, provided that we are conscious that no proposition or set of propositions can be true (or false) "in itself," but always and necessarily *about its domain of reference*. Now, since every science speaks only about its domain of reference, and since we can be confident that (despite never attaining an "absolute certainty") it is able to produce a reliable *image* of its domain, we must conclude that this image is *true relative to its domain of reference*. Precisely because truth is always relative in this referential sense, it would be absurd to pretend that any partial image is true also about other domains of reference, and even less about the whole of the thing from which the partial set of attributes has been selected. Coming back to our theme, we can say that any of the different sciences (natural and human) that offer scientific images of man *tell the truth* about man, but *do not tell all the truth*. One might think that in order to know "all the truth" it would be sufficient to accumulate the partial truths coming from all the single sciences, but this conclusion is untenable. First, it alludes to a kind of infinite and indefinite task (not only the present sciences, but also future ones should be taken into consideration); second, it is still biased by scientism, because it is said that only the accumulation of scientific images could contribute to the attainment of the *complete* truth. But this is simply a dogmatic presupposition that excludes the possibility that other kinds of truth could contribute to the attainment of complete truth or, maybe better, of the *whole* truth (i.e., the truth regarding "the whole" in its globality, in which the relations between the different partial images should also be considered).

The Richness of the Unity of Experience

In order to capture this global truth we have to rescue the cognitive relevance of many aspects of our experience *in its full richness*, as we have already characterized it. In particular those aspects that are not strictly bound to sensory evidence alone and that we nevertheless commonly qualify as "experience" (such as moral, aesthetic, religious, sentimental, affective experience), or are present to us in fundamental aspects of our cognitive activity, such as introspection or reflection. As we have already said, this unity of experience is, for every human, his or her *life* — what we could also call the *manifest image* of reality, not in the impoverished sense we encountered above, but in the sense of "what is immediately present" to us and, for this reason, is *methodologically* the starting point of any knowledge, but especially the *source of any fundamental problem*. This happens because the global unity of life, once it becomes the object of reflection, inevitably generates the problems of its sense and value. This is *the* problem for every conscious being and, characteristically, it generates the subquestion of whether the value of life is contained in the unity of experience or not. This is the *problem of the Absolute*, which coincides with the problem of giving a value to life, and it is of paramount interest for any human simply because *how one should concretely conduct one's life* depends on its solution. A conscious being, a being endowed with reason, inevitably wants to find the *true* solution to the problem of life relying upon *knowledge and reasoning*. This is tantamount to recognizing that a *postulate of the rationality of the real* is implicit in this fundamental attitude, a postulate to be understood simply as the claim that it is possible to provide a conception of the Absolute capable of granting the value of life. The effort will be that of transforming this postulate into a kind of theorem by actually finding this determination of the Absolute — and in this enterprise no element of truth can be disregarded. This is why the scientific truths must be included in this effort, because they become part of this unity of experience we cannot ignore; but at the same time we are brought to consider what problems regarding the sense and value of life overstep the possibility of treatment of these different scientific frameworks, and we easily find a great deal of them. In such a way we necessarily recover the full legitimacy of metaphysics as an intellectually uneliminable enterprise and the only rational discourse concerning the *whole* of reality, as well as the full intellectual legitimacy of the idea of *transcendence*, which (along with *immanence*) is one of the two alternatives open to the rational solution of the problem of the Absolute. Of course, the existence of this problem, and the postulate of the rationality of the real, do not guarantee that we will find the solution. But in any case the solution would be chosen as an act of *free faith*, a choice that is made, for-

The Scientific Images and the Global Knowledge of the Human Being

tunately, by many people who cannot devote themselves to philosophy. It is important, however, to see that this rational inquiry is possible and cannot be forbidden in the name of science.

The Peculiarly Human Feature of the Aesthetic Experience: The Teaching of Kant and the Challenge of Neuroscience

Franco Chiereghin

1. Introduction: Perceptual Activity and Artistic Expression

In 2004 an essay by Hideaki Kawabata and Semir Zeki, with the significant title "Neural Correlates of Beauty,"[1] appeared in the *Journal of Neurophysiology*. Here the authors, after having alluded to the Platonic dialogues in which the theme of beauty is discussed *(Hippias Major, Phaedrus, The Banquet)*, come to a stop with the *Critique of the Power of Aesthetic Judgment*, asking exactly the same questions of Kant as to the presuppositions that confer validity on our aesthetic judgment and about the conditions for the possibility of the phenomenon of beauty. Only, as Kant looks for the answers by traveling the path upward, toward the *a priori* structures of subjectivity, Kawabata and Zeki propose to answer by experimentally traveling the path downward, looking for the existence of specific neural connections, subject to the experimentation of the phenomenon of beauty, and asking themselves whether one or more cerebral structures in their workings condition the formulation of the judgment of taste. The research, conducted upon ten subjects (five males and five females), consisted of twice showing them 192 painting reproductions (abstract, still life, landscape, or portrait), asking them to push a button according to how they judged a painting: beautiful, ugly, or neutral. The data recorded using fMRI (functional magnetic resonance imaging) showed that for every pronouncement of an aesthetic

---

1. H. Kawabata and S. Zeki, "Neural Correlates of Beauty," *Journal of Neurophysiology* 91 (2004): 1699-1705. See on this experiment D. W. Zaidel, *Neuropsychology of Art: Neurological, Cognitive, and Evolutionary Perspectives* (Hove, UK: Psychology Press, 2005), p. 161.

judgment there is a corresponding activation of a complex of specific cerebral areas (visual cortex, orbitofrontal regions, anterior cingulate, parietal cortex, and motor cortex), operating interconnectedly, even though their quotients of activity were differentiated according to the type of experience.[2]

The relevance of this research is certainly indubitable, especially as regards the visual arts, and they have already attained highly significant results,[3] demonstrating how important or, better, necessary it is to recognize the neural structures active in the aesthetic experience in order to understand how much the characteristics of the perceptive processes might influence and condition both the creation and enjoyment of beauty. Nevertheless it is legitimate to ask: Is this side of research, in addition to being recognized as necessary, sufficient to explain the artistic phenomenon? Is this process of naturalization of aesthetic experience capable of exhausting the entire realm of the human experience of the beautiful?

In order to attempt to answer these questions I think it is appropriate first of all to find an understanding of the way to envisage the human capacity of making aesthetic experiences. It is known that art has always represented a problem that is nonmarginal to an evolutionary conception that intends to explain everything in terms of adaptation and natural selection. Darwin's ingenious attempts to explain humans' and animals' sensitivity to beauty through its original function of selecting the sexually most attractive mate[4] run into difficulties. For instance, the capacity to appreciate symmetries, harmonies, lively colors, or sound sequences (all features that will contribute to the aesthetic ex-

---

2. Contemporaneously with the study published by Kawabata and Zeki a study appeared, from which emerges the importance of the prefrontal cortex as the neural correlate of aesthetic judgment. Cf. C. J. Cela-Conde, G. Marty, F. Maestú, T. Ortiz, E. Munar, A. Fernández, M. Roca, J. Rosselló, and F. Quesney, "Activation of the Prefrontal Cortex in the Human Visual Aesthetic Perception," *Proceedings of the National Academy of Sciences* 101, no. 16 (April 2004): 6321-35. In a study appearing a year later, next to the importance of the prefrontal cortex, it is shown how aesthetic judgment activates cerebral areas that are in part coincidental with those activated by evaluative judgments of social order and morals. See T. Jacobsen, R. I. Schubotz, L. Höfel, and D. Y. V. Cramon, "Brain Correlates of Aesthetic Judgment of Beauty," *NeuroImage* 29 (2006): 276-85.

3. See, for example, S. Zeki, *Inner Vision: An Exploration of Art and the Brain* (Oxford and New York: Oxford University Press, 1999).

4. See C. Darwin, *The Descent of Man, and Selection in Relation to Sex* (London: Murray, 1871).

perience of beauty) is firmly interlaced with the reproductive function. However, despite the fact that these capacities and functions are interlaced, they are not identical. In fact, it is hard to deny that the capacity to appreciate symmetries, harmonies, lively colors, and sound sequences must be present as quite an autonomous capacity, or even as a capacity that precedes sexual attraction, in those subjects that select their mates.[5] If a subject were unable to recognize "beautiful" forms, the mate's efforts in unfolding sounds, forms, and colors in order to attract sexual attention to itself and be selected would not have any meaning. As it is not possible to identify the capacity of appreciation with the mechanisms of reproduction and survival, their appearance is yet to be explained.

As frequently happens, when faced with similar difficulties scholars fall back on the hypothesis of genetically determined dispositions present in all men universally, which might be at the origin of specific behaviors (among them the making of art) that are in themselves unnecessary, yet are successfully exploited to the ends of reproduction and survival. I remember a significant example of this in a text that appeared some eighteen years ago, *Homo aestheticus: Where Art Comes from and Why*, in which E. Dissanayake supports the thesis that there is in man a universal disposition, biologically based, that makes him be, precisely, *aestheticus,* and this consists in the capacity to "make things special."[6] For every considerable activity or event related to existence (birth, illness, death, nutrition, social bonds, etc.), all of the components of the determinate social groups would have exercised their ability to "make things special," attractive, and gratifying to the senses and to the intelligence, in order to distinguish them from the ordinary and thus to increase their importance and significance. The exercising of this aesthetic ability would have then favored a common recognition in behaviors capable of generating rites and ceremonies important to the ends of the cohesion and persistence of the group to which they belong. In this way, though indirectly achieved, even aesthetic activity would have found itself channeled into the great floodplain of behaviors directed toward survival.

5. See Geoffrey Miller, *Evolution of Human Music Through Sexual Selection*, in *The Origins of Music*, ed. N. L. Wallin, B. Merker, and S. Brown (Cambridge, MA: MIT Press, 2001), pp. 329-60.

6. E. Dissanayake, *Homo aestheticus: Where Art Comes from and Why* (New York: Free Press, 1992), p. 51.

Nevertheless, precisely because the "aestheticism" of man is assumed as something already present at the outset, it seems to me that from this perspective there is no room left to ask why on earth man has this irrepressible disposition to "make things special," and what renders it possible. Even if the hypothesis of genetic determinism had been completely demonstrated, it would still be left to explain why in the course of evolution, next to genes that preside over the formation of the heart, the liver, and all the other organs necessary for life, there are also genes that determine a predisposition seemingly "superfluous," not explicitly directed toward survival, even though useful in view of this.

If we don't want to stop at the "datum" of this *aestheticus* being of man, we need to make a step backward and ask ourselves: What renders possible this capacity to "make things special"? Is this capacity for "making things special" an exclusively human characteristic? Upon examination, I believe that it reflects a disposition to creativity that is widely present in the biosphere. Precisely in its specifically creative character, this capacity indeed has a long history and is the result of formation processes that, in addition to man and prior to his appearance, involve living organisms as such and take root, after all, in constitutive aspects of life itself.

Let us think, for example, about the extent to which perceptive capacity occurs in the living species in which it is present, at different levels of complexity and refinement. What the organism is in contact with (the world-environment) is a "cloud of atoms" that is specified in different forms of energy: chemical, electromagnetic, mechanical, thermal, etc. These are the "things" of the world-environment. And what does the organism that relates to them with its own sensory receptors do? It "renders them absolutely special": the olfactory system and that of gustation upon contact with chemical energy transform it into odors and tastes; the visual system, interacting with electromagnetic energy, transmutes it into lines, colors, surfaces, masses at rest or in motion; the auditory system, activated by the mechanical energy of the vibrations of air or liquids, transforms it into the entire range of sounds; the tactile system transforms thermal and mechanical energy into the sensations of hot, cold, pain, and so forth.

In all of these transformations, in which the sensory receptors select the "things" of the world and make them irreplaceable to the survival of the organisms, the part performed by the living subject is absolutely predominant. According to what the neurophysiologists tell us, in the visual perception of something, for example (but also true for the other perceptive systems), it would seem that environmental contributions constitute about 20 percent of the whole perceptive phenomenon, whereas the remaining 80 percent would be the work of subjectivity.

In perception, then, nothing is impression, reflection, imitation, or passive reception of preexistent meanings already packaged in the world. The world we see, hear, smell, taste, etcetera is in a preponderant way a construction of the subject that neither imitates nor reproduces anything, but operates according to the laws of its own activity. Several positions, as many authoritative as radical, have come to support the view that raw energy present in the environment has the sole task of activating the receptors, which do not filter "data," but rather fulfill their function in the firing of the neural populations' activity; once absolved of this task, the open door from the receptors to the diverse forms of energy present in the world closes, and the construction of the meanings of the world is uniquely the work of the subject.[7] Even without wholly accepting this position, the fact remains that the subject plays a predominant role in the construction of the manifestness of the world.

What consequences does this power have to the meaning of making art? The question arises whether the contrapositions of the past still make any sense, or if they still exist under different names: those between figurative and abstract, tonal and dodecaphonic, realism and surrealism, images of appearance and images of essence, and so on. On the contrary, they might be equal to those marks of simply diverse expressive styles, since even literary, musical, or depictive expression, which would like to be the most impersonal and adherent to "reality," or of that which from time to time is held to be "natural," is no less a construction of the subject than that which might appear as a more driven subjectivism. Even the traditional and more general antithesis, that between objectivism and subjectivism in art (in which many of the antitheses mentioned here might converge), once it is understood in the light of the predominant role performed by the subject in the construction of the meanings of the world, lends itself to a singular overturning of roles compared to its ordinary meaning.

---

7. See, for example, the position of W. J. Freeman, *How Brains Make Up Their Minds* (London: Weidenfeld & Nicolson, 1999). For some reservations regarding this position, refer to my *L'eco della caverna. Ricerche di filosofia della logica e della mente* (Padova: Il Poligrafo, 2004), pp. 231-39, 303-7, 321-24.

The Peculiarly Human Feature of the Aesthetic Experience

If the most elementary meaning of *subjective* is that of qualifying that which is produced by the subject, and if that which is produced by the subject is first and foremost, at the perceptive and motor-sense level, the temperate zone of average daily experience, then expressive styles placed in lines of continuity with the products of perceptive activity (such as naturalism, realism, verism, the figurative, etc.) should be organized preponderantly within "subjectivism." Though filtering and essentializing the current perceptive activity, they in fact maintain themselves inside the coordinates fixed by this and continue the work of construction of the meanings of a world characterized by sameness, equally distant from excess and from defect.

If, on the other hand, the most elementary meaning of *objective* is that of qualifying that which regards the reality of and for it itself (independently — as far as possible — from manipulations and subjective adaptations), then it would be necessary to recognize that from the point of view of perceptive activity, "reality" — which is at the foundation of perception — is constituted neither by the energy entering from the world nor by the products outgoing from the subject, but by the "way" in which the constituent activity of the subject produces the meanings of the world. "Objective," then, would be that artistic expression whose contents are organized and permeated by the power of its own configuration of the "ways" of producing the meanings on the part of the subject. Thus, for example, Molly's monologue at the end of Joyce's *Ulysses*, in its faithfulness to the method of production of the *stream of consciousness*, would be infinitely more "objective" than a chapter of Zola; and the painting of Mondrian, in manifesting the methods of organization of our visual perception, would be incomparably more objective than figurative Soviet realism.

In all of this there is obviously much of the paradoxical, but it can help produce that reshuffling of cards that, clearing the field of partial and inadequate levels of discussion, and allowing the emergence in all its plainness of what is taught to us by the elementary field of perception, a lesson that comes to coincide in a surprising manner with that which, starting from the other extreme of the subject's activity (the exercise of its higher "faculties"), was brought to light by Kant in the *Critique of the Power of Aesthetic Judgement*. "Beauty" or "sublime" are not characteristics of "things," but uniquely depend upon the way in which the imagination and the intellect harmonize themselves in a free game (in the experience of beauty) or by the way in which imagination and reason commit themselves to revealing all of the seriousness of their disproportion and contrast (in the sublime). It is only by beginning from this interior disposition that our capacity to "render things special" can reveal itself at a second and different level compared to that of perception. One could say that the properly human characteristic of artistic endeavor depends on the capacity to exercise upon the products of perception the same work of sense manifestation that perception exercises toward the different sources of energy present in the environment. The "things" of the world, already symbolized by the work of perception, become in their turn the occasions for the activating of a relation and a process among the faculties that constitute the only source of aesthetic experience.

In conclusion, and in exemplifying what has been asserted in this introductory note, a well-noted and often-cited case may be presented. When Beethoven wrote his sixth symphony, he titled it: "Pastoral-Symphonie oder Erinnerung an das Landleben (mehr Ausdruck der Empfindung als Malerey)." The attention of the interpreters is attracted (not wrongly so) above all by the annotation: "more expression of feeling than painting," in which it is customary to recognize properly the influx of Kant's teaching and thus the knowledge, on the part of the composer, that the source of artistic expression lies in the internality of feeling and not in the externality of imitative subjection to things. One could object that each movement of the symphony has one or more titles that would seem to indicate the contrary and thus a clear imitative intent toward the "things" that happen in rural life.[8] And in effect, Beethoven does not exclude the possibility that in his symphony there could be "painting": that which he underscores is the *prevailing* (not the exclusivity) of the expression of feeling with respect to the description *("mehr" . . . "als")*. But even this, which could appear as being a limited concession to descriptiveness, to *Tongemälde,* is again understood in light of the truly essential element and remains a little in the shadow

---

8. If the intentional annotation to Beethoven's first movement is still in the order of subjective impressions (*"Erwachen heiterer Empfindungen bei der Ankunft auf dem Lande"* [Awakening of Cheerful Feelings upon Arrival in the Country]), those relative to the other movements are clearly descriptive, from *"Szene am Bach"* (Scene by the Brook), to *"Lustiges Zusammensein der Landleute"* (Merry Gathering of Country Folk), to *"Gewitter Sturm"* (Thunderstorm), to *"Hirtengesang. Frohe und dankbare Gefühle nach dem Sturm"* (Shepherd's Song: Happy and Thankful Feelings After the Storm). At the end of the second movement there is then an explicit imitation of the song of the *"Nachtigall"* (nightingale), entrusted to the flutes, of the *"Wachtel"* (quail; oboe), and of the *"Kuckuk"* (cuckoo; clarinet).

(this time wrongly so) with respect to the Kantian statement. What is essential is the equation that Beethoven places at the beginning: "pastoral-symphony or memory . . ." This means: before expressing "feelings," the Pastoral gives voice to the "memory" of the feelings evoked by rural life. It is necessary then to acknowledge all the strength of this constructing of itself and living of the symphony inside the dimension of "memory," whose existence, differently from feelings that can be evoked by something other (here, rural life), depends entirely upon the work of the subject. The Pastoral *is* then "Er-innerung," and the significance of the German term indicates that the musical construction is identical to the delivery and projection in the profundity of the memory of the interior feeling of nature, which the recollecting power of the music draws up to expression.

2. The Experience of Beauty and the Characteristics of Aesthetic Judgment according to Kant

If one now wants to understand the properly human sense of aesthetic creativity, it is not possible to content oneself (as I have already mentioned) by accepting it as a given; rather it is necessary to examine it precisely as a way of being original to our human existence. It is not so much a case of going all the way back, starting from the given of an innate capacity to point out its consequences upon individual or group behaviors and lifestyles, as it is a case of going forward, to individuate the conditions that render possible the existence and exercising of that capacity.

On this path of research I believe that one of the most essential teachings we can turn to is that which comes to us from Kant, even if that makes us jump back a little more than two centuries. In the history of thought there is probably no philosophy that has posited the question about man with the intensity, extensiveness, and centrality of Kant's. In his last work, *Logik,* which appeared as edited by his student Jaesche but reviewed by Kant himself, he sums up the three fundamental questions that guided him throughout the elaboration of his own thought ("What can I know?" "What ought I to do?" "What can I hope for?") in the one, fundamental question, into which every other question flows: "What is man?" In each of his works there come to light aspects of the humanity in man that circumscribe in an ever more precise and essential way a proper and irreducible characteristic. In this way of approximation to the being of man the experience of beauty comes to have a singular place.

If we in fact look at what Kant states in the *Critique of the Power of Judgement*, we judge beauty beginning from the feeling of what is agreeable and disagreeable. If we consider the ways in which our representations refer to that feeling, we see three different experiences that spring forth: that of "pleasant," which can also be true for the simple animals; that of "good," which is true for rational beings in general (and thus true for those not affected by the limitations imposed by sensitivity); and finally that of "beautiful." "Beauty," affirms Kant, "[is valid] only for human beings, i.e., animal but also rational beings, but not merely as the latter (e.g., spirits), rather as beings who are at the same time animal."[9]

This attribution of the experience of beauty uniquely to humankind may provoke more than a little perplexity in the face of the results of contemporary research, which recognizes a sensitivity to beauty even in animals. It is then opportune to indicate precisely that that which Kant places as an exclusive characteristic of the human aesthetic experience is a "strong" concept of beauty, both from the point of view of enjoyment as well as from that of creativity. Kant would probably not have had great difficulty in placing the cases of animal sensitivity to beauty in that which he calls "pleasant." The experience of "beauty," on the other hand, is not only clearly distinct from "pleasant" and produces an absolutely disinterested pleasure, but (as we shall see more clearly in what follows) has its distinctiveness in the fact that every work of beauty is organized on the basis of a rule or a law, which, exhausting itself *in* it and being valid only *for* it, renders it communicable to all and potentially enjoyable by all.

How much the presence of a rule that is singularized in the work of art is essential to the human experience of beauty may be illustrated by an example that I hope persuades in spite of its apparent bizarreness. It may appear all the more bizarre because it deals with an artistic manifestation — dance — which in the Kantian treatment of the arts merits less than one line of citation. Yet I believe that it lends itself well to

---

9. I. Kant, *Kritik der Urteilskraft*, Ak. Ausg. V, § 5, p. 210 (*Critique of the Power of Judgement*, ed. P. Guyer, trans. P. Guyer and E. Matthews [Cambridge: Cambridge University Press, 2003], p. 95). Cited hereinafter as *KU*.

The Peculiarly Human Feature of the Aesthetic Experience

demonstrating the essentiality of a rule in the constitution of artistic experience.

When the capacity of contracting and relaxing the musculature is subjugated to that form of rule which is rhythm, then an expression of corporeity may manifest itself that connects on a different level than the skeletal and muscular in the dispatching of vital daily occupations. It is the level of that which we call "dance" both in humans and in animals (one speaks of the dance of bees, of dolphins, of schools of sardines, chimpanzees, etc.), even though in humans it is present with a truly "special" character, connected directly to the *way* in which the rule configures it and thus subjugated to rhythm. Indeed, that which characterizes human dance seems to consist in "a form of group behavior whereby an indefinite number of individuals start to move their muscles rhythmically, establish a regular rhythm, and continue doing so for long enough to arouse euphoric excitement shared by all participants, and (more faintly) by onlookers as well";[10] and exactly this intense emotive solidarity, provoked by dancing, renders plausible the hypothesis that dance was one of the prime causes of social cohesion that made the emergence of the human species possible.

The observation might verge on the banal in its apparent obviousness, but that which constitutes the distinctive character of human dance is exactly the capacity to "move together in tempo," naturally and spontaneously getting into a regular rhythmic articulation of measured time, shared by a group and maintained for sufficiently long periods. All of the elements that appear indispensable in producing human dance are also to be found in other animal species, except for the spontaneity of moving together in tempo. It might be said that even in animals forms of synchronized group movement are to be observed, which respect the distances between single components in a perfect way, as for instance in the maneuvers of flocks of birds, in the dance of dolphins or schools of fish. But the delicate and decisive point is just this: synchrony still does not signify moving together in tempo. Moving together contemporaneously (synchronously) is the necessary condition, yet it is still not sufficient to allow for the same rhythm, maintained in a regular and constant manner: synchronous movement

---

10. W. H. McNeill, *Keeping Together in Time: Dance and Drill in Human History* (Cambridge, MA: Harvard University Press, 1995), p. 13. See also B. Merker, *Synchronous Chorusing and Human Origins*, in Wallin, Merker, and Brown, *The Origins of Music*, pp. 315-27.

is possible also through the most casual of temporal articulations, and this is in effect what we encounter in the movements of groups of animals, where the unpredictability of synchronous movements may be the necessary result of fleeing from predators and deceiving them.

Even in chimpanzees "exhibitionistic" behaviors are present that closely recall human behaviors, such as the rhythmic tapping of feet in an erect position, shouts accompanied by emphatic gestures of the arms, and facial mimicry, in which emotive tension is released. Still more significant is how much takes place in environments such as animal reserves, where the wildness of nature has in part been modified by human endeavors. Here chimpanzees can be grouped together and taught by humans with relatively small effort to overcome the threshold that divides the world of animals from ours and learn to dance as we do. The fact remains, however, that the spontaneous production of something resembling the capacity of moving-together-in-tempo — with the rhythmic and protracted regularity that brings about the release of individual emotive tension, and its transformation into a group catharsis — has never been observed in chimpanzees that live in the wild, free from man's influence.[11]

The essential element, upon which the properly human artistry of dance depends, is therefore the capacity for members of a community to freely and communally subject themselves to a law of rhythmic articulation that is "invented," recognized, and practiced together: it is thanks to this capacity of "moving together in tempo" that the gestures and postures of corporeity are liable to take on a whole new order of meaning compared to that of their daily use.

One can then come back to Kant and better understand how the working together of rules, which are the expressions of an intellectual activity, and of corporeity, which is an expression of sensitivity, can distinguish in a characteristic way the human experience of beauty. What therefore surprisingly happens is that the peculiar intertwining of animality and rationality, which in other fields of actuation of the human faculties imposes severe limitations upon thought and action, in the experience of beauty is redeemed from those limits and transfigured in an experience that, as I hope to show, originates in freedom.

---

[11]. McNeill, *Keeping Together in Time*, pp. 14-18. Training on the part of man may, obviously, teach other species of animals to move together in tempo, as is possible to see, for instance, in riding schools or in circuses.

The Peculiarly Human Feature of the Aesthetic Experience

If we concentrate our attention not so much on the Kantian treatment of the beautiful in general, but rather upon the beauty of a work of art, this shows itself to have, both in its internal organization and in the means of its production, characteristics that do not permit going back to a mechanistic model of comprehension. As is well known, the third Kantian critique has as its theme, in the two parts of its division, the experience of beauty in the *Critique of the Power of Aesthetic Judgment* and the characteristics of natural organisms in the *Critique of the Power of Teleological Judgment.* It deals with two apparently heterogeneous classes of beings, brought together in reality by the same characteristic of not being fully comprehendable according to the mechanism of efficient causes.

That which in the work of art contrasts with its mechanistic reduction is constituted by many characteristics that collocate it into an intermediary position between the human techno-practical production, on the one hand, and the way in which nature produces organized beings, on the other. "In a product of art," affirms Kant, "one must be aware that it is art, and not nature; yet the purposiveness in its form must still seem *(aussehen)* to be as free from all constraint by arbitrary rules as if it were a mere product of nature."[12] In the production of beautiful art there is the discipline of rules, there is the concept of the object to be produced, there is the directed intention toward the actuation of an objective, and there is the material that waits to be formed; and yet everything must be composed and flow with that sovereign, unintentional "naturalness" that does not betray with the slightest trace "that the rule has hovered before the eyes of the artist and fettered his mental powers."[13] Now this can happen because the rule that organizes the work of art as a completed whole (not the rules that can be learned technically, but the rule that confers beauty to the work) has a wholly peculiar character. Before the act of production it does not exist; no one knows about it, not even the artist: it is all done in the deed; it is made in its making, and for this reason it can be recognized as "original." It has never appeared before and is not repeatable afterward. "The rule," says Kant, "must be abstracted from the deed,"[14] and this means that it has life and value uniquely in that deed. It can only organize that

---

12. *KU,* § 45, p. 306 (p. 185).
13. *KU,* § 45, p. 307 (p. 186).
14. *KU,* § 47, p. 309 (p. 188).

determined product, and it is not possible to lay a finger upon its generating principle in order to imitate it or to mechanistically reproduce it.

The inventions or ideations that are the basis for the originality and the beauty of the work of art, those which Kant calls "aesthetic ideas," are not in control, as to their origins, of the artist who brings them into being. They would not exist without him; yet they are not even intentionally willed by him. Certainly they spring forth from the creative force of his imagination, disciplined by the energies of rationale, but the artist knows not from where they come or how they come upon him, entirely dominating him. If they derive from an "intention of beauty" completely determinable through concepts, then there would be no one better than their author to explain in an exhaustive and definitive way the contents he wished to express and the rule of their organization. Not only does he not succeed in doing this, neither is anyone else capable except by an asymptotic process that can never come close to the inexhaustible, radiant power of the work.

If we ask ourselves, then, what the source might be upon which these prerogatives of the work of art depend, Kant's answer may seem disarming in its simplicity: at the origin of the creation of beauty there is a particular proportion in which the power of the imagination and the discipline of the intellect play freely with each other. As you can see, Kant uses the same elements as the basis of "common sense." In man there is an original accord between three heterogeneous faculties: imagination, as the faculty of intuitions; intellect, as the faculty of rules; and reason, as the faculty of ideas. Belonging to a world of "common" sense would not be possible if in each of us there were not present, and reciprocally finalized, the capacity to intuit individually and the capacity to conceive of the universal. This is the primary inheritance, shared by the common man and the genius, which makes it possible to express oneself, to communicate and comprehend each other. But in the creator of the work of art this common inheritance is present as a singular, inimitable proportion, from which is derived the originality, the exemplarity, the unintentionalness of the workings of the genius. Such are the gifts of this "favorite of nature," whose capacity "is apportioned immediately from the hand of nature" and "thus dies with him, until nature one day similarly endows another, who needs nothing more than an example in order to let the talent of which he is aware operate in a similar way."[15] This exceptional proportion of the capacities of the mind is the "rare phenomenon,"[16] through which nature is capable of giving the "rule to art,"[17] a talent that may be improved, formed, developed, yet never learned nor, through some artifice, taught or imitated.

3. Affinity of Structure between Products of the Beautiful Arts and the Beings Organized by Nature

Thus we have come close to the fundamental question: In what way is it possible to find in the products of beautiful art the traces and witnesses of the regulative activity of nature? What "natural" characteristics are present in the product of imagination, which, as Kant affirms, has the extraordinary power to create almost another nature with the materials it finds in the natural world outside of us?[18] On this point the *Critique of the Power of Aesthetic Judgement* is singularly weak. And yet I believe that Kant may be, at least partially, redeemed from any such failure if one only asks of him that which he was always capable of giving in an eminent manner, which is the individuation of the "conditions of possibility": in this case, the *a priori* conditions that make it possible for a product of art to bear resemblance to a product of nature. It is true that the criticisms start exactly from the comment that Kant concentrated almost exclusively on the subjective conditions in the experience of beauty, and that it is upon the extreme edge of subjectivity that there is a free interlacing of the imagination with the superior faculties of the intellect and reason. This would have led Kant to ignore the weight that the work of art has as a product to be considered in its independent objectivity, once it has left the hands of its creator. The preoccupation of the individuation of the subjective conditions of aesthetic experience would thus have been damaged in the internal analysis of the constitution of the work of art and the formal characteristics that make a unique and inimitable product of it.

Yet, beyond this, perhaps, in Kant's intentions themselves, I believe this analysis is well presented in his pages. But in order to find it, it is

15. *KU*, § 47, p. 309 (p. 188).
16. *KU*, § 49, p. 318 (p. 196).
17. *KU*, § 46, p. 307 (p. 186).
18. See *KU*, § 49, p. 314 (p. 192).

not possible to stay within the *Critique of the Power of Aesthetic Judgement*; rather, we must refer to §§ 64-65 of the *Critique of the Power of Teleological Judgement*, where Kant delineates the peculiar character that things take on when considered as natural ends. If the products of beautiful art must be seen with reference to the finality of their form, as if they were the products of nature, then it is to these products that we must turn to find a guide to the interpretation of the work of art's internal organization.

Let us try now to return to the Kantian text following these directives. That which is required in the first place for a thing to be a natural end is that "its parts (as far as their existence and their form are concerned) are possible only through their relation to the whole."[19] In saying this, it is very clear to Kant that this is valid not only for products of nature, but also for those of the arts (for the *technai*) in general. Technical activity, in fact, in order to produce something, must be guided by a concept or an idea of the totality of the thing, which precedes its accomplishment and "must determine *a priori* everything that is to be contained in it."[20] This deals with a rational principle, whose causality is determined by the idea of a whole, which is different from and external to the material of which it is comprised, and thus, to the single parts of which it is constituted.

Now even the products of the fine arts are preceded, in a sometimes considerable measure, by an idea of the whole that, different and external compared to the existence and the form of the parts, determines *a priori* the rules of their possible co-existence: let us consider, for example, the products of architecture, which is indebted to the science of construction, or the products of music and of the rules relative to mathematics (about which Kant speaks at length[21]), which govern musical composition in both its harmonic and contrapuntal aspects. And yet, until the causality of the idea of the whole expresses itself in this way, it is not possible to find in it the most aesthetically revealing characteristic, which is to say the capacity to generate beauty. Precisely because it can be entirely determined *a priori* (before the work), this idea of the whole is not yet an *aesthetic* idea, but has a "mechanical" character, not enlivened by beauty. As has been seen, the aesthetic idea is an

---

19. *KU*, § 65, p. 373 (pp. 244-45).
20. *KU*, § 65, p. 373 (p. 245).
21. See *KU*, § 53, pp. 328-29 (pp. 205-6).

intuition, to whose inexhaustible wealth no determinate thought or concept can be adequate. The aesthetic idea is certainly an idea of a whole, but the reference of the parts to the whole is not given *a priori*, but it is organized in its exemplary necessity with the making itself of the work. The aesthetic idea appears together with the work, showing itself in its objective existence.

If this is the way in which the aesthetic idea "acts," then it can be understood how the work's internal articulation might be strictly bound to that which, for Kant, is the second fundamental characteristic with which a thing that is a natural end is presented. Its independence from the "causality of the concepts of a rational being outside of it" makes it so that "its parts be combined into a whole by being reciprocally the cause and effect of their form."[22] This is what we can properly call "organization" in a natural entity and where the nexus among the parts is so binding that that which offers itself as an effect is at the same time the cause of its own cause (according to a causal nonlinear relationship, as with mechanical causes, but with circular reciprocity), so the whole that produces itself thus reveals as its basis an idea that neither precedes it as cause nor follows it as result. This idea is a principle of intelligibility that acts in the work itself — as an organized being that organizes itself.

If we transfer these criteria of comprehension from things as natural ends to works of art, I believe that each of us can immediately find examples as to how, in beautiful products of art, each part "exists only *through* all the others" and "thus as if existing *for the sake of the others* and *on account of* the whole."[23] To make use of one of the most noted examples, just think of how in a melody, taken as a unitary whole in its temporal articulation, each note exists in view of each of the others and at the same time; as it is embedded in the melodic development, it exists only through all of the others. Just as evident is that if each element of the work of art is in view of the single purpose of bringing into expression the fundamental sense of the aesthetic idea that governs it, then, relative to the production of the work's internal sense, the reciprocal linking of the parts makes of each of them not so much an *instrument (Werkzeug)*, which would have constant need of an external activity to demonstrate its suitability to the purpose, as it is rather an *organ (Or-*

22. *KU*, § 65, p. 373 (p. 245).
23. *KU*, § 65, p. 373 (p. 245).

gan), capable of production:[24] in the work of art each part fulfills exactly this "organic" function, so that each of them "produces" the sense of the others and at the same time is in debt to the others in the production of its own sense.

Certainly, as Kant reminds us, it becomes more difficult to transfer to the work of art other characteristics of a natural organization — for example, an organism's capacity of self-correction, the ability to substitute by itself a missing part or function. But it is worth acknowledging the nonmarginal analogies that the work of art has with the characteristics of autonomy and self-generation of a thing as a natural end that Kant sets out in § 64. Even though I am aware that here the metaphorical quotient in the Kantian lessons increases in a noteworthy manner, I nevertheless believe that it is worth the trouble to risk doing so.

To use one of Kant's examples: a tree generates itself above all as *species;* in addition to this it also generates itself as an *individual,* because its growth and development come about through substances whose nutritional characteristics, as much as their composition, are a product of itself; ultimately even a part of a plant can generate itself, as is shown by the practice of grafting a twig or a bud onto a plant of a different species.[25]

As bizarre as it may seem at first glance to look for a connection among these characteristics of plant life and works of art, I believe that it can first of all be recognized that the work of art generates itself according to species, if with this word the "type" of artistic manifestation (music, painting, poetry, etc.) is not intended — neither the school, the style, nor the trend — but that which differentiates the work of beauty in its specificity compared to every other technical production, in its own inimitable capacity for manifesting beauty. According to Kant, the example of a beautiful work is sufficient, so that a spirit endowed with a proportion of the capacity of the mind analogous to that of the genius is reawakened to the feeling of its own originality[26] and is driven to create in its turn a work that acts as an example and a solicitation for other like-minded spirits. The work of art thus generates new works of art; it preserves and continually reproduces in them the proper specific character: beauty in its exemplary function.

24. See *KU,* § 65, pp. 373-74 (p. 245).
25. See *KU,* § 64, pp. 370-72 (pp. 242-44).
26. See *KU,* § 49, p. 318 (pp. 195-96).

In the second place, when we are in front of a work of art, we can see that the aesthetic quality of the materials of which it is made totally depend on the internal principle of its organization; it is its own product. The pigments of color, the resonant material, the stone or the wood, are transfigured in expressive means and acquire an aesthetic sense determined uniquely thanks to the total organization of the work. A transformation of the materials certainly happens even in every other artifact, but relative to the products of genius we can repeat to the letter what Kant says regarding the process of the tree's self-generation as an individual: "in the separation and new composition of this raw material [the materials used in the work] there is to be found an originality of the capacity for separation and formation . . . that remains infinitely remote from all art [if it is not beautiful art]. . . ."[27]

Finally, the grafting. Notwithstanding that this might seem the most eccentric element vis-à-vis the work of art, we can nevertheless think of some extraordinary examples, in which a proper, original sense of existence finds a way to grow and express itself by grafting itself to a different conception of the world and feeding parasitically upon its beauty. I think, for instance, of the cathedral of Syracuse, where early Christian, Norman, and Baroque architectonic conceptions have been grafted onto a preexistent Doric temple, dedicated to Athena: the central nave and the symbols of a new redemption of the world "feed" on the space of Athena's cell just as in the lateral naves the space is articulated by the perimetrical Doric columns. Or one thinks of the radical change in the conception and function of space, vis-à-vis the preexistent architectonical lines, with which Michelangelo transformed the thermal baths of Diocletian in S. Maria degli Angeli. And the examples could be multiplied, above all in the field of music. To use only one: the initial theme of Beethoven's third symphony refers to the theme of the *Ouverture* of *Bastien und Bastienne,* the opera written by the young Mozart, almost as if the genius of Bonn wanted to take by the hand or be taken by that prodigious youthfulness and penetrate the new, unexplored world of his own original musicality.

---

27. *KU,* § 64, p. 371 (p. 243).

4. Mechanism and Teleology in the Interpretation of the Work of Art: The Naturalization of Aesthetic Judgment

If this possibility of transferring the characteristics of naturally organized beings to works of art has any plausibility, then it helps us not only to comprehend even better the legitimacy of the Kantian demand to look at beautiful art as if it were a product of nature, but also allows us to push our gaze even further, following the most profound inspiration that animates teleological judgment. At the end of the day, that which still remains to be cleared up here is the concept of "nature," which, referring both to the work of art and to the ability of its producer the genius, demonstrates being marked by a peculiar, significant ambiguity. Both the work of art, in its analogy to things as natural ends, and the genius, in the original proportion of his faculties, after all acknowledge something supersensible that makes itself known only at the limits of a way of comprehension entrusted to the categorical apparatus and to the judgment with which intellect determines completely its own objects.

For Kant, "it is quite certain that we can never adequately come to know the organized beings and their internal possibility in accordance with merely mechanistic principles of nature."[28] This insufficiency of a mechanistic explanation nevertheless does not authorize us to pose the finalistic perspective as the only plausible one. The distinction, worked out by Kant, is methodologically and epistemologically of great subtlety. Affirming that *all* generation of material things is possible only according to mechanistic laws or that *some* generations are not possible according to that law is a completely different thing from affirming that, in evaluating the events of material nature, I must use the principle of mechanism insofar as it is possible, while I can bring into play the principle of finality as soon as phenomena I cannot understand without it present themselves. In the first case I formulate determinant judgments that contradict each other precisely because they claim to say in themselves how natural things are constituted; in the second case I formulate reflective judgments compossible to each other, because through them I take on "maxims" of evaluation that are "regulative" to my way of knowing objects and not "constitutive" of their way of being.

28. *KU*, § 75, p. 400 (p. 663).

The Peculiarly Human Feature of the Aesthetic Experience

From this point of view the work of art is exposed, as with every other naturally organized being, to the same dialectic that arises from a mechanistic interpretation on the one hand (today we might speak of naturalistic reduction), which attempts to conquer as much ground as possible, and on the other hand a finalistic perspective, which attempts to protect its own indispensability.[29] In the age of Kant a naturalization in the mechanistic sense of the work of art would have probably appeared nonsensical, whereas today this is a real project. It aims for an even more ductile and exhaustive actuation of the naturalization, because it knows how to render functional to itself even those theoretical perspectives that have placed the mechanistic paradigm itself in crisis. Just think of the impetuous development in recent years with that branch of aesthetics that tries to apply the results of the most recent neurological research to the area of production and enjoyment of a work of art. This is not the place to go into the current debate about neuroaesthetics, which has all of the semblances of attempting an integral naturalization to the experience of beauty. But it is worth remembering that just the first part of the *Critique of the Power of Judgement* was highlighted as an exemplary reference text in the essay by Kawabata and Zeki that we quoted at the beginning.

So we can ask again the questions from which our inquiry began: Is the process of naturalization of aesthetic experience capable of exhausting the entire realm of the human experience of the beautiful? Or can this side of research reach exhaustive explanations by way of the neurophysiological point of view, but not yet exclusive explanations of the human aesthetic experience? It is precisely here that the Kantian teaching on the dialectic of teleological judgment continues to manifest its efficacy.

The authors quoted, Kawabata and Zeki, are particularly prudent and critically guarded, yet we frequently find with these scholars who are concerned with the mind-brain relationship a continual, significant lexical oscillation: those that are initially presented as neurally "correlated," as substrata or "involved" neural processes, "subtended" or "associated" with the experience of beauty, are transformed insensi-

---

29. If we were to rewrite today the antinomy of the teleological judgment, in the "thesis" we would not express the mechanistic perspective more uniquely, but we would speak more expansively of "naturalization" in all of its forms, of which mechanism is only a particular case.

tively or brusquely (with no forewarning, as with those of the authors) into neural processes that "generate" aesthetic judgment, "determine the creation" of the work of art, or "originate" the fundamental properties of the conscious experience of the beautiful.[30]

It would seem to be a useless redundancy (though evidently it is not) to remember that being associated with or correlated to something is very different from the generation or creation of that to which it is correlated, and that taking for granted the equivalency of significant terms does not bring about a true and proper *metabasis eis allo genos*. In reality, in the passage from one linguistic level to another we lay a finger upon that which Kant would call the transformation of a reflective judgment (regulative) into a determinant principle (constitutive) of the aesthetic experience. The maxim, on the basis of how we "evaluate" the involvement of the determinant cerebral areas when experiencing the beautiful, is in principle transformed into an exclusive "explanation" of the same. In this way, though, we finish by taking for granted exactly what we are trying to explain: the movements induced by electrochemical reactions, through which our nervous system codifies environmental interactions (listening to music, looking at a painting, etc.), are then decodified, interpreted, and expressed in a judgment of taste.

The reflective judgment, which evaluates a neural configuration in its concomitance with an aesthetic experience, knows very well that what it has before its eyes is a spatial distribution of nervous activity, and that this is still separated by an abyss from the processes of interpretation or decodification with which a significant aesthetic is conferred to the neural sequences. If we turn the reflective judgment into determinant judgment, either we don't perceive the problem or we take for granted that the interpreter coincides with the interpreted, identifying himself with it. Knowledge of the way in which the information contained in our sensorial receptors is codified in nervous impulses

---

30. Kawabata and Zeki explicitly recognize, at the end of their contribution, that "we cannot be said to have been able to determine what constitutes beauty in neural terms"; that does not take away from the Kantian problem from which they began ("what are the conditions implied by the existence of the phenomenon of beauty [or its absence] and of consciousness [or its absence] and what are the presuppositions that give validity to our esthetic judgments") they responded affirming that "In esthetics, the answer to both questions must be an activation of the brain's reward system with a certain intensity" ("Neural Correlates," p. 1704).

and how these are distributed at a cortical level is certainly necessary for the global comprehension of the aesthetic phenomenon. Nevertheless, deeming these processes of codification and distribution as alone sufficient for the explanation of the phenomenon means surreptitiously making them coincide with the activity of decodification and interpretation. And this is not at all taken for granted; rather, it is one of the points in which our ignorance becomes denser. It is in fact not infrequent to find among the more attentive experts of this delicate passage the frank acknowledgment that the way "the distribution of nervous impulses at the cortex level and in the successive phases of elaboration is decodified is *unknown.*"[31]

So, we can say, continuing to follow the Kantian suggestions, that even the work of art finds itself collocated inside a characteristically dialectical situation, in which two mutually irreducible perspectives nonetheless perform a positive function for its comprehension: one tends toward the naturalistic reduction of the aesthetic experience; the other tends to take away the finalized level to the interpretation and to the discovery of the sense. But, from the moment that both perspectives refer to the same object and find in the object itself sufficient reasons for existing one alongside the other it is legitimate to ask oneself if the unit, with which the work of art is presented, does not accede to a deeper principle, from which the two perspectives, given their irreducibility, spring forth as from a single root. In other words, we place the problem as to whether in that which remains unknown to us in the passage from one perspective to the other there is not hidden a foundation for their unity, inside the nature of the work of art.

As we are reminded above, according to Kant the work of art comes from an original accord of the faculties common to all men, which renders possible the expression, the communication, and the understanding of each other. But in the experience of the beautiful the original accord is configured like a game whose constitutive character is freedom. That for Kant the production and the enjoyment of beautiful art have their first and last source in an experience of freedom is demonstrated by the rich mass of expressions with which he characterizes not only the enjoyment of the beautiful in general, but also, specifically, the work of the genius. The agreement between the imagination and the

---

31. L. Maffei and M. Fiorentini, *Arte e cervello* (Bologna: Zanichelli, 1995), pp. 24-25 (my italics).

higher rational faculties, which is at the root of the aesthetic experience in its globality, does not only have the character of a disinterested game released from cognitive or practical purposes, but a game *free* from presupposed rules, a game that invents the rules as it is played: neither the enjoyment nor the creation of the finality of the form of beautiful art could exist without this original experience of being free from the restrictions of preestablished rules that are the basis for judgments of taste. When we then pass from a simple "evaluation" of the work of beauty to its "production," then something more is necessary: the intervention must take place in the "natural endowment of a subject for the *free* use of his cognitive faculties," which belongs only to the genius and to his capacity to create "a new rule by which the talent shows itself exemplary."[32]

In conclusion, if at the root of the human way to experience beauty is a free use of the relationship between sensitivity and cognitive faculties, its naturalization seems to meet a limit in precisely this fundamental experience of freedom.

---

32. *KU*, § 49, p. 318 (p. 455).

HUMAN DISTINCTIVENESS —
CLUES FROM SCIENCE

The Emergence of Human Distinctiveness: The Genetic Story

Graeme Finlay

The genome of a living creature is the genetic information needed to specify its body plan. This information is embodied in the order or sequence of four chemical letters that are linked to form the threadlike molecule we know as DNA. The DNA present in *each* cell of our bodies would extend over approximately two meters if laid out end-to-end. Present in that expanse of DNA are two sets of approximately 25,000 genes each.

The information present in the human genome has been determined by the Human Genome Project, celebrated in the much-heralded publication of a first draft in 2001.[1] Since then the information content of the genomes of several other mammals has been determined. These genomes include those of fellow primates (our closest living relative, the chimpanzee,[2] and the rhesus macaque[3]) and distantly related mammals such as the opossum.[4] One aim of these "big science"

---

1. International Human Genome Sequencing Consortium, "Initial Sequencing and Analysis of the Human Genome," *Nature* 409 (2001): 860-921; "Finishing the Euchromatic Sequence of the Human Genome," *Nature* 431 (2004): 931-45.

2. The Chimpanzee Sequencing and Analysis Consortium, "Initial Sequence of the Chimpanzee Genome and Comparison with the Human Genome," *Nature* 437 (2005): 69-87. For an analysis of the differences between the human and chimp genomes, see H. Kehrer-Sawatzki and D. N. Cooper, "Understanding the Recent Evolution of the Human Genome: Insights from Human-Chimpanzee Genome Comparisons," *Human Mutation* 28 (2007): 99-130.

3. Rhesus Macaque Genome Sequencing and Analysis Consortium, "Evolutionary and Biomedical Insights from the Rhesus Macaque Genome," *Science* 316 (2007): 222-33.

4. T. S. Mikkelsen, M. J. Wakefield, B. Aken, et al., "Genome of the Marsupial *Monodelphis domestica* Reveals Innovation in Non-coding Sequences," *Nature* 447 (2007): 167-77.

projects has been to make detailed comparisons between our genome and those of other primates, in the hope of reconstructing the way in which our genome has been assembled.

As a result of such comparisons, it may now be concluded that the human genome is the end-product of a very large number of DNA rearrangements over a very long period of time. Our genome has been continuously remodeled by a variety of processes with which geneticists are well acquainted. Segments of DNA have been copied-and-pasted to other locations in the genome. These events are recognizable by the presence of duplications. Other segments of DNA have been lost (seen as deletions), reversed in orientation relative to the surrounding DNA (inversions), cut-and-pasted elsewhere in the genome (translocations), or added from independent sources (insertions). These rearrangements originate as unique and unrepeatable events, but many of the DNA sequence features we possess are shared with other species. Such species must be related to us, because they have inherited the same unique novelties in their DNA. These patterns of relationships with other species enable us to reconstruct our evolutionary history.[5]

"What makes humans distinctive?" was a question uppermost in the minds of those who sequenced the genome of our closest relative, the chimpanzee.[6] Notwithstanding, Sean Carroll wrote in anticipation of the publication of the chimp genome sequence, "The sequencing of the chimpanzee genome will reveal no more directly about the origin of human traits than the sequence of the human genome tells us about how to construct a healthy baby."[7]

Searching for the "Genes That Make Us Human"

We are all Africans. The lineage that gave rise to humankind diverged from the chimp lineage at least five million years ago, and from the gorilla lineage soon before that.[8] For a long time, the study of human origins has been limited to comparing anatomical features. These studies

---

5. J. L. Bloore, "The Use of Genome-Level Characters for Phylogenetic Reconstruction," *Trends in Ecology and Evolution* 21 (2006): 439-46.
6. See note 2.
7. S. B. Carroll, "Genetics and the Making of *Homo sapiens*," *Nature* 422 (2004): 849-57.
8. See note 7.

themselves were limited by the scarcity of ancient fossils. All this has changed with the availability of genome sequences, because these provide a vast amount of detailed documentation of the genetic history shared by, and unique to, different species.

Mutations are generated in every generation of living creatures. It follows that the genomes of related species become more dissimilar (diverge) with the passage of time. DNA sequence comparisons have shown that different parts of the human and chimp genomes vary greatly in their degree of genetic divergence. The X chromosome is much less differentiated than the autosomal (nonsex) chromosomes. This has been interpreted to indicate that when the human and chimp lineages began to separate, there were transient hybridizations between the diverging populations, so that parts of the genome (especially the X chromosome) were subjected to selection that retained hybrid fertility and reduced sequence variation. The effect of this would be to reset the "genetic clock" for some parts of the genome, which started to diverge again only after a final separation of the two lineages.[9] Notwithstanding, simpler models involving abrupt geographic separation of populations that would later give rise to human and chimp lineages are also compatible with the data. It may not be possible to differentiate between models describing the origin of the human and chimp species.[10]

The genetic characteristics of another species within the hominid line are beginning to yield to genetic analysis. Neanderthals are close relatives who became extinct around 30,000 years ago. Traces of nuclear DNA extracted from Neanderthal bones have been subjected to sequence analysis. Early indications suggest that the DNA of Neanderthals and *Homo sapiens* diverged at least 516,000 to 706,000 years ago before anatomically modern humans appeared.[11] Evidence from a draft sequence of the Neanderthal genome has suggested that there was some gene flow (interbreeding) between Neanderthals and humans in Eurasia, but not in sub-Saharan Africa.[12]

9. N. Patterson, D. J. Richter, S. Gnerre, et al., "Genetic Evidence for Complex Speciation of Humans and Chimpanzees," *Nature* 441 (2006): 1103-8.

10. N. H. Barton, "How Did the Human Species Form?" *Current Biology* 16 (2006): R647-50.

11. R. E. Green, J. Krause, S. E. Ptak, et al., "Analysis of One Million Base Pairs of Neanderthal DNA," *Nature* 444 (2006): 330-36; J. P. Noonan, G. Coop, S. Kudaravalli, et al., "Sequencing and Analysis of Neanderthal Genomic DNA," *Science* 314 (2006): 1113-18.

12. E. Pennisi, "No Sex Please, We're Neanderthals," *Science* 316 (2007): 967; R. E.

Species arise and diverge with the appearance and spread of novel genetic variants that confer favorable characteristics upon the individuals that possess them. Genes on the human lineage that have been molded by the strongest pressures of natural selection are those that function in immunological protection, reproductive processes, and sensory perception. The process of genetic selection continues. For example, variants of the *hemoglobin-B* gene (causing sickle cell anemia) and the "Duffy antigen" gene confer resistance to malaria and exist at higher-than-expected frequencies in certain African populations. Variants of the lactase gene (allowing adults to digest cows' milk) are much commoner in groups that herd cattle;[13] no such variants have been found in DNA extracted from Europeans who lived earlier than 7,000 years ago.[14] The loss of skin color in northern Europeans may have occurred at the same time. This adaptation may have allowed farming populations living at high latitudes to absorb sufficient sunlight required for vitamin D synthesis in the skin. Current populations of Tibetans living at high altitudes vary in the oxygen-carrying capacity of their blood. Women with a high capacity have twice as many children as those with a low capacity.[15] Huge databases of genetic variation within human populations are being assembled and should lead to new understandings of how genetic forces have shaped our biology.

Such examples of gene selection may have contributed to an enduring expectation that comparative genetics will lead to the identification of "genes that make us human."[16] Geneticists will need, however, to sift through a large number of genetic changes before they identify critical ones. Considering only DNA that encodes proteins, the number of base changes that might have transformed a chimp-human an-

---

Green, J. Krause, A. W. Briggs, et al., "A Draft Sequence of the Neandertal Genome," *Science* 328 (2010): 710.

13. P. C. Sabeti, S. F. Schaffner, B. Fry, et al., "Positive Natural Selection in the Human Lineage," *Science* 312 (2006): 1614-20.

14. J. Burger, M. Kirchner, B. Bramanti, et al., "Absence of the Lactase-Persistence-Associated Allele in Early Neolithic Europeans," *Proceedings of the National Academy of Sciences of the USA* 104 (2007): 3736-41.

15. A. Gibbons, Meeting Briefs. American Society of Physical Anthropologists, *Science* 316 (2007): 364.

16. N. Mekel-Bobrov and B. T. Lahn, "What Makes Us Human: Revisiting an Age-Old Question in the Genomic Era," *Journal of Biomedical Discovery and Collaboration* 1 (2006): 18.

cestor into a modern human has been estimated to be in the tens of thousands.[17] But more important, the traits that interest us most — bipedalism, skeletal morphology, craniofacial morphology, brain size, and speech — are produced by the interaction of many genes,[18] compounded of course, by the effects of environment. It will be a very challenging task to relate the acquisition of such complex traits to particular changes in DNA sequence.

The manner by which DNA sequences are translated into the properties of living organisms is obscure. This applies supremely to the activity of the brain, which is central to considerations of human distinctiveness. Interesting work has been done on particular genes for which roles in neuronal development are expected *(FOXP2, ASPM, MCPH1, PDYN, GLUD2, COX8, CMAH)*. But given that 99 percent of the neuroscience literature features 1 percent of brain-expressed genes, this "candidate gene" approach is almost certainly too limited.[19] An alternative approach has been to compare entire genomes. Such surveys will be particularly informative when combined with clinical studies of neurological disorders. Whole-genome comparisons have identified twenty-eight genes that are expressed in the brain and that exist only in humans.[20] For example, "DUF1220 domain"-containing proteins comprise a gene family of which individual members are expressed in many tissues, including neurons associated with cognitive function. A high occurrence of amino acid-altering mutations suggests that the sequence divergence in these proteins has been driven by natural selection.[21] In general, however, the coding sequences of genes expressed in the brain do not seem to have changed more rapidly on the human lineage than they have on the chimpanzee lineage.[22]

---

17. Carroll, "Genetics and the Making of *Homo sapiens*"; N. Saitou, "Evolution of Hominoids and the Search for a Genetic Basis for Creating Humanness," *Cytogenetic and Genome Research* 108 (2005): 16-21.

18. See note 17.

19. J. M. Sikela, "The Jewels of Our Genome: The Search for the Genomic Changes Underlying the Evolutionarily Unique Capacities of the Human Brain," *PLoS Genetics* 2 (2006): 646-55.

20. A. Fortna, Y. Kim, E. MacLaren, et al., "Lineage-specific Gene Duplication and Loss in Human and Great Ape Evolution," *PLoS Biology* 2 (2004): 937-54.

21. M. C. Popesco, E. J. MacLaren, J. Hopkins, et al., "Human Lineage-specific Amplification, Selection, and Neuronal Expression of DUF1220 Domains," *Science* 313 (2006): 1304-7.

22. P. Shi, M. A. Bakewell, and J. Zhang, "Did Brain-specific Genes Evolve Faster in

From our perspective, we might intuit that humans are more "highly evolved" than chimps, and might expect to find more genes altered by natural selection on the human lineage than on the chimp lineage. However, a comparison of 14,000 gene sequences has indicated that fewer genes have been modified under the force of natural selection in humans than in chimps since our common ancestor. Perhaps 1.1 percent of human genes show signs of having been modified by natural selection, and 1.7 percent of chimp genes.[23] We might have to look elsewhere in the genome than in known genes in order to find a basis for our cognitive capacities.

Another approach has been to study the noncoding sequences that constitute most of the human genome. A study of DNA regions that are conserved in other primates but have undergone rapid change specifically on the human lineage showed that 96 percent of such rapidly evolving sequences occurred in DNA that did not code for proteins. The single sequence most highly altered in humans is one of these enigmatic segments of DNA; it is expressed in brain and reproductive tissue.[24] Human-specific sequences have been detected also near genes associated with neuronal cell adhesion.[25]

Noncoding DNA controls gene expression. Gene expression (as measured by the abundance of RNA copies) in the human brain is thus a focus of interest. Surprisingly, when humans and chimps are compared, the divergence of gene expression in the brain is less than that in other organs. Nevertheless, when data from a third species are added to provide baseline values pertaining to the time when the populations ancestral to the different species diverged from each other, the human lineage relative to the chimp lineage shows a greater *change* of gene expression in the brain relative to that of other organs. This increased

---

Humans Than in Chimpanzees?" *Trends in Genetics* 22 (2006): 608-13; H. Y. Wang, H. C. Chien, H. N. Osada, et al., "Rate of Evolution in Brain-expressed Genes in Humans and Other Primates," *PLoS Biology* 5 (2006): e13.

23. M. A. Bakewell, P. Shi, and J. Zhang, "More Genes Underwent Positive Selection in Chimpanzee Evolution Than in Human Evolution," *Proceedings of the National Academy of Sciences of the USA* 104 (2007): 7489-94.

24. K. S. Pollard, S. R. Salama, N. Lambert, et al., "An RNA Gene Expressed During Cortical Development Evolved Rapidly in Humans," *Nature* 443 (2006): 167-72.

25. S. Prabhakar, J. P. Noonan, S. Paabo, and E. M. Rubin, "Accelerated Evolution of Conserved Noncoding Sequences in Humans," *Science* 314 (2006): 786.

The Emergence of Human Distinctiveness

rate of change may have occurred relatively recently (<200,000 years) and is most marked in genes involved in energy generation.[26]

It will be a huge task to demonstrate that the changes in gene expression in human brain tissue are a cause and not merely a consequence of other developmental changes. Clearly, the unique *potential* of the human brain must be specified by the human genome, but the *realization* of the brain's potential is not genetically determined. It is not true that "genes make minds any more than a viola or a piccolo makes a sonata."[27]

It is important to establish that our distinctiveness as human cannot be defined in narrowly genetic terms. From the viewpoint of genetics, Varki and Altheide state, "Explaining 'humanness' is a vague and broadly philosophical question, not easily approached using the genome alone. We prefer to use the term 'the human condition' to refer to the entire suite of characters that make humans different from the great apes." These characters refer not only to physical aspects of human existence that science can tease apart, but "cognition, behavior, symbolic communication and culture."[28] In a similar vein, the theologian van Huyssteen states that biological and phylogenetic perspectives, together with our "intersubjective and social relationality," are all required to adequately define the "embodied human condition."[29]

In other words, our DNA sequence is necessary but not sufficient to explain the development of our humanity. The function of genes is modulated by environmental inputs. This is especially true for genes that work in neural tissue. Human brain and mind development and the full enjoyment of the richness of humanness are exquisitely sensitive to environmental factors. Critically important among these environmental inputs are the nonphysical cues mediated by relationship with those who provide the personal environment in which we are nurtured. Gene expression in the brain is modulated by the inductive environment created by relationship. The inability of genetics to generate the

---

26. P. Khaitovich, W. Enard, M. Lachmann, and S. Paabo, "Evolution of Primate Gene Expression," *Nature Reviews Genetics* 7 (2006): 693-702.

27. F. S. Collins, L. Weiss, and K. Hudson, "Heredity and Humanity: Have No Fear. Genes Aren't Everything," *The New Republic* 224 (2001): 27, or online at http://www.tnr.com/article/books-and-arts/heredity-and-humanity.

28. A. Varki and T. K. Altheide, "Comparing the Human and Chimpanzee Genomes: Searching for Needles in a Haystack," *Genome Research* 15 (2005): 1746-58.

29. J. Wentzel van Huyssteen, *Alone in the World? Human Uniqueness in Science and Theology* (Grand Rapids: Eerdmans, 2006), p. 278; also pp. 284, 288.

fullness of the human person may be illustrated by the mysterious phenomenon of feral children. History abounds with stories of children who (it is claimed) become isolated from human society and are nurtured in communities of animals. Following their discovery, attempts to integrate them into human society are at best partially successful. Reflecting on such claims, the philosopher Steeves concludes that humans are not defined genetically. On the contrary, it appears as if "the burgeoning consciousness of the infant will not necessarily develop into human intentionality on its own but rather requires the presence of a Significant Other who is human. This 'gracious act of attention' is thus responsible for 'creating' a human-person.... Without a human Other to attend to the child *as human,* the child does not become human — which is not to say that feral children have no sense of Self or Other, but rather that such senses do not include 'humanity.' ... Humanity is in some respect the result of specific treatment within one's community.... Being human is being treated by humans as human."[30]

An interesting perspective on the origins of humanness comes from history. The medieval Emperor Frederick II of Hohenstaufen attempted to investigate the role of social environment in the development of language. He ordered that some children be raised from birth in complete silence, in order to ascertain what language they would speak: perhaps they might spontaneously speak the Language of Heaven. Frederick's experiment was performed by "bidding foster-mothers and nurses to suckle and bathe and wash the children, but in no wise to prattle or speak with them; for he would have learnt whether they would speak the Hebrew language (which had been the first), or Greek, or Latin, or Arabic, or perchance the tongue of their parents of whom they had been born. But he labored in vain, for the children could not live without clappings of the hands, and gestures, and gladness of countenance, and blandishments."[31] It appears that the children failed to speak any language. Worse, they failed to flourish, and notwithstanding their normal set of genes, they died.

Genes do not work in isolation; they do not have the capacity to "make us human" if we are isolated from human community during

30. H. P. Steeves, "Illicit Crossings: The Other at the Human/Animal Boundary," Rhetoric of Identity: Conference paper, Centre for Rhetorics and Hermeneutics (2005): www.ars-rhetorica.net/Queen/VolumeSpecialIssue5/Articles/Steeves.html.

31. G. G. Coulton, *From St. Francis to Dante* (London: David Nutt, 1907), p. 242; see also G. Masson, *Frederick II of Hohenstaufen* (London: Secker & Warburg, 1957), p. 230.

infancy. Our humanity is the outcome of three kinds of adaptive history: the influence of biological evolution through the genes, the evolution of neural circuits through experience, and the influence of cultural evolution.[32] These effects are modulated by the relationships in which we are nurtured, and by exposure to the culture and stories that arise from the particulars of history. Gene expression is transcended by personal relationship during the formation of the richness of humanness: "culture and speech are essential for the making of the human mind," and may be part of a social trigger required to unleash genetic potential.[33] Language may be essential for consciousness.[34]

The experience of neglected children points to the need for loving nurture in the development of the brain, of the mind, and of the human person. Many children raised in environments of extreme neglect (experienced as reduced sensory input: words, touch, and social interactions) show developmental problems (language deficits, motor delays, behavioral problems) that lead to underdevelopment of both the cortex[35] and the corpus callosum.[36] Socio-emotional deprivation in Romanian orphans has been shown to exert long-term effects on brain function. Several areas of the brain show reduced glucose metabolism. Structural alterations in a tract of nerve fibers have been identified. The specificity of this effect indicates that abnormalities did not arise from nonspecific causes (like alcohol exposure *in utero* or malnutrition).[37] Sensory inputs arising from the attentions of a loving caregiver are necessary if an infant is to express its genetic potential to form and maintain healthy relationships.[38]

Such studies cannot address all possible confounding factors. How-

32. J. McCrone, "Feral Children," *Lancet Neurology* 2 (2003): 132.

33. See note 32.

34. J. Leiber, "Nature's Experiments, Society's Closures," *Journal for the Theory of Social Behaviour* 27 (1997): 325-43.

35. B. Perry, "Childhood Experience and the Expression of Genetic Potential: What Childhood Neglect Tells Us about Nature and Nurture," *Brain and Mind* 3 (2002): 79-100.

36. M. H. Teicher, M. L. Dumont, Y. Ito, C. Vatiuzis, et al., "Childhood Neglect Is Associated with Reduced Corpus Callosum Area," *Biological Psychiatry* 56 (2004): 80-85.

37. H. T. Chugani, M. E. Behen, O. Muzik, et al., "Local Brain Functional Activity Following Early Deprivation: A Study of Postinstitutionalised Romanian Orphans," *NeuroImage* 14 (2001): 1290-1301; T. J. Eluvathingal, H. T. Chugani, M. E. Behen, et al., "Abnormal Brain Connectivity in Children After Early Severe Socioemotional Deprivation: A Diffusion Tensor Imaging Study," *Pediatrics* 117 (2006): 2093-2100.

38. See note 35.

ever, animal studies have shown that enriched environments promote brain development. Animals raised in the wild have brains 15 to 30 percent larger than their domestically reared offspring.[39] An environment of sensorimotor and cognitive deprivation leads to underdevelopment of the cortex in rats, nonhuman primates, and humans, whereas "enriched animal environments — enclosures that stimulate the complexity of a natural habitat — lead to dramatic increases in both neurogenesis and the density of neuronal dendrites, the branches that connect one neuron to another. Complex surroundings create a complex brain." Our environments influence the structure of our brains.[40]

Genes are necessary but not sufficient to specify the neural circuits that provide vision. Sensory input from both eyes is needed during a critical period of development in order to generate normal binocular vision.[41] Structural change in the brain occurs in musicians, jugglers, taxi drivers, and students. Draganski and co-workers conclude that "plasticity is a characteristic of the nervous system that evolved for coping with changes in the environment."[42] This is genetics come of age, submitting to the tutelage of experience and relationship.

In the following sections of this chapter and in the Appendices we spell out some of the detailed genetic knowledge that underpins what has been written above. The final section will draw out some of the implications for our wider understanding of human distinctiveness that arises from the knowledge of our genetic substrate.

---

39. See note 35.

40. J. Lehrer, "The Reinvention of the Self," *Seed* 2 (2006): 58. This article discussed the work of Elizabeth Gould and Ronald Duman. See also J. Nithianantharajah and A. J. Hannan, "Enriched Environments, Experience-Dependent Plasticity and Disorders of the Nervous System," *Nature Reviews Neuroscience* 7 (2006): 697-709.

41. T. K. Hensch, "Critical Period Plasticity in Local Cortical Circuits," *Nature Reviews Neuroscience* 6 (2005): 877-88; more generally, see F. Fumagalli, R. Moltini, G. Racagni, and M. A. Riva, "Stress During Development: Impact on Neuroplasticity and Relevance to Psychopathology," *Progress in Neurobiology* 81 (2007): 197-217.

42. T. F. Munte, E. Altenmuller, and L. Jancke, "The Musician's Brain as a Model of Neuroplasticity," *Nature Reviews Neuroscience* 3 (2002): 473-78, B. Draganski, C. Gaser, V. Busch, et al., "Changes in Grey Matter Induced by Training," *Nature* 427 (2004): 311-12; E. Maguire, D. G. Gadian, I. S. Johnsrude, et al., "Navigation-related Structural Change in the Hippocampi of Taxi Drivers," *Proceedings of the National Academy of Sciences of the USA* 97 (2000): 4398-4403; B. Draganski, C. Gaser, G. Kempermann, et al., "Temporal and Spatial Dynamics of Brain Structure Changes During Extensive Learning," *Journal of Neuroscience* 26 (2006): 6314-17.

The Birth and Death of Genes

The distinctiveness of our humanity can be understood only in the context of our embodiedness as primates. Van Huyssteen emphasizes that "human uniqueness can be adequately addressed only if we take our own animality and embodied personhood seriously."[43] Analysis of our genome sequence and those of our primate relatives indicates that they are wholly interconvertible by genetic mechanisms that are familiar to molecular geneticists. A survey of these mechanisms will be of interest not only in terms of the genetic processes that have molded our biology, but also because they illuminate a theological understanding of our status as living beings created from "the dust of the earth." Indeed an understanding of those processes by which our genome has been generated will illustrate the nature of God's creativity as seen in biological history.

Duplications and Gene Birth

At least 5 percent of the human genome is composed of duplicated ("copied-and-pasted") segments of chromosomal DNA. An original sequence "A-B-C-D-E" may be duplicated on the same chromosome to form direct repeats "A-B-C-D-E-spacer-A-B-C-D-E" or inverted repeats "A-B-C-D-E-spacer-E-D-C-B-A." The duplicated segment may be spliced also into a different chromosome. These "segmental duplications" may be hundreds of thousands of bases in length. Donor sequences giving rise to duplicated segments may be located anywhere in the genome. The resulting duplications become concentrated in bumper-to-bumper configurations at sites along chromosome arms, adjacent to centromeres (structures that orchestrate chromosome movement), and adjacent to telomeres (chromosome ends). They provide raw material for the production of new genes, and so contribute to the characteristic features of species.[44]

---

43. Van Huyssteen, *Alone in the World?* p. 276.
44. E. E. Eichler and D. Sankoff, "Structural Dynamics of Eukaryotic Chromosome Evolution," *Science* 301 (2003): 793-97; X. She, J. E. Horvath, Z. Jiang, et al., "The Structure and Evolution of Centromeric Transition Regions within the Human Genome," *Nature* 430 (2004): 857-64; E. V. Linardopoulou, E. M. Williams, Y. Fan, et al., "Human Subtelomeres Are Hot Spots of Interchromosomal Recombination and Segmental Du-

Such duplications have shaped our genome over vast periods of time. We often share particular duplications (involving the same stretch of DNA spliced into the same chromosomal site) with other species. Each must have arisen as a unique event in a single cell, and all the species that share it may be presumed to be descended from the same progenitor. We share some large and very ancient DNA duplications with species as remotely related as mice and dogs. These duplicated segments form "gene deserts" at least one million bases long.[45]

Segments that have been duplicated more recently arose during primate evolution. They are possessed only by humans and other primates (Appendix 1).[46] Two-thirds of the segmental duplications in our genome are shared with chimps. The other one-third is unique to us. Since we diverged from the chimp lineage, duplicated DNA has accumulated at an estimated rate of 4-5 million bases per million years.[47] These processes are still active. There are several hundred locations in the human genome at which people vary in the number of copies of particular duplicated segments of DNA. Any two people may have dif-

---

plication," *Nature* 437 (2005): 94-100; J. A. Bailey and E. E. Eichler, "Primate Segmental Duplications: Crucibles of Evolution, Diversity and Disease," *Nature Reviews Genetics* 7 (2006): 552-64.

45. T. Itoh, A. Toyoda, T. D. Taylor, et al., "Identification of Large Ancient Duplications Associated with Human Gene Deserts," *Nature Genetics* 37 (2005): 1041-43.

46. X. She, G. Liu, M. Ventura, et al., "A Preliminary Comparative Analysis of Primate Segmental Duplications Shows Elevated Substitution Rates and a Great-Ape Expansion of Intrachromosomal Duplications," *Genome Research* 16 (2006): 576-86; M. E. Johnson, NISC Comparative Sequencing Program, Z. Cheng, et al., "Recurrent Duplication-driven Transposition of DNA During Hominoid Evolution," *Proceedings of the National Academy of Sciences of the USA* 103 (2006): 17626-31; V. Y. Kuryshev, E. Vorobyov, D. Zink, et al., "An Anthropoid-specific Segmental Duplication on Human Chromosome 1q22," *Genomics* 88 (2006): 143-51. For data on "inverted repeats," see P. E. Warburton, J. Giordano, F. Cheung, et al., "Inverted Repeat Structure of the Human Genome: The X-Chromosome Contains a Preponderance of Large, Highly Homologous Inverted Repeats That Contain Testes Genes," *Genome Research* 14 (2004): 1861-69; S. Rozen, H. Skaletsky, J. D. Marszalek, et al., "Abundant Gene Conversion Between Arms of Palindromes in Human and Ape Y Chromosomes," *Nature* 423 (2003): 873-76 [sequences were published electronically on the journal website as "Supplementary Information"]; Y. Kuroki, A. Toyoda, H. Noguchi, et al., "Comparative Analysis of Chimpanzee and Human Y Chromosomes Unveils Complex Evolutionary Pathway," *Nature Genetics* 38 (2006): 158-67.

47. Z. Cheng, M. Ventura, X. She, et al., "A Genome-wide Comparison of Recent Chimpanzee and Human Segmental Duplications," *Nature* 437 (2005): 88-93.

ferent copy numbers at ten to twenty of these sites. The process of genomic duplication (and deletion) that differentiated us from other primate species is ongoing, and may distinguish even closely related individuals.[48]

Segmental duplications generate spare copies of genes. With the passage of time, mutations accumulate in the copies. If the mutations inactivate the duplicated gene, no harm is done, because the gene copy was redundant. But if the mutations generate novel functions, the new gene copy may persist and acquire new characteristics. Single precursor genes spawn gene families by this means.[49] Examples of gene families arising by duplication are given below.

We detect the presence of volatile substances in the air by our sense of smell. Nerve cells in the lining of our noses express a great diversity of protein receptors that bind to airborne molecules and allow us to detect them as odors. Each such receptor is specified from one "olfactory receptor" gene. The size of this gene family varies widely in different mammals. The human olfactory receptor gene repertoire has expanded by gene duplication from an original group of genes (represented by a cluster on chromosome eleven) to multiple gene clusters distributed widely around the genome.[50]

Most of us enjoy the splendor of three-color vision. The capacity for three-color vision arose during primate history when a gene for a visual pigment protein called opsin was duplicated. This event gave rise

---

48. J. Sebat, B. Lakshmi, J. Troge, et al., "Large-scale Copy Number Polymorphism in the Human Genome," *Science* 305 (2004): 525-28; A. J. Iafrate, L. Feuk, M. N. Rivera, et al., "Detection of Large-scale Variation in the Human Genome," *Nature Genetics* 36 (2004): 949-51; G. H. Perry, J. Tchinda, S. D. McGrath, et al., "Hotspots for Copy Number Variation in Chimpanzees and Humans," *Proceedings of the National Academy of Sciences of the USA* 103 (2006): 8006-11.

49. For an introduction, see M. Hurles, "Gene Duplication: The Genomic Trade in Spare Parts," *PLoS Biology* 2 (2004): 900-904; also B. Conrad and S. E. Antonarakis, "Gene Duplication: A Drive for Phenotype Diversity and Cause of Human Disease," *Annual Review of Genomics and Human Genetics* 8 (2007): 17-35.

50. H. C. Mefford, E. Linardopoulou, D. Coil, et al., "Comparative Sequencing of a Multicopy Subtelomeric Region Containing Olfactory Receptor Genes Reveals Multiple Interactions Between Non-Homologous Chromosomes," *Human Molecular Genetics* 10 (2001): 2363-72; Y. Niimura and M. Nei, "Extensive Gains and Losses of Olfactory Receptor Genes in Mammalian Evolution," *PLoS One* (2007): e708; S. Rouquier and D. Giorgi, "Olfactory Gene Repertoires in Mammals," *Mutation Research* 616 (2007): 95-102.

to a new opsin protein with distinctive light-absorbing properties. The opsin locus remains unstable: some people have three pigment genes in tandem; others have one and are colorblind (Appendix 2).[51]

The functioning of our immune systems is controlled by the "human leukocyte antigen" gene complex. A large part of this genetic complex, spanning 1,800,000 bases, has been generated by several rounds of segmental duplications.[52] Comparison with other primate species confirms how this gene complex has been assembled in a stepwise fashion. The growth of gene families by duplication is widespread and ongoing.[53] This process has generated genes present only in humans. A comparison of gene copy numbers in great apes identified approximately 100 genes that have been duplicated on the human lineage. This rate of increase in the appearance of new gene copies is greater than that of any other great ape.[54]

51. K. S. Dulai, M. von Dornum, J. D. Mollon, and D. M. Hunt, "The Evolution of Trichromatic Colour Vision by Opsin Gene Duplication in New World and Old World Primates," *Genome Research* 9 (1999): 629-38; H. Ueyama, R. Torii, S. Tanabe, et al., "An Insertion/Deletion *TEX28* Polymorphism and Its Application to Analysis of Red/Green Visual Pigment Arrays," *Journal of Human Genetics* 49 (2004): 548-57.

52. T. Shiina, G. Tamiya, A. Oka, et al., "Molecular Dynamics of MHC Genesis Unraveled by Sequence Analysis of the 1,796,938-bp HLA Class I Region," *Proceedings of the National Academy of Sciences of the USA* 96 (1999): 13282-87; T. Anzai, T. Shiina, N. Kimura, et al., "Comparative Sequencing of Human and Chimpanzee MHC Class I Regions Unveils Insertions/Deletions as the Major Path to Genomic Divergence," *Proceedings of the National Academy of Sciences of the USA* 100 (2003): 7708-13; K. Fukami-Kobayashi, T. Shiina, T. Anzai, et al., "Genomic Evolution of MHC Class I Region in Primates," *Proceedings of the National Academy of Sciences of the USA* 102 (2005): 9230-34; J. K. Kulski, T. Anzai, and H. Inoko, "ERVK9, Transposons and the Evolution of MHC Class I Duplicons within the Alpha-block of the Human and Chimpanzee," *Cytogenetic and Genome Research* 110 (2005): 181-92.

53. N. Kouprina, M. Mullokandov, I. B. Rogozin, et al., "The *SPANX* Gene Family of Cancer/Testis Specific Antigens: Rapid Evolution and Amplification in African Great Apes and Hominids," *Proceedings of the National Academy of Sciences of the USA* 101 (2004): 3077-82; H. F. Rosenberg, K. D. Dyer, H. L. Tiffany, and M. Gonzalez, "Rapid Evolution of a Unique Family of Primate Ribonuclease Genes," *Nature Genetics* 10 (1995): 219-23; M. E. Johnson, L. Viggiano, J. A. Bailey, et al., "Positive Selection of a Gene Family During the Emergence of Humans and African Apes," *Nature* 413 (2001): 514-19; M. Ruault, M. Ventura, N. Galtier, et al., "*BAGE* Genes Generated by Juxtacentromeric Reshuffling in the Hominidae Lineage Are Under Selective Pressure," *Genomics* 81 (2003): 391-99; F. D. Ciccarelli, C. von Mering, M. Suyama, et al., "Complex Genomic Rearrangements Lead to Novel Primate Gene Function," *Genome Research* 15 (2005): 343-51.

54. See notes 20 and 47.

Segmental duplications can also cause problems. They may introduce a tendency for chromosomes to undergo harmful rearrangements. The presence of duplications that arose in species that were progenitors of humanity is implicated in a number of genetic diseases, such as leukemia and neurological diseases.[55] Segmental duplications unique to humans may be associated with diseases that are unique to humans.[56]

Deletions and Gene Death

Segments of DNA may also be deleted. As with duplications, unique deletions shared by multiple species are powerful markers of phylogenetic relationship.[57] The loss of tracts of DNA will at times result in the loss of entire genes, or parts of them. Such damaging mutations might be expected to be inimical to the development of species, but deletion events have contributed greatly to shaping of the human genome, leading to a hypothesis of "less is more": that the loss of some genetic functionality has contributed to the development of humanity.[58]

The human genome contains thousands of gene relics, disabled by deletions or other destructive mutations. Derelict genes that have lost the ability to specify the production of proteins are called "pseudogenes."[59] The largest gene family in our genome encodes the "olfactory

---

55. See note 47.

56. P. Stankiewicz and J. R. Lupski, "Molecular-evolutionary Mechanisms for Genomic Disorders," *Current Opinion in Genetics and Development* 12 (2002): 312-19; Conrad and Antonarakis, "Gene Duplication"; G. Saglio, C. T. Storlazzi, E. Giugliano, et al., "A 76-kb Duplication Maps Close to the BCR Gene on Chromosome 22 and the ABL Gene on Chromosome 9: Possible Involvement in the Genesis of the Philadelphia Chromosome Translocation," *Proceedings of the National Academy of Sciences of the USA* 99 (2002): 9882-87; M. P. Keller, B. A. Seifried, and P. F. Chance, "Molecular Evolution of the CMT1A Region: A Human- and Chimpanzee-specific Repeat," *Molecular Biology and Evolution* 16 (1999): 1019-26.

57. C. A. Matthee, G. Eick, S. Willows-Munro, et al., "Indel Evolution of Mammalian Introns and the Utility of Non-Coding Nuclear Markers in Eutherian Phylogenetics," *Molecular Phylogenetics and Evolution* 42 (2007): 827-37.

58. A. Wetterbom, M. Sevov, L. Cavelier, and T. F. Bergstrom, "Comparative Genomic Analysis of Human and Chimpanzee Indicates a Key Role for Indels in Primate Evolution," *Journal of Molecular Evolution* 63 (2006): 682-90.

59. D. Zheng and M. B. Gerstein, "The Ambiguous Boundary Between Genes and Pseudogenes: The Dead Rise Up, or Do They?" *Trends in Genetics* 23 (2007): 219-24;

receptors" required for our sense of smell. There are ≈1,000 olfactory receptor genes in our genome, of which over half are pseudogenes. The conversion of olfactory receptor genes into pseudogenes appears to have accelerated since the common ancestor of Old World monkeys and apes. It looks as if genes concerned with smell became less important after primates acquired three-color vision (Appendix 3). Two-thirds of these olfactory receptor pseudogenes are present also in chimps and have the same fingerprint mutations, indicating that they were inherited from a common progenitor. The other one-third of the olfactory receptor pseudogenes in our DNA were disabled only in the human lineage.[60]

It seems that the ancestors of humanity became less dependent on their sense of smell to survive. Evidence for this interpretation comes from a study of olfactory receptor genes in whales and dolphins, the ancestors of which returned to the sea from land. These creatures have the highest known proportion of olfactory receptor pseudogenes (generally above 60 percent).[61] "Use it or lose it" is a rule that seems to apply to the historical fates of our genes.[62]

Another form of chemosensation is that provided by the vomeronasal organ. This sensory organ is present in the nose and senses the presence of pheromones (chemical signals that regulate aspects of animal behavior such as aggression, mating, and nursing). The vomeronasal organ does not form in humans and higher primates, and

---

D. Zheng, A. Frankish, R. Baertsch, et al., "Pseudogenes in the ENCODE Regions: Consensus Annotation, Analysis of Transcription, and Evolution," *Genome Research* 17 (2007): 839-51.

60. Y. Gilad, O. Man, S. Paabo, and D. Lancet, "Human Specific Loss of Olfactory Receptor Genes," *Proceedings of the National Academy of Sciences of the USA* 100 (2003): 3324-27; Y. Gilad, O. Man, and G. Glusman, "A Comparison of the Human and Chimpanzee Olfactory Receptor Gene Receptor Repertoires," *Genome Research* 15 (2005): 224-30; Y. Gilad, V. Wiebe, M. Przeworski, et al., "Loss of Olfactory Receptor Genes Coincides with the Acquisition of Full Trichromatic Vision in Primates," *PLoS Biology* 2 (2004): 120-25.

61. J. Freitag, G. Ludwig, I. Andreini, et al., "Olfactory Receptors in Aquatic and Terrestrial Vertebrates," *Journal of Comparative Physiology (A)* 183 (1998): 635-50; T. Kishada, S. Kubota, Y. Shirayama, and H. Fukami, "The Olfactory Receptor Gene Repertoires in Secondary-Adapted Marine Vertebrates: Evidence for Reduction of the Functional Proportions in Cetaceans," *Biology Letters* 3 (2007): 428-30.

62. E. R. Liman, "Use It or Lose It: Molecular Evolution of Sensory Signalling in Primates," *Pflugers Archiv — European Journal of Physiology* 453 (2006): 125-31.

its signaling function seems to be defunct in these species. The genes that encode pheromone receptors (in excess of one hundred) and a key signaling molecule have been located in our DNA, but nearly all of them have sustained mutations that have disabled protein-coding function.[63] We have inherited an extensive suite of derelict pheromone-sensing genes. This is testimony to the fact that being human involves the loss of some of the sensory capabilities that drive the behavior of many of our fellow mammals.

At least 100 genes have been inactivated in humans since the human-chimp divergence.[64] Humans are unique in having weakened cheek muscles, arising from the inactivation of a muscle gene by a deletion mutation. There is current debate over whether the loss of this protein contributed to the evolution of the human skull.[65] The loss of particular genes that no longer serve essential functions is ongoing. This may be inferred in those instances when a gene and a defunct pseudogenic derivative currently coexist in the human population: some people retain the functional form while others have the inactive derivative.[66]

Rearrangements: Inversions and Translocations

Inversions are rearrangements that occur within chromosomes in which a segment of chromosomal DNA ("A-B-C-D-E") is flipped 180° with respect to the rest of the molecule ("A-D-C-B-E"). Translocations arise from the exchange of genetic material between chromosomes. Two orig-

---

63. Y. Niimura and M. Nei, "Evolutionary Dynamics of Olfactory and Other Chemosensory Receptor Genes in Vertebrates," *Journal of Human Genetics* 51 (2006): 505-17; N. I. Mundy, "Genetic Basis of Olfactory Communication in Primates," *American Journal of Primatology* 68 (2006): 559-67; J. M. Young and B. J. Trask, "V2R Gene Families Degenerated in Primates, Dog and Cow, but Expanded in Opossum," *Trends in Genetics* 23 (2007): 212-15.

64. See note 2.

65. H. H. Stedman, B. W. Kozyak, A. Nelson, et al., "Myosin Gene Mutation Correlates with Anatomical Changes in the Human Lineage," *Nature* 428 (2004): 415-18; M. A. McCollum, C. C. Sherwood, C. J. Vinyard, et al., "Of Muscle-bound Crania and Human Brain Evolution: The Story behind the *MYH16* Headlines," *Journal of Human Evolution* 50 (2006): 232-36.

66. X. Wang, W. E. Grus, and J. Zhang, "Gene Losses during Human Origins," *PLoS Biology* 4 (2006): 366-77.

inal chromosomes "A-B-C-D-E" and "V-W-X-Y-Z" may generate the derivative products "A-B-C-X-Y-Z" and "V-W-D-E." Inversions and translocations together have generated the diversity of chromosome sets that characterize species. Species that share a particular rearrangement have inherited it from the one ancestor in which the singular event occurred. Such rearrangements place genes in new environments and may influence the way they act.

The distribution of micro-inversions (<15,000 bases long) in different species confirms the phylogenetic relationships that have been derived using other molecular markers. Humans share a common ancestor with all the primates in possessing two primate-specific micro-inversions; with all simians by fourteen; with Old World primates by nine; and with the other great apes by five. A comparison of whole genome sequences has revealed that humans and chimps are distinguished by ≈300 such micro-inversions,[67] and by nine large inversions that are visible under the microscope. Two of these occurred on the human lineage; the other seven on the chimp lineage. Some genes situated near breakpoints are expressed differently in the two species. It is not known whether these changes are due to the inversion, or whether they have affected our biology.[68]

Also visible under the microscope is a chromosomal translocation that occurred on the lineage leading to humans. A single head-to-head fusion formed a human chromosome (chromosome 2) from two individual chromosomes retained as such in the other great apes, and differentiates our chromosome set from theirs.[69] The human chromosome set as a whole can be "cut-and-pasted" into that of an ancestor of apes, or of primates, or of mammals.[70]

---

67. M. J. Chaisson, B. J. Raphael, and P. A. Pevzner, "Microinversions in Mammalian Evolution," *Proceedings of the National Academy of Sciences of the USA* 103 (2006): 19824-29. Micro-inversion data are available on Supplementary Information on the *PNAS* website.

68. H. Kehrer-Sawatzki and D. N. Cooper, "Structural Divergence between the Human and Chimpanzee Genomes," *Human Genetics* 120 (2007): 759-78.

69. Y. Fan, E. Linardopoulou, E. Friedman, et al., "Genomic Structure and Evolution of the Ancestral Chromosome Fusion Site in 2q13-2q14.1 and Paralogous Regions on Other Human Chromosomes," *Genome Research* 12 (2002): 1651-62; L. W. Hillier, T. A. Graves, R. S. Fulton, et al., "Generation and Annotation of the DNA Sequences of Human Chromosomes 2 and 4," *Nature* 434 (2005): 724-31.

70. F. Yang, E. Z. Alkalaeva, P. L. Perelman, et al., "Reciprocal Chromosome Painting among Human, Aardvark, and Elephant (Superorder Afrotheria) Reveals the Likely Eutherian Ancestral Karyotype," *Proceedings of the National Academy of Sciences of the USA*

The Emergence of Human Distinctiveness

Human populations are distinguished by inversions that have occurred since the human species formed. Some people retain the original conformation, while others possess the rearrangement. An inversion of 900,000 bases on chromosome seventeen, found commonly in Europeans, may confer a selective advantage upon those who possess it.[71]

Insertions and New Genetic Functions

It is clear that through mammalian history, the genome that was to become ours has been formed by natural and haphazard genetic processes. If this seems demeaning, worse is to come. Bits of extraneous DNA have been spliced into the chromosomal DNA of our forebears. A sequence "A-B-C-D-E" may be converted to "A-B-X-X-X-C-D-Y-Y-E." Such insertions have been dismissed, perhaps presumptuously, as "junk."

DNA molecules may break spontaneously, perhaps as a result of damage from the background radiation to which we are inevitably exposed. Many of the extraneous units of DNA that have been inserted into our genomes may have been put there as molecular bandages at sites where DNA has been broken to hold the free ends together. In those cases in which these inserts are shared with other primate species, it may be concluded that our genome carries scars arising in the DNA of primate ancestors that lived millions of years ago (Appendix 4).[72]

On a much greater scale, 50 percent of our genome has accumulated from the activities of foreign invaders (viruses) and resident

---

100 (2003): 1062-66; M. Svartman, G. Stone, and R. Stanyon, "The Ancestral Eutherian Karyotype Is Present in Xenarthra," *PLoS Genetics* 2 (2006): 1006-11; W. J. Murphy, D. M. Larkin, A. Everts-van der Wind, et al., "Dynamics of Mammalian Chromosome Evolution Inferred from Multispecies Comparative Maps," *Science* 309 (2005): 613-17; S. Muller and J. Weinberg, "'Bar-coding' Primate Chromosomes: Molecular Cytogenetic Screening for the Ancestral Hominoid Karyotype," *Human Genetics* 109 (2001): 85-94.

71. H. Stefansson, A. Helgason, G. Thorleifsson, et al., "A Common Inversion under Selection in Europe," *Nature Genetics* 37 (2005): 129-37.

72. S. G. Nergadze, M. Rocchi, K. Azzalin, et al., "Insertion of Telomeric Repeats at Intrachromosomal Break Sites during Primate Evolution," *Genome Research* 14 (2004): 1704-10; E. Hazkani-Covo and D. Graur, "A Comparative Analysis of *Numt* Evolution in Human and Chimpanzee," *Molecular Biology and Evolution* 24 (2007): 13-18; E. E. Thomas, N. Srebro, J. Sebat, et al., "Distribution of Short Paired Duplications in Mammalian Genomes," *Proceedings of the National Academy of Sciences of the USA* 101 (2004): 10349-54.

"jumping genes" (unruly colonizers of our genome called transposons). These agents are "insertional mutagens." They splice themselves into chromosomal DNA as they please, and without consideration of the consequences. They are essentially parasites, and are potentially pathogenic. Human DNA contains several million inserted segments arising from these sources.[73] Over long timescales, many of these inserts have been recruited to assume new roles. They have become integrated into the functioning of the genome.

The foreign invaders are a class of virus called "retroviruses." When they infect cells, they insert their piece of DNA into the chromosomal DNA of the infected cell. The viral DNA is thus passed on to all the descendants of an infected cell. Some retroviruses infect blood cells and currently cause leukemia in human populations.[74] Other retroviruses have infected reproductive cells, and their DNA inserts thereby are passed on to future generations of organisms. These heritable retroviral inserts are called "endogenous retroviruses" (ERVs).[75] The DNA we have inherited contains several hundred thousand retroviral inserts.[76]

Nearly all of the ERV inserts in human DNA are shared by other great apes.[77] The majority are present also in the genomes of Old World monkeys.[78] All species that possess a particular ERV insert are descended from the one reproductive cell in which that particular insert arose. ERVs are strikingly powerful markers of evolutionary relatedness.[79]

During human history, invaders have often been assimilated into the cultures of the people whom they once overran. Mongol invaders

---

73. See note 1.

74. F. Mortreux, A.-S. Gabet, and E. Wattel, "Molecular and Cellular Aspects of HTLV-1 Associated Leukemogenesis," *Leukemia* 17 (2003): 26-38.

75. R. Gifford and M. Tristem, "The Evolution, Distribution and Diversity of Endogenous Retroviruses," *Virus Genes* 26 (2003): 291-315; N. Bannert and R. Kurth, "Retroelements and the Human Genome: New Perspectives on an Old Relation," *Proceedings of the National Academy of Sciences of the USA* 101 (2004): 14572-79; J. Mayer and E. Meese, "Human Endogenous Retroviruses in the Primate Lineage and Their Influence on Host Genomes," *Cytogenetic and Genome Research* 110 (2005): 448-56.

76. See note 1.

77. See note 2.

78. See note 3.

79. W. E. Johnson and J. M. Coffin, "Constructing Primate Phylogenies from Ancient Retrovirus Sequences," *Proceedings of the National Academy of Sciences of the USA* 96 (1999): 10254-60; E. D. Sverdlov, "Retroviruses and Primate Evolution," *Bioessays* 22 (2000): 161-71.

have repeatedly been assimilated into Chinese culture. In the same way, many ERVs have been domesticated to provide essential functions within the genomes in which they have come to reside. Small segments of DNA within ERVs now contribute to the essential regulation of nearby genes (Appendix 5).[80] ERVs that became resident in our DNA only since the human lineage diverged from that of the chimp exert an effect on the function of nearby DNA, the biological impact of which is not known.[81] Some ERVs have been added to the human genome so recently that only a minor proportion of people have them. It has been suggested that these recently integrated ERVs might disrupt genetic functions and cause disease.[82]

Once ERVs become resident in chromosomal DNA, they start to accumulate mutations and their genes decay. Against all odds, however, some ancient ERVs have retained functional genes with the capacity to direct the production of proteins. There is strong evidence that at least some of these ERV genes are now used during the development of the human embryo.[83] What was added to primate DNA as junk has been

---

80. L. N. van de Lagemaat, J.-R. Landry, D. L. Mager, and P. Medstrand, "Transposable Elements in Mammals Promote Regulatory Variation and Diversification of Genes with Specialised Functions," *Trends in Genetics* 19 (2003): 530-36; J. Ling, W. Pi, R. Bollag, et al., "The Solitary Long Terminal Repeats of ERV-9 Endogenous Retrovirus Are Conserved during Primate Evolution and Possess Enhancer Activities in Embryonic and Hematopoietic Cells," *Journal of Virology* 76 (2002): 2410-23; I. Bieche, A. Laurent, I. Laurendeau, et al., "Placenta-specific *INSL4* Expression Is Mediated by a Human Endogenous Retrovirus Element," *Biology of Reproduction* 68 (2003): 1422-29; H.-S. Sin, J.-W. Huh, D.-S. Kim, et al., "Endogenous Retrovirus-related Sequences Provide an Alternative Transcript of *MCJ* Genes in Human Tissues and Cancer Cells," *Genes and Genetic Systems* 81 (2006): 333-39; C. A. Dunn, L. N. van de Lagemaat, G. J. Baillie, and D. L. Mager, "Endogenous Retrovirus Long Terminal Repeats as Ready-to-use Mobile Promoters: The Case of β3GAL-T5," *Gene* 364 (2005): 2-12; M. T. Romanish, W. M. Lock, L. van de Lagemaat, et al., "Repeated Recruitment of LTR Retrotransposons as Promoters by the Anti-apoptosis Locus *NAIP* during Mammalian Evolution," *PLoS Genetics* 3 (2007): 51-62.

81. A. Buzdin, E. Kovalskaya-Alexandrova, E. Gogvadze, and E. Sverdlov, "At Least 50% of Human-specific HERV-K (HML-2) Long Terminal Repeats Serve in Vivo as Active Promoters for Host Nonrepetitive DNA Transcription," *Journal of Virology* 80 (2006): 10752-62.

82. D. Moyes, D. J. Griffiths, and P. J. Venables, "Insertional Polymorphisms; A New Lease of Life for Endogenous Retroviruses in Human Disease," *Trends in Genetics* 23 (2007): 326-33.

83. S. Blaise, N. de Parseval, L. Benit, and T. Heidmann, "Genomewide Screening for Fusogenic Human Endogenous Retrovirus Envelopes Identifies Syncytin 2, a Gene Conserved on Primate Evolution," *Proceedings of the National Academy of Sciences of the USA* 100

co-opted to provide essential services. It seems that we are at least partially what ancient ERVs have made us.

The second class of disruptive agents in our DNA are the resident "jumping genes." Our genome contains a veritable zoo of hundreds of classes of these semi-autonomous genetic elements. They have arisen in various ways, but share the property of copying-and-pasting themselves to new sites in the genome (Appendix 6).[84] A large number of the most ancient inserts in our DNA date from the earliest periods of mammalian history.[85] Others have proliferated vigorously only during primate history.[86] This process continues. It has been estimated that

---

(2003): 13013-18; L. Aagaard, P. Villesen, A. L. Kjeldbjerg, and F. S. Pedersen, "The ≈30 million-year-old ERVPbI Envelope Gene Is Evolutionarily Conserved among Hominoids and Old World Monkeys," *Genomics* 86 (2005): 685-91; C. A. Herve, G. Forrest, R. Lower, et al., "Conservation and Loss of the *ERV3* Open Reading Frame in Primates," *Genomics* 83 (2004): 940-43; H.-S. Kim, J.-M. Yi, H. Hirai, et al., "Human Endogenous Retrovirus (HERV)-R Family in Primates: Chromosomal Location, Gene Expression, and Evolution," *Gene* 370 (2006): 34-42; F. Mallet, O. Bouton, S. Prudhomme, et al., "The Endogenous Locus ERVWE1 Is a Bona Fide Gene Involved in Hominoid Placental Physiology," *Proceedings of the National Academy of Sciences of the USA* 101 (2004): 1731-36; B. Bonnaud, O. Bouton, G. Oriol, et al., "Evidence of Selection on the Domesticated ERVWE1 *Env* Retroviral Element Involved in Placentation," *Molecular Biology and Evolution* 21 (2004): 1895-1901; S. Prudhomme, G. Oriol, and F. Mallet, "A Retroviral Promoter and a Cellular Enhancer Define a Bipartite Element Which Controls *Env* ERVWE1 Placental Expression," *Journal of Virology* 78 (2004): 12157-68; M. Caceres, NISC Comparative Sequencing Program, and J. W. Thomas, "The Gene of Retroviral Origin Syncytin 1 Is Specific to Hominoids and Is Inactive in Old World Monkeys," *Journal of Heredity* 97 (2006): 100-106; B. Bonnaud, J. Beliaeff, O. Bouton, et al., "Natural History of the ERVWE1 Endogenous Retroviral Locus," *Retrovirology* 2 (2005): 57.

84. H. H. Kazazian, "Mobile Elements: Drivers of Genome Evolution," *Science* 303 (2004): 1626-32; D. J. Hedges and M. A. Batzer, "From the Margins of the Genome: Mobile Elements Shape Primate Evolution," *BioEssays* 27 (2005): 785-94; D. V. Babushok and H. H. Kazazian, "Progress in Understanding the Biology of the Human Mutagen LINE-1," *Human Mutation* 28 (2007): 527-39; J. Jurka, V. V. Kapitonov, O. Kohany, and M. V. Jurka, "Repetitive Sequences in Complex Genomes: Structure and Evolution," *Annual Review of Genomics and Human Genetics* 8 (2007): 241-59.

85. H. Nishihara, M. Hasegawa, and N. Okada, "Pegasoferae, an Unexpected Mammalian Clade Revealed by Tracking Ancient Retroposon Insertions," *Proceedings of the National Academy of Sciences of the USA* 103 (2006): 9929-34; J. O. Kriegs, G. Churakov, M. Kiefmann, et al., "Retroposed Elements as Archives for the Evolutionary History of Placental Mammals," *PLoS Biology* 4 (2006): 537-44.

86. I. Ovchinnikov, A. Rubin, and G. D. Swergold, "Tracing the LINEs of Human Evolution," *Proceedings of the National Academy of Sciences of the USA* 99 (2002): 10522-27; L. M. Mathews, S. Y. Chi, N. Greenberg, et al., "Large Differences between LINE-1 Amplification

The Emergence of Human Distinctiveness

the DNA of 10 percent of people possesses a new insert that arose during their own development and that is shared by no one else.[87] Most of these copy-and-paste events are innocuous. The presence of a new insert becomes apparent only when it disrupts an important gene and causes genetic disease. One in every thousand disease-causing mutations identified in medical genetics laboratories has arisen from an insertional mutagenesis event involving a misdirected "jumping gene."[88]

As with ERVs, many of these inserts have been domesticated to perform important functions in our DNA. The demonstrably random activities of "jumping genes" have helped to make us what we are. Many inserts now act to control the activities of nearby genes.[89] Others have donated segments of DNA that have been integrated into the information content of preexisting genes.[90] Some cases have been documented

---

Rates in the Human and Chimpanzee Lineages," *American Journal of Human Genetics* 72 (2003): 739-48; J. Xing, A.-H. Salem, D. J. Hedges, et al., "Comprehensive Analysis of Two Alu Yd Subfamilies," *Journal of Molecular Evolution* 57 (2003): S76-S89; A.-H. Salem, D. A. Ray, J. Xing, et al., "Alu Elements and Hominid Phylogenetics," *Proceedings of the National Academy of Sciences of the USA* 100 (2003): 12787-91; A.-H. Salem, D. A. Ray, D. J. Hedges, et al., "Analysis of the Human *Alu* Ye Lineage," *BMC Evolutionary Biology* 5 (2005): 18.

87. R. Cordaux, D. J. Hedges, S. W. Herke, and M. A. Batzer, "Estimating the Retrotransposition Rate of Human *Alu* Elements," *Gene* 373 (2006): 134-37.

88. J.-M. Chen, P. D. Stenson, D. N. Cooper, and C. Ferec, "A Systematic Study of LINE-1 Endonuclease-dependent Retrotranspositional Events Causing Human Genetic Disease," *Human Genetics* 117 (2005): 411-27; J.-M. Chen, C. Ferec, and D. N. Cooper, "LINE-1 Endonuclease-dependent Retrotranspositional Events Causing Human Genetic Disease: Mutation Detection Bias and Multiple Mechanisms of Target Gene Disruption," *Journal of Biomedicine and Biotechnology* 2006 (2006): 1 (Article ID 56182); P. A. Callinan and M. A. Batzer, "Retrotransposable Elements and Human Disease," *Genome Dynamics* 1 (2006): 104-15.

89. D. Laperriere, T.-T. Wang, J. H. White, and S. Mader, "Widespread Alu Repeat-driven Expansion of Consensus DR2 Retinoic Acid Response Elements during Primate Evolution," *BMC Genomics* 8 (2007): 23; J. Hasler and K. Strub, "*Alu* Elements as Regulators of Gene Expression," *Nucleic Acids Research* 34 (2006): 5491-97.

90. S. S. Singer, D. N. Mannel, T. Hehlgans, et al., "From 'Junk' to Gene: Curriculum Vitae of a Primate Receptor Isoform Gene," *Journal of Molecular Biology* 341 (2004): 883-86; M. Krull, J. Brosius, and J. Schmitz, "Alu-SINE Exonization: En Route to Protein-Coding Function," *Molecular Biology and Evolution* 22 (2005): 1702-11; G. Mola, E. Vela, M. T. Fernandez-Figueras, et al., "Exonization of *Alu*-generated Splice Variants in the Survivin Gene of Human and Non-human Primates," *Journal of Molecular Biology* 366 (2007): 1055-63; X. H.-F. Zhang and L. A. Chasin, "Comparison of Multiple Vertebrate Genomes Reveals the Birth and Evolution of Human Exons," *Proceedings of the National*

in which ancient "jumping gene" inserts have been recruited as raw material to form brand-new genes.[91]

Some classes of "jumping genes" contain enzymes that can copy cellular genes and splice those copies somewhere else in the genome. Most of these copied genes have lost the ability to produce the protein encoded by the parent gene.[92] But remarkably, this haphazard process has generated a trickle of new genes right through mammalian and primate history (Appendix 7).[93]

Humanness Transcends Genetics

Genomic science has revealed a detailed record of our genetic development. The incremental accumulation of myriad genetic rearrangements, deletions, and insertions has fashioned our genome from that of progenitors shared with other apes, and ever more remotely, with other primates, other mammals, and other vertebrates. Our status as a

---

Academy of Sciences of the USA 103 (2006): 13427-32; A. Damert, J. Lower, and R. Lower, "Leptin Receptor Isoform 219.1: An Example of Protein Evolution by LINE-1-mediated Human-specific Retrotransposition of a Coding SVA Element," *Molecular Biology and Evolution* 21 (2004): 647-51; M. Krull, M. Petrusma, W. Malakowski, et al., "Functional Persistence of Exonized Mammalian-wide Interspersed Repeat Elements (MIRs)," *Genome Research* 17 (2007): 1139-45.

91. V. Y. Kuryshev, B. V. Skryabin, J. Kremerskothen, et al., "Birth of a Gene: Locus of Neuronal BC200 snmRNA in Three Prosimians and Human BC200 Pseudogenes as Archives of Change in the *Anthropoidea* lineage," *Journal of Molecular Biology* 309 (2001): 1049-66; A. Courseaux and J.-L. Nahon, "Birth of Two Chimeric Genes in the *Hominidae* Lineage," *Science* 291 (2001): 1293-97.

92. Z. Zhang and M. Gerstein, "Large-scale Analysis of Pseudogenes in the Human Genome," *Current Opinion in Genetics and Development* 14 (2004): 328-35; A. Pavlicek, A. J. Gentles, J. Paces, et al., "Retrotransposition of Processed Pseudogenes: The Impact of RNA Stability and Translational Control," *Trends in Genetics* 22 (2006): 69-73; W. Ding, L. Lin, B. Chen, and J. Dai, "L1 Elements, Processed Pseudogenes, and Retrogenes in Mammalian Genomes," *IUBMB Life* 58 (2006): 677-85.

93. F. Burki and H. Kaessmann, "Birth and Adaptive Evolution of a Hominoid Gene That Supports High Neurotransmitter Flux," *Nature Genetics* 36 (2004): 1061-63; A. C. Marques, I. Dupanloup, N. Vinckenbosch, et al., "Emergence of Young Human Genes after a Burst of Retroposition in Primates," *PLoS Biology* 3 (2005): 1970-79; N. Vinckenbosch, I. Dupanloup, and H. Kaessmann, "Evolutionary Fate of Retrotransposed Gene Copies in the Human Genome," *Proceedings of the National Academy of Sciences of the USA* 103 (2006): 3220-25.

terminal twig of the phylogenetic tree has been established beyond reasonable doubt. Does this connection with the other animals bring into question our distinctiveness as human persons, or in any way undermine the biblical assertion that we are created by a purposive and loving God?

To be human is to wonder about our own distinctiveness. Integral to our humanity also is the capacity to conceive of a spiritual dimension to reality, to be able to entertain thoughts about "superempirical" realities that order our lives.[94] David Hay's study of human spirituality has led him to conclude that we possess a "relational consciousness" and are religious animals.[95] To van Huyssteen, we are praying, moral, and believing animals.[96] This capacity for religious thought is a product of our evolutionary development, and may have arisen from the interplay of behavioral selection and natural selection as a response to the consistent nature of the world.[97] The capacity to reflect on our place and purpose in the world and on God is all of a piece with our rational, symbolic, and aesthetic capacities.[98]

When the materialist Wolpert suggests that the mental *ability* or *capacity* for religious belief is genetically encoded,[99] he is stating the obvious. This is what he means when he asserts that *religion* or *religious beliefs* are genetically encoded. These ambiguous expressions should not be taken to imply that the *content* of religious beliefs is genetically encoded. For religious beliefs arise not from genetics but from human history and the specific events contributing to the development of human cultures, as Wolpert states.[100] Religious beliefs transcend genetics.[101]

Nor should these ambiguous expressions be taken to imply that certain people are religious because of their genes. As far as Collins is concerned, DNA sequence data "will never explain certain human at-

---

94. Van Huyssteen, *Alone in the World?* pp. 297, 291.
95. David Hay, *Something There: The Biology of the Human Spirit* (London: Darton, Longman & Todd, 2006), pp. 138f., 38, 127.
96. Van Huyssteen, *Alone in the World?* pp. 316, 274, 288-91.
97. Hay, *Something There*, pp. 37, 39, 145; Van Huyssteen, *Alone in the World?* pp. 237, 312.
98. Van Huyssteen, *Alone in the World?* p. 214.
99. Lewis Wolpert, *Six Impossible Things Before Breakfast* (London: Faber & Faber, 2006), pp. 117, 136-37, 217-18.
100. Wolpert, *Six Impossible Things*, pp. 120, 218.
101. Van Huyssteen, *Alone in the World?* pp. 269, 311-12.

tributes, such as the knowledge of the Moral Law and the universal search for God." We have all been dealt a particular set of (genetic) cards, and how we play the hand is up to us.[102] Indeed, human distinctiveness lies not just in having a thing called human nature, but in what we choose to do with our human nature. "Being human therefore is an act, not a thing, and its chief characteristic is not being, but what is done responsibly with being." It follows that the "human condition is a category of experience."[103]

Ultimately, genetic science — and indeed any branch of science — cannot provide an adequate account of our human distinctiveness.[104] If human mind arose (and in each one of us, arises) "only within the socially constructed context of linguistic communication,"[105] our human gene set gives us the uniquely human neural potential to respond to relational inputs, and only in so doing to become human. Our inclusion in a nurturing community of people is what makes us human. Descartes' statement, "I think therefore I am," described his epistemological starting-point. It may be adapted to describe the nature of human distinctiveness. If thinking comes only through knowing, the dictum, "I am known (and know) therefore I am," will be more fundamental.

We are anthropoid, hominoid primates, firmly rooted in our genetic history, but endowed with the capacity to respond to other self-revealing persons and to a self-revealing God. Any perspective that perceives our humanness as being dependent on knowing is compatible with biblical thought, which depicts personal knowledge of God as a reality that confers upon human life a fundamentally new quality. One of Israel's seers looked forward to the day when a personal knowledge of God would be the experience of a new humanity: "they will all know me from the least of them to the greatest," declares the Lord (Jer. 31:34). Jesus indicated that he was the inaugurator of this new humanity when he stated, "No one knows the Father except the Son and those to whom the Son chooses to reveal him" (Matt. 11:27; Luke 10:22; John 1:18).

Jesus' prayer, that "eternal life is knowing you, the only true God, and knowing Jesus Christ whom you sent" (John 17:3), expresses the

---

102. Francis S. Collins, *The Language of God* (New York: Free Press, 2006), pp. 140-41, 263.
103. Van Huyssteen (commenting on Heschel), *Alone in the World?* pp. 297, 299, 302-3.
104. Van Huyssteen, *Alone in the World?* pp. 289, 305, 325.
105. Van Huyssteen, *Alone in the World?* p. 231.

fundamental understanding of Christian faith. It firmly links "knowing" to the quality of life granted by God's grace to his creatures.

Social interaction and its attendant wonder of human self-awareness arise from the expression of genes in the inductive environment of personal human knowing. It seems that the very matter of our brains is organized in response to personal inputs that can only be described as "spiritual." We are formed as human persons by the experience of love, joy, peace, patience, kindness, goodness, faithfulness, gentleness, and self-control (Gal. 5:22-23). In the same way, the Christian hope to share in the life of God requires our genetic potential, induced to express mind by the attentions of the "gracious" human "Other," and thus prepared to receive, respond to, and to be formed by the self-disclosure of the divine "Other" who encounters us in the person known as Jesus of Nazareth.

Our genes provide the substrate for all that we are; and they provide the foundation by which personal encounter with other persons and with God confers upon us the fullness of human personhood. Christians should welcome the astonishing findings of genetics, not with anxiety, but with a sense of wonderment, as expressed by Francis Collins in his book *The Language of God*.[106]

We are firmly rooted in the biological world. This conclusion is not one that should be theologically surprising or threatening. The biblical creation stories record that both humankind and the other animals are made from dust or earth (Gen. 2:7, 19). The name Adam plays on the word "adamah," earth. Humanity was created along with the other terrestrial animals on the sixth day; and along with them was created "a living being," and told to "be fruitful and multiply."[107] And yet the Hebrews were aware of human distinctiveness. They recognized that being human entailed the possession of God's "image and likeness" (Gen. 1:22, 26-31): we are embodied creatures that uniquely possess the capacity of representing God's authority.[108]

Genetics and Scripture coincide in this self-understanding. The

---

106. Collins, *The Language of God*, pp. 140-41, 263.

107. Henri Blocher, *In the Beginning* (Downers Grove, IL, and Leicester, UK: InterVarsity Press, 1984), pp. 82-83; these insights were also stated by the ecologist Richard Storey, "Living at Home in God's Creation," in a sermon at West Hamilton Anglican Church, New Zealand, 2006.

108. R. S. Hess, "Genesis 1-2 and Recent Studies of Ancient Texts," *Science and Christian Belief* 7 (1995): 141-49.

Harvard botanist and Christian Asa Gray (friend and supporter of Darwin) said that man "is as certainly and completely an animal as he is certainly something more."[109] More expressively, a former Bishop of Edinburgh, Richard Holloway, has stated: "I am dust and ashes, frail and wayward, a set of predetermined behavioral responses, programmed by genetic inheritance and by social context, riddled with fears, beset with needs whose origins I do not understand and whose satisfaction I cannot achieve, quintessence of dust, and unto dust I shall return." He continued, however, "Dust I may be but troubled dust, dust that dreams, dust that has strange premonitions of transfiguration, of a glory in store, a destiny prepared, an inheritance that will one day be my own."[110]

We are an evolved species that is driven to reflect both on its evolutionary history and on its createdness. The evolutionary biologist and Russian Orthodox believer, Theodosius Dobzhansky, recognized the legitimacy of this twofold pursuit when he wrote, "Creation is not an event that happened in 4004 BC; it is a process that began some 10 billion years ago and is still underway."[111] This shows the inappropriateness of opposing "evolution" and "creation" as alternative theories between which we must choose. It also rightly denies that creation should be thought of as a single initiating event. But Dobzhansky did not get it quite right. The word "creation" does not in essence signify any physical or biological process. "Creation" rather denotes the activity of God — personal, rational, and purposive — that gives existence to the multibillion-year process of evolution. As Douglas Spanner put it, "Creation (in the biblical sense) is not a theory alternative to, and in competition with, theories offered by science. It has nothing to do with materials, mechanism and process. It is an ultimate concept that thrusts itself upon us when we look, not backwards in time, but away from our space-time altogether."[112]

Similarly, Howard Van Till stated that "To know God as Creator is not merely to know of one of his acts in the past. To know God as

---

109. James R. Moore, *The Post-Darwinian Controversies* (Cambridge: Cambridge University Press, 1979), p. 279.

110. R. J. (Sam) Berry, *Real Science, Real Faith* (Eastbourne, UK: Monarch, 1991), p. 162.

111. Quoted by Collins, *The Language of God*, p. 206.

112. Douglas Spanner, *Biblical Creation and the Theory of Evolution* (Exeter, UK: Paternoster, 1987), p. 34.

The Emergence of Human Distinctiveness

Creator is to experience one's continuing relationship to him — past, present and future." Thus biblically, creation does not stand "merely for an instantaneous act or event, but for an eternal covenantal relationship."[113] The processes of genetics that have provided an indelible record of our evolutionary past are expressions of God's creative activity. Human evolution is a process that owes its being to the will of God. It follows that to engage in the scientific study of evolutionary or comparative genetics must be done in rigorously genetic terms. As long as we are concerned with developing a genetic (scientific) account of our origins, our vocabulary must be limited to the starkly material story of DNA. This mechanistic framework is recognized as the creative and purposive work of God only by placing the narrowly genetic account into the rich context of the totality of our experience. It follows of course that any denial of divine authorship or of given purpose is also a faith position that can lay no claim to being scientific. Equally at fault are "Intelligent Design" theorists who deny the appropriateness of the genetic account so that they may introduce teleological considerations *into* science, and materialists who proclaim the all-encompassing sufficiency of the genetic account so that they may deny teleological considerations *beyond* science. Both flawed perspectives contribute to the destructive controversy that plagues discussion of our phylogenetic roots.

The randomness of genetic process may seem to be incompatible with the understanding that evolutionary history reflects the purposive action of God. But the occurrence of "chance" events (in the statistical sense of being probabilistic) cannot imply that a process is the outcome of "chance" (in the metaphysical sense of being unplanned). Even the exquisitely integrated system of cellular biochemistry arises from random molecular movement. In molecular engines, random "Brownian motion drives both the power and exhaust strokes." Brownian randomness is used by protein motors that move along intracellular tracks, secretory channels that pump products across membranes, enzymes that catalytically transform substrates, and mitochondrial generators that produce ATP.[114] Thus randomness is inherent to the workings of the material substrate out of which life arises.

Biological systems make use of randomness as a vital component

---

113. Howard J. Van Till, *The Fourth Day* (Grand Rapids: Eerdmans, 1986), p. 226.
114. G. Oster, "Darwin's Motors," *Nature* 417 (2002): 25.

of their operations. Genetic mechanisms that operate during sexual reproduction represent institutionalized randomness. The elaborate processes that function to ensure that genetic material is reshuffled in reproductive cells attests to the desirability of randomness in organismic self-perpetuation.[115] Our immune system has the capacity to adapt to unprecedented environmental provocations. It is so organized that intrinsic random genetic mechanisms continuously generate the diversity of responses that ensure the body can combat any foreign biomolecule that the biosphere can generate.[116] Randomness is an aspect of design.[117]

Evolution is like the immune system writ large. The ubiquity throughout the world of living organisms of parasitic genetic elements (those exuberant "jumping genes") implies that their disruptive activities are tolerated, if not cultivated, because of their capacity to generate novelty in the plant and animal genomes that play host to them. The randomness of genetic mechanism is a design feature built into living systems to sustain their dynamic responsiveness to environmental change; randomness is integrated into creative systems. Alternatively, we may say that order is generated in the environment of randomness, and is made possible by it. Phylogenetic mechanisms are a form of problem solving. For all the randomness of their process, genes are "smart." They share, distribute, and transmit information. Even software engineers have copied the strategies of genes to develop powerful problem-solving "genetic algorithms."[118]

To a mind conditioned by the biblical story, history is *created* history.[119] The divinely authored "Primal Testament," inscribed in our genome, documents the biological development of humanity. The Bible presents no *mechanism* of human origins, but the genetic record points

---

115. W. P. Pawlowski and W. Z. Cande, "Coordinating the Events of the Meiotic Prophase," *Trends in Cell Biology* 15 (2005): 674-81; R. U. Vallente, E. Y. Cheng, and T. J. Hassold, "The Synaptonemal Complex and Meiotic Recombination in Humans: New Approaches to Old Questions," *Chromosoma* 115 (2006): 241-49.

116. D. Jung, C. Giallourakis, R. Mostoslavsky, and F. W. Alt, "Mechanism and Control of V(D)J Recombination at the Immunoglobulin Heavy Chain Locus," *Annual Review of Immunology* 24 (2006): 541-70.

117. Richard Colling, *Random Designer* (Bourbonnais, IL: Browning Press, 2004).

118. Holmes Rolston III, *Genes, Genesis and God* (Cambridge: Cambridge University Press, 1999), ch. 1.

119. Adrio König, *New and Greater Things* (Pretoria: University of South Africa, 1988), p. 67.

The Emergence of Human Distinctiveness

to the way in which our species has arisen from the operation of the gift of freedom (random genetic process) in a world that is constituted lawfully, consistently, and fruitfully. These properties of our world reflect the Creator's love (conferring freedom),[120] rationality (conferring lawfulness), faithfulness (conferring consistency), and purpose (conferring fruitfulness). This evolutionary story reflects the productive interaction between chance (randomness) and necessity (lawful consistency). As John Polkinghorne[121] sees it, "The most striking example of all the fruitful interrelation of randomness and orderliness is provided by the insight that it is the interplay of chance and necessity which characterizes the evolution of the universe ... and of life ... and of humanity." The properties of matter manifest a remarkable potentiality, "which is explored through the shuffling operations of chance. . . . The raw material of novelty thus provided by chance is then explored by the intervention of lawful necessity to sift and preserve those configurations that manifest their fruitfulness by their survival and replication in a regularly behaving environment."

The climax of this story is but the starting point of the Bible story: the advent of humanity as the creature made in the "image of God" (Gen. 1:26-27). The tortuous route of human development may appear to be inconsistent with its being the creative work of God. It may seem incongruous that the genome of the creature described in such lofty terms has been assembled by such processes as the accretion of insertional mutagens.

Biblically, history shows a consistent pattern. The Old Testament describes the continuation of God's created history. It describes God's creation of a people through whom he purposed to bless humanity (Isa. 43:1; 44:1-2, 21, 24), a people who were created in the contingent and tumultuous ("random") events of history, unfolding in the context of God's faithfulness. Here is the "chance and necessity" motif in a new expression. The freedom graciously given to human beings has been abused in pride and selfishness. But superimposed upon this randomness, there is a consistent moral structure to the world, revealed in the directing necessity of God's mercy and judgment. There were suffering and extinctions in this history, but it reached its climax in the advent of

---

120. John Polkinghorne, *Science and Christian Belief* (London: SPCK, 1996), pp. 76-77.
121. John Polkinghorne, *Science and Creation* (London: SPCK, 1988), pp. 47-48; *One World* (London: SPCK, 1986), p. 54.

the paradigmatic "Image of God," Jesus Christ (2 Cor. 4:4; Col. 1:15; Heb. 1:3).

The New Testament describes the continuation of God's created history. Through Jesus and particularly in his death and resurrection, God effected the creation of a new humanity (Eph. 2:10, 15). This history too arises from the "chance and necessity" motif. The redeeming death of Christ reflected the contingent flow of human history ("You killed Jesus by letting sinful men crucify him"), and the necessity of God's inexorable purpose ("In accordance with his own plan"; Acts 2:23-24; 3:13-15). The purposed goal of this third phase of history is that the perfect Image of God who is Christ will be conferred on all who are part of the new humanity (1 Cor. 15:49; 2 Cor. 3:18; 1 John 3:2).

Evolutionary history, just like human history, progresses at the cost of ongoing suffering. Only mutational events that are beneficial or at least generally innocuous have survived the passage of time to contribute to the genome that we possess. Many other DNA duplications, deletions, rearrangements, and insertions have arisen during evolutionary history but have been lost from the record because their effects were harmful. Even though such suffering seems to be integral to the unfolding of a cosmos endowed with freedom, people may wonder how a God of love could have ordained such a system. The surprising biblical answer to this mystery is that God has shared in the travail. The God who is Author of this creation is a suffering God who bears the scars of a Roman gibbet on Mount Calvary as testimony to his commitment to the redemption and renewal of the world.[122]

The flow of human history seems to be all of a piece. The impersonal, genetic stage provided the biological substrate of a creature to whom God could reveal himself, and in whom God could become embodied in order to transform humanity into his own likeness. Redemption is God's act of reconciling and transforming an otherwise irremediably selfish creature. The completed sweep of human history envisions a perfected humanity as God's people living in unbroken fellowship with God (Rev. 21:3). It is harder than is commonly supposed to separate God's work of creation from his work of redemption.[123]

---

122. Charles Ohlrich, *The Suffering God* (London: SPCK, 1983).
123. König, *New and Greater Things*, p. 34.

Appendices

Appendix 1

Inverted repeats are abundant on the sex (X and Y) chromosomes. Most of these repeat structures are found not only in humans but also in other great ape species. The boundaries between the duplicated "arms" and intervening "spacers" in each such repeat are identical in all the species in which the repeat is found, indicating that the repeat arose in a unique event in a common ancestor. Such studies provide compelling evidence for the accepted evolutionary relationships of humans and other primates. Two examples are provided below. The letters A, C, G, and T represent the four chemical structures that provide the fundamental units of genetic information and that are strung in a linear sequence along the DNA molecule.

An example of the boundaries (↓) of a repeat from chromosome 1 is shown below:

```
          left repeated arm  /    spacer    /  right repeated arm
human  ... CTCTTTTCAGGGCCA↓CTTAA ... TTAAA↓TGGCCCTGAAAAGAG ...
chimp  ... CTCTTTTCAGGGCCA↓CTTAA ... TTAAG↓TGGCCCTGAAAAGAG ...
gorilla ... CTCTTTTCAGGGCCA↓CTTAA ... TTAAG↓TGGCCCTGAAAAGAG ...
```

The "male specific region" of the human Y chromosome contains eight inverted repeats. Most of these repeats have been identified in other great ape species, and the boundaries between the arms and spacers found to be identical. The spacer-arm boundaries (↓) of the repeat "P6" are shown:

```
          left repeated arm / spacer segment / right repeated arm
human   ... GTTGTGGGAG↓AGTGT ... GGGCC↓CTCCCACAAC ...
chimp   ... GTTGTGGGAG↓AGTGT ... GGGCC↓CTCCCACAAC ...
bonobo  ... GTTGTGGGAG↓AGTGT ... GGGCC↓CTCCCACAAC ...
gorilla ... GTTGTGGGAG↓AGTGT ... GGGCC↓CTCCCACAAC ...
```

Each copied-and-pasted structure is shared by all the African great apes, and demonstrates descent from the one progenitor in which it was uniquely generated. The data are from Warburton et al. (2004) and Rozen et al. (2003), respectively.[124]

124. See note 46.

GRAEME FINLAY

Appendix 2

Lower primates including New World monkeys (NWMs) have two-color vision and one opsin gene on the X chromosome. Higher primates, including the Old World monkeys (OWMs) and apes, have three-color vision. Trichromatic vision was acquired during primate history when the original opsin gene on the X chromosome (and a part of an adjacent gene called *TEX28*) was duplicated on a DNA segment 35,000 bases long. The arrow (below) indicates the site at which the duplicated segment was reinserted ("pasted") into the chromosomal DNA.

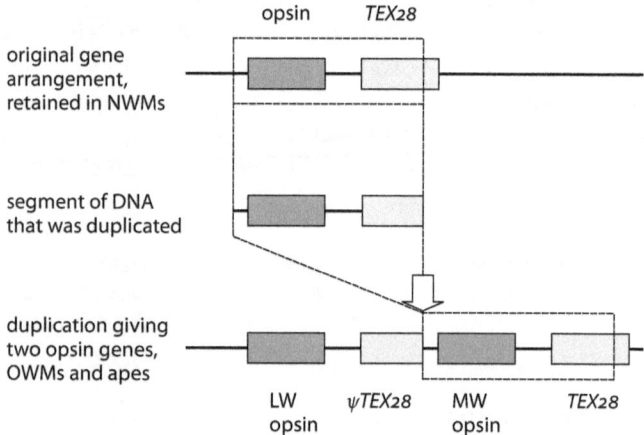

LW opsin: gene that encodes an opsin protein sensitive to long wave light; MW opsin: gene that encodes an opsin protein sensitive to medium wave light; *ψTEX28*: the *TEX28* pseudogene, a partial (truncated) copy of the *TEX28* gene that arose as a result of the duplication. The data are from Dulai et al. (1999).[125]

Appendix 3

Over half of the olfactory receptor genes in the human genome have been converted into pseudogenes that can no longer encode functional proteins. The distribution of the pseudogenes in different primate species reveals their phylogenetic relationships (as depicted in the figure

125. See note 51.

below). Symbols within boxes indicate a gene designation (as with "13E1p"), the location of the inactivating mutation (position 182), and the nature of that mutation (a deletion, "del"). This mutation is present in humans and chimps but in no other species, demonstrating that it occurred in an ancestor common to humans and chimps. The one exception to the pattern is seen with the "11K1p" pseudogene that underwent an inactivating "stop" mutation in an ancestor of macaques (OWMs) and apes. However, this simple mutation reverted to the normal sequence in an orang ancestor. Such revertant mutations are expected at low frequency. The data are from Gilad et al. (2003).[126]

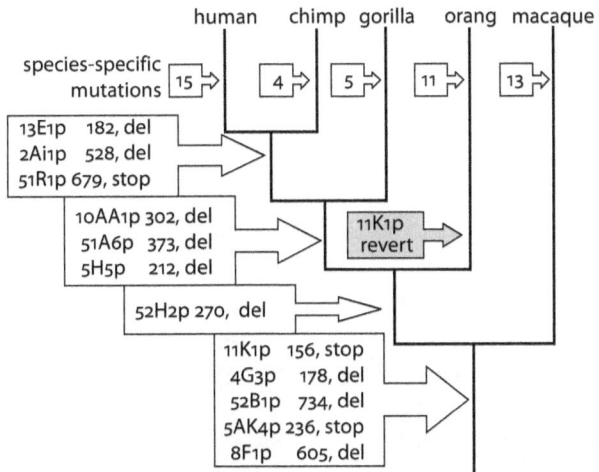

The large-scale loss of olfactory gene function is correlated with the acquisition of trichromatic vision. As shown below, at least 20 percent of olfactory receptor genes are disabled pseudogenes in all apes and OWMs (shaded and unshaded symbols), all of which have trichromatic vision. Fewer than 20 percent of the olfactory receptor genes are disabled in NWMs, lemurs, and mice (unshaded symbols), which have dichromatic vision. The striking exception is the howler monkey, which has a high frequency of pseudogenes, and that independently gained trichromatic vision. The data are from Gilad et al. (2004).[127]

126. See note 60.
127. See note 60. More recent studies on multiple primate genomes have supported the concept that the generation of olfactory receptor pseudogenes provides an outline

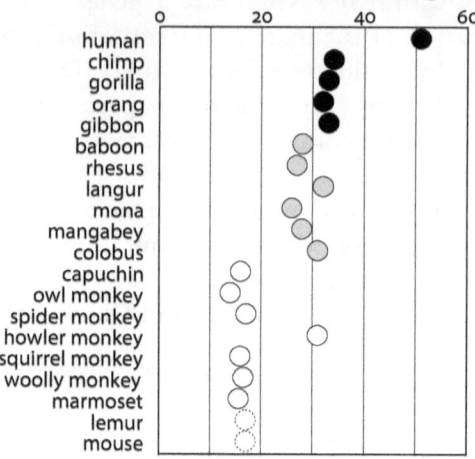

Appendix 4

Extraneous DNA may be inserted into the genome by several mechanisms. An enzyme called "telomerase" adds (TTAGGG)n units to the ends of chromosomes, but such repeats occur at many other sites within chromosomes. Particular instances of these molecular bandages are usually shared with other primate species, although some occur only in the human lineage.

An inserted telomeric repeat is found in the genomes of humans, chimps, and gorillas (the African great apes) as shown below. The uninterrupted sequence remains in all other species.

human	...GCTCAAGGT [TAGGGT(TAGGGT)5] GTAGGAAGC...	
chimp	...GCTCAAGGT [TAGGGT(TAGGGT)5] GTAGGAAGC...	
gorilla	...GCTCAAGTT [TAGGGT(TAGGGT)5] GTAGGAAGC...	
orang	...GGTCAGAGT	GTAGGAAGC...
leaf-eating monkey	...GGTCAGGGT	GTAGGAAGC...
olive baboon	...GGTCAGCGT	GTGGGAAGC...
rhesus macaque	...GGTCAGCGT	GTGGGAAGC...

---

of primate evolution. However, the loss of olfactory receptor pseudogenes is not greater in humans than in other primates, and is not correlated with the gain of trichromatic vision. See A. Matsui, Y. Go, and Y. Niimura, "Degeneration of Olfactory Receptor Gene Repertoire in Primates: No Direct Link to Full Trichromatic Vision," *Molecular Biology and Evolution* 27 (2010): 1192.

The Emergence of Human Distinctiveness

This insert arose in a germ-line cell from which the African great apes arose. The example is from Nergadze et al. (2004).[128]

Fragments of the mitochondrial genome have also been spliced into chromosomal DNA: 400 of these inserts are shared by humans and chimps, and thirty-four are unique to the human lineage. Thousands of small duplications occur as inserts in our DNA. Nine-tenths of these are shared with chimps. The rest arose on the human lineage, and some have appeared so recently that only a proportion of the human population possesses them. Whatever elicits the phenomenon, it is ongoing.[129]

Appendix 5

Retrovirus particles have a genome composed of RNA. When cells are infected, this RNA is introduced into the cytoplasm of the cell, and converted by a process called "reverse transcription" into DNA (paired dark line). This retroviral DNA genome (8,000-10,000 bases long) is then inserted into the DNA of infected cells. From thence it directs the production of new virus particles.

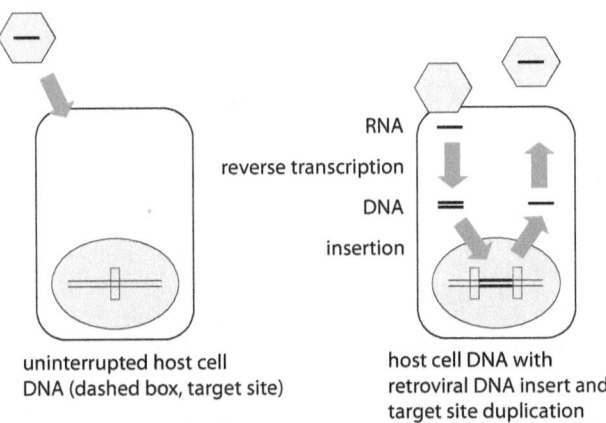

uninterrupted host cell DNA (dashed box, target site)

host cell DNA with retroviral DNA insert and target site duplication

If insertion occurs in reproductive cells, the insert may be inherited by all future generations of the organism, and will be known as an ERV.

128. See note 72.
129. See note 72.

Many ERVs and other inserts have been recruited to help in the transcription of genes. Genes function by being copied ("transcribed") into RNA. This process ("transcription") is controlled by short lengths of nearby DNA. Many ERVs have donated sequences that now regulate the activity of nearby genes. An ERV common to humans and mice drives transcription of the *CA1* gene in red blood cells. Two inserts (a "jumping gene" called an MIR and an ERV) common to humans and mice are present near the *MSLN* gene. They became resident in the DNA of an ancestor shared by humans and mice, but were recruited into the transcription unit only in the lineage that produced humans.

The roles of the inserted ERVs in the *CA1* and *MSLN* genes are depicted in the diagram below.

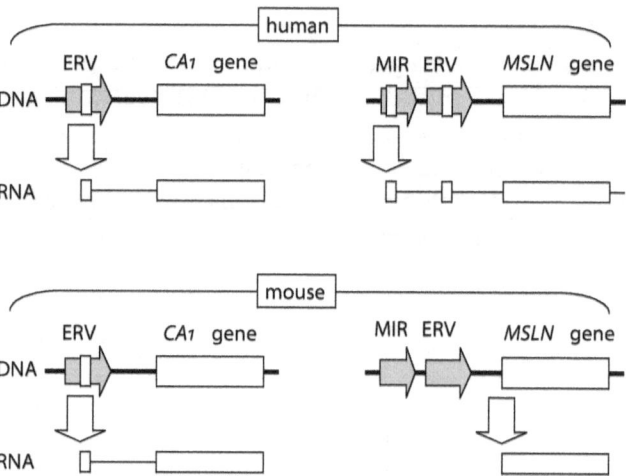

The left part of the figure indicates the ERV insert (gray arrow) that has contributed a short block of DNA sequence to the *CA1* gene transcription unit (open boxes). The right part depicts MIR and ERV inserts shared by humans and mice near the *MSLN* gene. Part of their sequence content has been incorporated into the *MSLN* transcription unit only in humans. The figures are based on van de Lagemaat et al. (2003).[130]

---

130. See note 80.

Appendix 6

Most of the "jumping genes" (transposons) in our genome have arisen through a copy-and-paste mechanism that involves an RNA intermediate. A parent insert (here called a "LINE element"; left-hand side in the figure below) is copied into RNA, from which are made proteins needed for the generation of a new insert. The proteins then use the original LINE RNA (or sometimes, other types of RNA) to make a DNA copy, which is spliced into a target site chosen largely at random in the genome (right-hand side). During this process, a small segment of chromosomal DNA at the target site becomes duplicated on each side of the insert. This is the telltale "target site duplication" (TSD, dashed box).

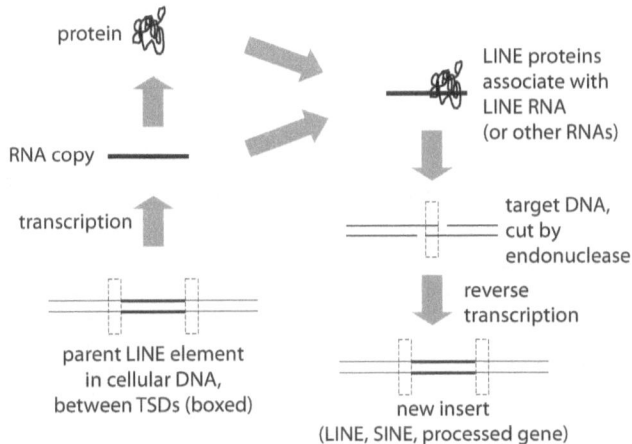

The DNA location of an inserted "jumping gene" shared by multiple primate species is shown below.

```
human   ... TAATCCTTACAGTGG [Alu] TCTTTACAGTGGATT ...
chimp   ... TAATCCTTACAGTGG [Alu] TCTTTACAGTGGATT ...
gorilla ... TAATCCTTACAGTGG [Alu] TCTTTACAGTGGATT ...
orang   ... TAATCCTTACAGTGG [Alu] TCTTTACAGTGGATT ...
gibbon  ... TAATCCTTACAGTGG [Alu] TCTTTACAGTGGATT ...
OWM     ... TAATCCTTACAGTGG             ATT ...
NWM     ... TAATCCTTACAGTGG             ATT ...
lemur   ... GAATAAAAACAGTGG             ATT ...
```

The short blocks of DNA sequence flank a "jumping gene" insert of the "Alu" class. The Alu insert itself is approximately 300 bases long. A twelve-base "target site" is underlined, together with the duplication that is produced during insertion of the Alu element. This insert is present in precisely the same site in all apes, and thereby can be shown to have formed in an ancestor of all the apes. A representative Old and New World monkey (OWM, NWM) and prosimian (lemur) retain the uninterrupted target site in their DNA. This insert has altered the expression of the important *"survivin"* gene. The example is taken from Mola et al. (2007).[131]

The distribution of "jumping genes" provides excellent markers of evolutionary relationships. Two families of "Alu" elements have been used to demonstrate how the apes have developed.

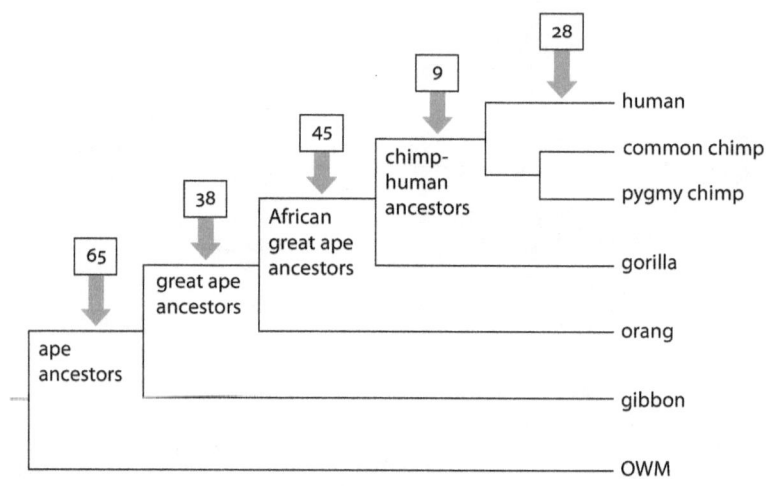

Numerals in boxes indicate the number of individual elements in the analysis that were added to the ape genome during particular periods of evolutionary history. For example, thirty-eight individual elements were identified in the human, chimp, gorilla, and orang genomes, but not in those of the gibbon or OWM, indicating that these elements were inserted into the primate genome in great ape ancestors. These results are from Xing et al. (2003) and Salem et al. (2003, 2005).[132]

    131. See note 90.
    132. See note 86.

Appendix 7

The enzymatic machinery of "jumping genes" may sometimes hijack RNA molecules transcribed from cellular genes, copy them back into DNA, and splice them into chromosomal DNA. Inserted gene copies arising from these unscheduled events are usually incapable of acting like the parent gene by directing the product of proteins, and are called "processed pseudogenes." There are ≈3,600 essentially full-length processed pseudogenes in our genomes, and many more gene fragments.[133]

Thirty percent of these pseudogenes are transcribed into RNA, and may have acquired novel functions. Indeed, 120 have retained protein-coding capacity and may function as authentic genes. Such "retrogenes" have added new functionality to the genome.

An example of a retrogene, copied-and-pasted from the original gene, courtesy of enzymes provided by "jumping genes," is shown below.

	left flanking sequence	[insert]	right flanking sequence
human	...GAAGT<u>ATAGAACAAA</u>CAG	[*GLUD2*]	<u>ATAGAACAAA</u>TAATG...
chimp	...GAAGT<u>ATAGAACAAA</u>CAG	[*GLUD2*]	<u>ATAGAACAAA</u>TAATG...
gorilla	...GAAGT<u>ATAGAACAAA</u>CAG	[*GLUD2*]	<u>ATAGAACAAA</u>TAATG...
orang	...GAAGT<u>ATAGAACAAA</u>CAG	[*GLUD2*]	<u>ATAGAACAAA</u>TAATG...
gibbon	...GAAGT<u>ATAGAACAAA</u>CAG	[*GLUD2*]	<u>ATAGAACAAA</u>TAATG...
OWM	...GAAGT<u>ATAGAACAAA</u>		TAATG...

The *GLUD2* retrogene insert, target site duplication (underlined), and an extra CAG are identical in all the ape species, but lacking from the OWM. This example is from Burki and Kaessmann (2004).[134]

Retrogenes have been formed at a rate of approximately one per million years through primate history. A study that defined the species range of thirty primate retrogenes generated a standard primate phylogenetic tree. Six of these retrogenes are human-specific.[135]

---

133. See note 92.
134. See note 93.
135. See note 93.

GRAEME FINLAY

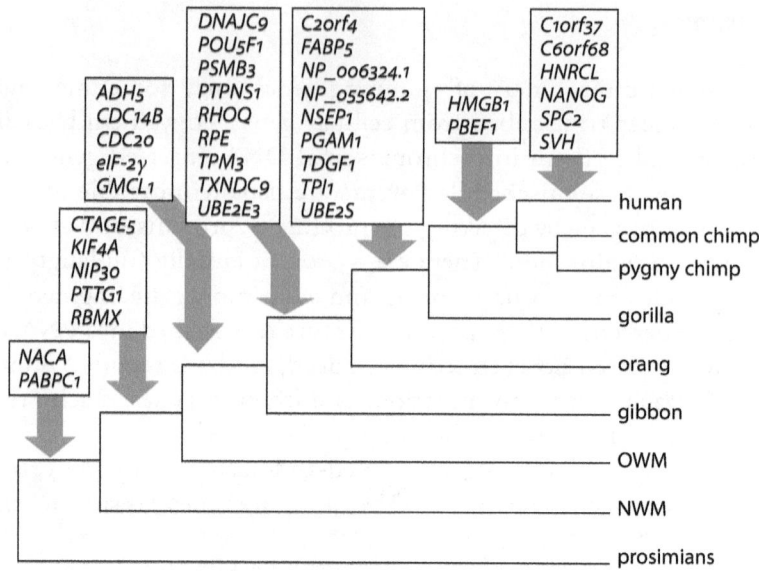

Evolution of *Homo sapiens*

R. J. Berry

The idea that human beings share a common ancestry with other animals — that we have evolved from a "lower form" — was repeatedly proposed long before the advent of modern science, at least as long ago as Gregory of Nyssa in the fourth century. Linnaeus classified humans as "Primates," in the same category as the apes. Another idea was that different human races evolved independently. Giordano Bruno argued in 1591 that no one could imagine that Jews and Ethiopians could share the same ancestry: either God created separate Adams or Africans were the descendants of pre-Adamic races. Isaac de La Peyrère[1] built on this, claiming the Bible taught that Adam and Eve were not the first human beings, but merely the first parents of the Jewish people. For him, the pre-Adamites helped to explain where Cain's wife came from and who had peopled the land of Nod (Gen. 4:16). La Peyrère was heavily criticized, but the idea of pre-Adamites persisted; in the seventeenth century it conveniently answered the question as to how the native inhabitants of the Americas related to those of the biblical world.[2]

In 1774, Henry Home suggested that different races were created for different environments, i.e., God created separate races of humans in

---

1. I. de La Peyrère, *Men Before Adam; or, A Discourse upon the Twelfth, Thirteenth and Fourteenth Verses of the Fifth Chapter of the Epistle of the Apostle Paul to the Romans, by Which Are Prov'd That Men Were Created Before Adam* (London, 1655).

2. D. N. Livingstone, "The Preadamite Theory and the Marriage of Science and Religion," *Transactions of the American Philosophical Society* 82, no. 3 (1992); G. B. Nelson, "'Men Before Adam': American Debates over the Unity and Antiquity of Humanity," in *When Science and Christianity Meet*, ed. D. C. Lindberg and R. L. Numbers (Chicago: University of Chicago Press, 2003), pp. 161-81.

different lands *(polygenism)*. Home later rejected this idea in favor of an explosion of diversity at the Tower of Babel, but polygenism remained popular, especially in the United States, ingenuously associated with the notion that some races were inferior to others.[3] This debate rumbled on in the secular world for more than a century.[4] For Christians, the issue became complicated by the publication (and general acceptance) of Darwin's ideas, plus evidence appearing around the same time from the excavation of Kent's cavern (near Torquay) that humans once lived among now extinct creatures,[5] and the discovery in 1856 of fossils of an apparently primitive form of human in the Neander Valley near Düsseldorf. Some Christians resolutely refused to accept that human origins were earlier than six thousand years or so, but more and more were forced to believe that pre-Adamic fossils had to be taken seriously. The problem was integrating them with the biblical record.

Did pre-Adamites really exist? Orthodox Judaism places creation in 3760 BCE, based largely on the biblical genealogies that go back to Adam (Gen. 5:1-3; 1 Chron. 1:1; Luke 3:38). Slightly older dates were put forward by others: Theophilus suggested 5529 BCE; Clement of Alexandria, 5590 BCE; Julius Africanus, 5531 BCE. Probably the best-known date is 4004 BCE, arrived at by Archbishop Ussher of Armagh in 1650. However, Isaac Newton (1642-1727) worked out that the Earth must have cooled for at least 50,000 years before it reached a temperature low enough to allow life to exist, although he felt something must be wrong with his sums because this was so much longer than the teaching of the church in his time. On a similar basis (based experimentally on the rate of cooling of iron balls), George-Louis (Count) Buffon calculated in 1779 that the world was 75,000 years old. In an attempt to harmonize his results with the Bible, Buffon suggested that there had been seven "epochs" of earth history, more or less matching the Genesis "days." In 1785 the founder of modern geology, James Hutton, maintained that the Earth "had no vestige of a beginning." This did not worry the influential Scottish minister, Thomas Chalmers (1780-1847). He declared, "The writings of Moses do not fix the antiquity of the globe. If they fix anything at all, it is only the antiquity of the species."

Stretching the history of the Earth increased the possibility of

3. J. Nott and G. Gliddon, *Types of Mankind* (Philadelphia, 1854).
4. S. J. Gould, *The Mismeasure of Man* (New York: W. W. Norton, 1981).
5. D. K. Grayson, *The Establishment of Human Antiquity* (New York: Academic, 1983).

change for its inhabitants. The Frenchman Jean-Baptiste Lamarck (1744-1829), inspired by the ideas of progress current in his time, regarded humanity as the end-product of an evolutionary unfolding. He wrote, "If some race of quadrumanous animals, especially one of the most perfect of them, were to lose by force of circumstances or some other cause, the habit of climbing trees and grasping the branches with their feet in the same way as their hands in order to hold on to them, and if the individuals of this race were forced to use their feet for walking, and to give up using their hands like feet there is no doubt . . . that these quadrumanous animals would at length be transformed into bimanous and that their thumbs on their feet would cease to be separated from the other digits when they use their feet for walking and that they would assume an upright posture in order to command a large and distant view."[6]

Lamarck's ideas were not widely accepted outside his native France. Darwin derided Lamarck's book as "veritable rubbish. I got not a fact or idea from it"; and he ridiculed "Lamarck's nonsense of . . . adaptations from the slow willing of animals." Notwithstanding, Lamarck raised public debate about evolution, along with his slightly older contemporary Erasmus Darwin (1731-1802), Charles's grandfather, who also suggested that evolution from simple forms had occurred. However, the most influential propagandist for evolution before the appearance of the *Origin of Species*[7] (in 1859) was the Edinburgh publisher Robert Chambers, with a book *The Vestiges of the Natural History of Creation*,[8] published anonymously in 1844. The *Vestiges* was effectively a tract against the prevailing deism of the time, most clearly represented by Archdeacon William Paley's *Natural Theology* of 1802.[9] Chambers wrote that when there is a choice between special creation and the operation of general laws instituted by the Creator, "I would say that the latter is greatly preferable as it implies a far grander view of the divine power and dignity than the other."

The *Vestiges* was an immediate bestseller.[10] In the ten years follow-

---

6. J.-B. Lamarck, *Philosophie Zoologique* (Paris, 1809); English translation Hugh Elliot (London: Macmillan, 1914), p. 170.

7. C. R. Darwin, *The Origin of Species* (London: John Murray, 1859).

8. R. Chambers, *Vestiges of the Natural History of Creation* (London: John Churchill, 1844).

9. W. Paley, *Natural Theology* (London, 1802).

10. J. A. Secord, *Victorian Sensation: The Extraordinary Publication, Reception and Secret*

ing its publication it sold more copies than did the *Origin* fifteen years later. But it was full of errors. For Darwin, "the writing and arrangement were certainly admirable, but the geology strikes me as bad and his zoology far worse." Its importance was in provoking debate about evolution. Darwin welcomed it on the grounds that "it has done excellent service in calling in this country attention to the subject, in removing prejudices. . . ." It certainly stirred controversy; it contradicted the current understanding of the Bible and of humanity as failed creatures in need of redemption. Adam Sedgwick, Professor of Geology at Cambridge University and Darwin's geological mentor, lambasted it in an eighty-five-page review. He wrote to his fellow geologist, Charles Lyell, "If the book be true, the labours of sober induction are in vain; religion is a lie; human law is a mass of folly, and a base injustice; morality is moonshine; our labours for the black people of Africa were works of madmen; and men and women are only beasts." Lyell himself fought against the idea of evolution largely because of his fears for the status of the human soul. Philip Gosse, a well-known and competent naturalist, wrote *Omphalos: An Attempt to Untie the Geological Knot* (1857), arguing that God made the world "as if" it was ancient.[11] In Gosse's thought, God had created the fossils along with everything else, so the "fossil record" was no evidence for evolution. Gosse believed that Adam was created *de novo* but with an "omphalos" (or navel) without being born in the normal way. There is no way to disprove this idea, but it portrays God as a deceiver; it never had many adherents. Most copies of *Omphalos* were pulped.

Charles Darwin and the Acceptance of Evolution

Darwin's main contribution to evolution was the discovery of a mechanism for adaptation (natural selection) that would lead to adaptive change in populations of living organisms, particularly in a changing environment. However, the chief effect of the *Origin of Species* was to convince the majority of Darwin's contemporaries of the fact that evolution had occurred. Darwin's work provided a framework for bio-

---

Authorship of Vestiges of the Natural History of Creation (Chicago: University of Chicago Press, 2000).

11. P. H. Gosse, *Omphalos* (London: Van Voorst, 1857).

Evolution of Homo sapiens

geography and taxonomy, and a reason for the existence of "rudimentary" organs (like the tail of primates or the hind-limbs of snakes and whales). The arguments of the *Origin* were quickly accepted, contrary to repeated assertions that they remain speculative and "only a theory."[12] Claims of a major conflict between science and religion are grossly over-exaggerated. Ironically, Darwin's ideas were assimilated more readily by conservative theologians than by liberals, apparently because of the stronger doctrine of providence of the former.[13] Many of the authors of the "Fundamentals," a series of booklets produced between 1910 and 1915 to expound the "fundamental beliefs" of Protestant theology as defined by the General Assembly of the American Presbyterian Church and which led to the word *fundamentalism* entering the language, were sympathetic to evolution. Princeton theologian B. B. Warfield, a passionate advocate of the inerrancy of the Bible, argued that evolution could provide a tenable "theory of the method of divine providence in the creation of mankind." The infamous debate between the Bishop of Oxford and Thomas Huxley at the 1860 meeting of the British Association for the Advancement of Science was not really about evolution versus creation, or even science versus religion. On the bishop's side it was about the danger of legitimizing change in an age when he believed it was having deleterious social and theological effects; Huxley was aiming for the secularization of society with the aim to establish the legitimacy of science against what he regarded as the improper influence of church leaders.

By 1884, ecclesiastical imprimatur had been given to the *Origin* by Frederick Temple, Bishop of Exeter and soon to become Archbishop of Canterbury. He wrote, "[God] did not make the things, we may say: no, but He made them make themselves. . . . It has often been objected to Paley's argument that it represents the Almighty as an artificer rather than a creator. . . . But this objection disappears when we put the argument into the shape which the doctrine of Evolution demands. . . ." Five years later, Oxford theologian Aubrey Moore wrote, "The break up of the mediaeval system of thought and life resulted in an atomism, which, if it had been more perfectly consistent with itself, would have

---

12. J. R. Moore, *The Post-Darwinian Controversies* (Cambridge: Cambridge University Press, 1979).

13. D. N. Livingstone, *Darwin's Forgotten Defenders: The Encounter between Evangelical Theology and Evolutionary Thought* (Grand Rapids: Eerdmans, 1987).

been fatal alike to knowledge and society.... God was 'throned in magnificent inactivity in a remote corner of the universe.' ... Science had pushed the deist's God farther and farther away, and at the moment when it seemed as if He would be pushed out altogether, Darwinism appeared and, under the disguise of a foe did the work of a friend."[14]

Contemporary "creationism" has no intellectual link with the debates of the nineteenth century and the historical acceptance of Darwinism. Rather it stems from the teaching of the Adventist Ellen White and the writings of her followers, notably George McCready Price, whose cry was "No Adam, no Fall; no Fall, no Atonement; no Atonement, no Savior."[15] The sticking point was — and for many, still is — the idea that humans are only upgraded monkeys and not individuals specially created in God's image.

However, there were significant scientific problems that did not appear until the beginning of genetics with the rediscovery of Mendel's work in 1900.

The inherited variation which had to be the basis of the variation on which natural selection could operate was found by the early Mendelists (as the geneticists were called) to have properties that seemed to render it useless for adaptation: the changes produced by the "mutant" genes of the geneticists tended to have major effects (such as the loss of wings in an insect or eyes in a mammal); it was almost always deleterious (resulting in the partial or entire loss of a structure or function), and (this emerged later) was usually inherited as a recessive character whereas "good" variation was inherited as a dominant trait. The widely drawn conclusion was that Mendelian genes could not form the basis of evolutionary change and that some other — and non-Darwinian — mechanism must be driving evolution. In the first decades of the twentieth century a range of guesses were put forward to explain the long-continued evolutionary trends being observed in the fossil record, many of them based on some sort of internal drive or *élan vital* toward progress and complexity.

The impasse between geneticists and Darwinian evolutionists was resolved during the 1930s, initially by the work of R. A. Fisher on mim-

---

14. A. Moore, "The Christian Doctrine of God," in *Lux Mundi*, ed. C. Gore (London: John Murray, 1889), pp. 57-109.

15. R. L. Numbers, *The Creationists: The Evolution of Scientific Creationism* (New York: Knopf, 1992).

icry in butterflies and his theory of the evolution of dominance, and more generally by the synthesis of his ideas with the mathematical studies of Haldane and Sewall Wright and the practical researches of Theodosius Dobzhansky and E. B. Ford, summarized by Julian Huxley with the publication in 1942 of *Evolution: The Modern Synthesis*.[16] This evolutionary or neo-Darwinian synthesis remains the basis for scientific consensus about evolution.[17] The split has retained more prominence than it deserves because three histories of biology describing the alleged inadequacies of Darwinian evolution were written at the end of the 1920s (by Nordenskiöld, 1928; Radl, published in English in 1930; and Singer, 1931). J. B. S. Haldane began his book *Causes of Evolution*, published in 1932, with an Introduction titled "Darwinism is dead — Any sermon," referring to attacks on evolution by the Roman Catholic apologists Hilaire Belloc and G. K. Chesterton.[18] Unfortunately the fact that many scientists (never mind the general public) in the presynthesis days did not really understand how natural selection operated led to some sort of purpose in evolution being influentially espoused by the zoologist Ray Lankester and the physiologist J. B. S. Haldane, the psychologists Lloyd Morgan, William McDougall, and E. S. Russell, physicists like Oliver Lodge, and the cosmologists A. S. Eddington and James Jeans, as well as by popularizers like Arthur Thomson and politicians such as Arthur Balfour. Not surprisingly with such apparently informed authorities, these ideas were seized upon by churchmen, prominent among them being Charles Gore, and somewhat later by W. R. Inge, Hensley Henson, Charles Raven, and E. W. Barnes. This crossover of evolutionary idealism from science to theology has been elegantly chronicled by Peter Bowler.[19]

The problem was that the scientific ideas about purpose and progression were wrong.[20] Most scientists realized this fairly quickly, but it took the theologians a long time to catch up. Indeed, Bowler's conclusion is that optimistic progressionism in theology did not suffer so

16. J. S. Huxley, *Evolution: The Modern Synthesis* (London: George Allen & Unwin, 1942).
17. R. J. Berry, *Neo-Darwinism* (London: Edward Arnold, 1982).
18. J. B. S. Haldane, *The Causes of Evolution* (London: Longmans, Green, 1932).
19. P. J. Bowler, *Reconciling Science and Religion: The Debate in Early-Twentieth Century Britain* (Chicago: University of Chicago Press, 2001).
20. M. Ruse, *Mystery of Mysteries: Is Evolution a Social Construction?* (Cambridge, MA: Harvard University Press, 1999).

much from conscious rejection as atrophy through its perceived ineffectiveness. "The Modernists," he wrote, "saw themselves marginalized not by the new science, of which many remained unaware, but by changing values within the churches, which brought back a sense of human sinfulness and alienation from God incompatible with the idea of progress."[21] One can have some sympathy with the theologians, because of the time that it took the scientists to reach the evolutionary synthesis, but this does not repair or excuse their error.

Darwin and Human Evolution

To return to the influence of Darwin's ideas on human evolution: Darwin was well aware of the furor that his thesis would produce. In the *Origin* he tried to divert attention from debates about human evolution by mentioning it only in passing at the end of the book: "In the future I see open fields for far more important researches. Psychology will be securely based on the foundation laid by Mr. Herbert Spencer, that of the necessary acquirement of each mental power and capacity by gradation. Much light will be thrown on the origin of man and his history." He set out his ideas in more detail in *The Descent of Man,* published in 1871.[22] He was clear about some things. As he wrote in one of his notebooks, "Man in his arrogance thinks himself a great work worthy of the interposition of a deity. More humble & I think truer to consider him created from animals." He did not believe that religion had any rational foundation ("Strange superstitions and customs would give way to the improvement of reason, to science, and our accumulated knowledge"); he compared religious devotion to the "love of a dog for its master."

However, he was careful to separate any instinctive urge to believe from any developing moral feelings. He wrote:

> It is extremely doubtful whether the offspring of the more sympathetic and benevolent parents, or of those who were the most faithful to their comrades, would be reared in greater numbers than the children of selfish and treacherous parents belonging to the same tribe. He who was ready to sacrifice his life, as many a savage has

---

21. Bowler, *Reconciling Science and Religion,* note 19, p. 417.
22. Charles Darwin, *The Descent of Man and Selection in Relation to Sex* (New York: D. Appleton & Co., 1896; original printed in London: John Murray, 1871).

been, rather than betray his comrades, would often leave no offspring to inherit his noble nature. The bravest men, who were always willing to come to the front in war, and who freely risked their lives for others, would on average perish in larger numbers than other men. Therefore it hardly seems probable, that the number of men gifted with such virtues, or that the standard of their excellence, could be increased through natural selection, that is, by the survival of the fittest. . . .[23]

This difficulty was resolved in principle by J. B. S. Haldane half a century later. He proclaimed he would be prepared to sacrifice his life for eight cousins or two brothers because the survivors would ensure the continuance of the genes for such unselfishness. For Haldane, "In so far as it makes for the survival of one's descendants and near relations, altruistic behaviour is a kind of Darwinian fitness, and may be expected to spread as the result of natural selection."[24] This claim was formalized in 1964 by W. D. Hamilton as the concept of "inclusive fitness," often called nowadays "kin selection," and popularized by E. O. Wilson in 1975 as the basis for "sociobiology."[25] An important element in the concept is that individuals have to be considered as members of a group; it is not sufficient to take them in isolation.

The basic idea of inclusive fitness is usefully complemented and extended beyond close relatives by the notion of "reciprocal altruism" — that self-sacrifice involves self-interest, providing there is a chance the beneficiary would repay the deed in the future.[26] There has been considerable discussion as to whether these mechanisms are really sufficient to explain human behavior.[27] (A major problem is that humans cooperate in much larger groups than nonhuman primates, extending beyond those with whom they routinely interact — sometimes called "imagined communities." They include people we have never met; such communities exist only in our mind.) Alexander has commented that "ethics, morality, human conduct, and the human psyche are to be un-

---

23. Darwin, *The Descent of Man*, p. 130.
24. Haldane, *The Causes of Evolution*, note 18, p. 131.
25. E. O. Wilson, *Sociobiology* (Cambridge, MA: Harvard University Press, 1975).
26. R. L. Trivers, "The Evolution of Reciprocal Altruism," *Quarterly Review of Biology* 46 (1971): 35-57.
27. P. Clayton and J. Schloss, eds., *Evolution and Ethics* (Grand Rapids: Eerdmans, 2004).

derstood only if societies are seen as collections of individuals seeking their own self-interest."[28] Responding to this, Gintis et al. have argued for "strong reciprocity," by which they mean a predisposition to cooperate with others and to punish those who violate the norms of cooperation, even when it is implausible to expect these costs to be repaid either by others or at a later date.[29]

Most of the controversy in Wilson's formulation of sociobiology was in his extrapolation of conclusions from (mainly) invertebrates to human beings. From this position, he argued, "Biology is the key to human nature, and social scientists cannot afford to ignore its rapidly tightening principles."[30] Philosopher Peter Singer has accepted this in full: "Sociobiology . . . enables us to see ethics as a mode of human reasoning which develops in a group context . . . so ethics loses its air of mystery. Its principles are not laws written up in Heaven. Nor are they absolute truths about the universe, known by intuition. The principles of ethics come from our own nature as social reasoning beings."[31]

Sociobiological ideas have been extremely important in biology, and have stimulated an immense amount of research. They have also provoked much dissent, particularly as they apply to mammals (especially humankind) because of their implications about determinism in behavioral choices.[32] These are scientific debates, but it is worth noting that the existence of apparently altruistic or self-giving behavior in nonhuman primates does not compromise Christian understanding. Frans de Waal has written: "Even if animals other than ourselves act in ways tantamount to moral behavior, their behavior does not necessarily rest on deliberations of the kind we engage in. It is hard to believe that animals weigh their own interests against the rights of others, that they develop a vision of the greater good of society, or that they feel life-

---

28. R. D. Alexander, *The Biology of Moral Systems* (New York: Aldine/de Gruyter, 1987), p. 3.

29. H. Gintis, S. Bowles, R. Boyd, and E. Fehr, "Explaining Altruistic Behaviour in Humans," *Evolution and Human Behavior* 24 (2003): 153-72.

30. E. O. Wilson, *On Human Nature* (Cambridge, MA: Harvard University Press, 1978).

31. P. Singer, *The Expanding Circle* (Oxford: Clarendon, 1981), p. 49.

32. A. L. Caplan, ed., *The Sociobiology Debate* (New York: Harper & Row, 1978); S. Rose, R. Lewontin, and L. Kamin, *Not in Our Genes* (Harmondsworth: Penguin, 1984); H. Cronin, *The Ant and the Peacock* (Cambridge: Cambridge University Press, 1991); M. Ridley, *The Origins of Virtue* (London: Viking, 1996); H. Rose and S. Rose, eds., *Alas, Poor Darwin* (London: Jonathan Cape, 2000).

Evolution of Homo sapiens

long guilt about something they should not have done."³³ From the Christian point of view, the self-giving of Christ was unique; it is by faith we affirm that the ultimate act of Christ's self-giving sets him and it apart from all others. This is not diminished in any way by the discovery of a fronto-mesolimbic network in the brain that is active when we engage in altruistic behavior.³⁴

It is clear that Darwin's concerns about the evolution of altruism are not as unanswerable as he thought. Notwithstanding, there is still much uncertainty about the determinants of behavior, particularly about the place of free will. MacKay argued forcefully that this was not a problem, since it is persons, not brains that choose.³⁵ For him, there was an indeterminacy at the level of our conscious experience, irrespective of any determinacy at the brain level.³⁶ Doye et al. summarize the range of proposed approaches: "the liberty of spontaneity can be more easily reconciled with God's sovereignty than the liberty of indifference."³⁷

Features of Human Evolution

1. Fossil history: Despite the fragmentary nature of many discoveries, *Homo* has a better fossil record than almost any other genus, although its credibility tends to be marred in popular understanding by overimaginative reconstruction of particular finds, notably the Piltdown debacle but also many fanciful attempts to portray human ancestors as either hulking brutes or mere variants of modern individuals. Unfortunately, the image of human fossil history for many is probably the much-reproduced frontispiece of T. H. Huxley's *Man's Place in Nature,* published in 1863, showing a parade of modern skeletons from a gibbon, through a series of stooping apes, to an upright man ("A grim

---

33. F. de Waal, *Good Natured: The Origin of Right and Wrong in Humans and Other Animals* (Cambridge, MA: Harvard University Press, 1996), p. 216.

34. J. Moll, F. Krueger, R. Zahn, M. Pardini, R. de Oliviera, and J. Grafman, "Human Fronto-meso-limbic Networks Guide Decisions about Charitable Donation," *Proceedings of the National Academy of Science of the USA* 103 (2006): 15623-28.

35. D. M. MacKay, *Behind the Eye* (Oxford: Blackwell, 1991), pp. 194-204.

36. See also M. A. Jeeves, "Brain, Mind and Behavior," in *Whatever Happened to the Soul?* ed. W. S. Brown, N. Murphy, and H. N. Malony (Minneapolis: Fortress Press, 1998), pp. 73-98.

37. J. Doye, I. Golby, C. Line, S. Lloyd, P. Shellard, and D. Tricker, "Contemporary Perspectives on Chance, Providence and Free Will," *Science & Christian Belief* 7 (1995): 117-39.

and grotesque procession" as Darwin's critic, the eighth Duke of Argyll, called it[38]). Notwithstanding and recognizing many uncertainties, there is general agreement that *Homo* originated from an *Australopithecus* stock in Africa, with *Homo habilis* existing 2-1.6 million years ago (mya), *Homo erectus* 1.8-0.3 mya, and *Homo sapiens* appearing 0.4-0.1 mya, more or less contemporaneous with the Neanderthals.

2. Genetic homology: Genome maps enable the genetic constitutions of different organisms to be compared. Even though the widely quoted figure that humans and chimps share 98.4 percent of their genes is probably an overestimate, there is identity between more than 95 percent of the genes in the two species; put another way, this means that the distinguishing sequences add up to about 35 million nucleotide differences.[39] The high proportion of genes that we share with chimpanzees led Jared Diamond to suggest that we would be classified as a third chimpanzee species if normal taxonomic criteria were applied.[40] Most of the differences between the species are due to fairly small duplications; the other differences are small insertions or deletions.[41] Around 8 percent of the human genome apparently consists of retroviral inserts influencing gene regulation in significant ways.[42] Bustamante et al. examined 11,624 loci that had different alleles in chimps and humans and found that the differences in 304 were apparently due to positive selection; another 813 had apparently been subjected to negative or stabilizing selection.[43] Pollard et al. have shown

---

38. T. H. Huxley, *Evidence as to Man's Place in Nature* (London: Williams & Norgate, 1863).

39. R. J. Britten, "Divergence between Samples of Chimpanzee and Human DNA Sequences Is 5%, Counting Indels," *Proceedings of the National Academy of Sciences of the USA* 99 (2002): 13633-35.

40. J. Diamond, *The Rise and Fall of the Third Chimpanzee* (London: Radius, 1991).

41. Z. Cheng, M. Ventura, X. She, P. Khaitvich, T. Graves, K. Oseogawa, D. Church, P. DeJong, R. K. Wilson, S. Pääbo, M. Rocchi, and E. E. Eichler, "A Genome-wide Comparison of Recent Chimpanzee and Human Segmental Duplications," *Nature* 437 (2005): 88-93.

42. P. Medstrand, L. N. van de Lagemaat, C. A. Dunn, J-R. Landry, D. Svenback, and D. L. Mager, "Impact of Transposable Elements on the Evolution of Mammalian Gene Regulation," *Cytogenetic & Genome Research* 110 (2005): 342-52; C. Biemont and C. Vieira, "Junk DNA as an Evolutionary Force," *Nature* 443 (2006): 521-24.

43. C. D. Bustamante, A. Fledel-Alon, S. Williamson, R. Nielsen, M. T. Hubisz, S. Glanowski, D. M. Tanenbaum, T. J. White, J. J. Sninsky, R. D. Hernandez, D. Civello, M. D. Adams, M. Cargill, and A. G. Clark, "Natural Selection on Non-Coding Genes in the Human Genome," *Nature* 437 (2005): 1153-57.

that virtually all the genomic regions showing the greatest divergence are ones concerned with regulation of coding sequences, the most notable one being a locus expressed in the developing cortex between two and four gestational months. (It has eighteen substitutions compared with an expected rate of 0.27, based on the rate in other amniotes.[44]) Most of the same genes found in different species (over 90 percent of the genes in mouse and human are common to both) occur in conserved blocks (i.e., in the same order in the two species).

Putative relationships can also be derived from chromosomes.[45] All the great apes except humans have twenty-four pairs of chromosomes; humans have twenty-three pairs. Individual chromosomes can be identified cytochemically. The large human chromosome no. 2 is the result of an end-to-end (telomeric) fusion of two individual ape chromosomes.[46] Such "Robertsonian translocations" are not infrequent between (and within) close species.

3. Life history: We know our own life history in considerable detail — fertility, fecundity, gestation period, development pre-natally and post-natally, both anatomical and behavioral, morbidity and mortality at different stages, longevity, and so on. In many respects we are similar to the great apes, but we also differ in specific ways. For example, the primary dentition appears at around six months in humans and secondary dentition at about six years, compared to three months and three years respectively in the closest apes; humans grow for twenty years and live for seventy years compared with ten and thirty-five years in the apes; sexual maturity in human females takes place at twelve years of age, compared with six to eight in the apes; humans never have a complete covering of hair, while in the apes this is complete soon after birth.[47]

    44. K. S. Pollard, S. R. Salama, N. Lambert, M-A. Lambot, S. Coppens, J. S. Pederson, S. Katzman, B. King, C. Onodera, A. Siepel, A. D. Kern, C. Dehay, H. Igel, M. Ares, P. Vanderhaegen, and D. Haussler, "An RNA Gene Expressed during Cortical Development Evolved Rapidly in Humans," *Nature* 443 (2006): 167-72.

    45. S. J. O'Brien, M. Menotti-Raymond, W. J. Murphy, W. G. Nash, J. Wienberg, R. Stanyon, N. G. Copeland, N. A. Jenkins, J. E. Wornack, and J. A. M. Graves, "The Promise of Comparative Genomics in Mammals," *Science* 286 (1999): 458-81.

    46. J. W. Ijdo, A. Baldini, D. C. Ward, et al., "Origin of Human Chromosome 2: An Ancestral Telomere-telomere Fusion," *Proceedings of the National Academy of Science of the USA* 88 (1991): 9051.

    47. A. A. Abbie, "Timing in Human Evolution," *Proceedings of the Linnean Society of New South Wales* 83 (1958): 197-213.

4. *Communication:* The efficiency and precision of communication between individual humans and groups distinguish us from all other animals. There is a wide consensus that a key human characteristic is the complexity of language, without denying or denigrating the sophistication and complexity of communication in many nonhuman groups. Many people have argued that the key difference between chimpanzees and us is our ability to communicate in a spoken language with a large vocabulary, while the apes are apparently incapable of uttering some of the commonest vowel sounds. For example, Jared Diamond suggests that a significant stage in human differentiation involved "the structure of the larynx, tongue and associated muscles that give us fine control over spoken sounds. . . . The missing ingredient [which prevented the chimps developing more complex speech] may have been some modification of the proto-human vocal tract to give us finer control and permit formation of a much greater variety of sounds."[48]

The human supralaryngeal pathway is entirely different from that of all other mammals. We do not know for certain when humans diverged in this respect; it was probably in the early history of the human lineage. However, between 10,000 and 100,000 years ago, two nucleotide differences appeared in the latter in a gene *(FOXP2)* that codes for a transcription factor controlling genes that affect grammar, speech production, nonverbal intelligence, and nonspeech-related movement of the mouth and face, plus cerebellar development. This gene is highly conserved: mice and primates differ in only one out of its 715 amino acids.[49] Intriguingly, a single-point mutation on the long arm of chromosome 7 (the same section involved in the determination of autism) carried by fifteen out of thirty-one individuals in three generations of a human family produced a complex of symptoms, including an inability to speak intelligibly; an induced mutation in the homologous segment in mice leads to inability to produce ultrasonic sounds and also to cerebellar defects, probably as a result of effects on neuronal migration of maturation in the cerebellum.[50]

48. Diamond, *The Rise and Fall of the Third Chimpanzee,* p. 47.
49. W. Enard, M. Przeworski, S. E. Fisher, C. S. L. Lai, V. Wiebe, T. Kitano, A. P. Monaco, and S. Pääbo, "Molecular Evolution of *FOXP2,* a Gene Involved in Speech and Language," *Nature* 418 (2002): 869-72.
50. W. Shu, J. Y. Cho, Y. Jiang, M. Zhang, D. Weisz, G. A. Elder, J. Schmeidler, R. de Gasperi, M. A. Gama Sosa, D. Rabidou, A. C. Santucci, D. Perl, E. Morrisey, and J. D. Bux-

Evolution of Homo sapiens

W. H. Thorpe[51] and Robert Hinde[52] argue from the perspective of animal behavior that the differences between animal and human language are so great that they should be regarded as qualitative. Indeed, Thorpe believed that only humans are capable of recognizing abstract moral law, which he defined as "eternal values which are in themselves good."[53]

5. Culture: "Humans are uniquely reliant on culture as a means of adaptation. . . . Culture differs from individual learning because variations are acquired from other individuals."[54] This brings us back to the evolution of altruism and the importance of the group. The determinants and flexibility (or volatility) of culture are irrelevant in the present context (a critical discussion is given by McGrath[55]); there is no dispute from either natural or social science that we are differentiated and characterized by a multiplicity of cultures, some climatically dependent (i.e., those dominated by particular foods or seasons), others by history (e.g., local tribes or clans).

Early sites in Africa show some evidence of the use of fire, but clear evidence of its controlled creation occurs only in the past 10,000 to 20,000 years; fire use should be distinguished from fire making.[56] Colonization of temperate latitudes may have been impossible without it. Populations that moved north from Africa in an interglacial period would have had a difficult time as the climate worsened. In such circumstances the management of hunting and gathering must have moved from mere opportunism to a need for planning and cultural specialization.[57]

---

baum, "Altered Ultrasonic Vocalization in Mice with a Disruption in the *Foxp2* Gene," *Proceedings of the National Academy of Sciences of the USA* 102 (2005): 9643-48.

51. W. H. Thorpe, *Animal Nature and Human Nature* (London: Methuen, 1974).

52. R. A. Hinde, "Animal-human Comparisons," in *The Oxford Companion to the Mind*, ed. R. L. Gregory (Oxford: Oxford University Press, 1987), pp. 25-27.

53. W. H. Thorpe, *Biology, Psychology and Belief* (Cambridge: Cambridge University Press, 1961).

54. R. Richardson and R. Boyd, "Cultural Inheritance and Evolutionary Ecology," in *Evolutionary Ecology and Human Behaviour*, ed. E. A. Smith and B. Winterhalder (Hawthorne, NY: Aldine/de Gruyter, 1992), pp. 61-92, esp. p. 61.

55. A. McGrath, *Dawkins' God: Genes, Memes and the Meaning of Life* (Oxford: Blackwell, 2004).

56. Alison Brooks, this volume.

57. D. Erdal and A. Whiten, "Egalitarianism and Machiavellian Intelligence in Human Evolution," in *Modelling the Early Human Mind*, ed. P. Mellars and P. Gibson (Cambridge: McDonald Institute for Archaeological Research, 1996), pp. 139-50.

However, the most rapid change in culture took place around 10,000 years ago with the beginning of agriculture. The change of humankind from itinerant hunter-gatherer to resident farmer is a special case of the relationship between species. The consensus is that both animal and plant cultivation arose in the Middle East around 10,000 years ago and spread rapidly to other areas where the available species and climate were favorable.[58]

6. "Chance" and adaptation: On a different level but relevant in debates about the status of humankind is the widespread perception that evolution by natural selection is driven by chance, dependent on randomly occurring mutation. This is a common misapprehension of "creationists," but extends much wider than the beliefs of anti-evolutionists. It was the basis of Jacques Monod's nihilistic *Chance and Necessity*.[59] The Darwinian process does not depend on chance: adaptation results from the selection of advantageous variants, and this is a deterministic process. The confusion arises because variation is a random process, depending on mutation or, much more significantly in sexual organisms, on the phenotypic expression of new variants through recombination. Selection experiments on organisms where mutants have been induced by ionizing radiation show that recombination produces variation much more commonly than fresh mutation.[60] While it is true that adaptation relates to survival and the possibility of gene transmission rather than long-term purpose, it is wrong to claim that "Darwinian evolution" is an entirely fortuitous process. Indeed Simon Conway Morris has shown that the range of viable options for any trait is so limited that it may lead to the appearance of progress.[61]

Fossils of the genus *Homo* show fairly consistent trends in increasing brain and decreasing tooth size. Some changes were rapid. For example, brain size increased by about 50 percent between the earliest *Australopithecus* and the earliest *H. erectus*, and by 50 percent again be-

---

58. J. Diamond, *Guns, Germs and Steel* (London: Jonathan Cape, 1997).

59. J. Monod, *Chance and Necessity* (London: Collins, 1971); see also W. H. Thorpe, *Purpose in a World of Chance* (Oxford: Oxford University Press, 1978).

60. K. Mather, *Genetical Structure of Populations* (London: Chapman & Hall, 1973), p. 86.

61. S. Conway Morris, *Life's Solution: Inevitable Humans in a Lonely Universe* (Cambridge: Cambridge University Press, 2003); see also R. J. Berry, "Nothing in Biology Makes Sense Except in the Light of Evolution," *Science & Christian Belief* 18 (2006): 23-29.

Evolution of Homo sapiens

tween *H. erectus* and the present. Cavalli-Sforza and Bodmer have calculated that the second phase of increase could be achieved with a selection differential of only 0.00004 per generation, which is very small compared to other selection pressures operating in the wild (10,000 times less than observed in the Galapagos Islands finches).[62] Notwithstanding, they comment that the evolution of human brain size is among the most rapid of known evolutionary processes.

Four conservative inferences can be drawn from these studies:

1. Neoteny: Human maturation takes twice as long as in the chimpanzee or gorilla, although gestation length is similar in all three groups. Human brains are one-fourth of the adult size at birth (compared to one-half in chimpanzees) and continue growing at the fetal rate for a year after birth (compared to only a month or two in chimpanzees). A slow rate of skull ossification allows this expansion to take place.

Large brains require large amounts of energy: about 20 percent of resting metabolism in humans supports brain metabolism, compared with 9 percent in chimpanzees and 2 percent in marsupials. Larger brains have a low tolerance for variations in temperature, maternal blood pressure, and oxygenation and may cause obstetric risks,[63] implying that there must be considerable positive tradeoffs to balance these costs.

Louis Bolk developed a theory of "fetalization" as the cause of human evolution.[64] His ideas were confused by his espousal of Haeckel's Theory of Recapitulation (i.e., that ontogeny repeats phylogeny), but his underlying argument about the significance of differential growth rates stands, and has been championed by de Beer and Gould.[65] This asserts that many of our traits are the allometric or incidental results of reduced growth or maturation rate. Contrary to earlier speculation,[66] it seems fairly certain that our large brains are the consequences

---

62. L. L. Cavalli-Sforza and W. F. Bodmer, *The Genetics of Human Populations* (San Francisco: Freeman, 1971), p. 692; R. Boyd and J. B. Silk, *How Humans Evolved* (New York: Norton, 2006), p. 21.

63. B. H. Smith, "The Cost of a Large Brain," *Behavioural and Brain Sciences* 13 (1990): 365-66.

64. L. Bolk, *Das Problem der Menschwerdung* (Jena: Gustav Fischer, 1926).

65. G. R. de Beer, *Embryos and Ancestors* (Oxford: Oxford University Press, 1940); S. J. Gould, *Ontogeny and Phylogeny* (Cambridge, MA: Harvard University Press, 1977).

66. For example, S. L. Washburn, "Tools and Human Evolution," *Scientific American* 203 (1955): 63-75.

of neoteny, rather than the result of selection from brain size as such. Life-cycle features have shaped behavioral possibilities rather than the other way around.

We can go further: study of skull size and of tooth eruption order indicates that the change in growth patterns took place in *Homo erectus* around a million years ago. John Napier comments, "it would seem likely that the major intellectual advances of the genus *Homo* occurred at the *Homo erectus* stage, accompanying progress in tool making, advances in big-game hunting techniques, the discovery of fire, and the development of speech and language."[67]

2. Supralaryngeal tract: Social and natural scientists seem to agree that a major key to human-ness is language and its possibilities for communication. However, the differentiating feature between ape and human is not the ability to make sounds; the structure of the larynx is similar in all the great apes, including humans. "The missing ingredient may have been some modifications of the proto-human vocal tract to give us finer control.... A tiny change in anatomy resulting in capacity for speech would produce a huge change in behaviour."[68]

This "tiny change" seems to be the route of the supralaryngeal airway. This differs in adult humans from all other mammals. Until the age of three months, humans have the same-shaped airway as nonhumans, and can breathe and drink at the same time, liquid moving to either side of the larynx. In adult humans, the larynx has descended into the neck; air, liquids, and solid food have a common pathway. The human vocal tract can seal off the air pathway that leads from the nose to the mouth, enabling the production of non-nasal, more precise, and readily identifiable sounds.

3. Migration and group size: Darwin is conventionally taken to have advocated gradual and progressive evolutionary change. In fact, he wrote in the *Origin*, "I do not suppose that the process goes on so regularly... it is far more probable that each form remains for long periods unaltered, and then again undergoes modification." Jumps or "punctuations" in fossil sequences may represent gaps or imperfections in fossilization, or they may be a true record of a change that is rapid in paleontological terms but long in biological terms, marking tens of hundreds of generations and allowing ample time for major genetical changes.

67. J. R. Napier, *The Roots of Mankind* (London: Allen & Unwin, 1971), p. 205.
68. Diamond, *The Rise and Fall of the Third Chimpanzee*, p. 47.

Evolution of Homo sapiens

In fact, the colonial nature of primate and human communities provides a clear basis for genetical heterogeneity, since each group is likely to have been founded by a small group of individuals that will differ from their ancestral population for no reason other than the sampling of variants in a small group. The total population of Britain in the later Paleolithic was probably only a few hundred, scattered in mainly coastal sites.[69] Any new groups that form will face the challenges of the environment in which they find themselves, and may disappear or (rarely) flourish.[70] Such descendant groups may differ significantly from their parental population and provide a situation for trying out new gene combinations. There is thus a well-known mechanism for testing hitherto untried genomes, such as ones producing neoteny.

Recurrent founder situations are very much more plausible than a progressive co-evolutionary scenario. The constraints of a species changing in adaptive concert with another make co-evolution an unlikely event.[71] The common situation is like an arms race, where one species reacts and adapts to a new challenge (which may be biotic or abiotic), and then the challenger (if a living organism) has to respond.[72] Common examples of this are host-parasite and predatory-prey relationships. The notion of "hopeful monsters," i.e., novel variants appearing at the right time and in the right place is unfashionable, but ought not to be ignored. As Miriam Rothschild has written, "Parasitism can develop gradually or suddenly. It can be the outcome of complicated interactions or the result of isolated accidents which occurred a million years ago or only this morning. . . . There is only one vital factor in the genesis of a parasitic relationship, and that is opportunity."[73]

4. Energy requirements: Work on foraging and diet in nonhuman primates now extends into anthropology, and even paleoanthropology.

---

69. H. J. Fleure, *A Nature History of Man in Britain* (London: Collins, 1951), p. 33.

70. R. J. Berry, "The Significance of Island Biotas," *Biological Journal of the Linnean Society* 46 (1992): 3-12.

71. P. R. Ehrlich and P. H. Raven, "Butterflies and Plants: A Study in Coevolution," *Evolution* 18 (1964): 586-608; D. Futuyma and M. Slatkin, eds., *Coevolution* (Sunderland, MA: Sinauer, 1983).

72. R. J. Berry, "The Processes of Pattern: Genetical Possibilities and Constraints in Coevolution," *Oikos* 44 (1985): 222-28.

73. M. Rothschild and T. Clay, *Fleas, Flukes and Cuckoos* (London: Collins, 1952), p. 48.

There is a linear relationship in mammals between body mass and resting metabolic rate (Kleiber's Law). The slope of this relation is 0.75, indicating that smaller mammals have higher metabolic rates per unit body mass than larger ones. This in turn means that smaller animals need more energy-rich foods than larger ones. A larger animal can exist on a low-energy diet like leaves, but also has some flexibility to divert food from maintenance into reproduction and struggle (both inter- and intra-specific); a species that extracts higher-quality foods (i.e., fruit or animals rather than leaves) has a greater variety of life-history options than one that depends on a low-quality diet.

Leonard and Robertson[74] have compared and modeled the daily energy expenditure of a number of primate species and some human hunter-gatherer groups. They confirmed that more active foragers tend to favor energy-rich diets; their data from human populations showed high-energy demands, large ranges, and very high-quality diets. From their model, they estimated that the Australopithecines had energy needs similar to that of chimpanzees, assuming they lived in a relatively wooded environment. However, at the time of the emergence of *Homo* 2.5 to 1.5 million years ago there was a drastic reduction in the forests of eastern and southern Africa,[75] requiring and promoting an expansion of home range as the food resources became patchily distributed.[76] *Homo habilis* and *H. erectus* were larger than *Australopithecus* and would have required about 40 percent more energy. If the increase in size coincided with an increase in foraging range, they would have needed 85 percent more energy. The obvious way to improve their energy intake would have been to move to more energy-rich food.

This has led to the suggestion that *Homo* survived because it changed from vegetarianism to carnivory[77] (meat provides 100-200 kcal of metabolizable energy for every 100 g of food consumed, compared with 10-20 kcal/100 g for leaves or 50-100 kcal/100 g for fruits). A

---

74. W. R. Leonard and M. A. Robertson, "Comparative Primate Energetics and Hominid Evolution," *American Journal of Physical Anthropology* 102 (1997): 265-81.

75. E. S. Vrba, "Late Pliocene Climatic Events and Hominid Evolution," in *Evolutionary History of the "Robust" Australopithecines*, ed. F. E. Grine (Hawthorne, NY: Aldine/de Gruyter, 1988), pp. 405-26.

76. R. Foley and P. C. Lee, "Finite Social Space, Evolutionary Pathways and Reconstructing Hominid Behaviour," *Science* 243 (1989): 901-6.

77. K. Milton, "A Hypothesis to Explain the Role of Meat-Eating in Human Evolution," *Evolutionary Anthropology* 8 (1999): 11-21.

hominid feeding on animals could have a significantly increased caloric input. This fits with the archaeological evidence of animal bones and stone tools in early *Homo* sites,[78] and a shift from tough and fibrous foods is also consistent with the reduction of facial robustness (prognathism) and posterior tooth size at the same time.

Wrangham et al. have reviewed the evidence and suggested other correlates of diet being an important element in social and sexual differentiation of early hominids.[79] Their proposal is that cooking, particularly of underground plant organs, might have been a key factor. They believe that this could have led to social groupings for defense and food storage, and an increase in male-female bonding for increased stability. The details of their hypothesis do not matter for the present. The importance is that there seems to be agreement that food availability and caloric value were a significant element in the environment to which our ancestors had to adapt (and adapt they did, as shown by their success in survival).

"Natural Selection Could Not Have Done It All"

Alfred Russel Wallace, co-discoverer of natural selection with Charles Darwin, originally argued that natural selection had acted in the earlier stages of human evolution, but as our intellectual and moral faculties became "fairly developed," the body ceased to be subject to selection, and subsequently adaptation was solely "through the action of the mind."[80] Darwin welcomed these ideas, writing to J. D. Hooker (May 22, 1864) that they were "*most* striking and original and forcible," although they were contained in a paper that Wallace later claimed to have "quite distressed" Darwin because of his conclusion that "natural selection could not have done it all."[81] However, Wallace did not let the matter rest. He believed that brain size was a reliable indicator of mental capaci-

---

78. For example, H. T. Bunn and E. M. Kroll, "Systematic Butchery by Plio/Pleistocene Hominids at Olduvai Gorge, Tanzania," *Current Anthropology* 27 (1986): 431-52.

79. R. W. Wrangham, J. Holland Jones, G. Laden, D. Pilbeam, and N. Conklin-Brittain, "The Raw and the Stolen," *Current Anthropology* 40 (1999): 567-94.

80. A. R. Wallace, "The Origin of Human Races and the Antiquity of Man Deduced from the Theory of Natural Selection," *Journal of the Anthropological Society* 2 (1864): 157-87.

81. A. R. Wallace, *My Life: A Record of Events and Opinions*, 2 vols. (London: Chapman & Hall, 1905), vol. 1, p. 418.

ties; he regarded the mind as a composite entity, subdivided into many faculties that have developed independently of each other. His problem was that both fossil humans and "savages" had skulls (and therefore brains) of similar size to those of civilized people, and consequently all must be presumed to have had the same mental capacities. However, for Wallace, such traits as mathematical ability and the ability to carry out complex trains of abstract reasoning were useless (if not harmful) in the struggle for existence in primitive cultures. As it was both unneeded and unused, the brain could not have evolved by natural selection alone. Consequently, and certainly influenced by his newfound belief in spiritualism, he proposed that a "Higher Intelligence" had guided human evolution in a "definite direction and for special ends."[82]

Darwin was horrified. Wallace responded to him: "I can quite comprehend your feeling with regard to my 'unscientific' opinions as to Man, because a few years back I should myself have looked at them as equally wild and uncalled for. . . . My opinions on the subject have been modified *solely* by the consideration of a series of remarkable phenomena, physical and mental, which I have now had every opportunity of fully testing, and which demonstrate the existence of forces and influences not yet recognised by science."[83]

Darwin was prepared to accept that some human physical and mental attributes had never had any direct selective value, although he disagreed strongly with Wallace that "man in the rudest state" lacked intellectual ability and achievements.[84] Stephen Jay Gould comments, "Wallace emerges from most historical accounts as a lesser man than Darwin for one of three reasons, all related to his position on the origins of human intellect: for simple cowardice; for inability to transcend the constraints of culture and traditional views of human uniqueness; and for inconsistency in advocating natural selection so strongly (in the debate on sexual selection), yet abandoning it at the most crucial moment of all."[85]

---

82. A. R. Wallace, "Sir Charles Lyell on Geological Climates and the Origin of Species," *Quarterly Review* 126 (1869): 359-94.

83. A. R. Wallace, *Alfred Russel Wallace: Letters and Reminiscences*, ed. J. Marchant (New York: Harper, 1916), p. 200.

84. M. J. Kottler, Charles Darwin, and Alfred Russel Wallace, in *The Darwinian Heritage*, ed. D. Kohn (Princeton: Princeton University Press, 1985), pp. 367-432.

85. S. J. Gould, "Natural Selection and the Human Brain: Darwin *vs.* Wallace," in *The Panda's Thumb* (New York: W. W. Norton, 1980), pp. 47-58.

Evolution of Homo sapiens

Wallace's version of human evolution illustrates a recurring theme in evolutionary studies: the legitimate but mistaken interpretation of scientific data (in Wallace's case, his assumptions that brain size and mental capacity were the same and that all evolutionary change is adaptive), compounded by seemingly relevant extra-scientific convictions (Wallace's commitment to spiritualism). There is no easy way to solve this dilemma, other than continually to reexamine all information in its contexts and to brutally exclude any alien input. Michael Ruse has chronicled a progressive improvement by evolutionary scientists in distinguishing objectivity from subjectivity. He draws three conclusions pertinent for the understanding of science in general, never mind evolution: the objectivists (the Popperians) have triumphed over the subjectivists (the Kuhnians); evolutionary studies have shown an "ever greater manifestation and adherence to the epistemic norms"; and, although there are people who specialize in "popular-science-level evolutionary theorizing," we have seen a decreasing inclusion of cultural values within science to the extent that modern professionals actively spurn them.[86]

Ruse had two starting points for his exploration of evolutionary science: the "creationist" complaint that evolution is "only" a theory, implying that there are a host of other ways of interpreting the data that evolutionists use in their studies, and much more generally, that "cultural studies" are little more than gobbledygook.[87] His investigation focused on both the overt and inadvertent obfuscations that have plagued the perception of evolution from before the time of Darwin. They are implicit, for example, in the pre-Darwinian debates between the diluvialists and uniformitarians; in the Huxley-Wilberforce confrontation, which was about authority not science; in Herbert Spencer's "social Darwinism"; in the mystical metaphysics of gradualism during the 1920s; in the continuing eugenics-in-the-cupboard saga, which stretches from Francis Galton to contemporary paranoia about gene therapy and stem-cell research; but most acutely in the recurring and imaginative explanations for the determinants of human behavior. Evolutionary just-so stories abound; they are easy to invent but usually lack the data for their refutation. There have been legitimate scientific

---

86. Ruse, *Mystery of Mysteries*, p. 237.
87. A. D. Sokal, "A Physicist Experiments with Cultural Studies," *Lingua Franca* (May/June 1996): 62-64.

debates about (mainly) the mechanisms of evolution from 1859 onward. In the nonbiological world these debates tend to be interpreted as showing the existence of doubts about the occurrence of evolution itself or the relative impotence of natural selection, and often lead to highly dubious extrapolations about what might have happened in the past. Nowhere have these speculations been so common or their protagonists more passionate than around questions on human nature.

Could natural selection have done it all? On a purely scientific level the answer is no: adaptation for any trait brings a suite of other changes that may be advantageous or disadvantageous. But this could be regarded as pedantry; our ancestry has certainly been shaped by selection. However, this does not mean that we will fully understand human nature even if we successfully bring together embryology, anatomy, genetics, ecology, and behavioral studies. Certainly such a synthesis is a necessary preliminary step, but it would be foolish to expect this to give us all the answers we want, even if we could develop a rational synthesis. Nor do we have to go along with Wallace and postulate a guiding "Higher Intelligence." But before we can advance, we have to reconcile the arch-reductionists who insist that we are nothing but survival machines controlled by selfish genes to those who focus on personal and sexual relationships and group dynamics. Between them are those who believe that the insights and models of sociobiology and its children provide all the bases for truly knowing ourselves. E. O. Wilson, prophet of this middle road, argues that there are two sorts of people, empiricists and transcendentalists, and that the robustness of this bi-polarity is testable "by the continuance of biological studies of complex human behaviour."[88]

If Wilson is right, we would then have a straightforward research program to sort out our past, and possibly guide our future. His way is certainly better than illegitimately transferring the material and methodology of one discipline to solve the problems of another — like the claim that Darwinian analysis can be used to study culture, because both are transmitted.[89] Analogies may be useful in stimulating ideas, but can cause confusion if extended too far.[90] However, from a theolog-

---

88. E. O. Wilson, *Consilience* (New York: Knopf, 1998), p. 264.

89. Richardson and Boyd, "Cultural Inheritance and Evolutionary Ecology," pp. 61-92; McGrath, see note 34.

90. E. P. Martins, ed., *Phylogenies and the Comparative Method in Animal Behavior* (New York: Oxford University Press, 1996).

Evolution of Homo sapiens

ical point of view we do not have to take sides in scientific debates, because the biblical distinction between animals and humankind is that only we are made "in the image and likeness of God" (Gen. 1:26); we are divinely "inbreathed" dust (i.e., existing material into which God "breathed into his nostrils the breath of life") (Gen. 2:7). Joel Green points out that the word translated "'breath of life' is used [in Genesis 1] with reference to 'every beast of the field . . . every bird of the air . . . everything that creeps on the earth' . . . demonstrating incontrovertibly that 'soul' is not under this accounting a unique characteristic of the human person. One might better translate Genesis 2:7 with reference to the divine gift of life, 'the human being became a living person.'"[91] God could have created humans *de novo*, with no continuity with the rest of creation, or he could have transformed an existing animal into one made "in his image." As we have seen, it is impossible to distinguish between these from the biblical record alone.

The most likely explanation, and one that accords with the scientific data, is that God implanted his image into an existing animal. In Genesis 1, *bara* is used for the creation of matter (v. 1), the creation of the "great sea-beasts" (v. 21), and the creation of humankind (v. 27). The notion that God entered his world to imbue humankind with his image at a particular time is supported by the use of *bara*, which suggests a specific act of God; in this it is distinguished from the "molding" of existing forms described by the word *asah* (a general word for making or shaping), which is the more usual word for God's "creating" or "making" in the creation stories. If this is accepted, the species *Homo sapiens* whose fossil history we know and whose genetic history we can infer, could be described as being transformed into *Homo divinus*, a distinction apparently made first by John Stott.[92] There is no reason why this divine work should have produced any morphological or genetical change: God's image implies relationship and not any trait that would have left a mark in the paleoanthropological record. How it occurred is unknown. The essential point is that, whatever the mechanism turns out to be, the witness of Scripture is that it was part of the divine upholding of all things.

Did God make a single person (or pair), or did his image emerge in

---

91. J. B. Green, "What Does It Mean to Be Human?" in *From Cells to Souls — and Beyond*, ed. M. A. Jeeves (Grand Rapids: Eerdmans, 2004), p. 196,
92. J. R. W. Stott, *Understanding the Bible* (London: Scripture Union, 1972), p. 63.

a group of individuals? The word translated "Adam" could imply corporate humanity, but the idea of Adam as a historic individual seems to be the biblical thrust: Paul compares the "one man" through whom sin entered into the world with the "one man" who brought the gift of righteousness (Rom. 5:12-19; see also 1 Cor. 15:21, 45). Leon Morris supports this interpretation, while cautioning that "Paul's argument in Romans 5 is very condensed and in all translations and comments we must allow for the possibility that Paul's meaning may at some point be other than we think."[93] Notwithstanding, he asserts that "the one man [Adam] is very important and underlies the whole discussion. Twelve times in verses 12-19 we have the word *one*; repeatedly Paul refers to one man Adam (and to one sin of that one man) and opposes to him (and it) the one man Jesus Christ (and his one world of grace). The one man and his sin and the one Savior and his salvation are critical to the discussion." James Dunn discusses and rejects the possibility that Adam can be regarded as merely a representative man: "Paul does not use *anthropos* here to characterize humankind as a whole; the concept of corporate responsibility is more of a hindrance than a help here";[94] he cites H. W. Robinson and F. F. Bruce in support.

The exegesis of this point must be left to theological debate. However, it can be regarded as irrelevant for this discussion, because the Bible story of the creation of humankind and the secular account of human evolution do not inevitably conflict, so long as we accept that the image that characterizes us is a sovereign act of the Creator. There is no reason why this would be transmitted like a Mendelian characteristic; it could have been conferred on an individual and then spread by divine *fiat* to all other members of *Homo sapiens*. Likewise, the effects of the disobedience of the first pair could have spread "laterally."[95] This understanding underlines the responsibility of the individual to respond to God in obedience, whereas interpreting "Adam" as corporate humanity minimizes personal commitment and the consequences of disobedience. The "death" that entered the world the day that Adam sinned is, of course, primarily separation from God (e.g., Eph. 2:1-5).

93. L. Morris, *The Epistle to the Romans* (Downers Grove, IL: InterVarsity Press, 1988), p. 228.

94. J. Dunn, *Romans 1-8*, Word Biblical Commentary 38A (Dallas: Word, 1988), p. 272.

95. R. J. Berry, "This Cursed Earth: Is 'the Fall' Credible?" *Science & Christian Belief* 11 (1999): 29-49, 165-67.

Physical death was part of creation from the beginning, not least in the Creator's provision of plants for animals to eat (Gen. 1:29, 30; 2:16). Adam can legitimately be seen as a descendant of a "pre-Adamic" lineage, but at the same time a unique historical individual, divinely created "in the image of God."

The Emergence of Human Distinctiveness: The Story from Neuropsychology and Evolutionary Psychology

Malcolm Jeeves

Introduction

Research at the interfaces of contemporary psychology with neuroscience and evolutionary biology is exceptionally active, fruitful, and heavily funded. The media, almost daily, give a high profile to the latest discoveries. One reason is that leading researchers are aware of how advances in neuropsychology and evolutionary psychology prompt rethinking of commonly shared, and often deeply held, views of our nature. The issues raised concern not only Christians but also attentive humanists.

In the case of neuropsychology, the subtitle of a recent book *The New Brain Sciences: Perils and Prospects* edited by Sir Dai Rees, former head of the British Medical Research Council, and brain researcher Steven Rose, alerts readers to how accumulating evidence for the tightening links between mind and brain raises questions about the extent to which we are free to think and act as we choose.[1] Neuropsychological research repeatedly underlines the intimate interdependence between mind and brain, what used to be called soul and body. In so doing, it calls into question a widespread religious belief that each of us has, or is, an immaterial soul untouched by what is happening in our material bodies. Such research reopens old questions about how to understand our complex makeup. Which are the best models of our complex nature — dualistic, monistic, or pluralistic?

---

1. Dai Rees and Steven Rose, eds., *The New Brain Sciences — Perils and Prospects* (Cambridge: Cambridge University Press, 2004).

Evolutionary psychology challenges the supposed distinctiveness of one feature of our human nature after another. Research reveals that some of our nonhuman primate cousins show, albeit in rudimentary form, skills and abilities that were previously thought to make us unique and distinctive. Developments in evolutionary psychology certainly prompt us to revise ideas about human uniqueness if they are based solely on philosophy or theology. For example, views about what is meant by the claim that we are made in "the image of God" have varied widely down the centuries. Sinclair Ferguson reminds us that while references to the image or likeness of God are relatively infrequent in Scripture, nevertheless, the interpretation of humanity it enshrines is all-pervasive.[2]

We shall examine three of the most enduring past theological interpretations of in what sense we are made in the image of God. Is it because we possess a separate immaterial soul in which resides our unique capacity to reason? Is it that we alone are capable of moral agency and moral behavior? Or is it because we are endowed with special capacities for entering into relationships? Each calls for reexamination in light of findings from neuropsychology and evolutionary psychology. Before examining the relevant scientific evidence we shall briefly put today's questions in historical context.

From "Soul Talk" to "Mind Talk"

When we talk about the human person in a religious context, words that come readily to mind are *soul, spirit, heart,* and *body*. Although many parts of the human body are mentioned in Scripture, never the brain. Contrast that with the scientific context, where discussions of brain and mind dominate.

How did the focus move from "soul talk" to "mind talk," and how are they related? In the seventeenth and eighteenth centuries, philosophers' "soul" talk changed to "mind" talk. Kenan Malik observed that "the difficulty in finding a common language in which to talk of the immortal soul and the body-machine led many seventeenth- and eighteenth-century natural philosophers to speak increasingly of the

---

2. S. B. Ferguson, entry on "The Image of God," in Sinclair B. Ferguson and David Wright, eds., *New Dictionary of Theology* (Leicester: InterVarsity Press, 1988).

'mind' rather than of the 'soul'. The mind was not simply a synonym for the soul in a more mechanistic language," he observed.

> Rather, those aspects of the soul's relationship with a world that were amenable to naturalistic explanations — memory, perception, emotions and so on — were recast as problems of the mind. This transformation helped minimise conflict between theologians and natural philosophers: the soul eventually became the domain purely of theology, while natural philosophers developed the "science of mind." But it did not resolve the underlying problem of how to talk about an immaterial entity using a language developed for describing machines. It simply transformed the terms of that problem: the question of how the transcendental soul acted upon the physical body became replaced by the question of how the immaterial mind could arise out of fleshy matter. It still remains a central question for the science of mind.[3]

Stevenson and Haberman have reminded us, however, that the issues are not quite as straightforward as Malik suggested.[4] As a broad generalization we may still say that for the past two millennia the dominant view of soul-body or mind-brain relations was expressed in terms of some form of dualism. There were other views such as those of Aristotle, Spinoza, and materialists such as Hobbes and La Mettrie. It is because past "soul-body" talk in the history of religious thought raised so many of the same issues as today's "mind-brain" talk that what is happening in contemporary psychology and neuroscience is immediately relevant to exploring current views of human nature. As Vidal reminds us, in some contemporary discussions, so dominant has become the focus on the brain that "personhood" has been replaced by "brainhood."[5] The strange thing is that it should be Michael Gazzaniga who has most emphasized what he calls "brainhood."[6] Strange because Gazzaniga's distinguished early work was carried out with Nobel laureate Roger Sperry on the so-called "split-brain" experiments, and it was Roger Sperry who, perhaps

---

3. Kenan Malik, *Man, Beast and Zombie* (London: Weidenfeld & Nicolson, 2000), pp. 36 and 41.

4. Leslie Stevenson and D. L. Haberman, *Ten Theories of Human Nature*, 4th ed. (New York: Oxford University Press, 2004).

5. Fernando Vidal's chapter in this book.

6. Michael Gazzaniga, *The Ethical Brain* (New York: Dana Press, 2005).

more than any other high-profile scientist at that time, insisted upon the importance of "mind-talk" and warned of the errors of metaphysical reductionism.[7]

The Neuropsychological Story

Twenty-seven years ago the Nobel laureate neurophysiologist David Hubel[8] wrote that "fundamental changes in our view of the human brain cannot but have profound effects on our view of ourselves and the world." There has been an explosive rise in the number of neuroscience researchers since Hubel's declaration. At the inaugural meeting in 1969 of the Society for Neuroscience there were fewer than 100 participants; today more than 30,000 attend. Our view of the human brain has changed dramatically. It is these changes that prompt a reconsideration of some of our views of ourselves. What are the salient features of the current neuropsychological landscape, and how are they relevant to our understanding of human nature?

The rapid growth in brain science went largely unnoticed until the U.S. Government declared the 1990s "The Decade of the Brain" and our newspapers and magazines began, occasionally, and now almost daily, to show graphic pictures from brain-imaging studies of how our brains change as we view our changing world, experience beautiful paintings, witness harrowing scenes, or engage in our favorite hobbies.[9] A quick count shows that in 1995, there were 87 articles on brain imaging and behavior on CNN and the major American news networks; by 2000, there were 340 — a quadrupling in five years. And the trend continues. In a word, the general public is becoming increasingly aware that there are remarkably tight links between our minds and our brains and that today we can monitor these links.

There is a long history from neurology and experimental neuropsychology demonstrating how remarkably localized some mental processes are in the brain. This localization does not necessarily imply fixity. With the advent of new techniques for monitoring brain activity it

---

7. R. W. Sperry, "Psychology's Mentalistic Paradigm and the Religion/Science Tension," *American Psychologist* 43, no. 8 (1988): 607-13.
8. D. H. Hubel, "The Brain," *Scientific American,* September 1979, pp. 45-53.
9. Rapaal Malach, *Neuron* (May 2006).

is clear that plasticity of function is also a key feature of mind-brain relations.

Localization and Specificity

A century and a half of steadily accumulating evidence has shown regions and systems in the brain selectively specialized for specific abilities. Studies of localization of function within the brain, until relatively recently investigated mainly through so-called "bottom-up" approaches, have given rise to a widespread belief that there is a fixity about the neural embodiment of cognitive and conceptual abilities. This fixity has frequently been described as specificity. While substantially correct, nevertheless, in some instances (see below) specificity has been misleadingly overstated in a way that fails to do justice to the more recent evidence for plasticity.

More than half a century ago researchers showed how the physical and social environments in which animals grow up can shape and mold their brains.[10] Similar research, using increasingly sophisticated methods, has demonstrated the long-term effects of the early environment on adult behavior in the form of quite specific changes in the biochemistry of the brain and in concentrations of different neurotransmitters.[11]

More recently, advances in brain-imaging techniques have led to a fresh awareness of how cognitive processes and the social, as well as the physical environment, including habitual ways of behaving, can "mold" or "sculpture" the brain (see, for example, Ian Robertson's 1999 book *Mind Sculpture*[12] and Sharon Begley's 2006 book *Train Your Mind, Change Your Brain*[13]). These reviews by Robertson and Begley together give new prominence to the actual and potential importance of so-called "top-down" processes.

---

10. M. R. Rosenzweig, D. Krech, and E. I. Bennett, "Brain Chemistry and Adaptive Behavior," in *Biological and Biochemical Bases of Behavior*, ed. H. H. Harlow and C. N. Woolsey (Madison: University of Wisconsin Press, 1958), pp. 367-400.

11. K. Matthews, J. W. Dalley, C. Matthews, Hu Tsai Tung, and T. W. Robbins, "Periodic Maternal Separation of Neonatal Rats Produces Region and Gender-specific Effects on Biogenic Anime Content in Post-mortem Adult Brain," *Synapse* 40 (2001): 1-10.

12. Ian Robertson, *Mind Sculpture* (London: Bantam Press, 1999).

13. Sharon Begley, *Train Your Mind, Change Your Brain: How a New Science Reveals Our Extraordinary Potential to Transform Ourselves* (New York: Random House, 2006).

The Emergence of Human Distinctiveness

The increasing demonstration of the intimate links between cognitive processes and brain processes may give clues to the possible neurobiological effects of beliefs and expectations. Advances in understanding the possible power of top-down effects have been so fast that what ten years ago leading researchers could see as "only a dream" have already been partially realized by researchers such as O'Craven and Kanwisher, described later in this chapter.[14]

This clear evidence for the embodiedness of our cognitive processes and our behavior generally has implications for our "spirituality." There are well-documented changes in the dimensions of life, loosely called spirituality, that are dependent upon the intactness and normal functioning of our brain. Detailed studies of distressing changes in spirituality in Alzheimer's patients graphically illustrate this. The spiritual dimension to life is embodied.[15] At the same time, awareness of the importance of "top-down" processes points to the importance of cognitive processes, such as beliefs, expectations, including religious ones, as well as the social context in which these are held. All this underscores the need to remember that spirituality is firmly embedded in a context of shared beliefs and social relationships.

Bottom-Up Approaches to the Study of Mind-Brain Links

Using the bottom-up methods, which dominated for a century and a half, typical experimental procedures involved making changes in selective neural and/or biochemical substrates of the brain and then observing how behavior or cognitive capacities changed as a result. Soon it was not even necessary to produce surgical lesions since, following on the pioneering work of David Hubel and Torsten Wiesel, there was a rapid expansion in methods that depended on implanting very small electrodes in columns of cells in the brain. Researchers then monitored the activity in those cells, as the subjects — usually animals — were presented with a variety of sensory stimuli.

14. K. M. O'Craven and N. Kanwisher, "Mental Imagery of Faces and Places Activates Corresponding Stimulus-Specific Brain Regions," *Journal of Cognitive Neuroscience* 12 (2000): 1013-23.

15. Glenn Weaver, "Embodied Spirituality: Experiences of Identity and Spiritual Suffering among Persons with Alzheimer's Dementia," in *From Cells to Souls — and Beyond*, ed. Malcolm Jeeves (Grand Rapids: Eerdmans, 2004).

An example from the laboratories where I worked for three decades illustrates the remarkable specificity of some aspects of neural processing. Twenty-five years ago, David Perrett and his colleagues at St. Andrews used single-cell recording techniques to map regions in monkeys' brains that responded selectively to the sight of human faces.[16] Every new study seemed to tighten the links between what the monkey was seeing and how the cells of the brain were responding. There was a remarkable specificity in the cells' responses to facial stimuli. Among other things, Perrett found, for example, that changing the view of a face in its horizontal orientation from side profile to full face and back had a dramatic effect on the level of activity of face-responsive neurones.[17] All this suggested to Perrett that one of the key functions of these neurones may be to determine the direction of another's gaze. He proposed that the information provided by the eyes, the face, and the body was selectively processed by different columns of neurones, all part of a processing hierarchy for attention direction or social attention. Other researchers demonstrated this was a part of a larger system.[18]

With the advent of the so-called cognitive revolution, which was in part a reaction against behaviorism, and, in part, reflected rapid developments by experimental psychologists of new methods to study mental events, new efforts were made to study how psychological processes were physically embodied in the brain. Research efforts by psychologists focused on memory, attention, and perception. It was not long before researchers such as Tulving could present a taxonomy that divided memory into working, or short-term, memory and long-term memory.[19] The latter was further subdivided into explicit and implicit long-term memory. Explicit long-term memory was further subdivided into

---

16. D. I. Perrett, P. A. J. Smith, D. D. Potter, A. J. Mistlin, A. S. Head, A. D. Milner, and M. A. Jeeves, "Neurons Responsive to Faces in the Temporal Cortex: Studies of Functional Organisation, Sensitivity to Identity and Relation to Perception," *Human Neurobiology* 3 (1984): 197-208.

17. D. I. Perrett, J. K. Hietanen, M. W. Oram, and P. J. Benson, "Organization and Functions of Cells Responsive to Faces in the Temporal Cortex," *Philosophical Transactions of the Royal Society: Biological Sciences* 335, no. 1273 (January 29, 1992): 23-30.

18. See D. I. Perrett, M. W. Oram, and E. Wachsmuth, "Understanding Minds and Expression from Facial Signals: Studied at the Brain Cell Level," *IEEE International Workshop on Robot and Human Communication* (1993): 3-12.

19. See E. Tulving, *Elements of Episodic Memory* (Oxford: Clarendon Press, 1983).

episodic memory (for events) and semantic memory (for facts). Implicit long-term memory was divided into procedural and conceptual representational memory. Experimental psychologists devised ingenious techniques for studying these different sorts of memory empirically. Once this fractionation of cognitive processes had taken place, it led to a natural search for possible specific neural mechanisms upon which each of these forms of memory were dependent for their normal functioning. Such neural systems could be localized or widely spread throughout the brain.

Links between brain and mind are not confined to perception and cognition but also extend to the understanding of differences in human personality and behavior. Occasional reports of such changes appear in the clinical literature and have a long and checkered history. Most who tell the story start with the account of how Phineas Gage, a foreman working on the Rutland & Burlington Railroad in Vermont, accidentally suffered damage to the frontal part of his brain and thereafter was a changed person. A dramatic example of a similar change was reported recently.[20] It described how a schoolteacher had begun collecting sex magazines and visiting pornographic websites and focusing his attention on images of children and adolescents. This was something that, according to him, he simply could not stop himself doing. He was arrested for child molestation, convicted, and underwent a rehabilitation program that was unsuccessful. The day before his final sentencing he went voluntarily to the hospital emergency department complaining of a severe headache. He was distraught and contemplating suicide, aware that he could not control his impulses — so much so that he propositioned the nurses in the hospital. An MRI scan of his brain revealed a large tumor pressing on his right frontal lobe. The surgeons removed it, and the lewd behavior and pedophilia faded away. Sadly, after a year he began to manifest pedophilia afresh. New MRI scans showed that the tumor was beginning to regrow. It was removed and once again his urges subsided. This case, not surprisingly, received wide publicity and comment. One thing, however, is clear: it demonstrated the remarkably tight links between what is happening in the brain and how we behave. This in turn, as McCall Smith has noted, prompts us to "consider the question of how far greater understanding

---

20. J. M. Burns and R. H. Swerdlow, "Right Orbitofrontal Tumor with Pedophilia Symptom and Constructional Apraxia Sign," *Archives of Neurology* 60 (2003): 437-40.

in neuroscience might enable us to reformulate the criminal law analysis of human action."[21]

Smith believes that behavioral geneticists have already been able to produce sufficient evidence to justify serious thought being given to the legal and ethical issues of this field of activity. Although so far there have not been many studies linking specific genes to particular forms of behavior, work in this field has attracted a good deal of attention. For example, researchers looked at three generations of a widely dispersed family in the Netherlands in which a small number of male members were claimed to have been involved in various forms of unacceptable behavior including arson, rape, and "having a violent temper." Eight of these "aggressive" male members had a defect in a gene on their X chromosome known to be responsible for the production of monoamine oxidase, an enzyme that affects serotonin levels. This was followed up by a study of 500 male children which suggested that children who had a gene resulting in lower levels of monoamine oxidase were more likely to behave violently in adult life, but only if they were exposed to maltreatment and abuse in childhood. Smith suggests that "from both a moral and legal point of view, the fact that a person has acted in a particular way because of a characteristic of the brain or of the genotype may not exculpate but may lead us to mitigate blameworthiness to some extent."[22]

When evidence from brain damage in adult humans is the only or even the main source of evidence about the remarkable specificity of localization of functions within the brain, it can lead to a serious failure to recognize the plasticity of the developing brain. Such an overemphasis is present at times in the writings of Steven Pinker, who drew evidence mainly from adult neuropsychology and genetic disorders.[23] However, other leading workers in the field, such as Karmiloff-Smith, have pointed out that Pinker's interpretation of the data is flawed. She notes that it is based on a static model of the human brain that ignores the complexities of gene expression and the dynamics of post-natal development.[24] We agree with Karmiloff-Smith's critique.

21. A. McCall Smith, "Human Action, Neuroscience and the Law," in Rees and Rose, *The New Brain Sciences — Perils and Prospects,* p. 105.
22. McCall Smith, "Human Action, Neuroscience and the Law," p. 121.
23. Steven Pinker, *Words and Rules: The Ingredients of Language* (London: Weidenfeld & Nicolson, 1999).
24. A. Karmiloff-Smith, "Elementary, My Dear Watson, the Clue Is in the Genes. . . . Or Is It?" *The Psychologist* 15 (2002): 608-11.

The Emergence of Human Distinctiveness

When Karmiloff-Smith received the 2004 Latsis Prize awarded by the European Science Foundation, the citation summed up the importance of her corrective remarks. It observed that "her research aimed to show that the brain is neither hardwired nor a blank slate, but that both genes and environment interact in complex ways and that the actual process of post-natal development plays a crucial role in this dynamic interaction." The judges added: "This highlights the fact that the adult neuropsychological model is inappropriate for explaining developmental disorders."

A similar point has been made by Nancy Kanwisher and Galit Yovel, who adduce a large body of evidence for the specificity of neural mechanisms for face perception in the fusiform face area. They argue that in the ongoing debate about "the extent to which the mind/brain is composed of (i) special-purpose ('domain-specific') mechanisms, each dedicated to processing a specific kind of information (e.g. faces, according to the face specificity hypothesis), versus (ii) general-purpose ('domain-general') mechanisms, each capable of operating on any kind of information," their work "supports the face specificity hypothesis and argues against its domain-general alternatives." At the same time they note that "evidence that very early experience is also crucial in the development of normal adult face recognition comes from studies of individuals born with dense bilateral cataracts." They conclude: "In sum, substantial evidence indicates important roles for both genetic factors and specific early experience, in the construction of the Fusiform Face Area."[25]

Clearly there is a remarkable specificity in the neural mechanisms for some of our most important perceptual and cognitive functions in social interactions and for daily living. At the same time all this further underlines that, with specificity, there is also plasticity as emphasized by Karmiloff-Smith. Recognizing the key importance of psychological processes and the evidence for plasticity, we turn now to consider the special relevance of top-down effects.

---

25. Nancy Kanwisher and Galit Yovel, "The Fusiform Face Area: A Cortical Region Specialised for the Perception of Faces," *Philosophical Transactions of the Royal Society of London B* (2006): 2109 and 2122.

MALCOLM JEEVES

Top-Down Approaches to the Study of Mind-Brain Links

As the cognitive revolution has spread, so coincidentally, we have witnessed over the past three decades a plethora of publications using ever more sophisticated brain-imaging techniques. These research reports point to the importance of "top-down" effects, referring to changes in cognition being paralleled by localized changes in the brain. Two striking examples of top-down effects illustrate their potency. Maguire and his colleagues noted that licensed London taxi drivers are renowned for their extensive and detailed navigation experience and skills. They collected structural MRIs of the brains of a group of taxi drivers and of matched controls, and discovered that, as a result of two years of intensive training in navigation, the anterior hippocampi of the taxi drivers were significantly larger. Moreover, the volume of gray matter in the right hippocampus correlated significantly with the amount of time spent as a taxi driver. The researchers concluded that "it seems that there is a capacity for local plastic changes in the structure of the healthy adult human brain in response to environmental demands."[26] They have recently followed up their earlier researches with laboratory studies that have demonstrated how the relative sizes of the brain regions change as training on spatial tasks progresses.

The second example is a study by O'Craven and Kanwisher, whose work on specificity was described above, which beautifully illustrates how the mind can selectively mobilize specific brain systems.[27] They asked volunteers to look at pictures of faces or houses or to imagine these pictures. They demonstrated how imagining faces or houses selectively activated the same areas of the brain as when the subjects were seeing the pictures of houses or faces. Specifically, seeing or thinking about faces activated the fusiform face area, while seeing or thinking about houses activated the parahippocampal place area. The experimenters, in effect, showed that they could actually "read the minds" of their subjects by observing their brain activity. They could tell whether

26. Eleanor A. Maguire, David G. Gadian, Ingrid S. Johnsrude, Catriona D. Good, John Ashburner, R. S. J. Frackopwiak, and C. D. Frith, "Navigation-related Structural Change in the Hippocampi of Taxi Drivers," *Proceedings of the National Academy of Sciences* 97, no. 8 (2000): 4398.

27. K. M. O'Craven and N. Kanwisher, "Mental Imagery of Faces and Places Activates Corresponding Stimulus-Specific Brain Regions," *Journal of Cognitive Neuroscience* 12 (2000): 1013-23.

the subjects were thinking about faces or houses by measuring activity in respective brain areas.

Maintaining a Balance

The picture that emerges from the science sketched above points to the intimate relationships between mind, brain, and behavior. We described some of these as "bottom-up" and some as "top-down." There is now an emerging consensus about how to portray these intimate relationships. The neurologist Antonio Damasio wrote that "the distinction between diseases of brain and mind, and between neurological problems and psychological/psychiatric ones, is an unfortunate cultural inheritance that permeates society and medicine. It reflects a basic ignorance of the relation between brain and mind."[28] A similar view was expressed by Robert Kendell, a recent past president of the Royal College of Psychiatrists in Britain. He wrote, "Not only is the distinction between mental and physical ill founded and incompatible with contemporary understanding of disease, it is also damaging for the long-term interests of patients themselves."[29]

In drawing inferences about the relations between psychological processes and their neural substrates, it is important to remember that "the integration of methods and data from bottom-up and top-down approaches provides a means of circumventing some of the thornier interpretative problems of either approach alone and thereby permits strong inferences in cognitive neuroscience."[30] In this way we can simultaneously remember that cognitive processes are embedded within the brain and at the same time sculpture the brain. It is clear that while there is a remarkable specificity about how some of our most fundamental perceptual and cognitive processes are embodied in our brains, there is also striking evidence of how cognition and behavior sculpture our brains, demonstrating equally remarkable plasticity.

---

28. Antonio Damasio, *Descartes' Error* (New York: Putnam, 1994), p. 40.

29. R. E. Kendell, "The Distinction between Mental and Physical Illness," *British Journal of Psychiatry* 178 (2001): 490-93.

30. Martin Sarter, Gary G. Berntson, and John T. Cacioppo, "Brain Imaging and Cognitive Neuroscience," *American Psychologist* (January 1996): 13-21.

Mind and Brain: Soul and Body Relationships — Irreducible, Intrinsic, or Interdependent?

It is one thing to demonstrate the intimate interrelationship between what is happening at the conscious mental level and what is happening at the level of the brain and the body, but the unanswered question is: How can we most accurately characterize this intimate relationship without making claims or assumptions about what we know of the relationship between the two that have not yet been demonstrated?

Some discussions of human nature and mind-brain or soul-body relations quickly focus on the relative claims of dualism and monism. When this happens monistic views are often made synonymous with physicalism and are further portrayed as necessarily materialist and reductionist. In short, a great deal of philosophic baggage invariably gets attached to the terms *monism, dualism,* and *physicalism.* Is there any way this can be avoided by underlining the unity of the person while, at the same time, recognizing the need for a *duality* of accounts if we are to do full justice to the way the world is?

Studies by neuropsychologists such as those described above underline the dependence of the mental aspects of our life on their physical embodiments, in the brain and the body. Such evidence indicates the remarkable *interdependence* between what is happening in the physical substrates, in terms of brain and body mechanisms, and what is happening in terms of mental abilities and individual and social behavior. While interdependence per se is not denied by Cartesian dualists, the nature of the interdependence increasingly uncovered by scientific research, we believe, makes a belief that there are two substances — one an immaterial soul or mind substance and the other a material body/brain substance — difficult to defend without tortuous and convoluted reasoning. The burgeoning field of psychoneuroimmunology produces example after example of how changes in the social situation and mental life are reflected in changes in cerebral and endocrine processes.

What is clear is that there is a remarkable interdependence between what is occurring at the cognitive level and what is occurring at the physical level. We could perhaps describe this as a relationship of *intrinsic interdependence,* using the word *intrinsic* to mean that, as far as we can see, it describes the way the world is in this regard (*Concise Oxford Dictionary:* intrinsic, *adj.,* belonging naturally, inherent). We can perhaps go further than this and say that on our present knowledge it is an *irreduc-*

ible intrinsic interdependence: we cannot reduce the mental to the physical any more than we can reduce the physical to the mental. In this sense, there is an important duality to be recognized, but it is a duality without dualism.

In attempting to think further about this irreducible intrinsic interdependence, which manifests duality without dualism, an analogy some have found helpful is in terms of computer software and computer hardware — an apt analogy when so many of us make daily use of computers. Even here, however, there are traps for the unwary. All too easily analogies of the relationship between mental events and physical events, or software and hardware, are smuggled in as if they were explanations.

Donald MacKay suggested that it was silly to pit the mental and physical levels of description against one another; rather, they should be seen as harmoniously complementary. The mental, at the conscious level, is spelling out the personal significance of a unitary situation; the physical is dealing with another aspect of it, the so-called "brain" story. Professor MacKay was keen, when using the computer analogy, to emphasize that between the descriptions of the software (the mental) and hardware (the neurobiological) levels there is a correlation but not a translation. The example he liked to use was that if we have a mathematical equation that has two roots and it is embodied in a computer, then the facts about the equation are not facts about the computer — except, as he put it, in a "Pickwickian" sense. He wrote, "computers don't have roots. And yet if the computer is solving the equation there is a direct physical correlate for the statement 'the equation has two roots' and any engineer can tell you what it is."[31] But no one is suggesting that if you look hard enough you can find roots in the computer!

A number of eminent neuroscientists such as Roger Sperry emphasized the importance of the cognitive aspect of behavior, with reference to "top-down" effects. At times, Sperry went so far as to refer to mental activity "pushing and hauling" the activity of the brain. We do not need to endorse that view. What we are suggesting is that if the one is embodied in the other, then the *interdependence* is even closer than just "pushing and hauling." What we are anxious to affirm, as was MacKay, is that the mental activity is efficacious in determining the activity of the brain. That does not mean that you spend your time trying to find

---

31. D. M. MacKay, *Behind the Eye* (Oxford: Blackwell, 1991), p. 60.

elements in the physics of the computer "sensitive" to influences from the hypothetical mathematical world. Hence between the mental and the physical there is an irreducible (in the sense that to get rid of either is to tell less than the whole story), intrinsic (in the sense that it is part of the way the world is), interdependence (the mental and physical are correlated and complementary), reflecting duality but not necessitating dualism of substance.

There is an ongoing debate among thoughtful Christians about the best way to characterize the intimate links between mind and brain. Some advocate substance dualism, some emergent dualism, some nonreductive physicalism, and others what they call a constitution view of persons (e.g., Green et al., 2004[32]). I have elsewhere labeled my view "dual aspect monism."[33]

Belief in an immaterial soul played an important role in debates about what was meant by saying that we are made in the image of God. It was in the immaterial soul that our capacity to reason was said to be located, and hence the need for an immaterial soul was foundational to one of the most widely held and enduring views of what it means to say that humans are uniquely made "in the image of God."

The Natural Light of Reason and the Image of God

The belief that we are bipartite, that we are body plus an immaterial soul, was assumed by such thinkers as Plato, Aristotle, Origen, Nemesius, and, particularly significant because of his persisting influence on Christian theology, Augustine of Hippo (354-430). Augustine differed from the Greeks in believing that a human being is a rational soul using a mortal and material body, rather than simply being imprisoned in a body. For Aquinas (1225-74), nearly a thousand years later, the soul was an "incomplete" substance produced by special creation at the moment the embryonic organism was able to receive it. The classical tripartite division of body, mind, and soul became, with Descartes, a bipartite separation of material and thinking substances.

---

32. Joel B. Green, ed., *What about the Soul?* (Nashville: Abingdon Press, 2004).
33. Malcolm Jeeves, "Brain, Mind and Behaviour," in *Whatever Happened to the Soul?* ed. Warren S. Brown, Nancey Murphy, and H. Newton Malony (Minneapolis: Fortress Press, 1998).

The Emergence of Human Distinctiveness

For long dualism remained both scientific and theological orthodoxy. In some ecclesiastical circles it still is. For example, the *Catechism of the Catholic Church*[34] states:

> God ... can be known ... by the natural light of reason.... Man has this capacity because he is created "in the image of God."

As regards the claim that humans alone can reason, there are remarkable similarities between the cognitive capacities of animals — and more especially of nonhuman primates — and ourselves. Rapid developments in evolutionary psychology offer a large body of evidence pointing to the conclusion that animals also think. There is also an expanding research literature discussing whether or not chimpanzees have a "theory of mind." There is clear evidence for behavior in animals that, if it were seen in humans, would be described as imagination and as involving inventiveness and means-end reasoning.

Studies at the interface with neuroscience indicate how these emerging capacities may be related to the development of the brain. In each instance any attempt to set down a clear demarcation between the reasoning abilities of nonhuman primates and humans is found to have become blurred. This, of course, is not to deny that there are distinctive capacities in humans that have led to the explosive development of learning, philosophy, literature, music, art, science, and so on and so forth. No one is claiming that. The point is a simple one that evidence for reasoning and thinking abilities in nonhuman primates is available. While rudimentary, they are today seen to overlap with similar abilities in developing small children. It therefore becomes increasingly difficult to seek to anchor a belief in the uniqueness of humans created in the image of God in terms of reasoning located in an immortal soul.

As we saw above, the idea of a separate immaterial soul (mind) is difficult to defend in light of the tightness of the links between mind and brain, soul and body. Rather, a holistic view of ourselves is both compatible with the science and consonant with much contemporary theological thought; see, for example, Joel Green's review.[35]

---

34. *Catechism of the Catholic Church,* Chapter One, Part One, III. The Knowledge of God According to the Church, p. 36.

35. See Joel Green's chapter in this book.

Evolutionary Psychology and Human Distinctiveness

Philosophers have long agonized over the question of what makes us human. Are the differences between ourselves and animals in kind or merely in degree? The question is not new. Pascal wrote that "it is dangerous to show a man too clearly how much he resembles the beast, without at the same time showing him his greatness. It is also dangerous to allow him too clear a vision of his greatness without his baseness. It is even more dangerous to leave him in ignorance of both."[36] Evolutionary psychology can help to reduce that ignorance.

There is a checkered history of attempts to establish the uniqueness of humankind on scientific grounds. That there are no necessary religious stakes in this should be apparent from the comments of Richard Dawkins, a prominent atheist who readily lists four things that illustrate human uniqueness. Richard Passingham notes how man has always considered himself to be set apart from animals. He reminds us how the nineteenth-century anatomist Richard Owen (1858), writing about the basis of brain differences, put man in a separate subclass, set apart from another subclass containing all the other mammals.[37] Owen called our subclass the Archencephala, or "ruling brains," claiming that there were three structures unique to the human brain. In 1836, T. H. Huxley convincingly refuted these claims, demonstrating that all three structures, including the hippocampus minor, could be seen in the brains of other primates. Huxley was scornful of those who, as he put it, sought "to base Man's dignity upon his great toe," all those who thought "we are lost if an Ape has a hippocampus minor." Others have sought to pin the uniqueness of humans on our possession of a soul contrasted with the parallel assertion that animals do not have souls. Today some see evolutionary psychology as blurring what they regard as essential distinctions between humans and nonhuman primates.

Comparative Psychology and Evolutionary Psychology

The first psychologist elected a Fellow of the Royal Society of London, Lloyd Morgan, worked primarily on animals. At that time the field was

---

36. Blaise Pascal, *Pensées* (1659).
37. Richard Passingham, *The Human Primate* (Oxford: Freeman, 1982).

labeled comparative psychology, a name it still retains but one that, in recent years, has been largely superseded by evolutionary psychology.

Many of the early studies by comparative psychologists looked for a neat natural scale in which changes in sensory processes and learning would parallel the position of an animal in the phylogenetic scale.[38] This in turn led to a search for ways in which, with more complex nervous systems, more elaborate behaviors and learning capacities would emerge. Such studies were mainly carried out on animals that are easily kept in laboratories, such as rats, pigeons, cats, and monkeys. Evolutionary psychology as it is conceived today has only tenuous links with such earlier comparative psychology. One of the best early examples was Norman Munn's 1971 book *The Evolution of the Human Mind*.[39]

Evolutionary psychology refers to the study of the evolution of behavior and of the mind using principles of natural selection. The presumption is that natural selection has favored genes that designed both behavioral tendencies and information-processing systems that solved problems faced by our ancestors, thus contributing to their survival and the spread of their genes.

The main focus of research in evolutionary psychology is the question of how humans came to be the apparently special animal we are today. A leading researcher in the field, Richard Byrne, lists some of the central questions in evolutionary psychology, such as: "When did a particular cognitive trait enter the human lineage? What was its original adaptive function? (and has it been retained for the same reason, or is it now valuable for some different purpose)? What is the cognitive basis for the trait, and how does its organisation relate to other mental capacities?"[40]

One of the most actively researched topics in evolutionary psychology is the so-called "theory of mind." Much debate in recent years has been and continues to be whether or not humans are unique by virtue of possessing "mind-reading" behavior and a "theory of mind."

---

38. Duane Rumbaugh and Malcolm Jeeves, "A Comparison of Two Discrimination-reversal Indices Intended for Use with Diverse Groups of Organisms," *Psychoneurological Science* (1966).

39. Norman L. Munn, *The Evolution of the Human Mind* (Boston: Houghton Mifflin, 1971).

40. Richard W. Byrne, "Evolutionary Psychology and Sociobiology: Prospects and Dangers," in *Human Nature*, ed. Malcolm Jeeves (Edinburgh: Royal Society of Edinburgh Publications, 2006).

There has also been intensive research in the last decade investigating the possible neural substrates for mind-reading behavior, a topic that forms a natural bridge between neuropsychology and evolutionary psychology. As far back as 1978, Premack and Woodruff had described animals that had the ability to understand the mind of another as possessing a "theory of mind."[41] According to two of the leaders in the field, Andrew Whiten and Richard Byrne, "having a theory of mind or being able to mind-read concerns the ability of an individual to respond differentially, according to assumptions about the beliefs and desires of another individual, rather than in direct response to the other's overt behaviour."[42]

Another of the main contentions in evolutionary psychology is that any straightforward separation between cognitive and social capacities is likely to be unsatisfactory. It is argued that the unprecedented complexity of human beings, as compared to monkeys and great apes, has come about precisely because these two domains are integrated in mutually reinforcing ways. Of relevance for our discussions is whether all this has any implications for our understanding of what constitutes human uniqueness.

In evaluating the evidence for sophisticated social behavior in animals, we should follow Byrne's warning of the dangers of drawing inferences from field observations alone. He writes that "researchers have to be very cautious, then, in attributing to non-human primates the ability to understand social behaviour or how things work in the mechanistic way of adult humans. Rapid learning in social circumstances, a good memory for individuals and their different characteristics, and some simple genetic tendencies are capable of explaining much that has impressed observers as intelligent in simian primates."[43] It is evident that there are serious scientific issues to be addressed here and it is tempting, in a search for human uniqueness, to seize upon so-called mind-reading behavior as one way of uniquely separating off humans from non-humans. One theologian who recently found this temptation irresistible was Christopher Fisher. In an otherwise excellent review of trends in evo-

41. David Premack and Guy Woodruff, "Does the Chimpanzee Have a Mind?" *Behavioural and Brain Sciences* 4 (1978): 515-26.

42. Richard Byrne and Andrew Whiten, *Machiavellian Intelligence: Social Expertise and the Evolution of Intellect in Monkeys, Apes, and Humans* (Oxford: Clarendon Press, 1988).

43. Richard W. Byrne, "Evolutionary Psychology and Sociobiology: Prospects and Dangers," in Jeeves, *Human Nature*.

lutionary psychology, he identified, as a key piece of scientific evidence to settle a theological issue, the then dominant view that having a theory of mind was a differentiating factor between humans and animals.[44]

In his paper, Fisher recorded that one of the leading workers in the field, Daniel Povinelli, had found "no evidence that chimpanzees reason about intentions as internal states," and he quoted another leader, Michael Tomasello, as seeing "the social nature of human cognition more than anything else as unique to the human mind."[45] The problem is that both Povinelli[46] and Tomasello have since changed their views. Tomasello has written that "in our 1997 book *Primate Cognition*, we reviewed all the available evidence and concluded that nonhuman primates understand much about behavior of conspecifics but nothing about their psychological states [but] in the last five years new data have emerged that require modification of this hypothesis. The form that a new hypothesis should take is not entirely clear but we are now convinced that at least some nonhuman primates — the research is mainly on chimpanzees — do understand at least some psychological states in others." He asserts that "for the moment we feel safe in asserting that chimpanzees can understand some psychological states in others — the question is only which ones and to what extent."[47]

There is an equal temptation faced by those who are unthinkingly over-enthusiastic about new developments in evolutionary psychology. When similarities between the behavior of humans and some nonhuman primates are identified, there will always be a temptation to say that humans are therefore "nothing but" unusually complex primates, and to ignore the distinctiveness of the ethical, moral, and religious aspects of human cognition and behavior.

We turn now to ask how the evidence from evolutionary psychology may help, if at all, in evaluating another former widely held view of

---

44. Christopher Fisher, "Animals, Humans and X-men: Human Uniqueness and the Meaning of Personhood," *Theology and Science* 3, no. 3 (2005): 291-314.

45. Fisher, "Animals, Humans and X-men," pp. 291-314. Fisher criticizes in particular D. J. Povinelli, M. Bering, and S. Giambrone, "Towards a Science of Other Minds: Escaping the Argument by Analogy," *Cognitive Science* 24 (2000): 531.

46. D. J. Povinelli and J. Vonk, "Chimpanzee Minds: Suspiciously Human?" *Trends in Cognitive Science* 7 (2003): 157-60.

47. M. Tomasello, J. Call, and B. Hare, "Chimpanzees Understand Psychological States — the Question Is Which Ones and to What Extent," *Trends in Cognitive Science* 7 (2003): 153-56.

what constitutes being made "in the image of God." Does our distinctiveness rest in our unique capacity to demonstrate moral agency and moral behavior?

Moral Behavior, Moral Agency, and the Image of God

The capacity for moral agency and moral behavior has, in the past, been seen as a defining feature of what it means to be made in the image of God. The illustrious North American theologian Jonathan Edwards wrote, "herein does very much consist that image of God wherein He made man . . . viz. in those faculties and principles of nature whereby he is capable of moral agency."[48] If Edwards was claiming that this capacity was unique to humans then we may ask how does such a claim stand today in light of developments in evolutionary psychology? Over the past three decades, evidence has been steadily accumulating of behavior, which if we were to witness it in humans, we would attribute to the possession of a moral sense and moral agency. Because there is an evolutionary history to the emergence of a moral sense, however, does not make that behavior any less worthy. Frans de Waal has written that "aiding others at the cost or risk to oneself is widespread in the animal kingdom," adding: "The fact that the human moral sense goes so far back in evolutionary history that other species show signs of it plants morality firmly near the center of our much-maligned nature."[49] The theologian Jürgen Moltmann has said that self-giving is "God's Trinitarian nature, and is therefore a mark of all his works."[50] Clearly self-giving is found not just in God's human work.

Some fear that there goes another claim to human uniqueness. But as we just saw, leaders in the field remind us that because two behaviors are superficially similar is no reason to assume that the underlying mechanisms and thinking patterns are identical. Self-giving, self-

---

48. Jonathan Edwards, *On the Freedom of the Will*, Part 1, Section V (Concerning the Notion of Liberty and of Moral Agency), pp. 19f. in vol. 1 of *The Works of President Edwards* (New York: Wiley & Putnam, 1844), a reprint of the Worcester Edition digitized October 12, 2007.

49. Frans de Waal, *Good Natured: The Origin of Right and Wrong in Humans and Other Animals* (Cambridge, MA: Harvard University Press, 1996).

50. Jürgen Moltmann, "God's Kenosis in the Creation and Consummation of the World," in *The Work of Love*, ed. John Polkinghorne (Grand Rapids: Eerdmans; London: SPCK, 2001), pp. 140f.

sacrificing behavior appears in different animals. But that in itself tells us nothing about what underlies those behaviors. Self-giving behavior may, for example, occur with or without self-awareness.

It seems that there are good arguments for believing that some aspects of self-giving and self-limiting behavior have developed over our evolutionary history and become more pronounced among nonhuman primates.

When similarities between the behavior of humans and some nonhuman primates are identified, there is an automatic temptation to say that humans are "nothing but" unusually complex primates and to ignore the distinctiveness of the ethical, moral, and religious aspects of human cognition and behavior. Because there is increasing evidence for the beginnings of behavior in animals that, if it were to occur in humans would be labeled as moral, suggests that human moral sense goes back a long way in our evolutionary history.

In a similar vein, Richard Byrne, commenting on a reported trend for stepfathers to murder their partners' babies under three years old, warns about forcing such findings into assumptions about so-called evolutionary stable strategies:

> [T]hese are not carefully thought out by beasts; nor are any genes really selfish or altruistic since they are no more than pieces of DNA molecules. Nor is an understanding of "kinship" likely to be remotely similar to our own. They are human applied labels based on the superficial appearance of the actions of individual animals whose behaviour is partially governed by genes.... Natural selection is a mechanistic process and thus morally neutral; discovering a genetic influence on murder does not condone it.... Human social behaviour is influenced by our culture and our extensive information transmission by spoken and written language in ways not well described by biology.[51]

In order to defend the uniqueness of the developed human capacities for moral agency it is not necessary to deny evidence of their emergence in animals and in particular in nonhuman primates. The more important question for Christians, however, is whether there is any evidence in Scripture to support the view that the image of God in hu-

---

51. Richard W. Byrne, "Evolutionary Psychology and Sociobiology: Prospects and Dangers," in Jeeves, *Human Nature*, pp. 94, 96, and 99.

mans is to be defined in terms of a unique capacity for moral behavior and moral agency? If there is, we await its identification.

For those who begin from theistic presuppositions it means we can see embedded within creation the seeds, development, and fruits of self-giving behavior. We do not need to deny the emergence of self-giving altruism in primates in order to defend the unique self-emptying sacrifice of Christ. That, we believe, was a unique and ultimate act that sets Christ apart from all others in heaven and on earth.

The Imago Dei as a Unique Capacity for Personal Relatedness

Sinclair Ferguson, referred to earlier, has pointed out that two of the leading theologians of the last century, Emil Brunner and Karl Barth, both emphasized that the image of God is not the possession of the isolated individual but of the person in community. Barth developed the idea characteristically in a Christocentric manner. More recently the theologian Colin Gunton has stated explicitly that "[i]f God is a communion of persons inseparably related, then it is in our relatedness to others that our being human consists."[52]

It is interesting that a similar focus on relatedness is found today in the writings of neuropsychologists and evolutionary psychologists. Warren Brown, for example, has written that "a theory of mind is involved in extending our relatedness both to others and to ourselves,"[53] and evolutionary psychologists Byrne and Corp have written that "learning in social contexts may be constrained by neocortical size" and that "neocortical expansion has been driven by social challenges among the primates."[54]

But the capacity for relatedness is not some capacity free-floating above the head or out there in space. The evidence from neuroscience and evolutionary psychology both point to the beginnings of an understanding of the neural substrates required to be functioning normally for the possession of a full capacity for personal interrelatedness.

One of the most significant discoveries in the last decade in neuro-

---

52. Colin Gunton, *The Promise of Trinitarian Theology* (Edinburgh: T. & T. Clark, 1997).

53. Warren S. Brown, "Neurobiological Embodiment of Spirituality and Soul," in Jeeves, *From Cells to Souls — and Beyond*, pp. 58-76.

54. R. W. Byrne and N. Corp, "Neocortex Size Predicts Deception Rate in Primates," *Proceedings of the Royal Society of London* (2004): Biology 271:1693-99.

science was the identification of a small specialized group of neurones in the frontal part the brain labeled the "mirror neurones," which seemed to be part of the essential substrate for interpersonal interactions. These mirror neurones were discovered by Giacomo Rizzolatti and his colleagues,[55] and commenting on their importance Ramachandran wrote: "I predict that mirror neurones will do for psychology what DNA did for biology: they will provide a unifying framework and help explain a host of mental abilities that have hitherto remained mysterious and inaccessible to experiments... and thus I regard Rizzolatti's discovery as the most important unreported story of the last decade."[56]

It is becoming clear that these mirror neurones are part of a wider network upon which the capacity for personal relatedness depends.[57] The evidence for this comes from ongoing studies of the brains of autistic individuals. It is widely known that one of the difficulties experienced in some forms of autism is the capacity to relate to other people. It is already evident that in certain autistic individuals the brain is functioning abnormally as compared with that of controls when they perform tasks that are known to mobilize the so-called mirror neurones. It will be some time before the full details have been worked out experimentally, and they will undoubtedly turn out to be far more complicated than we currently suspect. The important point here, however, is that the capacity for relatedness, if this is to be seen as the key to understanding the imago dei, is itself dependent upon our wholeness as persons and intimately dependent upon our biology. It is an embodied capacity.

The Continuing Search for Human Distinctiveness

It is clear that lots of Rubicons keep getting bridged between animals and humans as research advances. And it is likely this trend will continue. As we have seen, the most recent case of this has to do with the

---

55. G. Rizzolatti, L. Fadigo, V. Gallese, and L. Fogassi, "Premotor Cortex and the Recognition of Motor Actions," *Cognition, Brain Research* 3 (1996): 131-41.

56. V. S. Ramachandran, The Third Culture, June 1, 2000, www.edge.org/3rd.

57. N. J. Emery and D. I. Perrett, "How Can Studies of the Monkey Brain Help Us Understand 'Theory of Mind' and Autism in Humans?" in *Understanding Other Minds 2: Perspectives from Autism and Cognitive Neuroscience,* ed. Baron-Cohen et al. (Oxford: Oxford University Press, 2000).

intense interest in whether or not animals show a theory of mind. Not only have Tomasello and his colleagues changed their views and are now convinced on the basis of laboratory studies that there is evidence for theory of mind in monkeys, but it is also evident that some birds can show evidence for theory of mind. For example, see Nicola Clayton's demonstration that scrub jays give evidence that in other species would be interpreted as a theory of mind. She has commented that "future planning is a complex cognitive skill that was thought to be unique to humans. The present study shows that scrub jays can plan what and where to cache for tomorrow's breakfast."[58]

As things stand, if an animal does something remarkable and an explanation is given in cognitive terms, we find some scientists, in what remains of the behaviorist tradition, working overtime to explain how it could all have been learned by the animals on the basis of associative learning theory. It always seems possible to give an alternative explanation, given sufficient time and ingenuity.

Given the closely similar brain architecture of humans and nonhuman primates together with the close similarities between their respective genomes, where is the most promising place to look to discover why it is that humans differ so much in their potential for showing achievements that set them apart from all other primates?

In the view of many, the essential difference that sets humans apart is language. It is a capacity for language that allows two mental streams to develop so that we are able both to look into the future and also to look over the past. We are able to look at both of these streams, because we code them linguistically and they are then available for comparison and analysis. How, when, and where language developed in evolutionary history we do not yet know. Richard Byrne believes that nothing that any living apes do looks like syntax except for food processing with their hands. In this there seems to be evidence of a manual planning system, and this would tie in with gesture as being an important forerunner of language. As yet there is no evidence that any primates can copy a sound.

Despite the concern that some Christians may have about the apparent narrowing of the gap between themselves and some nonhuman primates, there are no necessary theological issues at stake in this re-

---

58. Nicola S. Clayton, "Animal Cognition: Crows Spontaneously Solve a Metatool Task," *Current Biology* 17 (2007): R894-895.

search. Scholarly and careful workers in the field are often dismayed by some of the media interpretation of their findings. A Christian can be enthusiastically open-minded about developments in evolutionary psychology — not gullible, but discerning, glimpsing fresh pointers to the greatness of the Creator in the wonders of his creation. We may see these as another area of science where we may be able to exercise the stewardship to which we are called by engaging in new research. We may also take encouragement from the fact that from time to time research on nonhuman primates may give clues that will help in the understanding of some distressing forms of behavior in humans. For example, intensive study on theory of mind and its neural substrates is already giving new clues that are helping in the understanding of autism. Basic scientific research properly understood and applied is found to give new ways of exercising the care and compassion to which Christians are called.

The Way Ahead

Keep in mind Sinclair Ferguson's reminder that while references to the image or likeness of God are relatively infrequent in Scripture, the interpretation of humanity it enshrines is all-pervasive. We have reviewed some interpretations that, down the centuries, have been accepted as being essential to a proper understanding of the meaning of the image of God in humans. We have also seen how advances in neuropsychology and evolutionary psychology prompt a reexamination of what constitutes the image of God in humans, which in turn prompts a reexamination of what was hitherto taken as the biblical basis for such views.

In his recent biography of Jonathan Edwards, George Marsden wrote that "Edwards regarded Scripture alone as truly authoritative, so earlier interpreters could be revised. The project of understanding Scripture's true meaning was an ongoing progressive enterprise to which Edwards hoped to contribute."[59] This is a timely reminder. It is Scripture that is authoritative, not the interpretation given by a particular group of Christians at a particular time. Scientists who are Chris-

---

59. George Marsden, *Jonathan Edwards: A Life* (New Haven: Yale University Press, 2003), p. 474.

tians believe that using the talents God has given enables us to discover more about the wonders of his creation. They also believe that ultimately the truth they discover in this way will not contradict or conflict with truth that has been revealed in Scripture. However, as the history of past interactions of science and faith amply illustrates, from time to time the discoveries we make from within science prompt us to reexamine some of our earlier interpretations of Scripture. Perhaps we are passing through another one of these periods when we need to listen carefully to what God is telling us through science about our mysterious human nature as we seek to interpret and understand Scripture in a new but appropriate way.

Relating this to the focus of this chapter we have seen how evidence from neuropsychology and evolutionary psychology sheds new light on our understanding of human distinctiveness, permitting the following tentative conclusions:

1. A holistic model of the human person does most justice to the scientific understanding of ourselves. Dualisms of parts or substances will not do. There is no scientific evidence for them, and there is no biblical warrant for them. Our unity is central. We know each other, not as brains in bodies, but as embodied persons. We are people who relate to each other as beings created in the image of God, but this image is not a separate thing. It is not the possession of an immaterial soul, it is not the capacity to reason, and it is not the capacity for moral behavior.

We have seen how the results of research at the interface of psychology and neuroscience have underlined the intimate relationships between mind and brain. We suggested that a helpful way to think about the relationship between the mental and physical aspects of our life is one of irreducible intrinsic interdependence that manifests duality without dualism.

While some of the research findings as reported in the media are dramatic, many unanswered questions remain about how properly to interpret them. It is also clear that this is very much a report of work "in progress." We have acknowledged that there is an ongoing lively debate among those at the cutting edge of the research, as well as among philosophers, about how best to make sense of it all. There are no slick and simple answers.

2. We noted that the spiritual dimensions to our lives are firmly embodied. On the one hand, research based on bottom-up approaches gives special insights into understanding how changes in the neural

structures of the brain, such as those occurring in Alzheimer's disease, manifest themselves in the subjective awareness and the objective expression of the religious life. On the other hand, we may see how the top-down effects might give clues to how beliefs and expectations may operate in phenomena such as the placebo effect. In other words, the spiritual dimensions of our lives are both firmly embodied so that they do not remain immune to the effects of changes in brain, and also embedded so that they may sculpture our brains and be efficacious in healing.

3. Various abilities claimed in the past to discriminate humans uniquely from animals have now been seen to be present in rudimentary forms in animals. Where there are close similarities, as Richard Byrne reminded us, it is tempting immediately to apply human labels on the basis of a superficial appearance of the actions of individual animals whose behavior is partly governed by genes. He reminds us that natural selection is a mechanistic process that is morally neutral. As Byrne put it, "discovering the genetic influence on murder does not condone it... human social behaviour is influenced by our culture and our extensive information transmission by spoken and written language in ways not well described by biology."[60] We noted that, in a similar vein, Alexander McCall Smith, former professor of medical law and expert in bioethics, writing on the impact of neuroscience and insights that it provides, cautioned that "from both the moral and legal point of view, the fact that a person has acted in a particular way because of a characteristic of the brain or of the genotype, may not exculpate but may lead us to mitigate blameworthiness to some extent. Returning to the psychopath, or indeed to the paedophile, such persons may behave anti-socially and may be held responsible for what they do, but they still deserve some pity at least on the grounds that the starting point for their choices is so much more difficult than it is for those are not affected by such conditions."[61] In a word, the more we discover about the genetic and neural underpinnings of behavior the more it should generate the compassion which according to Scripture is a Christian hallmark.

---

60. Richard W. Byrne, "Evolutionary Psychology and Sociobiology: Prospects and Dangers," in Jeeves, *Human Nature,* pp. 84-105.

61. A. McCall Smith, "Human Action, Neuroscience and the Law," in Rees and Rose, *The New Brain Sciences — Perils and Prospects,* p. 121.

4. In a concluding chapter to the book *The New Brain Sciences — Perils and Prospects* mentioned at the beginning, Sir Dai Rees and Barbro Westerholm emphasize that "these insights (from neuroscience) can only heighten the sense of mystery at the workings of the human mind rather than encourage any idea that the remorseless march of the new brain sciences will soon arrive at a 'total explanation' or 'final synthesis' of them. On the contrary, the picture seems to expand and become ever more elaborate."[62] If we believe that all truth comes from God, we can, as Christians who are scientists, while marveling at what we discover, be quite relaxed about the increasing wonders revealed every day about the most intimate details of human nature. What we already know will seem so small in the light of what will be revealed in the coming decades and will add even further to our conviction that we are indeed "fearfully and wonderfully made" (Ps. 139:14).

5. The contemporary focus of much current theological thinking on the imago dei is that it is seen primarily in our capacity for relatedness: relatedness to our Creator, relatedness to one another, and relatedness to the creation. To understand and accept this has enabled us to recognize the need to show greater compassion to those struggling to make and then maintain normal interpersonal relations, and to those struggling to conform with the "standing orders" for all Christians. At the same time we have no scriptural warrant for appealing to this or that special cognitive, conative, or mystical capacity to establish our uniqueness or in order to identify the imago dei in each of us. Rather, we should recognize that above all, Scripture teaches that our distinctiveness is to be found in our special calling and destiny. It is a calling to a personal relationship of love and obedience to our Creator and a destiny to fulfill his invitation and command to be faithful stewards of his creation.

6. But as Christians we should not leave it there. Biblical scholars and theologians forcibly remind us that any attempt to interpret and understand the imago dei without reference to the Lord Jesus Christ falls far short of what Scripture teaches. It is in him and him alone that we have the clearest vision of what the imago dei is and how it is to be understood.

The Old Testament scholar Patrick Miller, for example, has writ-

---

62. Dai Rees and Barbro Westerholm, "Conclusion," in Rees and Rose, *The New Brain Sciences — Perils and Prospects,* p. 267.

ten, after reviewing the evidence from the Psalms concerning what it means to be a human being and then comparing this with the book of Hebrews, that "the writer to the Hebrews hears in the Psalms the word that whatever we say about the human reality must take into account the face of Jesus Christ. The New Testament underscores this in spades when it makes Psalm 22, the model lament, the interpretive key to understanding the passion and death and resurrection of Jesus Christ." He later goes on to note that "the Hebrews writer says the critical words 'But we do see Jesus.' We do see Jesus, who for a little while was made lower than the angels, crowned with glory and honor because of the suffering of his death, so that by the grace of God he might taste death for everyone" (Heb. 2:9). And he later continues, "Whatever therefore is to be said about the human cannot be confined to general statements about humanity apart from God. It cannot be said apart from the discovery that in Jesus Christ we see who we are and we also see God for us. And what he said about the human cannot be said as a general statement that assumes that what we see now is all there is to see. The answer to the question about who we are is finally eschatological, where tears are no longer part of the human reality, where joy is the order of eternity, and where our transience disappears in the disappearance of death. We cannot see that yet. But we do see Jesus. That will have to do. I think it is enough."[63]

---

63. P. D. Miller, "What Is a Human Being? The Anthropology of Scripture," in Green, *What about the Soul?* p. 73.

The Social Animal

David G. Myers

"It is not good that the man should be alone."

Genesis 2:18

Imagine awakening to find oneself alone on a deserted island. The weather is pleasant. Food and water are abundant. Predators are absent. Comfortable shelter is at hand. But there is not another soul on the island and no possibility of contacting anyone.

From the creation story's perspective, even an idyllic existence devoid of relationship with other humans would be an impoverished, incomplete existence. In our individuality we are incomplete. "The Bible presents no conception of individual man as existing in and for himself," said biblical scholar G. Ernest Wright.[1] "The individual was created for society. . . . There is no man apart from a people in which he lives and moves and has his being."

So it is elsewhere in the Bible, as humans existed in community. After the creation, at which God finds "Adam" to be incomplete, and needing a complementary "thou," individuals merged into families which merged into clans which merged into tribes which merged into a

---

1. G. Ernest Wright, *The Biblical Doctrine of Man in Society* (London: SCM Press, 1954).

Parts of this essay are adapted from David Myers's previous writings, including *The Pursuit of Happiness* (New York: Avon Books, 1992); *The American Paradox* (New Haven and London: Yale University Press, 2000); *What God Has Joined Together* (co-authored by Letha Dawson Scanzoni) (HarperSanFrancisco, 2005); and *Psychology*, 8th ed. (New York: Worth Publishers, 2007).

people. So it was for Aristotle, in declaring our species "the social animal." So it was in the 2000 movie *Cast Away* in which the marooned Chuck Noland (played by Tom Hanks) combated the agony of social starvation by talking with his girlfriend's photo and a volleyball he named Wilson. And so it is for today's social psychologists who have discerned a deep human "need to belong."[2]

The Need to Belong

We humans thrive in relationship, especially close, supportive relationships. Cast away on an island, isolated in prison, alone at a new school, living in a foreign land, people feel keenly their lost connections. "Without friends," wrote Aristotle in *Nichomachean Ethics*, "no one would choose to live, though he had all other goods." Indeed, echoed the early personality theorist, Alfred Adler, we have an "urge to community."[3] Social psychologists Roy Baumeister and Mark Leary have assembled evidence that confirms the human need to belong.

Belonging promotes survival. Among our several infant social responses — anger, fear, love — the greatest is love. Shortly after birth, we begin to prefer familiar voices and faces. By eight months, we display powerful attachment. We seek out our caregivers. Separated from them, when being handed to a stranger, we wail. Reunited, we cling.

Biological wisdom underlies this need to attach. By keeping children connected to their caregivers with invisible elastic bands, attachments helped keep them from danger and ensured their survival. As adults, they also formed attachments with other adults that led to reproduction, and then to sustaining relationships that helped protect their offspring and nurture them to reproductive maturity.

Group bonds further supported survival. When hunting, eight hands were often better than two. When foraging, groups offered protection from predators and enemies. Any who preferred to live and hunt and gather alone were less likely to survive to have grandchildren to carry on their genes.

2. Roy Baumeister and Mark Leary, "The Need to Belong: Desire for Interpersonal Attachment as a Fundamental Human Motivation," *Psychological Bulletin* 117 (1995): 497-529.

3. Eva Dreikurs Ferguson, "Adler's Motivational Theory: An Historical Perspective on Belonging and the Fundamental Human Striving," *Individual Psychology* 45 (1989): 354-61.

As social animals with "social identities," today we cheer on our groups, kill for our groups, die for our groups. When our groups triumph, we feel social pride. Social psychologist Robert Cialdini observed that after a big football victory, the winning school's students typically report that "we" won. Asked the outcome after their team's defeat, students often report that "they" lost.

The group definition of who we are also implies who we are not. Social psychological experiments reveal that forming people into groups promotes "ingroup bias." Ask children, "Who's better, the children in your school or the children at [another nearby school]?" Virtually all will say their own school has better children. Cluster people into groups defined by nothing more than their birth date or even the last digit of their driver's license, and they'll feel a certain kinship with their number mates, and will show them favoritism. So strong is our group consciousness that "we" seem better than "they" even when "we" and "they" are randomly defined.

We long to belong. Our need to belong pervades our thoughts and feelings. We contemplate actual and desired relationships. Falling in love, we feel joy. We think often of our loved one. Asked "What is necessary for your happiness?" or "What is it that makes your life meaningful?" most people's first answer is close, satisfying relationships with friends, family, or romantic partners.[4]

Kennon Sheldon and his colleagues asked American and South Korean collegians to consider: What was your most satisfying moment in the past week?[5] Then they asked the students to rate how much this peak experience had satisfied various needs. In both countries, the satisfaction of self-esteem and the need to belong were the top two contributors to the peak moment. Another study found that "very happy" university students are distinguished not by their money but by their "rich and satisfying close relationships."[6] The need to belong greatly outweighs any drive to be rich.

---

4. Ellen Berscheid, "Interpersonal Attraction," in *The Handbook of Social Psychology*, ed. Gardner Lindzey and Elliott Aronson, vol. 2 (New York: Random House, 1985), pp. 413-84.

5. Kennon M. Sheldon, Andrew J. Elliot, Youngmee Kim, and Tim Kasser, "What Is Satisfying about Satisfying Events? Testing 10 Candidate Psychological Needs," *Journal of Personality and Social Psychology* 80, no. 2 (2001): 325-39.

6. Ed Diener and Martin E. P. Seligman, "Very Happy People," *Psychological Science* 13, no. 1 (2002): 81-84.

When we feel included, valued, and loved, our self-esteem rides high. Indeed, self-esteem mirrors our sense of belonging and being valued, observe Mark Leary and his colleagues; it is a gauge that monitors the level of our social connections.[7] To win friendships and to avoid rejection is to sustain our self-esteem. And that motivates us to conform to expectations and to look and act in ways that create favorable impressions. Seeking approval and belonging, we spend billions on clothes, cosmetics, and diets.

South Africans have a word for the longing for belonging. *Ubuntu*, explained Desmond Tutu, expresses the idea that "my humanity is caught up by, is inextricably bound up, in yours."[8] *Umuntu ngumuntu ngantu*, says a Zulu maxim: "A person is a person through other persons."

We seek to maintain relationships. If an important relationship fractures, we suffer. Uprooted to a foreign land, we may ache over our lost connections. Even after being randomly thrown together at school, at summer camp, or on a vacation cruise, we lament the separation upon parting. We promise to call, to write, to return for reunions. If, as Barbra Streisand sang, "people who need people are the luckiest people in the world," then virtually everyone is lucky.

Because being alone often seems intolerable, attachments can even keep people in abusive relationships. Even when bad relationships break, people suffer. In U.S. National Opinion Research Center surveys, only one in five separated and divorced people report being "very happy."

When death or other forms of separation break our social ties, the frequent result is loneliness, homesickness, jealousy, or anxiety. Refugees in a new land may be depressed by the isolation, which is why modern immigration policies now encourage "chain migration" that enables people to connect with compatriots from their home country.[9] The second Bosnian family in a small town generally has an easier adjustment than the first.

We feel the pain of ostracism. Many people can recall a time when their need to belong was thwarted by ostracism — when they felt ignored or

7. Mark R. Leary, Alison L. Haupt, Kristine S. Strausser, and Jason T. Chokel, "Calibrating the Sociometer: The Relationship Between Interpersonal Appraisals and State Self-Esteem," *Journal of Personality and Social Psychology* 74, no. 5 (1998): 1290-99.

8. Desmond Tutu, *No Future without Forgiveness* (New York: Doubleday, 1999).

9. Mary Pipher, *The Middle of Everywhere: The World's Refugees Come to Our Town* (New York: Harcourt Brace, 2002).

excluded. What was it like to be shunned, to be avoided, to be met with averted eyes, even to be given the silent treatment?

Purdue University social psychologist Kipling Williams and his colleagues have studied ostracism — social exclusion — in both natural and laboratory settings.[10] Across the world, they report, humans use ostracism to control social behavior, with punishing effects. When ostracized, people respond with hurt feelings, anxious fretting, and depressed mood. Those who have experienced the silent treatment from a family member or co-worker have called it "emotional abuse" and "a terrible, terrible weapon to use." Lea, a lifelong victim of the silent treatment by her mother and grandmother, reflected that "It's the meanest thing you can do to someone, especially if you know they can't fight back. I never should have been born." During two years of silent treatment by his employers, reported Richard, "I came home every night and cried. I lost twenty-five pounds, had no self-esteem and felt that I wasn't worthy."

If rejected and unable to remedy the situation, people often withdraw and sometimes turn nasty. In a series of studies, psychologist Jean Twenge and her collaborators told some participants "everyone chose you as someone they'd like to work with."[11] They told the rest that the others *didn't* want them in their group. Compared to those feeling wanted, those excluded became much more likely to engage in self-defeating behaviors and to underperform on aptitude tests. They also exhibited more antisocial behavior, such as disparaging someone who had insulted them or, when given the option, blasting them with noise. "If intelligent, well-adjusted, successful university students can turn aggressive in response to a small laboratory experience of social exclusion," noted the research team, "it is disturbing to imagine the aggressive tendencies that might arise from a series of important rejections or chronic exclusion from desired groups in actual social life."

---

10. Kipling D. Williams, *Ostracism: The Power of Silence* (New York: Guilford, 2002).

11. Jean M. Twenge, Roy F. Baumeister, Dianne M. Tice, and Tanja S. Stucke, "If You Can't Join Them, Beat Them: Effects of Social Exclusion on Aggressive Behavior," *Journal of Personality and Social Psychology* 81 (December 2001): 1058-69; Jean M. Twenge, Kathleen R. Catanese, and Roy F. Baumeister, "Social Exclusion Causes Self-Defeating Behavior," *Journal of Personality and Social Psychology* 83, no. 3 (2002): 606-15; Roy G. Baumeister, Jean M. Twenge, and Christopher K. Nuss, "Effects of Social Exclusion on Cognitive Processes: Anticipated Aloneness Reduces Intelligent Thought," *Journal of Personality and Social Psychology* 83, no. 4 (October 2002): 817-27.

Most socially excluded teens do not commit violence, but some do. Charles "Andy" Williams, whom peers derided as a "freak, dork, nerd, stuff like that," went on a shooting spree at his suburban California high school, killing two and wounding thirteen.[12] Columbine, Colorado, killers Eric Harris and Dylan Klebold were similarly on the fringes of their school's social networks. Virginia Tech mass murderer Seung-Hui Cho was reportedly bullied and mocked by high school classmates for his extreme shyness.

Experiments have probed the ostracism effect. People who are left out of a simple ball-tossing game feel deflated and stressed. Kipling Williams and his colleagues were surprised to discover a toll even from "cyber-ostracism" by faceless people whom one will never meet. Such ostracism elicits heightened activity in a brain area, the anterior cingulate cortex, that also is activated in response to physical pain. Ostracism, it seems, *is* a real pain.

Williams and four of his colleagues personally experienced ostracism's effects in a little experiment on themselves, as each was ignored for an agreed-upon day by the four others. Contrary to their expectations that this would be a laughter-filled role-playing game, the simulated ostracism disrupted work, interfered with pleasant social functioning, and "caused temporary concern, anxiety, paranoia, and general fragility of spirit." To frustrate our need to belong is to unsettle our lives.

When prolonged, an unmet need to belong can foster depression. American Psychological Association past-president Martin Seligman notes that rates of depression have soared as kinship connections have waned.[13] He believes that depression is especially common among young Westerners because of the epidemic hopelessness that stems from the rise of individualism and the decline of commitment to faith and family. When facing failure or rejection, contends Seligman, the self-focused individual takes on personal responsibility for problems and has nothing to fall back on for hope. A well-connected person is a well-supported person. A lonely person is an unhappy person.

To be "wretched" literally means, in its Middle English origin

---

12. Scott Bowles and Martin Kasindorf, "Friends Tell of Picked-On but 'Normal' Kid," *USA Today*, March 6, 2001, p. 4A.

13. Martin E. P. Seligman, *Learned Optimism* (New York: Knopf, 1991). See also Ed Diener and Martin Seligman, "Beyond Money: Toward an Economy of Well-Being," *Psychological Science in the Public Interest* 5, no. 1 (2004): 1-31.

(*wrecche*), to be without kin nearby. Indeed, children reared in institutions without normal social attachments, or locked away at home under extreme neglect, often do become wretched — withdrawn, frightened, speechless. After studying the mental health of homeless children for the World Health Organization, psychiatrist John Bowlby asserted that "intimate attachments to other human beings are the hub around which a person's life revolves" and that this is true in every stage of life from infancy to old age. He wrote that intimate attachments reciprocally provide strength and enjoyment to each individual in the relationship. "These are matters about which current science and traditional wisdom are at one," he concluded.[14]

Among adults, jealousy, guilt, and loneliness all involve a disrupted need to belong. With their need to belong thwarted, the bereaved often feel life is empty and pointless. Exile, imprisonment, and solitary confinement are progressively more severe forms of punishment.

A caveat: Cultures vary in individualism and connectedness. Although people everywhere are social creatures, cultures differ. In 1831, the French writer Alexis de Tocqueville coined the term "individualism" after traveling in America. Individualists, he noted, owe no one "anything and hardly expect anything from anybody. They form the habit of thinking of themselves in isolation and imagine that their whole destiny is in their hands." A century and a half later, psychotherapist Fritz Perls (1972) epitomized this radical individualism in his "Gestalt prayer":

> I do my thing, and you do your thing.
> I am not in this world to live up to your expectations.
> And you are not in this world to live up to mine.

Psychologist Carl Rogers (1985) agreed: "The only question which matters is, 'Am I living in a way which is deeply satisfying to me, and which truly expresses me?'"

That is hardly the only question that matters to people in many other cultures, including those of Asia, South America, and most of Africa, note cross-cultural psychologists. Where *community* is prized, conformity is accepted. Schoolchildren often display their solidarity by wearing uniforms; many workers do the same. To maintain harmony,

---

14. John Bowlby, *Loss, Sadness, and Depression*, vol. 3 of *Attachment and Loss* (London: Basic Books, 1980).

confrontation and dissent are muted. "The stake that stands out gets pounded down," say the Japanese.

The distinction between Western individualism and Asian "collectivism" can be overstated. Americans, for example, score high on belonging to groups, welcoming others' advice, and valuing personal relationships.[15] Yet they do place less priority on group harmony and doing one's duty. Sociologist Amitai Etzioni (1993) therefore advocates a "communitarian" individualism that balances our nonconformist individualism with a spirit of community. Fellow sociologist Robert Bellah (1996) concurs. "Communitarianism is based on the value of the sacredness of the individual," he explains. But it also "affirms the central value of solidarity . . . that we become who we are through our relationships."

As Westerners in various nations, most readers of this book enjoy the benefits of nonconformist individualism. Communitarians remind us that we also are social creatures having a basic need to belong. Conformity is neither all bad nor all good. We therefore do well to balance our "me" and our "we," our needs for independence and for attachment, our individuality and our social identity.

Social Support

Massive survey and epidemiological evidence further confirms our essential social nature. Social support — feeling liked, affirmed, and encouraged by intimate friends and family — promotes both happiness and health. Supportive family members, marriage partners, close friends, and even companionable pets help people live longer, happier lives and to cope with stressful events.

Social support and happiness. Among the strongest predictors of self-reported happiness are human attachments. Being attached to friends with whom we can share intimate thoughts has two effects, observed Francis Bacon: "It redoubleth joys, and cutteth griefs in half."[16] And so it seems from answers to a question asked of Americans by the National Opinion Research Center: "Looking over the last six months,

---

15. Marilyn Brewer and Ya-Ru Chen, "Where (Who) Are Collective in Collectivism? Toward Conceptual Clarification of Individualism and Collectivism," *Psychological Review* 114 (2007): 133-51.

16. Francis Bacon, "Of Friendship," in *Essays, Civil and Moral* (New York: P. F. Collier & Son, 1909).

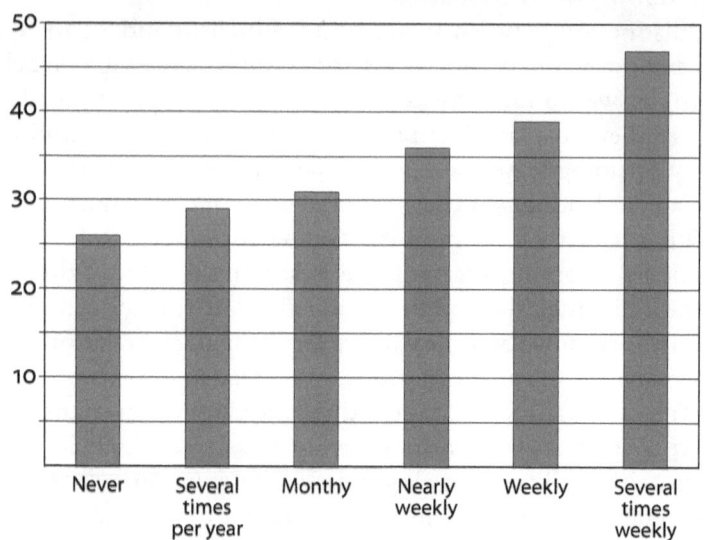

who are the people with whom you discussed matters of importance to you?" Compared to those who could name no such intimate, those who named five or more such friends were 60 percent more likely to feel "very happy."[17]

Social support is one explanation for the common finding that actively religious people express relatively high levels of happiness (see the graph above). For their active members, faith communities are social support networks — people who are there for one another in life's good times and bad.

Close friendships enable us to be known and accepted as we are. When social anxiety is replaced by trust, we become free to open up, to *self-disclose*. To lack opportunities for self-disclosure — for sharing our likes and dislikes, our proud and embarrassing moments, our worries and our dreams — is to feel lonely. "When I am with my friend," reflected the Roman statesman Seneca, "methinks I am alone, and as much at liberty to speak anything as to think it."[18]

17. Ronald S. Burt, "Strangers, Friends and Happiness," *GSS Technical Report*, no. 72 (Chicago: National Opinion Research Center, University of Chicago, 1986).
18. Seneca (60 CE), *Seneca of a Happy Life*, in *Morals*.

Percent "Very Happy" among Married and Never Married Americans
(NORC surveys, 1972-2004)

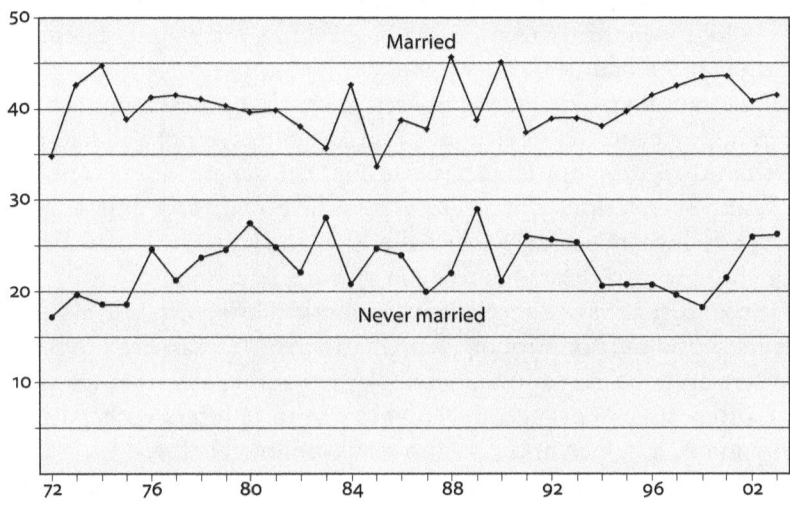

Happiness promotes self-disclosure (in a good mood we open up; in a bad mood we clam up). But intimacy also promotes happiness. Having someone with whom to discuss threats to our well-being helps us cope. Experiments confirm the benefits of sharing rather than suppressing stressful experiences. In one, Stephen Lepore and his colleagues[19] had students view a stressful slide show and video on the Holocaust and either talk about it immediately afterward or not. Two days later, those who talked were experiencing less stress and fewer intrusive thoughts. Even mentally revisiting a recent problem that was still "stressing you out" — vividly recalling the incident and associated feelings — served to boost active coping and mood.[20]

For many people, marriage is intimate friendship sealed with commitment. The graph above, which presents data from nearly 43,000 randomly sampled Americans, indicates that marital status is one of the strongest predictors of happiness. The marriage-happiness correla-

---

19. Steven J. Lepore, Jennifer D. Ragan, and Scott Jones, "Talking Facilitates Cognitive-Emotional Processes of Adaptation to an Acute Stressor," *Journal of Personality and Social Psychology* 78, no. 3 (March 2000): 499-508.

20. Inna D. Rivkin and Shelley E. Taylor, "The Effects of Mental Stimulation on Coping with Controllable Stressful Events," *Personality and Social Psychology Bulletin* 25, no. 12 (1999): 1451-62.

tion isn't perfect. There are miserable marriages and joyful singles. But it extends across countries and both genders (contrary to one of pop psychology's myths that, emotionally speaking, marriage is a good deal for men and a bad deal for women).

The causal arrows between marriage and happiness run both ways. First, happy people are better natured, more outgoing, and less irritable than their unhappy counterparts, and thus enjoy more — and more enduring — relationships. Misery may love company, but company does not love misery. To be unhappy (and therefore self-focused, grouchy, and withdrawn) is to be at risk for rejection.

Second, marriage, especially when marked by equity, self-disclosing intimacy, and mutual support, helps satisfy the human need to belong. It offers an antidote to loneliness. It offers additional roles (as spouse and, often, as parent) to one's identity. And it offers each partner a companion, a helper, and a secure and comfortable lover.

Whether through friendship or committed partnership, to have one's need to belong well met — to have people who celebrate when you're born, care about you as you live, and will miss you when you're gone — is a giant step toward the happy life.

Social support and health. Social connections also reduce one's risk of ill health and premature death. They foster stronger immune functioning, calm the cardiovascular system, and lower blood pressure. Consider the evidence:

Relationships can sometimes be stressful, especially in crowded living conditions lacking privacy.[21] "Hell is others," wrote Jean-Paul Sartre. Peter Warr and Roy Payne asked a representative sample of British adults what, if anything, had emotionally strained them the day before. Their most frequent answer? "Family."[22]

But asked what prompted yesterday's times of pleasure, the same British sample, by an even larger margin, again answered, "Family." For most of us, family relationships provide not only our greatest heartaches (even when well-meaning, family intrusions can be stressful) but also our greatest comfort and joy. Moreover, seven massive investigations, each following thousands of people for several years, revealed that

21. Gary W. Evans, M. N. Palsane, Stephen J. Lepore, and Janea Martin, "Residential Density and Psychological Health: The Mediating Effects of Social Support," *Journal of Personality and Social Psychology* 57, no. 6 (December 1989): 994-99.
22. Peter Warr and Roy Payne, "Experiences of Strain and Pleasure Among British Adults," *Social Science and Medicine* 16, no. 19 (1982): 1691-97.

close relationships predict health. Compared with those having few social ties, people are less likely to die prematurely if supported by close relationships with friends, family, fellow workers, members of a faith community, or other support groups.[23] Leukemia and heart disease patients also have enjoyed markedly increased survival rates if married or supported by family or friends. "Woe to one who is alone and falls and does not have another to help," observed the writer of Ecclesiastes (4:10).

Carefully controlled studies indicate that married people live longer, healthier lives than the unmarried. The National Center for Health Statistics reports that regardless of people's age, sex, race, and income, they tend to be healthier if married.[24] Married folks experience less pain from headaches and backaches, suffer less stress, drink and smoke less, and, despite being slightly more overweight, are generally healthier. A seven-decades-long Harvard study found that a good marriage at age 50 predicts healthy aging better than does a low cholesterol level at 50.[25]

Given a supportive marital partner, people receive medical attention sooner. They sleep better, cope better with stresses, and find their

---

23. Sheldon Cohen, "Psychosocial Models of the Role of Social Support in the Etiology of Physical Disease," *Health Psychology* 7, no. 3 (1988): 269-97; James S. House, Karl R. Landis, and Debra Umberson, "Social Relationships and Health," *Science* 241 (July 1988): 540-45; Nanette Nelson, *A Meta-Analysis of the Life-Event/Health Paradigm: The Influence of Social Support* (Ph.D. dissertation, Temple University, 1988); R. B. Case, A. J. Moss, N. Case, M. McDermott, and S. Eberly, "Living Alone After Myocardial Infarction: Impact on Prognosis," *Journal of the American Medical Association* 267, no. 4 (January 22/29, 1999): 515-19; Eduardo A. Colon, Allan L. Callies, Michael K. Popkin, and Philip B. McGlave, "Depressed Mood and Other Variables Related to Bone Marrow Transplantation Survival in Acute Leukemia," *Psychosomatics* 32, no. 4 (Fall 1991): 420-25; R. B. Williams, J. C. Barefoot, R. M. Califf, T. L. Haney, W. B. Saunders, D. B. Pryor, M. A. Hlatky, I. C. Siegler, and D. B. Mark, "Prognostic Importance of Social and Economic Resources Among Medically Treated Patients with Angiographically Documented Coronary Artery Disease," *Journal of the American Medical Association* 267, no. 4 (January 22/29, 1992): 520-24; John E. Murray, "Marital Protection and Marital Selection: Evidence from a Historical-Prospective Sample of American Men," *Demography* 37, no. 4 (2000): 511-21; Chris M. Wilson and Andrew J. Oswald, "How Does Marriage Affect Physical and Psychological Health? A Survey of the Longitudinal Evidence," working paper, University of York and Warwick University, 2002.

24. National Center for Health Statistics, Charlotte A. Schoenborn, "Marital Status and Health: United States, 1999-2002," *Advance Data from Vital and Human Statistics*, no. 351, Centers for Disease Control and Prevention (December 15, 2004).

25. George Vaillant, *Aging Well: Surprising Guideposts to a Happier Life from the Landmark Harvard Study of Adult Development* (Boston: Little, Brown, 2002).

self-esteem bolstered when wounded by others' slings and arrows. They also eat better, exercise more, and drink and smoke less. (One study of 50,000 young adults found that unhealthy behaviors dropped sharply after marriage; another study of 30,000 men found that when a marriage ended, vegetable consumption plummeted and fried food and alcohol consumption spiked.[26])

Does the marriage-health correlation mean merely that healthy people more often marry and stay married? After controlling for various possible explanations, two recent analyses independently concluded that marriage supports health. Marriage "improves survival prospects" and "makes people healthier and longer-lived."[27]

But the quality of a marriage relationship also matters. Conflict-laden marriages are not conducive to health; positive, happy, supportive ones are.[28] One five-year study following 1532 older married adults found it was even better to give than to receive. After controlling for preexisting health and personality differences, researchers observed a markedly lower risk of dying during the five-year period among those who frequently reached out to help friends and neighbors and who made their spouse feel loved and cared for.[29]

Environments that support our need to belong also foster stronger immune functioning. Given ample social support, spouses of cancer patients exhibit stronger immune functioning.[30] Social ties and positive sociability even confer resistance to cold viruses. Sheldon Cohen and his colleagues demonstrated this by putting 276 healthy volunteers in quarantine for five days after administering nasal drops laden with a cold vi-

26. Hara Estroff Marano, "Debunking the Marriage Myth: It Works for Women, Too," *New York Times,* August 4, 1998 (www.nytimes.com); Patricia Mona Eng, Ichiro Kawachi, Garrett Fitzmaurice, and Eric B. Rimm, "Effects of Marital Transitions on Changes in Dietary and Other Health Behaviours in U.S. Male Health Professionals," *Journal of Epidemiology & Community Health* 59, no. 1 (January 2005): 56-62.

27. Murray, "Marital Protection and Marital Selection," pp. 511-21; Wilson and Oswald, "How Does Marriage Affect Physical and Psychological Health?"

28. Janice K. Kiecolt-Glaser and Tamara L. Newton, "Marriage and Health: His and Hers," *Psychological Bulletin* 127, no. 4 (2001): 472-503.

29. Stephanie L. Brown, Randolph M. Nesse, Amiram D. Vinokur, and Dylan M. Smith, "Providing Social Support May Be More Beneficial Than Receiving It: Results from a Prospective Study of Mortality," *Psychological Science* 14, no. 4 (2003): 320-27.

30. Robert S. Baron, Carolyn E. Cutrona, Daniel Hicklin, Daniel W. Russell, and David M. Lubaroff, "Social Support and Immune Function Among Spouses of Cancer Patients," *Journal of Personality and Social Psychology* 59, no. 2 (August 1990): 344-52.

rus, and then repeating the experiment with 334 more volunteers.[31] (In both experiments, the volunteers were paid $800 each to endure this experience.) The cold fact is that the effect of social ties is nothing to sneeze at. Age, race, sex, smoking, and other health habits being equal, those with the most social ties were least likely to catch a cold and they produced less mucus. More sociability meant less susceptibility. More than fifty studies further reveal that social support calms the cardiovascular system, lowering blood pressure and stress hormones.[32]

Close relationships also provide the opportunity to *confide* painful feelings, a social support component that has now been extensively researched in studies of health as well as happiness. In one study, health psychologists James Pennebaker and Robin O'Heeron contacted the surviving spouses of people who had committed suicide or died in car accidents.[33] Those who bore their grief alone had more health problems than those who could express it openly. Talking about our troubles can be "open heart therapy." Friendships are good medicine.

Older people, many of whom have lost a spouse and close friends, are somewhat less likely to confide often. Moreover, suppressing emotions is sometimes detrimental to our physical health. When Pennebaker surveyed more than 700 undergraduate women, he found that about one in twelve reported a traumatic sexual experience in childhood. Compared with women who had experienced nonsexual traumas, such as parental death or divorce, the sexually abused women — especially those who had kept their secret to themselves — reported more headaches and stomach ailments.

In a simulated confessional, Pennebaker asked volunteers to share with a hidden experimenter some upsetting events that had been prey-

---

31. Sheldon Cohen, W. J. Doyle, D. P. Skoner, B. S. Rabin, and J. M. Gwaltney Jr., "Social Ties and Susceptibility to the Common Cold," *Journal of the American Medical Association* 277, no. 24 (1997): 1940-45; Sheldon Cohen, "Social Relationships and Health," *American Psychologist* 59, no. 8 (November 2004): 676-84.

32. Bert N. Uchino, John T. Cacioppo, and Janice K. Kiecolt-Glaser, "The Relationship Between Social Support and Physiological Processes: A Review with Emphasis on Underlying Mechanisms and Implications for Health," *Psychological Bulletin* 119, no. 3 (1996): 488-532; Bert N. Uchino, Darcy Uno, and Julianne Holt-Lunstad, "Social Support, Physiological Processes, and Health," *Current Directions in Psychological Science* 8, no. 5 (1999): 141-48.

33. James W. Pennebaker and Robin C. O'Heeron, "Confiding in Others and Illness Rate Among Spouses of Suicide and Accidental-Death Victims," *Journal of Abnormal Psychology* 93, no. 4 (November 1984): 473-76.

ing on their minds. He asked some of the volunteers to describe a trivial event before they divulged the troubling one. Physiological measures revealed that their bodies remained tense the whole time they talked about the trivial event; they relaxed only when they later confided the cause of their turmoil.

Writing about personal traumas in a diary can also help.[34] When volunteers in one experiment did this, they had fewer health problems during the ensuing four to six months.[35] As one participant explained, "Although I have not talked with anyone about what I wrote, I was finally able to deal with it, work through the pain instead of trying to block it out. Now it doesn't hurt to think about it."

Pennebaker and his colleagues also invited thirty-three Holocaust survivors to spend two hours recalling their experiences.[36] Many did so in intimate detail never before disclosed. In the weeks following, most watched a videotape of their recollections and showed it to family and friends. Those who were most self-disclosing had the most improved health fourteen months later. Talking about a stressful event can temporarily arouse people, but in the long run it calms them.[37] Confiding is good for the soul and good for the body. And confiding most often comes not with fleeting relationships and hookups, but with enduring, close relationships and lifelong partnerships.

So, it is indeed not good for the human to be alone. We humans have a basic need to belong. We seek relationships. We thrive most happily and healthily when supported by close, intimate, enduring relationships. "The sun looks down on nothing half so good as a household laughing together over a meal," offered C. S. Lewis.[38]

---

34. Scott H. Hemenover, "The Good, the Bad, and the Healthy: Impacts of Emotional Disclosure of Trauma on Resilient Self-Concept and Psychological Distress," *Personality and Social Psychology Bulletin* 29, no. 10 (October 2003): 1236-44. Sonja Lyubomirsky, Laura King, and Ed Diener, "The Benefits of Frequent Positive Affect: Does Happiness Lead to Success?" *Psychological Bulletin* 131, no. 6 (2005): 803-55.

35. James W. Pennebaker, *Opening Up: The Healing Power of Confiding in Others* (New York: W. Morrow, 1990).

36. James W. Pennebaker, Steven D. Barger, and John Tiebout, "Disclosure of Traumas and Health Among Holocaust Survivors," *Psychosomatic Medicine* 51, no. 5 (September-October 1989): 577-89.

37. Marilyn Mendolia and Robert E. Kleck, "Effects of Talking about a Stressful Event on Arousal: Does What We Talk about Make a Difference?" *Journal of Personality and Social Psychology* 64, no. 2 (February 1993): 283-92.

38. C. S. Lewis, *The Weight of Glory and Other Addresses* (New York: Macmillan, 1949).

The human need to belong has practical implications for our private lives and our public policies. It reminds us to attend to our relationships, to not take our friends and partners for granted, to show them the same kindness we display to those we wish to impress, to affirm them, to play, pray, and share together. It also mandates a more relationships-supportive ecology. Given that well-being "rests on strong family and relationship ties," note happiness researchers Ed Diener and Martin Seligman, "we would argue that government policies should be aimed at cementing social ties. This could mean offering tax breaks to married couples (a conservative proposal) and it could mean adopting marriage for gay and lesbian couples (a liberal position)."[39]

Family Connections and Children's Well-Being

What's true of adults is also true of children: stable relationships predict well-being. Compared to children without two co-supportive parents (and usually without involved fathers), children raised in stable two-parent homes are at decreased risk for poverty, school dropout, delinquency, emotional disorder, and substance abuse. The association between divorce and teen pathology "is a closer association than between smoking and cancer," observed developmental psychologist E. Mavis Hetherington.[40]

We need to be careful not to overstate the point: most kids in nontraditional families grow up healthy, and some kids in nurturing two-parent families struggle with depression, delinquency, and drugs. Still, the correlation between family structure and pathology occurs across families, across neighborhoods, and over time. Show a social scientist a place and time where nearly all children are co-parented by two adults who are enduringly committed to each other and their children, and the scientist will show you a place and time with relatively low rates of poverty, disorder, and social pathology.[41] (This effect results *not* pri-

---

39. Diener and Seligman, "Beyond Money: Toward an Economy of Well-Being," pp. 1-31.

40. E. Mavis Hetherington, "Marriage and Divorce American Style: A Destructive Marriage Is Not a Happy Family," *American Prospect*, April 8, 2002 (www.prospect.org).

41. Behavior geneticists remind us that biological parents and their children share genes. For example, compared to men who propagate and stay, those who propagate and leave may be more impulsive (and therefore crime-prone) — and so may the children

marily from married parents shaping their children differently or having different values, but rather from healthier school, neighborhood, and peer influences that ride along with intact families.[42])

Although poverty is associated with (and is a consequence of) family dissolution, a little-known set of studies reveals that there's more to the family structure effect than income loss. First, stepparent families have incomes similar to those of originally intact families, but higher rates of child pathology. Consider, too, the National Center for Health Statistics' 1981 Child Health Survey of 15,416 randomly sampled children and its 1988 repeat of this survey with 17,110 more children.[43] The lead researcher, Nicholas Zill, recognized that intact and broken families differ in many ways: race, children's ages, parental education, income, and family size. So he statistically adjusted scores to extract such influences. In the first survey, those living with both parents were nonetheless *half* as likely as those living with a never or formerly married mother to have been suspended or expelled from school or to have had misbehavior reported by the school.[44] The follow-up survey confirmed these essential findings. Ergo, family breakup is not just a proxy for poverty.

Perhaps, then, conservatives and liberals find common ground in welcoming a more marriage- and family-supportive culture — one that

- welcomes children into families with parents that love them, and into an environment that nurtures families,
- encourages close relationships within extended families and with supportive neighbors and caring friends,

---

who carry their genes. Genetics cannot, however, account for the joint decline of both marriage and child well-being between 1960 and the early 1990s. Cultures can change quickly; genes cannot.

42. See Judith Rich Harris, *The Nuture Assumption* (New York: Free Press, 1998).

43. Nicholas Zill, "Behavior, Achievement, and Health Problems Among Children in Stepfamilies: Findings from a National Survey of Child Health," in *Impact of Divorce, Single Parenting, and Stepparenting on Children,* ed. E. Mavis Hetherington and Josephine D. Arasteh (Hillsdale, NJ: Erlbaum, 1988). The 1988 survey is summarized in a 1991 report by Deborah A. Dawson, "Family Structure and Children's Health: United States, 1988," *Vital Health Statistics, Series 10: Data from the National Health Survey, No. 178* (Hyattsville, MD: National Center for Statistics, U.S. Department of Health and Human Services, DHHS Publication No. PHS 91-1506).

44. James L. Peterson and Nicholas Zill, "Marital Disruption, Parent-Child Relationships, and Behavior Problems in Children," *Journal of Marriage and the Family* 48, no. 2 (May 1986): 295-307.

- values our diversity while finding unity in shared ideals,
- develops children's capacities for empathy, self-discipline, and honesty,
- provides media that offer social scripts of kindness, civility, attachment, and fidelity,
- and regards sexuality as life-uniting and love-renewing.

Whether liberal or conservative, feminist or fundamentalist, these are among our shared values. With such common values and aspirations agreed upon, could we engage a national dialogue about how best to realize them? Could we affirm liberals' efforts to reduce the demoralizing effects of poverty and conservatives' efforts to encourage positive media? Liberals' support for family-friendly workplaces and conservatives' support for marriage? Liberals' advocacy for children in all sorts of families and conservatives' support for co-parenting?

Conclusion

Contemporary psychological science strongly affirms ancient biblical wisdom: it is not good for humans to be alone. We humans have a basic need to belong, which historically has supported human survival and is manifest in our longing for belonging, our desire for approval and close relationships, and our experiences of the pain of ostracism. We flourish with greatest happiness and health when supported by close, enduring relationships. Children also tend to flourish when co-parented in stable, supportive families. We are indeed, as Aristotle recognized, social animals, made for relationship.

ARCHAEOLOGY AND
PALEOANTHROPOLOGY

What Is a Human? Anthropological Perspectives on the Origins of Humanness

Alison S. Brooks

[I]t would be impossible to fix on any point when the term "man" ought to be used.

Charles Darwin, *The Descent of Man*

Defining Human, Early Scientific Efforts

During the late seventeenth and eighteenth centuries, natural historians and biologists wrestled with the problem of defining humans within new conceptualizations of the natural world. In the context of the first anatomical studies of great apes, they found morphology (anatomical shape) alone was insufficient to achieve the appropriate degree of distinctiveness they felt was warranted, so many definitions and discussions fell back on distinctions in behavior such as language, innovation, or technology. In 1699, Tyson, in the first description of chimpanzee anatomy, named the chimpanzee *Homo sylvestris*, arguing that it was only the soul that differentiated this animal from ourselves, the brain and other anatomical parts being remarkably similar. Buffon (1749-67) wrote: "If our judgement were limited to figure [morphology] alone, I acknowledge that the ape might be regarded as a variety of the human species." Linnaeus in 1735 put *Homo sapiens* in the same order as the chimpanzee *(Homo troglodytes)* (Bendysche 1863), but Blumenbach (1779-80) and Lamarck (1809) put humans in a separate order, *Bimana*, emphasizing our reliance on bipedalism and free hands for making tools. However, Blumenbach's (1779-80) definition of human, *"Homo, erectus bimanus, mentum prominulum, dentes aequaliter approximati, incisores inferiores erecti,*" would have excluded not only all the apes but also the large number of fossil human ancestors without chins. Lacking fossil evidence for human evolution, some early systematists who dealt only with living populations saw behavioral continuity from humans to "wild children" who lacked the essential ability to speak, to apes. Newly discovered peoples, such as the "Hottentots" of southern Africa, were sometimes accorded a less-than-human status.

The Fossil Record of Human Evolution

Beginning in the nineteenth century, the discovery of fossil remains attributable to human ancestors forced scientists to develop more explicit anatomical criteria for inclusion in the human lineage. Although the first discoveries bore the clearest resemblance to current humans and were associated with the bones of extinct animals, their robust skeletons were seen as evidence for a life of hard labor and possible disease in historic (e.g., Roman) times, and their great antiquity and associations were questioned. One of the earliest was the discovery by William Buckland (1823), reader in mineralogy at Oxford, of the "Red Lady of Paviland," which later research showed to be a ca. 26,000-year-old male burial in Paviland Cave near Swansea in Wales, with red ocher and ivory ornaments (Aldhouse-Green 1998). Despite the associated bones of extinct animals, Buckland interpreted this skeleton to be the remains of a camp follower of the Roman army, encamped nearby. "Whatever may have been her occupation, the vicinity of a camp would afford a motive for residence as well as the means of subsistence in what is now so exposed and uninviting a solitude" (Buckland 1823, p. 90). When even older fossils of Neanderthals began to turn up, beginning around 1835 with the first fossil Neanderthals from Engis in Belgium (Schmerling 1833-34), these also were attributed by Buckland and others (Grayson 1983) to socially marginal historic Europeans, as were the finds from the Neander Valley itself in 1856.[1]

---

1. It should be noted that nineteenth-century physical anthropologists and anatomists argued that skeletons of the European lower classes were physically distinctive, bearing a slightly closer resemblance to apes in the shape of the forehead, chin, and upright stance (Gould 1996).

Yet by the 1860s, the great antiquity of human ancestors and their association with extinct faunas in Europe had been demonstrated to the satisfaction of many natural scientists through archaeological finds in France and elsewhere. Beads, engraved bones, and other objects that were clearly of human manufacture had been recovered in association with extinct animals, including fossil elephants, rhinoceroses, monkeys, and cave bears (Lartet 1861). The establishment of the antiquity of life thus depended on parallel discoveries in stratigraphy, comparative anatomy, and geology, while acceptance of the antiquity of humanity depended in addition on emerging discoveries in paleontology.

Comparative anatomy and the geographic distribution of the apes most similar to humans had led Darwin (1871) to locate the likely origin place of humans in Africa. Only in 1891, however, was the first fossil attributed to a human ancestor recovered from outside Europe, not from Africa but from Trinil in Indonesia (Dubois 1894). Haeckel (1868) had already named the putative "missing link" between apes and humans *"Pithecanthropus alalus"* ("ape-man without speech"), but Dubois, struck by the human aspect of the femur found at Trinil (now thought to be the femur of a modern person and not associated with the fossil skull) preferred to emphasize the erect bipedal gait of his fossil: *"Pithecanthropus erectus."* This fossil, with its cranial capacity of only 900 cc, was incorporated later into the genus *Homo* as a separate species: *Homo erectus*. It had two important implications: that bipedalism was well established before the brain became modern, and that the early chapters in the story took place outside the European continent.

The first African fossils of Pliocene or Pleistocene Age relevant to human evolution were recovered only in 1924 at Singa (Sudan) and Taung (South Africa) (Woodward 1938, Dart 1925). The ca. 2-2.5 million-year-old Taung specimen of a small child with a chimpanzee-sized brain became the type fossil of *Australopithecus* (Dart 1925), a genus that is probably ancestral to our own *(Homo)*, and provided support for Darwin's inference that humans originated in Africa. The Singa skull, on the other hand, at prior to ca. 133 thousand years ago (kya) had a relatively large brain cavity, high forehead, but robust brow ridges, placing it close to the origin of our own species *Homo sapiens* in the late Middle Pleistocene (McDermott et al. 1996).

Since the 1920s, Pleistocene-age (1.8-0.01 million years ago [mya]) fossil specimens belonging in the hominin lineage[2] have been recovered at an accelerating pace from Europe, Asia, Africa, and Australia, and now total more than a thousand individuals, many represented only by isolated teeth. Africa has yielded the oldest members of the lineage (Senut et al. 2001, Brunet et al. 2002, Haile-Selassie 2001, Haile-Selassie and WoldeGabriel 2009), the oldest artifacts (Semaw 2000, Semaw et al. 2003, Roche et al. 1999), the oldest members of our genus *Homo* (Kimbel et al. 1996, Deino and Hill 2002, Sherwood et al. 2002), and the oldest members of the species *Homo sapiens* (White et al. 2003, McDougall et al. 2005). Multiple genetic studies of mitochondrial, Y-chromosome, and nuclear DNA conclude that the greatest variability, the most ancestral lineages, and the likely region of origin all concur in indicating an African homeland for modern humans.

The hominin tree is bushiest at its Pliocene (5-1.8 million years ago) base, where we have relatively little fossil evidence (Figure 1). After ca. 1.4 mya, at the end of the early Pleistocene, all subsequent fossils are attributed to a small number (2-7) of species within the genus *Homo,* and most of these named species are either geographically or temporally distinct, rather than living at the same place and time.

The impressive complexity of the hominin fossil record has clarified some of the features that distinguished our lineage at an early stage from that of our closest simian relatives, as well as the order in which these distinctions appear. While we have very little evidence of chimpanzee or gorilla ancestry during the Plio-Pleistocene epochs of human emergence, studies of ancestral apes who lived more than 7 mya, prior to the ape-human split, together with comparative studies of present-day apes can help delineate what is peculiarly human. These unique human anatomical features include adaptations for bipedal locomotion, canine teeth that are similar in size and function to adjacent teeth in the dentition, adaptations for manual dexterity, and a large brain for our body size.

Bipedalism appears to have been present in the very oldest fossils attributed to the human lineage around 6 to 7 mya, based on the forward placement of the foramen magnum of *Sahelanthropus* where the spinal column enters the skull (Zollikofer et al. 2005), and on the morphology of the femur of *Orrorin tugenensis* (Richmond and Jungers

---

2. "Hominin" refers to humans and our extinct ancestors and close relatives, from the time of our divergence from the lineage of the African apes (Wood 2005).

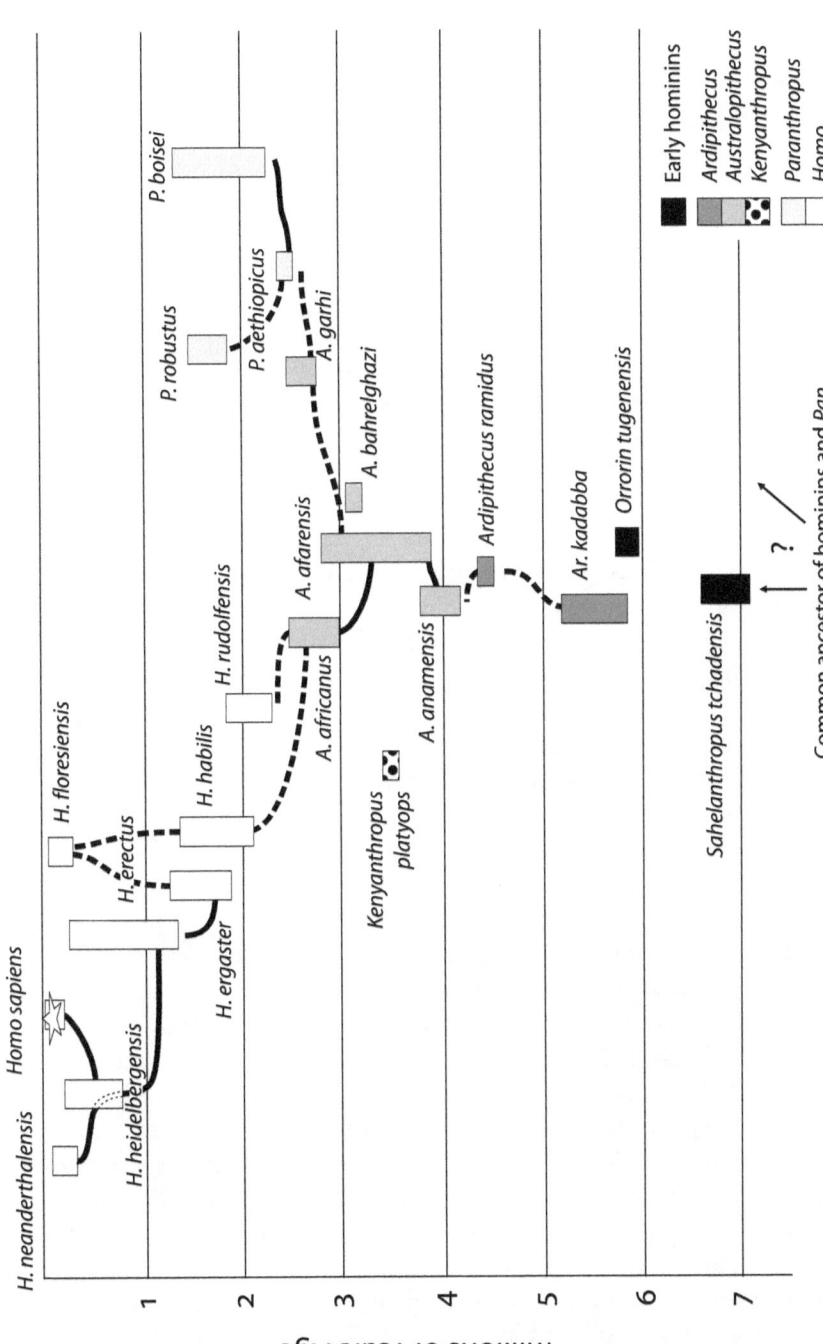

Figure 1. The hominin lineage, with dashed lines suggesting likely lines of decent (courtesy Brian Richmond). Note that relationships of the earliest hominins and of *Kenyanthropus* are unclear. *H. floresiensis* is the recently discovered small hominin from the Late Pleistocene of Flores in Indonesia, nicknamed "the Hobbit."

2008). Fully committed or obligate bipedalism, however, only appears in the genus *Homo* after 2.3 mya, and signals a commitment to terrestrial habitats, possibly including the development of endurance running as a major adaptation (Bramble and Lieberman 2004).

Ardipithecus fossils from Ethiopia, along with *Orrorin* and *Sahelanthropus*, suggest that while canine teeth, used by male apes in threat displays and occasionally as weapons in aggressive contests over social ranking, were reduced in the earliest fossils, their slashing function persisted to a certain degree in the earliest hominins (Haile-Selassie et al. 2004). While canines were further reduced in the earliest *Australopithecus afarensis* fossils from Ethiopia and Tanzania, only after 2.9 mya in the later australopithecines and early *Homo* did they reach proportions and morphology more similar to ours, suggesting a commitment to other forms of aggression or communication.

The small bones of the hand are rare in the fossil record, but those from *A. afarensis* such as "Lucy" (Figure 2a) and her Ethiopian fossil contemporaries of 3.7 to 2.9 mya and *A. africanus* (ca. 2.8-2.5 mya) show that hands by this time were capable of greater manual dexterity, with shorter palms and with fingers that could more adeptly grasp objects in opposition with the thumb (D. Green and Gordon 2008). The toe and finger bones were still somewhat curved, however, to promote tree-climbing (Stern and Susman 1983), and the wrist still exhibited a small projection, inherited from their ape ancestors, that stabilizes the wrist in African apes when walking on their knuckles (Richmond and Strait 2000).

The fossil record has demonstrated unequivocally that large brains were not a feature of early hominin evolution, but emerged only later within the genus *Homo*. The oldest members of this genus are found in Ethiopia at 2.3 mya (Kimbel et al. 1996), although a fossil temporal bone from Kenya points to the same early age for this genus throughout the East African Rift Valley (Deino and Hill 2002, Sherwood et al. 2002). Initially brain enlargement was not remarkable, teeth remained large, and body proportions suggested continued ability to navigate in the trees (Wood and Collard 1999). But by ca. 1.8 mya, brain size had increased to an average of about three-fourths the size of modern *H. sapiens*, along with full commitment to bipedalism, technology and manual dexterity, and something other than canine display for communicating relative dominance. Another increase in brain size to modern levels occurred about 700-600 kya, with no increase in body size, suggesting new and as-yet poorly understood cognitive developments. The

What Is a Human?

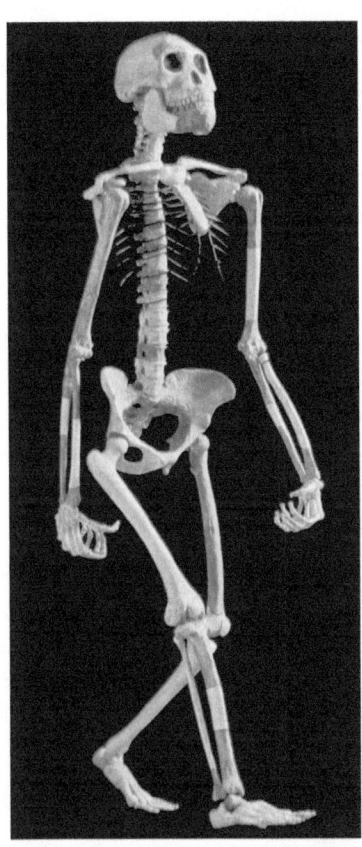
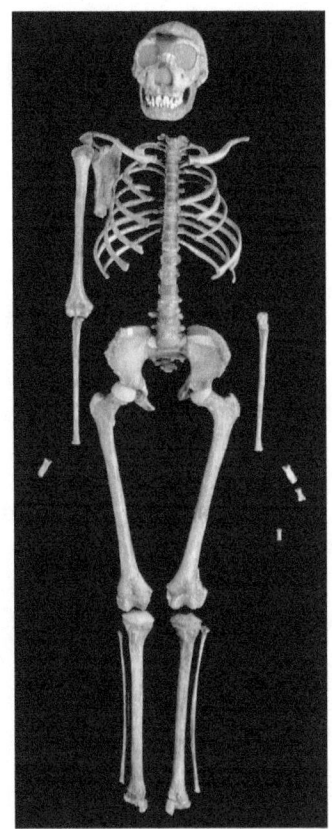
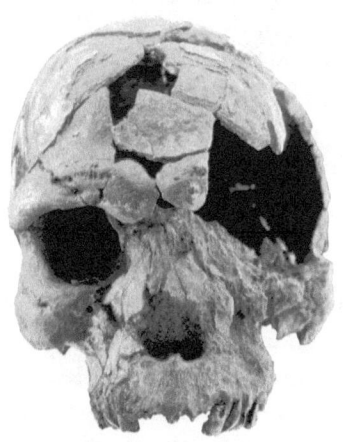

Figure 2. Fossil hominins: a) *(above left)* "Lucy" (Ethiopia) *(Australopithecus afarensis)*, reconstructed by Owen Lovejoy. Note very long arms relative to legs, curved digits. Large face, small brain, ca. 3.7-2.9 mya (courtesy Owen Lovejoy, *National Geographic*); b) *(above right)* the Nariokotome "boy" (Kenya) *Homo ergaster/erectus* 1.5 mya (species range is ca. 1.8-0.8 mya, or younger in E/SE Asia) (courtesy National Museums of Kenya or *National Geographic*?); c) *(below right)* Homo sapiens idaltu (Herto, Ethiopia) 1.61 mya, one of the oldest fossil representatives of our own species (courtesy David L. Brill/Atlanta).

oldest fossils with modern brain sizes are also African and include fossils from South, Central, and East Africa.

Clearly the expanding fossil record has blurred the morphological distinction between human and nonhuman primates that Blumenbach saw so clearly. But were all of these ancestors fully human? What do we mean by human? Are even all members of the genus *Homo* human? For that matter, anthropologists do not even agree on what should be placed in the genus *Homo*. Does it start with the appearance of stone tools 2.6 mya, the first signs of brain enlargement in Ethiopian and Kenyan fossils from 2.3 mya, or only with the humanlike suite of characteristics reflected in a complete skeleton (Figure 2b) with a larger brain, smaller teeth, modern body size, and modern limb proportions found in Kenya at 1.5 mya (Wood and Collard 1999)? Should we limit the definition of "fully human" only to members of the species *sapiens*, defined morphologically (Pearson 2000, Lieberman et al. 2004) by their large brains in relation to their body size, by their small teeth, their gracile skeletons, their chins, their minimal brow ridges and vertical foreheads, and by the way the face is tucked under the braincase, bringing the larynx closer to the mouth and tongue to facilitate speech? Can behavioral contrasts provide the distinction we seek?

Behavioral Perspectives on "What Is Human?"

Even for eighteenth- and nineteenth-century scholars, behavior played a major role in the definition of humans, as it did for Aristotle, Horace, and other ancient writers. Distinctions cited by these and other early scholars included language, shame, reason, use of fire and tools, a sense of justice, and a sense of the sacred. Once the great apes were known, these distinctions like the morphological ones became more nuanced. James Burnett (Lord Monboddo) argued in 1779-99 that orangutans and chimpanzees were human in every way — they had a guttural form of communication believed by native Indonesians to be language, and used simple stick tools. He also argued they had a sense of shame, built huts, used fire, and buried their dead, for which there is no modern evidence (Burnett 1779-99).

New research on great ape behavior has further blurred the behavioral distinctiveness of humans. All the great apes make and use simple tools, and for both chimpanzees and orangutans, tool use and other behaviors vary between populations, suggesting that a rudimentary form of "culture" is being handed down from one great ape generation to the next (Whiten et al. 1999). While spoken language is still a major defining feature of humans, many humans use other forms of communication, and apes have proven capable of learning and passing on a rudimentary ability for sign language[3] (Savage-Rumbaugh et al. 1989, Jackendorf 1999). Furthermore, there is now evidence that babies, who share with apes some of the same anatomical disadvantages in speaking, can communicate ideas in sign language long before they can talk, suggesting, if ontogeny recapitulates phylogeny, that sign language may have an older history in humans than spoken language (Petitto and Marentette 1997, Petitto et al. 2001). Psychologists (evolutionary and otherwise) are focusing on the expression, in humans, of such characteristics as "theory of mind," "ability to imitate," "empathy," "problem-solving abilities," and so on, but in almost every case, at least one of the great apes (and other animals as well) have shown a degree of these features that will not permit an absolute distinction between humans and other animals (Tomasello and Call 1997, Tomasello et al. 2005).

Genetics appears to provide another biological definition of humans, or at least of modern humans since the full decoding of the human genome in 2001. But genetic sequences, even those derived from fossils, actually do not shed much light on whether the bearers were fully human or not — only on their degree of relatedness to ourselves. The differences between the Neanderthal mitochondrial genome (R. Green et al. 2006, Noonan et al. 2006) and ours tell us nothing about the complexity of Neanderthal language(s) or whether Neanderthals shared ethical constraints, whether they held complex beliefs about death and the afterlife, whether they sang or made up poems or told stories about their ancestors. Genetics may be more informative on this issue in the future. Animal studies of behavioral genetics and the genetics of brain growth and development are just beginning to yield results (Fisher and Marcus 2006). Due to the essential unity of the genetic code in all living things, such results may carry implications for the evolution of human behavior.[4]

---

3. Their anatomy does not facilitate the rapid production and distinction of multiple speech sounds.

4. According to some calculations, humans share 98.5 percent of their DNA with chimpanzees but also about 50 percent with bananas (Wood and Constantino 2004).

ALISON S. BROOKS

Defining Human: The Archaeological Approach

If we want to study the evolution of human behavior, we must necessarily turn to the fossil and archaeological records (Brooks 1996). Fossils can reflect behavior — in the shape of bones, their chemical composition, the position and strength of muscle markings, the damages suffered over a lifetime, and the disposition of the skeletal remains. Archaeological sites are formed by definition only through human activities, although Mercader et al. (2002, 2007) have shown that chimpanzees also leave archaeological traces of their behavior. The fossil and archaeological records are limited, however, in what they can say about the past, as they require definitions of humanness that are amenable to recovery in the material record. For example, one cannot recover fossil languages, at least not until the development of writing, although dead languages can be reconstructed up to a point from words preserved in living languages. But one can recover traces of symbolic behavior (D'Errico et al. 2003), or morphological traces of changes in brain or vocal tract morphology, that suggest an ability for language. Ideologies or the capacity for abstract thought are not preserved, but one can recover traces of practices that seem to conform to ideas about spirituality — burial of the dead and cave art. Problem solving and innovativeness cannot be directly observed in the past, but one can document increases in technological sophistication and rates of innovation. And while the social networks and societies in which humans live are abstractions that must be inferred from physical evidence even in living populations, through geochemical characterization of sources, one can trace the movement of materials over very long distances, rule out natural transport, and infer the size of such networks (Gamble 1998, Féblot-Augustins 1997, 1999). In addition, from patterns of variability in the material record, it is possible to infer whether or not people distinguished themselves from their neighbors through their material culture, and what the size of the distinctive groupings might have been. Signs of empathy may also be evident in the survival of individuals with crippling injuries or major deficits, who could not have survived long on their own.

From the perspective of modern humans, behavioral definitions of humanness include what could be called "living in our heads" — in reference to the fact that we do not live in a natural world but in one of our own imagination — an imagination that has led in many cases, perhaps inadvertently, to actual transformation of the natural world. Humans think up cultural solutions to scarcity, risk, and the quest for food, shelter, and mates, resulting in an astounding diversity of cultural forms, and the transformation (and endangerment) of vast areas of the earth's surface. Since humans' teeth and their two-legged gait are utterly inadequate for defense against natural predators, humans are totally dependent on invented technologies. Rather than living in a physical herd or a pack, humans live in what Anderson (1983) has called "imagined communities," populated by individuals one may never physically encounter — distant relatives, compatriots, ancestors, and spiritual beings. Humans use symbols extensively to represent themselves, their social groups, and their thoughts. In addition, symbols are used to reify social groups to the extent that disrespect to a symbol, especially a religious symbol, is tantamount to an act of violence against a person. And humans have the ability to imagine the feelings and lives of those around us as both separate from and similar to one's own — in a way that leads to extraordinary capacities for altruism and sympathy, even for individuals one may never meet.

The capabilities of modern humans must involve at least six different faculties:

- *Abstract thinking.* This is the ability to act with reference to concepts not limited in time and space. A chimpanzee can be taught to use symbols correctly to solicit a reward, but not to go to the grocery store with a shopping list and remember that she forgot to write down the milk.
- *Planning depth.* This is the ability to strategize in group context. Social carnivores share this ability in the immediate future, but lack our ability to plan for next year, or for contingencies that may never happen.
- *Problem solving through behavioral, economic, and technological innovation.* Many animals are good problem solvers, but modern humans solve problems that have not yet arisen, and devise entirely new ways of living in the process.
- *Imagined communities* (Anderson 1983). Our present communities, from family to nation, may include people we have never met, spirits, animals, people who have died, and the not-yet-born. These communities exist in our heads, and never meet face-to-face as a group.

- *Symbolic thinking* particularly regards information storage. This involves the ability to reference both physical objects/beings and ideas with arbitrary symbols, and to act on the symbol even if the person who planted it is no longer present. It is both the arbitrariness of such symbols and their freedom from time and space constraints that distinguish our symbolic behavior from that of animals.
- *Theory of mind* (C. Sherwood et al. 2008) involves the ability to recognize oneself as a separate intelligence but at the same time to read the emotions and thoughts of others (empathy). Apes and even domestic carnivores possess this to a degree, but only modern humans possess shared intentionality (Tomasello et al. 2005) and can even recognize and respond to humanity in individuals they will never meet.

The Early Record of Behavioral Evolution 2.6-0.6 MYA

When do these abilities first appear? It is difficult to say, not only because the record is sparse and patchy but because the capability may or may not be expressed for hundreds or thousands of years after it appears, and may depend on the development of other factors, or historical events. The capability for inventing computers may have existed in the late Pleistocene, but could not be expressed without the appropriate cultural and technological milieu. The limited evidence for early expression of some of these characteristics suggests, however, that the total package was not assembled over a short period.

Problem solving and technological innovation. The first stone tools date to 2.6 mya from Ethiopia (Semaw 2000, Semaw et al. 2003), slightly later in Kenya (Kibunjia et al. 1994, Roche et al. 1999). There is little evidence for abstract thinking in these artifacts as they consist of simple flakes directly related to the form of the raw material, although the ability to choose appropriate raw materials (Stout et al. 2005) and to derive multiple flakes from a single block (Delagnes and Roche 2005) is far beyond what even the smartest apes can be taught to do. The rate of change or innovation is initially very slow; new forms such as bifacially worked symmetrical hand-axes appear only after the first 900,000 years, and tools remain very static for more than 1 mya after that. Nevertheless, such tools made it possible for early humans to shift from the largely frugivorous diet of the great apes to one involving substantial carnivory (De Heinzelin et al. 1999, e.g.), and also to expand into the Near East, Indonesia, and China, far beyond their original range, by 1.9-1.6 mya (Anton and Swisher 2004, Gabunia et al. 2000, Zhu et al. 2001, 2008, Belmaker et al. 2002, Belmaker in press). Technology also seems to have made possible a shift in food preparation from teeth to tools, so that teeth become smaller while body size increases. Early human diets were probably omnivorous, with meat obtained largely by scavenging, although the "early access" pattern of marks on some bones suggests that at least some early humans confronted felid or canid carnivores at kill sites. Fire was controlled by 0.8 mya or earlier (Goren-Inbar et al. 2004), facilitating a new diet, the use of caves, hunting, new technologies, and social time at night.

There is no evidence from this time for *imagined communities* or *symbolic thinking*. Stone and other materials appear to have largely derived from within twenty-five km of the site (Féblot-Augustins 1997, 1999), and the shapes and technologies are very similar from India to England and from France to South Africa (Petraglia and Korisettar 1997). The early presence of language in some form is also debatable, as brain asymmetries exist in early *Homo,* but modern speech would have been difficult (Lieberman and McCarthy 2007). The symmetrical forms of stone tools after 1.7 mya may have carried a symbolic meaning, but since they are also utilitarian objects, their symbolic meaning, if any, is obscure.

Empathy, which appears very early in children before competent speech, may already be reflected in a very early human skull from Dmanisi in the Caucasus at 1.9 mya (Lordkipanidze et al. 2005), of an individual who had lost almost all his teeth a considerable time before death, a condition that is rarely found in wild primates. Survival of this toothless individual required either a new, very soft diet or the assistance of others. The 1.5 mya *Homo ergaster* skeleton from Kenya also appears pathological in its vertebral column, yet survived into adolescence (Ohman et al. 2002).

The early appearance of these features does not mean they were as fully expressed as in modern humans or even that the full capacity existed as in ourselves. But it does indicate that the human capacity did not arise suddenly in full-blown form but developed or evolved over time from nonhuman antecedents.

Late Archaic Humans and Neanderthals

After 600 kya, most fossils exhibit essentially modern brain sizes, yet evidence of an increase in technological innovation, larger social networks, or symbolic behavior is minimal until ca. 400 kya. A new stone technology (Levallois) required a degree of abstract thought to imagine the flakes whose shapes were predetermined by the shaping of the

Figure 3. The oldest artifacts: a, b) *(above left top and middle)* flake and core from Gona, Ethiopia, 2.6 mya (courtesy Dietrich Stout); c) *(above right)* animal bones cut and broken open with stone tools, Bouri, Ethiopia, 2.6 mya (National Museum of Ethiopia, Addis Ababa; © 1999 David L. Brill/Atlanta); d) *(above left bottom)* refitted core and flakes, showing complexity of flaking sequence, Lokalalei 2C, Kenya, 2.34 mya (courtesy Hélène Roche; © MPK/WTAP).

What Is a Human?

Figure 4. Early traces of symbolic behavior before the oldest *Homo sapiens:* a) *(above top)* possible crude human figure — natural stone with groove delimiting the head, Berekhat Ram, Israel, ca. 250-280 kya (courtesy Francesco D'Errico); b) *(above middle and bottom)* ocher, Olorgesailie, Kenya, 220 kya (A. S. Brooks).

cores (Boeda 1995, Schlanger 1996, Tryon 2006, Monnier et al. 2006). The increased use of ocher in Africa might suggest body painting or alternatively a more utilitarian function (McBrearty and Brooks 2000, Barham 1998, Lombard 2005). And in Israel and Morocco, two slightly modified stones with traces of ocher dating to between 500 and 200 kya may or may not represent crude human images (D'Errico and Nowell 2000, Bednarik 2003). Wooden spears or javelins from Germany and numerous remains of large animals imply a more complex hunting technology (Thieme 1997), which may have facilitated the occupation of much higher temperate latitudes by 600 kya, especially in Europe (Parfitt et al. 2005). One cave in Spain contains the remains of more than thirty individuals, mostly children and young adults, who lived ca. 400 kya. It is unclear if this concentration was due to deliberate disposal of the dead or some other factor (Arsuaga et al. 1997).

Neanderthals, who occupied Eurasia as far east as Uzbekistan between ca. 250 and 40 kya, were significantly more like modern humans in their behavior than their predecessors. They buried their dead, but without clear evidence of grave goods or associated symbols (Pettit 2001), used black and red mineral pigments found as powder, lumps, and "crayons," made stone-tipped spears (Boëda et al. 1998), and were competent hunters of large game (Mellars 1996, Chase 1989). Their fossil remains bear traces of both interpersonal aggression, in the form of a knife wound (Trinkaus 1983), and empathy, as elderly and handicapped individuals survived for much longer periods than previously. Evidence of cannibalism is also found at many sites (Defleur et al. 2000). Although Neanderthals occupied Europe for at least 200 kya, their technology shows very little innovation or regional differentiation until the end of this time. The Neanderthal brain was similar in size to ours when adjusted for their large body mass, but the relationship of the tongue and soft palate to the laryngeal space suggests that they may still not have been capable of all the complex speech sounds made by modern humans (Lieberman and McCarthy 2007). Clear evidence of symbolic behavior in the form of personal ornaments is only found at the most recent Neanderthal sites, dating to a time when anatomically modern humans were already on their periphery (Mellars 2006). Does this mean they possessed a capacity for innovation and symbolic behavior, or only a facility for imitation (Zilhao 2006)?

Into the 1970s it was thought that modern humans evolved in Europe. But with the advent of new fossils and better dating techniques, it became clear that the oldest anatomically *"Homo sapiens"* fossils were African. The oldest fossil attributed to *Homo sapiens* in Africa (McDougall et al. 2005) is more than five times as old as the oldest *Homo sapiens* in Europe. At the same time, genetic studies demonstrated that all living humans share a "recent" African common ancestor who lived between 100 and 200 kya, or more, while one group of African genetic lineages shares a common ancestor with all non-Africans that is considerably younger, perhaps 40-80,000 years ago. Although at first this result was disputed, repeated genetic analyses have confirmed our African origin. DNA sequences have been recovered from twelve Neanderthals who lived as far apart as Spain and Siberia, and the resulting sequences share similarities with one another but indicate at least three regional populations (Fabre et al. 2009) and contain many sequences not shared with living humans, suggesting around 600 kya or more of separate evolution (R. Green et al. 2006, Noonan et al. 2006).

The rapid appearance of modern-looking people in Europe was not some punctuated "human revolution" or "great leap forward" but was clearly an invasion of people with long tropical limb proportions (Pearson 2001). Asia has a more complicated but equally punctuated history, also suggesting invasion and ultimate dominance by outsiders (Akazawa et al. 1998). Indeed the first "out-of-Africa" migrations of *Homo sapiens* were to the Near East, with modern humans appearing first at Skhul and Qafzeh in Israel between ca. 110 and 90 kya, an initial wave that does not appear to have spread beyond this region until 50-60 ka. Modern humans then disappear from the Levant, as Levantine fossils from 90-50 ka are all Neanderthals (Hublin 2000), then re-expand at or before ca. 50 kya. Whether they used a northern route out of Africa via the Nile valley, or another "southern route" over the Bab-el-Mandeb strait (Foster and Matsumara 2005), they reached Australia by at least 50 kya and possibly slightly earlier (Stringer 1999, O'Connell and Allen 2004).

Becoming Fully Human: The Later Evolution of Behavior

The earliest *Homo sapiens* in Europe and Asia, ca. 40 kya and later, were almost certainly capable of the same range of behaviors as we are, as indicated by their cave paintings (Clottes 2000), sculptures (Conard 2003), musical instruments, beads and other jewelry (D'Errico et al. 2003), trade networks, technological innovations, regional diversity, economic flexibility, and ability to colonize the entire globe. About earlier humans in Africa who were physically similar to ourselves in many ways, there is considerable debate. Scholars like Richard Klein (2001 e.g.) argue that they were physically modern but behaviorally primitive. To him and others, modern behavior came about suddenly, a "Human Revolution" tied to a rapidly spreading genetic mutation for language. Sally McBrearty and I have argued otherwise, that the capabilities for these behaviors began to be expressed and therefore existed *before* modern physical appearance, with a gradual assembly of the kinds of behaviors we see later (McBrearty and Brooks 2000). This assembly was not unilineal but geographically and temporally spotty, with many reversals.

As archaeologists, we look especially for technological innovation and complexity as proxies for problem solving, long-distance exchange as a proxy for both planning depth and imagined communities, economic intensification (another proxy for problem solving and planning depth), regional styles that change over time (proxies for symbolic thinking and/or imagined communities), and beads, images, and notational pieces along with burial of the dead as proxies for symbolic thinking and theory of mind. For all of these material expressions of behavioral capabilities, there are modern, even living groups that lack them. While demonstrably capable of producing such items, they clearly lack the impetus or the history to do so, so absence may not be a good marker of nonmodernity. But absence of all of these over long archaeological stretches of time cannot be characterized as "modern behavior."

The rest of this paper will focus on three particular expressions of behavioral capabilities: technological innovation, long-distance exchange, and symbolic behavior. Since modern humans evolved in Africa, one should look particularly at the African evidence, which is still very scanty. There are more excavated sites dating to 250-35 kya in southwestern France than in the vast African continent. In particular the more typical tropical regions of Africa are poorly known; most of the evidence comes from the temperate regions at the northern and southern edges of the continent. Despite the limited quality of the evidence, more than 150 sites testify to the gradual assembly of innovative, social, and symbolic behaviors, and to a complex interrelationship between behavior and morphology, leading to modern humans.

Before ca. 200 kya, there are no known fossils attributed to *Homo sapiens sensu strictu*. The oldest examples to date are from Ethiopia, from the Middle Awash (160 kya, White et al. 2003), and from a second region in the far south, on the Omo river (195 kya, McDougall et al. 2005). All human remains found in Africa after this date are grouped in *Homo sapiens,* distinguished by smaller teeth, a chin, a vertical face tucked under the cranium, a vertical forehead, and vocal tract proportions conducive to spoken language. Several lines of evidence converge to suggest that East Africa rather than South Africa could be the cradle not only of our physical selves but also of our behavior. Not only are the oldest hafted points and the oldest *Homo sapiens* from there, but new mtDNA and Y-chromosome studies suggest that an East African population, the Sandawe, may reflect as deep a root of the human genetic tree as the southern African San (Tishkoff et al. 2007, Brooks et al. 2008). Genetics also suggests that the ancient East African population was larger. In central Kenya, as well as in northern Tanzania and areas of Ethiopia, archaeological remains suggest a density of human occupation that is quite rare outside this area, with the possible exception of the South African coast, where colder temperatures, a winter rainfall pattern, and rich marine resources concentrated human habitation in coastal areas (Marean et al. 2007).

But after more than a million years with little change in technology, the African record suggests that well before the appearance of *Homo sapiens,* before 285 kya, behavior had begun to change. New technologies produced standardized stone flakes and long thin blades (Johnson and McBrearty 2009, Gibbons 2009), ocher processing increased, and many sites have small quantities, up to 5 percent, of stone material derived from sources a considerable distance away — as much as 200 km or more, the first sign of an expanded social network. The increased use of ocher in Africa might suggest body painting or possibly a more utilitarian function. And in Israel and Morocco, two slightly modified stones with traces of ocher dating to between 500 and 200 kya may or may not represent crude images (D'Errico and Nowell 2000). The behavioral changes reflected in these finds are not sudden or directional. The evidence for them is interspersed with sites containing the old symmetrical large cutting tools, or simple flake technologies, or lacking evidence for ocher or exotic stone. But the general trend is toward more complex behaviors with time. By ca. 267 kya (e.g., Morgan and Renne 2008), several sites in South and East Africa include carefully made stone points, designed for hafting onto spear shafts.

ALISON S. BROOKS

New Technologies

More dramatic changes in behavior occur after the appearance of *Homo sapiens*. From South Africa to Egypt and from the western Sahara to Ethiopia, evidence for complex technologies and new tools increases especially after 100 kya. In the Middle Awash region of Ethiopia, the first *Homo sapiens* at ca. 160 kya are associated with both advanced flake technologies and the older symmetrical large cutting tools (Clark et al. 2003). Before 90 kya, stone points are large or thick, and were likely hafted onto thrusting spears in close encounters with prey. But after 90 kya, the points become tiny and light (Brooks et al. 2006, Yellen et al. 2005). We measured points from a number of other sites of about the same age from North, South, and East Africa and compared them to contemporaneous points made by Neanderthals. In comparing these to the range of points made by historic groups of hunter-gatherers, we concluded that the ancient African examples had to have served as armatures for a complex projectile weapons system, involving a point, a haft, and some sort of propulsion system, either a bow or a spear-thrower. It is also likely that these very small points, which could not have delivered a lethal blow to a large animal, were associated with the use of poison.

A projectile weapons system has some parallels to a grammar (Ambrose 2001) in that it involves noninterchangeable forms: point, haft, binding, and propulsion agent, which can be combined in a limited number of ways, with each point or haft filling a role that can only be interchanged with another point or haft. Such a system provides tremendous advantages to the hunter, who can now kill at a distance, with much more success and less risk to himself (or herself), resulting in greater survivorship. What were they doing with these weapons? In the western Kalahari desert, we excavated a site dating to 77 kya on a seasonal pan, which today serves as an ambush hunting venue at the end of the rainy season, when other water sources are dry and game is concentrated around this resource (Brooks and Yellen 1987, Helgren and Brooks 1983). More than 600 small, finely made points constitute the dominant tool class, and associated animal remains suggest that humans were hunting large dangerous animals such as African buffalo, extinct giant zebra, and warthog with points weighing less than 10 grams, well within the range of arrowheads and spear-thrower darts known from historic peoples. At Klasies River in South Africa, one of

What Is a Human?

these small points was actually stuck into the cervical vertebra of a giant buffalo (Milo 1998), providing proof of its use as a weapon.

At Mumba Shelter in Tanzania, there are also small projectile armatures, in levels dated to between 40 and 60-70 kya (Mehlman 1979, 1989, 1991, Hare et al. 1993, Prendergast et al. 2007). These are not only triangular but geometric crescents and trapezoids, designed for hafting multiple elements in a single haft in the manner of pre-dynastic Egyp-

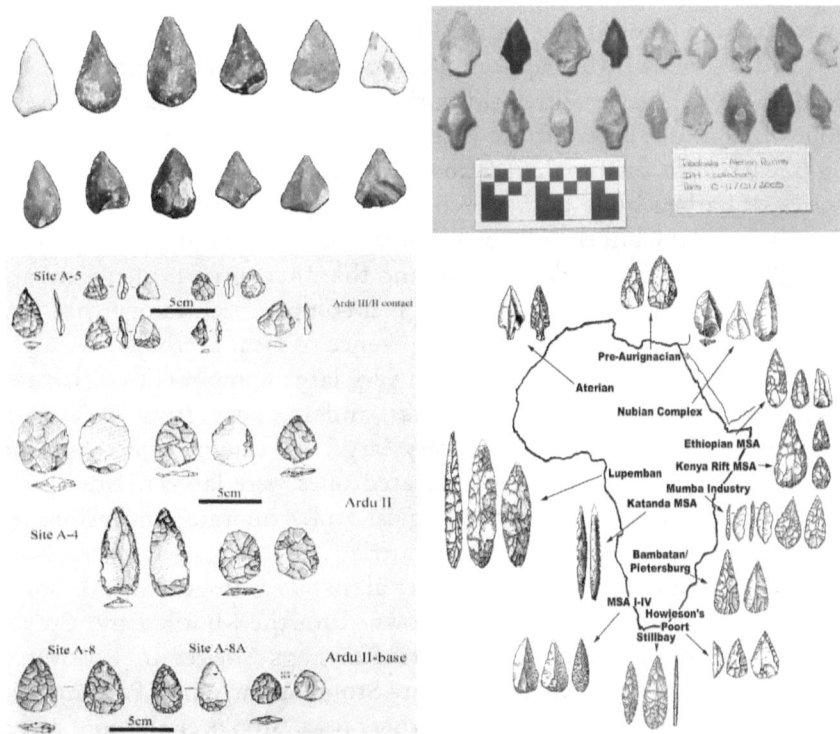

Figure 5. Small African projectile points dating to between 130 and 60 kya, which suggest early *Homo sapiens'* use of complex projectile technologies such as the spear-thrower and/or bow and arrow: a) *(above top left)* triangular points from ≠Gi, Botswana, 77 kya (A. S. Brooks); b) *(above top right)* tanged points from Tabelbala, Algerian Sahara, ca. 60-130 kya (A. S. Brooks); c) *(above bottom left)* point sequence from youngest (top) to older (base) at Aduma, Middle Awash Valley, Ethiopia, all younger than 90 kya (A. S. Brooks); d) *(above bottom right)* point diversity in Africa 90-60 kya, suggesting the possibility of large-scale ethnic or interactive groups (S. McBrearty and A. S. Brooks).

tian arrowheads. Again, this level of technological sophistication is also found in a very limited time and space in southern Africa, 60-65 kya. What is even more interesting in the Tanzanian case is that some of the tools are made of obsidian, not from Tanzania but from central Kenya, almost 300 km away (Merrick and Brown 1984). So we are not only looking at technological sophistication, but also at a likely exchange network. A few other African sites show comparable exchange distances in small amounts.

As early as 130 kya, another set of technological innovations appears to have focused on fishing. In eastern DR Congo (Zaire), we discovered a series of what appeared geologically and typologically to be Middle Stone Age localities along the river at a place called Katanda, following an old land surface (Brooks et al. 1995). We excavated three sites, each with mammalian fauna and lithic artifacts but also with a series of barbed bone points (Yellen et al. 1995).[5] The dates for these sites have varied, but the trapped charge dating techniques suggest that an age of 80-90 kya would be likely, and that there is no evidence for an age of less than 60 kya. Again, this is a complex technology that appears to have been outside the competence of Neanderthals.

The associated fauna includes a very large component of fish remains, all of the same species *(Clarias)* and age, suggesting a seasonal fishing activity. The fish were very large; we caught one weighing seventy-four pounds, and the excavated ones were larger. Thus these three sites testify to both technological and economic innovation. In addition, fish provides important nutrients — omega-3 fatty acids — which nourish the brain (Crawford et al. 1999, Parkington 2003). Bone points very much like these are known from the Middle-Later Stone Age intermediate industry at White Paintings Shelter in Botswana (Robbins et al. 2000). The earliest Late Stone Age at White Paintings is dated to between 40 and 57 kya (Feathers 1997, Brooks et al. 2008). Very different cylindrical bone points resembling historical bone arrow points are known from ca. 77 kya at Blombos Cave (Henshilwood et al. 2001), from Peers Cave, and a number of other South African coastal sites, predating 65 kya. In each case, fish bones have also been recovered. Bone points are a major technological advance, requiring consid-

---

5. Francesco d'Errico is studying the manufacture and use of these points and has suggested that there is wear from some sort of line or string on the base, indicating probable use as a harpoon (Brooks et al. 2004).

What Is a Human?

Figure 6. Fishing and harpoon technology by early *Homo sapiens* at Katanda, eastern DR Congo, at 60-80 kya: a) *(above left top)* a few of the thousands of very large catfish bones recovered in excavations at three sites (A. S. Brooks); b) *(above left bottom)* very large catfish caught in 1990 in the Semliki River below the sites (A. S. Brooks); c) *(above right)* barbed bone harpoons with string wear in the basal grooves (A. S. Brooks).

erably more time and effort to manufacture. Their advantage, according to ethnographic accounts, is that they float, allowing the fisherman to retrieve them easily.

Small projectile armatures in a complex weapons system could have given the edge to later modern humans, allowing populations to expand both within and outside Africa at the expense of the Neanderthals and other archaic populations. Neanderthals had many injuries from personal encounters with large dangerous animals (Berger and Trinkaus 1995); later moderns had very few. Neanderthals also had many more signs of dietary stress in their bones and teeth than the early moderns who succeeded them (Ogilvie et al. 1989).

These projectiles are also quite variable in time and space – at least as variable as the small arrow tips that succeed them. The patterning of regional variation is to a large extent independent of climate and raw material – a stone industry with geometric shapes (the Howiesons Poort), for example, is found from southern Namibia to the Cape Province of South Africa in a limited time band and is made on a wide variety of raw materials, from quartz to silcrete and chert. The distribution of regional styles of early *Homo sapiens* is thus as suggestive of ethnic or regional differences as any later African stone tools.

Symbolic Behavior

So far, we have demonstrated the presence of technological innovation, economic intensification, long-distance exchange, and regional styles in the behavioral repertoire of early modern humans. But is there hard evidence for symbolic behavior? Until very recently, there was little evidence before 40 kya. An image from the Apollo 11 Cave of an antelope with human hind legs was found in a level with an old date of 27,000 (Wendt 1976), although we have dated the industry found with it to 65,000 at that site (Miller et al. 1999). In 2002, an extraordinary piece of engraved ocher was described from Blombos cave in South Africa (Henshilwood 2002). It and a second similar piece clearly suggest that ocher had more than a utilitarian function. Many other pieces of ocher, bone, and eggshell with engraved geometric or linear designs are known from both this site and other sites in southern Africa, including fragments of decorated ostrich eggshell containers from ca. 65 kya at the Atlantic coastal site of Diepkloof (Rigaud et al. 2006).

Bead and other body ornaments are unequivocal evidence for symbolic behavior and for fully human status, as they have little utilitarian function. In traditional hunting societies, beads provide the basis of exchange networks that serve to tie distant people together in a mutual support network, which can be activated when times are bad. Individuals deliberately build these networks up as they grow into middle age,

What Is a Human?

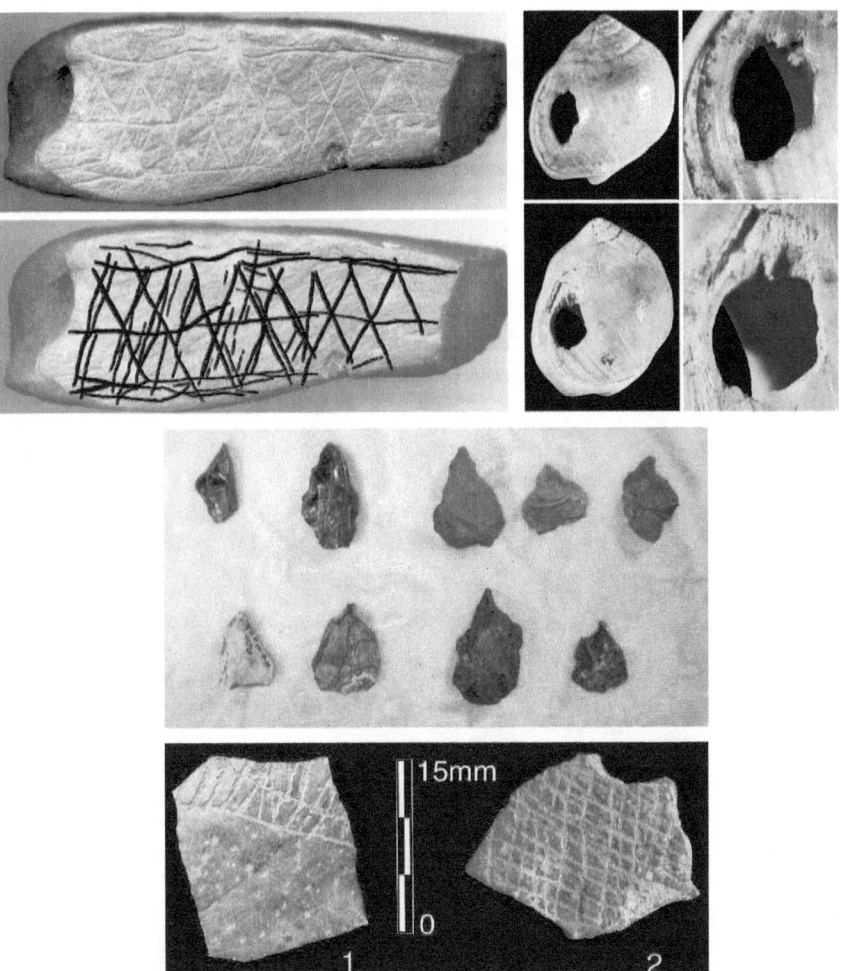

Figure 7. Symbolic behavior by early *Homo sapiens* in Africa: a) *(above top left)* geometric design engraved on ocher from Blombos Cave, South Africa, 76 kya (courtesy Francesco D'Errico); b) *(above top right)* perforated shell beads from Blombos, 76 kya, with string wear in the holes. Beads from the same or similar species have now been found at multiple sites in South and North Africa, and the Levant, between 105 and 60 kya. Other shell beads have been recovered from East Africa dating to a similar antiquity (courtesy Francesco D'Errico); c) *(above middle)* small perforators for making holes or engraving from Aduma, Middle Awash, dating to ca. 80-90 kya (A. S. Brooks); d) *(above bottom)* geometric design engraved around lip of ostrich eggshell "canteen" (fragments), Diepkloof Rock Shelter, South Africa, ca. 60-65 kya (courtesy J.-Ph. Rigaud?).

and acquire major responsibilities for raising and marrying off children or for supporting elderly parents (Wiessner 1984). As they age and their needs decrease, individuals begin to reduce the size of these networks. Beads and personal ornaments such as rings, or headpieces, also serve as markers of social identity or status worldwide, from wedding bands to the colorful collars of the Maasai to the diamond necklaces of society women (or men). Despite extensive excavation, no beads are known from Europe before ca. 40 kya. Early African sites have yielded a few ostrich eggshell beads in early sites — an unfinished one from South Africa (Boomplaas) dated to ca. 60-80 kya, and several from Tanzania (Mumba) dated directly to between 45 and 52 kya (Hare et al. 1993). In 2004, a series of perforated shell beads from the coast of South Africa, dated to 76 kya, made headlines as the oldest evidence for personal ornaments (Henshilwood et al. 2004, 2005). Newer finds of shell beads, of the same genus, have been published from even older sites in North Africa and the Middle East, in direct association with modern humans at one site, but dated to as much as 110 kya (Vanhaeren et al. 2006, Bouzouggar et al. 2007). More and older bead sites are being reported as we excavate more sites with modern technologies.

Figure 8. Oldest known figurative image from South Africa, Apollo 11 Cave, 27,000 BP (courtesy Heinrich Barthe Institut, Ralph Vogelsang).

What Is a Human?

The evidence for human burial practices with grave offerings indicative of symbolic behavior within Africa is limited, due in part to the relative dominance of open-air excavations where bone preservation is poor, and in part to probable cultural practices of burial away from living sites. Two relatively elaborate cave burials at early dates, however, confirm the antiquity of this practice among modern humans at opposite ends of their early geographic range: the burial of a child at Border Cave in South Africa dated to 66-90 kya (Beaumont et al. 1978, Beaumont 1980, Miller et al. 1999, Millard 2006, Jacobs et al. 2008,) and an elaborate modern human burial at Qafzeh in Israel dated to 90-100 kya (Vandermeersch 1970, 1981, Hovers et al. 2003). The child burial is associated with what appears to be ocher and has a large perforated *Conus* shell in its chest area. The nearest source for the shell is the Indian Ocean ca. eighty km away. The Qafzeh individual was associated with seventy-one pieces of red ocher, and also with a perforated bivalve shell *(Glycymeris)* (D. Bar-Yosef 2005). Although the perforation could have been natural, the shell was brought to the site and placed in the burial, along with some possible offerings of animal remains. These two sites constitute the earliest clear evidence for symbolic burial with grave goods and red ocher, practices that suggest a belief in the survival of a spirit after death.

Summary: Why Humanness Is a Gradual Process, Not a Sudden Event

The accelerating rate of technological innovation was a stepwise process, not a sudden event related to language. By 70 to 60 kya, well before the out-of-Africa event that apparently led to Neanderthal extinction, anatomically modern humans in Africa (and occasionally in the Levant) had light, complex projectile weaponry, fishing and bone fishing spears, long-distance exchange networks, ocher, deliberate burial with grave goods, regionally distinctive point styles, symbolic engravings, and personal ornaments. Within Africa, there is probably a complex web of interregional migration and local extinction that makes the record patchy and discontinuous. In addition, demographic and climatic factors may affect the degree to which any of these modern human capabilities are expressed; ethnographic studies suggest that symbolic expression, subsistence practices, and regional networks in-

ALISON S. BROOKS

 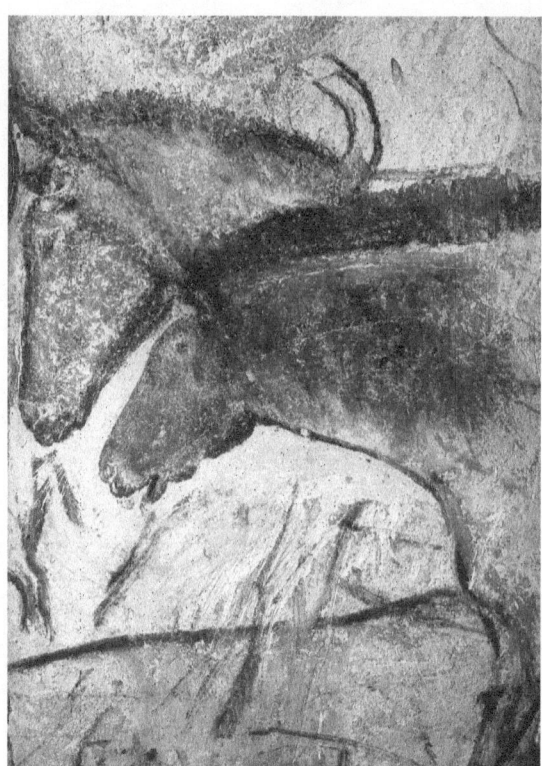

Figure 9: Examples of some of the first figurative sculptures and painted images from Europe: a) *(above left)* the "lion-man" in mammoth ivory, Hohlenstein-Stadel, Baden-Württemberg, Germany, ca. 32 kya (courtesy Ulmer Museum, Der Löwenmennsch: *Tier und Mensch in der Kunst der Eiszeit*, cover image and plate 13); b) *(above right)* a panel of horses from Chauvet Cave, France, ca. 30 kya (courtesy Jean Clottes et al., plate III.108 of *Cheavet Cave: The Art of Earliest Times*, photo by C. Fritz and G. Tosello).

tensify under conditions of resource stress. It is also interesting that the first Australians, who must have come from Africa but entered an empty continent ca. 50 kya, lack evidence for any of these behaviors until after 30 kya when the population had grown to fill the available regions, and the climate turned hyper-arid.

Neanderthals, on the other hand, before 50 kya, had hafted spear points (Boeda et al. 1998), used a large amount of black coloring materials (they probably had light-colored skin), and practiced simple burials without offerings or ocher. There is little evidence in this early time range for Neanderthal fishing[6] and none for bone tools, musical instruments, cave art, or personal ornaments. After 40 kya, when the modern humans were already on their periphery or perhaps in their midst, Neanderthals responded to pressure by developing or adopting some of the same traits — particularly the beads, and stone technologies. But they still lacked small, light projectile armatures, they rarely if ever went fishing, and really long-distance raw material transport is only marginally present toward the end at the northeast end of their range in Eastern Europe and Central Asia, where we would expect human territories to be very large and populations sparse.

Why was *Homo sapiens* able to replace Neanderthals in Eurasia after 50 kya but not before? There seem to be three possibilities: one is the sudden genetic mutation theory, one is about technological superiority, and one concerns the development of more sophisticated social networks, supported by a greater use of symbols, which buffered human populations against risks, much like the naming and gift-giving relationships of the Kalahari hunter-gatherers.

While the answer is almost certainly more complicated than any of these simple hypotheses, and may involve combinations of them and other arguments, I would argue that the evidence against a revolutionary genetic event is strong when you look at Africa. That continent is characterized by the earlier appearance of technological and economic complexity, as well as of complex symbolic behavior. The patterning of change both during and at the end of the Middle Stone Age period of early *Homo sapiens* is also very different from that consistent with a revolution, as it is both spotty and gradual. Such patterning is much better explained by the existence in earlier anatomically modern humans of modern behavioral capabilities that are variably expressed when conditions call for them — when either climate or population growth creates effective crowding, in an otherwise sparsely inhabited landscape.

At what point did *Homo* become fully human? The more we know, the harder it is to draw a line between human and nonhuman or prehuman. The evidence suggests that the capabilities for "living in

---

6. Neanderthal fishing was argued for late Gibraltar Neanderthals by Stringer et al. (2008), but the fish remains in question are very limited and derive from small fish that possibly could have been brought in by a nonhuman mammal or avian predator.

our heads" were present before 130 kya, and developed in a stepwise fashion, possibly in a feedback relationship with our morphology. Capacities for some of the most human qualities — creativity, empathy, reverence, spirituality, aesthetic appreciation, abstract thought, and problem solving (rationality) — were already evident soon after the emergence of our species.[7]

References

Akazawa, T., K. Aoki, and O. Bar-Yosef, eds. *Neanderthals and Modern Humans in Western Asia.* New York: Plenum Publishers, 1998.

Aldhouse-Green, Stephen. "Paviland Cave: Contextualizing the 'Red Lady,'" *Antiquity* 72, no. 278 (1998): 756-72.

Ambrose, Stanley. "Paleolithic Technology and Human Evolution," *Science* 299, no. 5509 (2001): 1748-53.

Anderson, Benedict. *Imagined Communities: Reflections on the Origin and Spread of Nationalism.* London: Verso Books, 1983.

Anton, S. C., and C. C. Swisher III. "Early Dispersals of *Homo* from Africa," *Annual Review of Anthropology* 33 (2004): 271-96.

Arsuaga, J. L., I. Martínez, A. Gracia, J. M. Carretero, C. Lorenzo, N. García, and A. I. Ortega. "Sima de los Huesos (Sierra de Atapuerca, Spain): The Site," *Journal of Human Evolution* 33, nos. 2-3 (1997): 109-27.

Barham, L. S. "Possible Early Pigment Use in South-Central Africa," *Current Anthropology* 39 (1998): 703-20.

Bar-Yosef Mayer, Danielle E. "The Exploitation of Shells as Beads in the Palaeolithic and Neolithic of the Levant," *Paléorient* 31, no. 1 (2005): 176-85.

Beaumont, Peter B. "On the Age of the Border Cave Hominids 1-5," *Paleontologica Africana* 23 (1980): 21-33.

Beaumont, Peter B., Hertha de Villiers, and John C. Vogel. "Modern Man in Sub-Saharan Africa Prior to 49000 BP: A Review and Evaluation with Particular Reference to Border Cave," *South African Journal of Science* 74 (1978): 409-19.

Bednarik, Robert. "A Figurine from the African Acheulian," *Current Anthropology* 44, no. 3 (2003): 405-13.

Belmaker, Miriam, Eitan Tchernov, Sylvana Condemi, and Ofer Bar-Yosef. "New Evidence for Hominid Presence in the Lower Pleistocene of the Levant," *Journal of Human Evolution* 43, no. 1 (2002): 43-56.

---

7. I am extremely grateful to Brian Richmond for his comments on this manuscript and to Mary Ann Meyers for careful editing of the paper and its references.

Belmaker, Miriam. "On the Road to China: The Environmental Landscape of the Lower Pleistocene in Western Eurasia and Its Implication for the Dispersal of *Homo*," in *Asian Paleoanthropology: From Africa to China and Beyond*, edited by Christopher J. Norton, David R. Braun, and John W. K. Harris. New York: Springer (Vertebrate Paleobiology and Paleoanthropology Series), in press.

Bendysche, Thomas. "On the Anthropology of Linnaeus: 1735-1776," in "The History of Anthropology," *Memoirs of the Anthropological Society of London*, 1 (1863): 421-26.

Berger, Thomas D., and Eric Trinkaus. "Patterns of Trauma among the Neanderthals," *Journal of Archaeological Science* 22 (1995): 841-52.

Blumenbach, Johann Friedrich. "I. Ordn. Bimanus. II. Quadrumana," in *Handbuch der Naturgeschichte*. Dietrich, Göttingen (1779-1780) translated by R. T. Gore, as "Order I: Bimanus, II: Quadrumana," in *A Manual of the Elements of Natural History*, Section 4, 34-42. London: W. Simpkin and R. Marshall, 1825.

Boëda, Eric. "Levallois: A Volumetric Construction, Methods, and Technique," in *The Definition and Interpretation of Levallois Technology*, edited by Harold Dibble and Ofer Bar-Yosef. Philadelphia: University of Pennsylvania Press, 1995.

Boëda, Eric, Jacques Connajn, and Sultan Mohesen. "Bitumen as Hafting Material on Middle Paleolithic Artifacts from El Kowm Basin, Syria," in *Neanderthals and Modern Humans in Western Asia*, edited by Aoki Akazawa and Ofer Bar-Yosef, pp. 193-214. New York: Plenum Publishers, 1998.

Bouzouggar, A., N. Barton, M. Vanhaeren, F. d'Errico, S. Collcutt, T. Higham, S. Parfitt, E. Rhodes, J. L. Schwenninger, C. Stringer, E. Turner, S. Ward, A. Moutmir, and A. Stambouli. "82,000-Year-Old Shell Beads from North Africa and Implications for the Origin of Modern Human Behavior," *Proceedings of the National Academy of Sciences* 104 (2007): 9964-69.

Bramble, Dennis M., and Daniel E. Lieberman. "Endurance Running and the Evolution of *Homo*," *Nature* 432 (2004): 345-52.

Brooks, Alison S. "Behavior and Human Evolution," in *Contemporary Issues in Human Evolution*, edited by W. E. Meikle, F. C. Howell, and N. G. Jablonski, pp. 135-66. Memoirs of the California Academy of Sciences no. 21, 1996.

Brooks, Alison S., David M. Helgren, Jonathan M. Cramer, Alan Franklin, William Hornyak, Jody M. Keating, Richard G. Klein, W. John Rink, Henry P. Schwarcz, J. N. Leith Smith, Kathryn Stewart, Nancy E. Todd, Jacques Verniers, and John E. Yellen. "Dating and Context of Three Middle Stone Age Sites with Bone Points in the Upper Semliki Valley, Zaire," *Science* 268 (1995): 548-53.

Brooks, A. S., and J. E. Yellen. "The Preservation of Activity Areas in the Archaeological Record: Ethnoarchaeological and Archaeological Work in Northwest Ngamiland, Botswana," in *Method and Theory of Activity Area Research*, edited by S. Kent, pp. 63-106. New York: Columbia University Press, 1987.

Brooks, A. S., and J. E. Yellen. "Bones of Contention: Bone Tools and the Emergence of Modern Human Behavior," in *Abstracts of the 69th Annual Meeting of the Society for American Archaeology, March 31-April 4, Montreal, Canada*, p. 65 (Washington, DC: Society for American Archaeology, 2004).

Brooks, Alison S., F. James Feathers, Gideon Hartman, Noreen Tuross, Francesco d'Errico, and John E. Yellen. "Middle Stone Age Bone Points from Katanda (D. R. Congo): New Perspectives on Age and Association," in Abstracts of the Annual Meeting of the Palaeoanthropology Society, Montreal, Canada, March 30-31, 2004, *PaleoAnthropology* 1 (2004): p. A04.

Brooks, A. S., J. E. Yellen, L. Nevell, and G. Hartman. "Projectile Technologies of the African MSA: Implications for Modern Human Origins," in *Transitions before the Transition: Evolution and Stability in the Middle Paleolithic and Middle Stone Age*, edited by E. Hovers and S. Kuhn, pp. 233-55. New York: Kluwer Academics/Plenum, 2006.

Brooks, Alison S., Sarah A. Tishkoff, and John E. Yellen. "Origins of Modern African Diversity: Archaeological and Genetic Perspectives," in *Abstracts of the 73rd Annual Meeting of the Society for American Archaeology, Vancouver, BC, Canada, March 24-30, 2008*. Washington, DC: Society for American Archaeology, 2008.

Brunet, Michel, et al. "A New Hominid from the Upper Miocene of Chad, Central Africa," *Nature* 418 (2002): 145-51.

Buckland, William. *Reliquiae Diluvinae, or Observations on the Organic Remains Contained in Caves, Fissures and Diluvial Gravel, and on Other Geological Phenomena, Attesting the Action of a Universal Deluge.* London: J. Murray, 1823.

Buffon, Georges Louis Leclerc, Comte de. "Nomenclature des Singes," in *Histoire Naturelle, Générale et Particulière.* Paris: Imprimerie Royal (1749-67). Translated by W. Smellie, "The Nomenclature of Apes," in *Natural History, General and Particular,* vol. 10, pp. 1-36. London: T. Cadell and M. Davies, 1812.

Burnett, James (Lord Monboddo). "Of the Several Steps of the Human Progression from the Brute to the Man, Etc.," in *Ancient Metaphysics: or the Science of Universals,* book 1, ch. 2, pp. 25-34. Edinburgh: J. Balfour and Co., 1779-99.

Chase, P. G. "How Different Was Middle Palaeolithic Subsistence?: A Zooarchaeological Perspective on the Middle to Upper Palaeolithic Transition," in *The Human Revolution: Behavioral and Biological Perspectives on the Origins of Modern Humans,* edited by P. Mellars and C. B. Stringer, pp. 321-27. Edinburgh: Edinburgh University Press, 1989.

Clark, J. D., Y. Beyene, G. WoldeGabriel, W. K. Hart, P. R. Renne, H. Gilbert, A. Defleur, G. Suwa, S. Katoh, K. R. Ludwig, J-R. Boisserie, B. Asfaw, and

T. D. White. "Stratigraphic, Chronological and Behavioral Context of Pleistocene *Homo sapiens* from Middle Awash, Ethiopia," *Nature* 423 (2003): 747-52.

Clottes, Jean. "Art between 30,000 and 20,000 bp," in *Hunters of the Golden Age: The Mid-Upper Palaeolithic of Eurasia 30,000-20,000 BP*, edited by Wil Roebroeks, Margherita Mussi, Jiri Svoboda, and Kelly Fennema, pp. 87-103. Leiden: University of Leiden Press, 2000.

Conard, N. J. "Palaeolithic Ivory Sculptures from Southwestern Germany and the Origins of Figurative Art," *Nature* 426 (2003): 830-32.

Crawford, M. A., M. Bloom, C. L. Broadhurst, W. F. Schmidt, S. C. G. C. Cunnane, K. Gehbresmeskel, F. Linseisen, J. Lloyd-Smith, and J. Parkington. "Evidence for the Unique Function of Docosahexaenoic Acid during the Evolution of the Modern Human Brain," *Lipids* 34 Supplement (1999): S39-S47.

Dart, Raymond. "*Australopithecus africanus*: The Man-Ape of South Africa," *Nature* 115 (1925): 195-99.

Darwin, Charles R. *The Descent of Man and Selection in Relation to Sex*. London: John Murray, 1871.

De Heinzelin, J., J. D. Clark, T. White, W. Hart, P. Renne G. Woldegabriel, Y. Beyene, and E. Vrba. "Environment and Behavior of 2.5-Million-Year-Old Bouri Hominids," *Science* 284, no. 5414 (1999): 625-29.

Deino, A., and A. Hill. "40Ar/39Ar Dating of Chemeron Formation Strata Encompassing the Site of Hominid KNM-BC 1, Tugen Hills, Kenya," *Journal of Human Evolution* 42, no. 1 (2002): 141-51.

Deino, A., and S. McBrearty. "40Ar/39Ar Chronology for the Kapthurin Formation, Baringo, Kenya," *Journal of Human Evolution* 42 (2002): 185-210.

Delagnes, A., and H. Roche. "Late Pliocene Hominid Knapping Skills: The Case of Lokalalei 2C, West Turkana, Kenya," *Journal of Human Evolution* 48 (2005): 435-72.

D'Errico, F., C. Henshilwood, G. Lawson, M. Vanhaeren, A.-M. Tillier, M. Soressi, F. Bresson, B. Maureilllle, A. Nowell, J. Lakarra, L. Backwell, and M. Julien. "Archaeological Evidence for the Emergence of Language, Symbolism, and Music — An Alternative Evolutionary Perspective," *Journal of World Prehistory* 17, no. 1 (2003): 1-70.

D'Errico, Francesco, and April Nowell. "A New Look at the Berekhat Ram Figurine: Implications for the Origins of Symbolism," *Cambridge Archaeological Journal* 10 (2000): 123-67.

D'Errico, F., and C. S. Henshilwood. "Additional Evidence for Bone Technology in the Southern African Middle Stone Age," *Journal of Human Evolution* 52 (2007): 142-63.

Defleur, Alban, Tim White, Patricia Valensi, Ludovic Slimak, and Évelyne

Crégut-Bonnoure. "Neanderthal Cannibalism at Moula-Guercy, Ardèche, France," *Science* 286, no. 5437 (2000): 128-31.

Dubois, Eugene. *Pithecanthropus erectus. Eine Menschenähnliche Uebergangsform aus Java*. Batavia: Landesdruckerei, 1894.

Fabre, Virginie, Silvana Condemi, and Anna Degioanni. "Genetic Evidence of Geographical Groups among Neanderthals," *PLoS One* 4, no. 4 (2009): e5151.

Feathers, James K. "Luminescence Dating of Sediment Samples from White Paintings Rockshelter, Botswana," *Quaternary Science Reviews* 16, nos. 3-5 (1997): 321-31.

Féblot-Augustins, J. *La Circulation des Matières Premières au Paléolithique* (2 vols.). Liège: ERAUL/CNRS no. 75, 1997.

Féblot-Augustins, Jehanne. "Raw Material Transport Patterns and Settlement Systems in the European Lower and Middle Palaeolithic: Continuity, Change and Variability," in *The Middle Palaeolithic Occupation of Europe*, edited by W. Roebrucks and C. Gamble, pp. 193-214. Leiden: University of Leiden, 1999.

Fisher, Simon E., and Gary F. Marcus. "The Eloquent Ape: Genes, Brains and the Evolution of Language," *Nature Reviews: Genetics* 7 (2006): 9-20.

Fitzsimmons, F. W. "Palaeolithic Man in South Africa," *Nature* 95 (1915): 615-16.

Forster, P., and S. Matsumura. "Did Early Humans Go North or South?" *Science* 308, no. 5724 (2005): 965-66.

Gabunia, Leo, Abesalom Vekua, David Lordkipanidze, Carl C. Swisher III, Reid Ferring, Antje Justus, Medea Nioradze, Merab Tvalchrelidze, Susan C. Antón, Gerhard Bosinski, Olaf Jöris, Marie-A.-de Lumley, Givi Majsuradze, and Aleksander Mouskhelishvili. "Earliest Pleistocene Hominid Cranial Remains from Dmanisi, Republic of Georgia: Taxonomy, Geological Setting, and Age," *Science* 288, no. 5468 (2000): 1019-25.

Gamble, Clive. "Palaeolithic Society and the Release from Proximity: A Network Approach to Intimate Relations," *World Archaeology* 29, no. 3 (1998): 426-49.

Gibbons, Ann. "Oldest Stone Blades Uncovered," *ScienceNOW* (April 2, 2009): http://sciencenow.sciencemag.org/cgi/content/full/2009/402/2 4/2/2009.

Goren-Inbar, N., et al. "Evidence of Hominin Control of Fire at Gesher Benot Ya'aqov, Israel," *Science* 304 (2004): 725-27.

Gould, Stephen J. *The Mismeasure of Man* (rev. ed.). New York: W. W. Norton, 1996.

Grayson, Donald K. *The Establishment of Human Antiquity*. New York: Academic Press, 1983.

Green, David J., and Adam D. Gordon. "Metacarpal Proportions in *Australopithecus africanus*," *Journal of Human Evolution* 54, no. 5(2008): 705-19.

Green, Richard E., Johannes Krause, Susan E. Ptak, Adrian W. Briggs, Michael T. Ronan, Jan F. Simons, Lei Du, Michael Egholm, Jonathan M. Rothberg, Maja Paunovic, and Svante Pääbo. "Analysis of One Million Base Pairs of Neanderthal DNA," *Nature* 444 (2006): 330-36 (and supplemental data).

Haeckel, Ernst. *The History of Creation: Or the Development of the Earth and its Inhabitants by the Action of Natural Causes: A Popular Exposition of the Doctrine of Evolution in General, and That of Darwin, Goethe, and Lamarck in Particular.* Chapter 23: "Migration and Distribution of Mankind. Human Species and Human Races," pp. 325-33. Translated from the German by E. Ray Lankester. New York: D. Appleton, 1868.

Haile-Selassie, Yohannes. "Late Miocene Hominids from the Middle Awash, Ethiopia," *Nature* 412 (2001): 178-81.

Haile-Selassie, Yohannes, Gen Suwa, and Tim D. White. "Late Miocene Teeth from Middle Awash, Ethiopia, and Early Hominid Dental Evolution," *Science* 303, no. 5663 (2004): 1503-5.

Haile-Selassie, Yohannes, and Giday WoldeGabriel, eds. *Ardipithecus Kadabba: Late Miocene Evidence from the Middle Awash, Ethiopia.* Berkeley: University of California Press, 2009.

Hare, P. Edgar, Glenn A. Goodfriend, Alison S. Brooks, Julie E. Kokis, and David W. von Endt. "Chemical Clocks and Thermometers: Diagenetic Reactions of Amino Acids in Fossils," *Carnegie Institution of Washington Yearbook* 92 (1993): 80-85.

Helgren, David H., and Alison S. Brooks. "Geoarchaeology at Gi, a Middle Stone Age and Later Stone Age Site in the Northwest Kalahari," *Journal of Archaeological Science* 10 (1983): 181-97.

Henshilwood, C. S., F. d'Errrico, M. Vanhaeren, K. von Niekerk, and Z. Jacobs. "Middle Stone Age Beads from South Africa," *Science* 304 (2004): 404. (See accompanying online material for pictures: DOI: 10.1126/science.1095905.) NB there is a longer treatment in *JHE* 48, no. 1 (2005): 3-24.

Henshilwood, C. S., F. D'Errico, C. W. Marean, R. G. Milo, and R. Yates. "An Early Bone Tool Industry from the Middle Stone Age at Blombos Cave, South Africa: Implications for the Origins of Modern Human Behaviour, Symbolism and Language," *Journal of Human Evolution* 41 (2001): 631-78.

Henshilwood, C. S., Christopher S. Henshilwood, Francesco d'Errico, Royden Yates, Zenobia Jacobs, Chantal Tribolo, Geoff A. T. Duller, Norbert Mercier, Judith C. Sealy, Helene Valladas, Ian Watts, and Ann G. Wintle. "Emergence of Modern Human Behavior: Engravings from South Africa," *Science* 295 (2002): 1278-80.

Hovers, Erella, Shimon Ilani, Ofer Bar-Yosef, and Bernard Vandermeersch. "An Early Case of Color Symbolism: Ochre Use by Modern Humans in Qafzeh Cave," *Current Anthropology* 44, no. 4 (August-October 2003): 491-522.

Hublin, Jean Jacques. "Modern-Non-Modern Hominid Interactions: A Mediterranean Perspective," in *The Geography of Neanderthals and Modern Humans in Europe and the Greater Mediterranean,* edited by Ofer Bar-Yosef and David Pilbeam, pp. 157-82. Cambridge, MA: Peabody Museum of Archaeology and Ethnography, Harvard University, 2000.

Jackendorf, Ray. "Possible Stages in the Evolution of the Language Capacity," *Trends in the Cognitive Sciences* 3, no. 7 (1999): 272-79.

Jacobs, Zenobia, Richard G. Roberts, Rex F. Galbraith, Hilary J. Deacon, Rainer Grün, Alex Mackay, Peter Mitchell, Ralf Vogelsang, and Lyn Wadley. "Ages for the Middle Stone Age of Southern Africa: Implications for Human Behavior and Dispersal," *Science* 322 (2008): 733-35.

Johnson, Cara Roure, and Sally McBrearty. "Cutting Edge: A New Date for the Earliest Blade Technology," in Abstracts of the Paleoanthropology Society 2009 Meetings. *PaleoAnthropology* 2009: A18.

Kibunjia, Mzalendo, Hélène Roche, Frank H. Brown, and Richard E. Leakey. "Pliocene and Pleistocene Archaeological Sites West of Lake Turkana, Kenya," *Journal of Human Evolution* 23 (1992): 431-38.

Kimbel, W. H., R. C. Walter, D. C. Johanson, K. E. Reed, J. L. Aronson, Z. Assefa, C. W. Marean, G. C. Eck, R. Bobe, E. Hovers, Y. Rak, C. Vondra, T. Yemane, D. York, Y. Chen, N. M. Evensen, and P. C. Smith. "Late Pliocene *Homo* and Oldowan Tools from the Hadar Formation (Kada Hadar Member), Ethiopia," *Journal of Human Evolution* 31 (1996): 549-61.

Klein, R. G. "Southern Africa and Modern Human Origins," *Journal of Anthropological Research* 67 (2001): 1-16.

Lamarck, Jean Baptist Pierre Antoine de Monet, Chevalier de. "Degradation and Simplification of Organization from one Extremity to the Other of the Animal Chain, Proceeding from the Most Complex to the Simplest. Bimana," in *Zoological Philosophy,* translated by H. Elliot, chapters 6 and 8, pp. 68-72 and 169-73. London: Macmillan Co., 1914. Original publ. *Philosophie Zoologiques.* Paris: Dentu, 1809.

Lartet, Édouard. "Nouvelles recherches sur la coexistence de l'Homme et des grands mammifères fossils," *Annales des Sciènces Naturelles (Zoologie)* 4ième série 15 (1861): 177-253.

Lieberman, Daniel E., Brandeis M. McBratneym, and Gail Krovitz. "The Evolution and Development of Cranial Form in *Homo sapiens,*" *Proceedings of the National Academy of Sciences* 99, no. 3 (2002): 1134-39.

Lieberman, Phillip, and Robert C. McCarthy. "Tracking the Evolution of Language and Speech: Comparing Vocal Tracts to Identify Speech Capabilities," *Expedition* 49, no. 2 (2007): 15-20. (See also "Recent Origin for Modern Human Speech Capabilities," *Robert McCarthy, Florida Atlantic University* online computer reconstruction of Neanderthal speech at http://www.nasonline.org/site/DocServer/RobertMcCarthy.pdf?docID=38761.)

Lombard, Marlize. "Evidence of Hunting and Hafting during the Middle

Stone Age at Kwa Zulu, Natal: A Multianalytical Approach," *Journal of Human Evolution* 48 (2005): 279-300.

Lordkipanize, David, Abesalom Vekua, Reid Ferring, G. Philip Rightmire, Jordi Agusti, Gocha Kiladze, Alexander Mouskhelishvili, Medea Nioradze, Marcia S. Ponce de León, Martha Tappen, and Christoph P. E. Zollikofer. "Anthropology: The Earliest Toothless Hominin Skull," *Nature* 434 (2005): 717-18.

Marean, C. W., M. Bar-Matthews, J. Bernatchez, E. Fisher, P. Goldberg, A. I. Herries, Z. Jacobs, A. Jerardino, P. Karkanas, T. Minichillo, P. J. Nilssen, E. Thompson, I. Watts, and H. M. Williams. "Early Human Use of Marine Resources and Pigment in South Africa during the Middle Pleistocene," *Nature* 449 (2007): 905-8.

McBrearty, S., and A. Brooks. "The Revolution That Wasn't: A New Interpretation of the Origin of Modern Human Behavior," *Journal of Human Evolution* 39 (2000): 453-563.

McDermott, F., C. Stringer, R. Grün, C. T. Williams, V. K. Din, and C. J. Hawkesworth. "New Late-Pleistocene Uranium-Thorium and ESR Dates for the Singa Hominid (Sudan)," *Journal of Human Evolution* 31, no. 6 (1996): 507-16.

McDougall, Ian, Francis H. Brown, and John G. Fleagle. "Stratigraphic Placement and Age of Modern Humans from Kibish, Ethiopia," *Nature* 433 (2005): 733-36.

Mehlman, Michael J. "Mumba-Höhle Revisited: The Relevance of a Forgotten Excavation to Some Current Issues in East African Prehistory," *World Archaeology* 11 (1979): 80-94.

Mehlman, Michael J. "Late Quaternary Archaeological Sequences in Northern Tanzania," Ph.D. diss., University of Illinois, 1989.

Mehlman, M. J. "Context for the Emergence of Modern Man in Eastern Africa: Some New Tanzanian Evidence," in *Cultural Beginnings: Approaches to Understanding Early Hominid Lifeways in the African Savanna*, edited by J. D. Clark, pp. 177-196. Bonn: Forschunginstitut fur Vor- und Fruhgeschichte, Romisch-Germanisches Zentralmuseum, Monographien 19, 1991.

Mellars, P. A. *The Neanderthal Legacy: An Archaeological Perspective from Western Europe*. Princeton: Princeton University Press, 1996.

Mellars, P. "The Impossible Coincidence: A Single-Species Model for the Origins of Modern Human Behavior in Europe," *Evolutionary Anthropology* 14 (2005): 12-27. (But see also Zilhao 2007, below.)

Mercader, Julio, Melissa Panger, and Christophe Boesch. "Excavation of a Chimpanzee Stone Tool Site in the African Rainforest," *Science* 296, no. 5572 (2002): 1452-55.

Mercader, Julio, Huw Barton, Jason Gillespie, Jack Harris, Steven Kuhn, Robert Tyler, and Christophe Boesch. "4,300-Year-Old Chimpanzee Sites and the

Origins of Percussive Stone Technology," *Proceedings of the National Academy of Sciences* 104, no. 9 (2007): 3043-48.

Merrick, Harry V., and Frank H. Brown. "Obsidian Sources and Patterns of Source Utilization in Kenya and Northern Tanzania: Some Initial Findings," *African Archaeological Review* 2 (1984): 129-52.

Millard, Andrew. "Bayesian Analysis of ESR Dates with Application to Border Cave," *Quaternary Geochronology* 1, no. 2 (2006): 159-66.

Miller, Gifford H., Peter B. Beaumont, Hillary J. Deacon, Alison S. Brooks, P. Edgar Hare, and A. J. T. Jull, "Earliest Modern Humans in Southern Africa Dated by Isoleucine Epimerization in Ostrich Eggshell," *Quaternary Science Reviews* 8, no. 13 (November 1999): 1537-48.

Milo, R. "Evidence for Hominid Predation at Klasies River Mouth, South Africa, and Its Implications for the Behaviour of Early Modern Humans," *Journal of Archaeological Science* 25 (1998): 99-133.

Monnier, Gilliane F. "The Lower/Middle Paleolithic Periodization in Western Europe," *Current Anthropology* 47, no. 5 (2006): 709-44.

Morgan, Leah F., and Paul R. Renne. "Diachronous Dawn of Africa's Middle Stone Age: New 40Ar/39Ar Ages from the Ethiopian Rift," *Geology* 36, no. 12 (2008): 967-70.

Noonan, James P., Graham Coop, Sridhar Kudaravalli, Doug Smith, Johannes Krause, Joe Alessi, Feng Chen, Darren Platt, Svante Pääbo, Jonathan K. Pritchard, and Edward M. Rubin. "Sequencing and Analysis of Neanderthal Genomic DNA," *Science* 314, no. 5802 (2006): 1113-18.

O'Connell, J. F., and J. Allen. "Dating the Colonization of Sahul (Pleistocene Australia-New Guinea): A Review of Recent Research," *Journal of Archaeological Science* 31 (2004): 835-53.

Ogilvie, M. D., B. K. Curran, and E. Trinkaus. "Incidence and Patterning of Dental Enamel Hypoplasia among the Neanderthals," *American Journal of Physical Anthropology* 79 (1989): 25-41.

Ohman, J. C., C. Wood, B. Wood, R. H. Crompton, M. M. Günther, L. Yu, R. Savage, and W. Wang. "Stature-at-Death of KNM-WT 15000," *Human Evolution* 17, nos. 3-4 (2002): 129-42.

Parfitt, Simon A., René W. Barendregt, Marzia Breda, Ian Candy, Matthew J. Collins, G. Russell Coope, Paul Durbidge, Mike H. Field, Jonathan R. Lee, Adrian M. Lister, Robert Mutch, Kirsty E. H. Penkman, Richard C. Preece, James Rose, Christopher B. Stringer, Robert Symmons, John E. Whittaker, John J. Wymer, and Anthony J. Stuart. "The Earliest Record of Human Activity in Northern Europe," *Nature* 438 (2005): 1008-12.

Parkington, J. "Middens and Moderns: Shellfishing and the Middle Stone Age of the Western Cape, South Africa," *South African Journal of Science* 99, nos. 5-6 (2003): 243-47.

Parkington, J., C. Poeggenphl, J.-Ph. Rigaud, and P.-J. Texier. "From Tool to

Symbol: The Behavioural Context of Intentionally Marked Ostrich Eggshell from Diepkloof, Western Cape," in *From Tools to Symbols: From Early Hominids to Modern Humans,* edited by F. d'Errico and L. Backwell, pp. 475-92. Johannesburg: Witwatersrand University Press, 2005.
Pearson, Osbjorn M. "Postcranial Remains and Modern Human Origins," *Evolutionary Anthropology* 9, no. 6 (2001): 229-47.
Petitto, Laura Ann, and P. F. Marentette. "Babbling in the Manual Mode: Evidence for the Ontogeny of Language," *Science* 251, no. 5000 (1991): 1493-96.
Petitto, Laura Ann, Siobhan Holowka, Lauren E. Sergio, and David Ostry. "Language Rhythms in Baby Hand Movements," *Nature* 413 (2001): 35-36.
Petraglia, Michael D., and Ravi Korisettar, eds. *Early Human Behaviour in Global Context: The Rise and Diversity of the Lower Paleolithic Record.* London: Routledge, 1997.
Pettitt, Paul A. "The Neanderthal Dead: Exploring Mortuary Variability in Middle Paleolithic Eurasia," *Before Farming* 1 (2001): 1-19.
Prendergast, M. E., L. Luque, M. Domínguez-Rodrigo, F. Diez-Martin, A. Z. P. Mabulla, and R. Barba. "New Excavations at Mumba Rockshelter, Tanzania," *Journal of African Archaeology* 5, no. 2 (2007): 163-89.
Richmond, Brian G., and William L. Jungers. "*Orrorin tugenensis* Femoral Morphology and the Evolution of Hominin Bipedalism," *Science* 319, no. 5870 (2008): 1662-65.
Richmond, Brian G., and David S. Strait. "Evidence That Humans Evolved from a Knuckle-Walking Ancestor," *Nature* 404 (2000): 382-85.
Rigaud, Jean-Philippe, Pierre-Jean Texier, John Parkington, and Cedric Poggenpoel. "Le mobilier Stillbay et Howiesons Poort de l'abri Diepkloof. La chronologie du *Middle Stone Age* sud-africain et ses implications," *Comptes Rendus Palévol* 5 (2006): 839-49.
Robbins, L. R., M. L. Murphy, G. A. Brook, A. Ivester, A. C. Campbell, R. G. Klein, R. Milo, and W. Downey. "Archaeology, Paleoenvironment, and Chronology of the White Paintings Rock Shelter, Tsodilo Hills, Northwest Kalahari Desert, Botswana," *Journal of Archaeological Science* 27 (2000): 1085-1113.
Roche, H., A. Delagnes, J. Brugal, C. Feibel, M. Kibunjia, V. Mourre, and P-J. Texier. "Early Hominid Stone Tool Production and Technical Skill 2.34 Myr Ago in West Turkana, Kenya," *Nature* 399 (1999): 57-60.
Savage-Rumbaugh, Sue, Stuart G. Shanker, and Talbot J. Taylor. *Apes, Language and the Human Mind.* New York: Oxford University Press, 1998.
Schlanger, Nathan. "Understanding Levallois: Lithic Technology and Cognitive Archaeology," *Cambridge Archaeological Journal* 6, no. 2 (1996): 231-54.
Schmerling, P.-C. *Recherches sur les Ossements Fossiles Découverts dans les Cavernes de la province de Liège, Vol 1 et 2.* Liège: Collardin, 1833-34.
Semaw, S., M. Rodgers, J. Quade, P. Renne, R. Butler, M. Dominguez-Rodrigo,

D. Stout, W. Hart, T. Pickering, and S. Simpson. "2.6 Million-Year-Old Stone Tools and Associated Bones from OGS-6 and OGS-7, Gona, Afar, Ethiopia," *Journal of Human Evolution* 45 (2003): 169-77.

Semaw, S. "The World's Oldest Stone Artifacts from Gona, Ethiopia: Their Implications for Understanding Stone Technology and Patterns of Human Evolution between 2.6-1.5 Million Years Ago," *Journal of Archaeological Science* 27 (2000): 1197-1214.

Senut, Brigitte, Martin Pickford, Dominique Gommery, Pierre Mein, Kiptalam Cheboi, and Yves Coppens. "First Hominid from the Miocene (Lukeino Formation, Kenya)," *Comptes Rendus de l'Académie des Sciences — Series IIA — Earth and Planetary Science* 332, no. 2 (January 30, 2001): 137-44.

Sherwood, Chet C., Francys Subiaul, and Tadeusz Zawidzki. "A Natural History of the Human Mind: Tracing Evolutionary Changes in Brain and Cognition," *Journal of Anatomy* 212, no. 4 (2008): 426-54.

Sherwood, Richard J., Steven C. Ward, and Andrew Hill. "The Taxonomic Status of the Chemeron Temporal (KNM-BC 1)," *Journal of Human Evolution* 42, nos. 1-2 (2002): 153-84.

Stern, J. T., and R. L. Susman. "The Locomotor Anatomy of *Australopithecus afarensis*," *American Journal of Physical Anthropology* 60, no. 3 (1983): 279-317.

Stout, D., J. Quade, S. Semaw, M. J. Rogers, and N. E. Levin. "Raw Material Selectivity of the Earliest Stone Toolmakers at Gona, Afar, Ethiopia," *Journal of Human Evolution* 48 (2005): 365-80.

Stringer, Chris. "Has Australia Backdated the Human Revolution?" *Antiquity* 73, no. 282 (1999): 876-79.

Stringer, C. B., J. C. Finlayson, R. N. Barton, Y. Fernández-Jalvo, I. Cáceres, R. C. Sabin, E. J. Rhodes, A. P. Currant, J. Rodriguez-Vidal, J. F. Giles-Pacheco, and J. A. Riquelme-Cantal. "Neanderthal Exploitation of Marine Mammals in Gibraltar," *Proceedings of the National Academy of Sciences* 105 (2008): 14319-24.

Thieme, Hartmut. "Lower Palaeolithic Hunting Spears from Germany," *Nature* 385 (1997): 807-10.

Tishkoff, Sarah A., Mary Katherine Gonder, Brenna M. Henn, Holly Mortensen, Alec Knight, Christopher Gignoux, Neil Fernandopulle, Godfrey Lema, Thomas B. Nyambo, Uma Ramakrishnan, Floyd A. Reed, and Joanna L. Mountain. "History of Click-Speaking Populations of Africa Inferred from mtDNA and Y Chromosome Genetic Variation," *Molecular Biology and Evolution* 24, no. 10 (2007): 2180-95.

Tomasello, Michael, and Josep Call. *Primate Cognition*. New York: Oxford University Press, 1997.

Tomasello, Michael, Malinda Carpenter, Josep Call, Tanya Behne, and Henrike Moll. "Understanding and Sharing Intentions: The Origin of Cultural Cognition," *Behavioral and Brain Sciences* 28 (2005): 675-91.

Trinkaus, Eric. *The Shanidar Neanderthals.* New York: Academic Press, 1983.

Tryon, Christian A. "'Early' Middle Stone Age Technology from the Kapthurin Formation, Kenya," *Current Anthropology* 47 (2006): 367-75.

Tyson, Edward. *Orang-Outang: Or the Anatomy of a Pygmy Compared with that of a Monkey, an Ape and a Man. To which is Added a Philosophical Essay Concerning the Pygmies, the Cynocephalie, the Satyrs, and Sphinges of the Ancients. Wherein it will Appear that They are All either Apes or Monkeys and not Men, as formerly Pretended.* London: T. Bennett, 1699. (Note that "Orang Outan" was the general designation for all apes in the seventeenth and eighteenth centuries.)

Vandermeersch, Bernard. "Une sépulture moustérienne avec offrandes découverte dans la grotte de Qafzeh," *Compte Rendus de l'Académie des Sciences* 268 (1970): 298-301.

Vandermeersch, Bernard. *Les hommes fossiles de Qafzeh (Israël).* Paris: Editions du CNRS, 1981.

Vanhaeren, Marian, and Francesco d'Errico. "Aurignacian Ethno-Linguistic Geography of Europe Revealed by Personal Ornaments," *Journal of Archaeological Science* 33, no. 8 (2005): 1105-28.

Vanhaeren, M., F. d'Errico, C. B. Stringer, S. L. James, J. A. Todd, and H. K. Mienis. "Middle Paleolithic Shell Beads in Israel and Algeria," *Science* 312 (2006): 1785-88.

Wendt, W. E. "Art Mobilier from the Apollo 11 Cave, Southwest Africa: Africa's Oldest Dated Works of Art," *South African Archaeological Bulletin* 31 (1976): 5-11.

White, Tim D., Berhane Asfaw, David deGusta, Henry Gilbert, Gary D. Richards, Gen Suwa, and F. Clark Howell. "Pleistocene *Homo sapiens* from Middle Awash, Ethiopia," *Nature* 423 (2003): 742-47.

Whiten, A., J. Goodall, W. G. McGrew, T. Nishida, V. Reynolds, Y. Sugiyama, C. E. G. Tutin, R. W. Wrangham, and C. Boesch. "Cultures in Chimpanzees," *Nature* 399 (1999): 682-85.

Wiessner, Pauline. "Reconsidering the Behavioral Basis for Style: A Case Study Among the Kalahari San," *Journal of Anthropological Archaeology* 3, no. 3 (1984): 190-234.

Wood, Bernard A. *Human Evolution: A Very Short Introduction.* New York: Oxford University Press, 2005.

Wood, Bernard A., and Paul Constantino. "Human Origins: Life at the Top of the Tree," in *Assembling the Tree of Life,* edited by Joel Cracraft and Michael J. Donoghue, pp. 517-35. New York: Oxford University Press, 2004.

Wood, Bernard A., and Mark Collard. "The Changing Face of Genus *Homo.*" *Science* 284, no. 5411 (1999): 65-71.

Woodward, Sir Arthur Smith. "A Fossil Skull of an Ancestral Bushman from the Anglo-Egyptian Sudan," *Antiquity* 12, no. 46 (1938): 190-95, Plate I-VII.

Yellen, J., A. S. Brooks, E. Cornelissen, M. Mehlman, and K. Stewart. "A Middle Stone Age Worked Bone Industry from Katanda, Upper Semliki Valley, Zaire," *Science* 268 (1995): 553-56.

Yellen, J. E., A. S. Brooks, D. Helgren, M. Tappen, S. Ambrose, R. Bonnefille, J. Feathers, G. Goodfriend, K. Ludwig, P. Renne, and K. Stewart. "The Archaeology of Aduma: Middle Stone Age Sites in the Awash Valley, Ethiopia," *PaleoAnthropology* 10 (2005): 25-100.

Zhu, R. X., K. A. Hoffman, R. Potts, C. L. Deng, Y. X. Pan, B. Guo, C. D. Shi, Z. T. Guo, B. Y. Yuan, Y. M. Hou and W. W. Huang. "Earliest Presence of Humans in Northeast Asia," *Nature* 413 (2001): 413-17.

Zhu, R. X., R. Potts, Y. X. Pan, H. T. Yao, L. Q. Lu, X. Zhao, X. Gao, L. W. Chen, F. Gao, and C. L. Deng. "Early Evidence of the Genus *Homo* in East Asia," *Journal of Human Evolution* 55 (2008): 1075-85.

Zilhão, J. "Neanderthals and Moderns Mixed, and It Mattered," *Evolutionary Anthropology* 15, no. 5 (2006): 183-95.

Zollikofer, Christoph P. E., Marcia S. Ponce de León, Daniel E. Lieberman, Franck Guy, David Pilbeam, Andossa Likius, Hassane T. Mackaye, Patrick Vignaud, and Michel Brunet. "Virtual Cranial Reconstruction of *Sahelanthropus tchadensis*." *Nature* 434 (2005): 755-59.

THEOLOGICAL ACCOUNTS OF HUMAN DISTINCTIVENESS: THE IMAGO DEI

Humanity — Created, Restored, Transformed, Embodied

Joel B. Green

In his preface to *The Anatomy of the Brain and Nerves,* Thomas Willis (1621-75), the celebrated Father of Neurology, gave poignant witness to the Christian tradition's longstanding indebtedness to two sources of knowledge. Likening his dissection table to "the most holy Altar of Your Grace" — Gilbert Sheldon, Archbishop of Canterbury — Willis referred to his work as a study of "the Pandects of Nature, as into another Table of the Divine Word, and the greater Bible: For indeed, in either Volume there is no high point, which requires not the care, or refuses the industry of an Interpreter; there is no Page certainly which shews not the Author, and his Power, Goodness, Trust, and Wisdom."[1] This sentiment, so prevalent in the Middle Ages,[2] can be found much earlier in Augustine, who wrote, "Some people read books in order to find God. But the very appearance of God's creation is a great book."[3] More recently, Alister McGrath has likewise argued in his important work, *A Scientific Theology,* for two modes of knowing God — the natural order and Scripture; the metaphor also reverberates in the title of R. J. Berry's theology of nature, *God's Book of Works.*[4] Since the onset of "the New Science" in the seventeenth

---

1. Thomas Willis, *The Anatomy of the Brain and Nerves,* Latin original trans. Samuel Pordage, ed. William Feindel (Birmingham: Classics of Medicine Library; Montreal: McGill-Queens University Press, 1978 [1681]), pp. 51-52.

2. Peter Harrison, *The Bible and Protestantism and the Rise of Natural Science* (Cambridge: Cambridge University Press, 1998).

3. Augustine, *Sermo Mai* 126; ET in Karlfried Froehlich, "'Take up and Read': Basics of Augustine's Biblical Interpretation," *Interpretation* 58 (2004): 5-16 (12).

4. Alister E. McGrath, *A Scientific Theology,* vol. 1: *Nature* (Grand Rapids: Eerdmans,

century, the utility of this metaphor has rested especially in carving out a space for the natural sciences in theological discourse. It is not too much of an exaggeration to say that today, the tables are turned. After a half-century of spectacular expansion in our understanding of genetics and neuroscience, as well as more recent advances in evolutionary psychology, the particular voice of God's Book of Words, the Bible, and with it the witness of Christian theology, is often muted if not silenced in discussions of the nature of the human person.[5] When neurobiology speaks not only to the issues of memory and circadian rhythms, but also to topics formerly reserved for theology, like free will and responsibility, personal identity and religious experience, or empathy and altruism, what space is left for the biblical theologian?

Of course, the way I have phrased this question is itself the problem, since it assumes the relevance or significance of theology only in those gaps unoccupied (or not yet occupied) by the natural sciences. Although situating our theological work in relation to the natural sciences can help to open hermeneutical vistas to which we might otherwise have been blind, it is simply not the case that biblical and theological studies have only an adjunct role to play vis-à-vis the natural sciences. Rather, even when both theology and neuroscience explore the same phenomenon — for example, religious experience or free will — each has its own explanatory role and value. In fact, the real problems come when theological studies masquerade as empirical science, or when empirical science confuses its physical findings with metaphysical accounts.

Theology possesses no trump card in the face of competing data from the sciences; in fact, it would be unthinkable for theology to set itself over against empirical research. After all, as a world-encompassing discipline, theology regards the sciences potentially as a means of revelation, though, contrary to some claims made on behalf of science, not the only means of revelation. Consequently, even when theology and science speak separately, as today they often do, theological affirmations

---

2001); R. J. Berry, *God's Book of Works: The Nature and Theology of Nature* (Glasgow: The Gifford Lectures; London: T. & T. Clark, 2003).

5. Among many efforts to debunk theology in favor of biology, see John McGraw, *Brain and Belief: An Exploration of the Human Soul* (Del Mar, CA: Aegis, 2004); and, more famously, Richard Dawkins, *The God Delusion* (Boston: Houghton Mifflin, 2006).

about the human person cannot ignore the findings of science; indeed, theological explanation should account for laboratory findings. Moreover, the work of biblical interpretation in an age of science increases our awareness of the scientific assumptions of earlier centuries at work already in the shaping of biblical studies — including those now-antiquated scientific assumptions that artificially set the parameters for our own reading of biblical texts. Hence, situating the work of exegesis in relation to the sciences has the potential to liberate us from certain predilections that might guide our work unawares, and to allow questions to surface that might otherwise have remained buried.

My concern in this essay, then, is to set out some of the primary contours of the Bible's portrait of humanity — that is, a biblical-theological anthropology or, more simply, a biblical anthropology. In doing so, my initial focus will be the Bible's own starting-point with regard to humanity: the creation of humanity in the "image of God." Although the phrase "image of God" appears outside of Genesis 1-2 only infrequently, beginning here will provide the rubrics with which to pursue other aspects of the biblical witness.

"In the Image of God He Created Them" (Gen. 1:27)

Two immediate affirmations derive from the perspective on humanity provided in Genesis 1:27-31 and 2:4-25 — namely, continuity and difference: the continuity of humanity with all other animals and, indeed, with the rest of creation; and the difference between humanity and other animals.

Humans are like other living things in their being created by God and thus in their relation to him. Moreover, like them, humanity is formed from the stuff of the earth. Vegetation is for both humans and animals (Gen. 1:30). Animals share with humans the command to reproduce, increase, and fill the seas and the earth (Gen. 1:22). The additional vocation given humanity, "to subdue" and "to have dominion" over the earth (Gen. 1:26, 28), does not call for the human exploitation of nature, but must be understood in the context of the order set forth in the creation account. True, the creation account imbues humanity with royal identity and task, but this is a nobility granted without conquest; its essence is realized in co-existence with all of life in the land, and in the cultivation of life. Similarly, Psalm 8:7 portrays humanity in a stance of dominion over creation, as though standing over its defeated enemies, but with no hint of military action. Stewardship of creation, management and care without conquest or domination — the human family has this responsibility in relation to God's creation because this is how God has made us.

Humans are unlike other creatures in that only humanity is created after God's own likeness, in God's own image (imago dei). Only to humanity does God speak directly. Humanity alone receives from God this divine vocation. The imago dei tradition has been the focus of diverse interpretations among Jews and Christians — ranging widely from some physical characteristic of humans (such as standing upright) to a way of knowing (especially the human capacity to know God), and so on. What is obvious is that humanity is thus defined in relation to God in terms of both similarity and difference: humanity is in some sense "like" God, but is itself not divine. Humanity thus stands in an ambivalent position — living in solidarity with the rest of the created order and yet distinct from it on account of humankind's unique role as the bearer of the divine image, called to a particular and crucial relationship with Yahweh and yet not divine.[6]

Taken within its immediate setting in Genesis 1, "the image of God" in which humanity is made is set in relation to the exercise of dominion over the earth on God's behalf. This observation does not take us far, however, since we must then ascertain what it means to exercise dominion in this way — that is, in a way that reflects God's own ways of interaction with his creatures. Additionally, this way of putting the issue does not grapple with the profound word spoken over humanity and about humanity, that human beings in themselves (and not merely in what they do) reflect the divine image. What is this quality that distinguishes humanity? God's words affirm the creation of the human family in its relation to himself, as his counterpart, so that the nature of humanity derives from the human family's relatedness to God. The concept of the imago dei, then, is fundamentally relational, or covenantal, and takes as its ground and focus the graciousness of God's

---

6. See McGrath, *Nature,* p. 197. For recent surveys of ways in which creation of humanity "in the divine image" has been interpreted, together with a contemporary proposal, see Stanley J. Grenz, *The Social God and the Relational Self: A Trinitarian Theology of the Imago Dei* (The Matrix of Christian Theology; Louisville: Westminster John Knox, 2001); and especially J. Richard Middleton, *The Liberating Image: The Imago Dei in Genesis 1* (Grand Rapids: Brazos, 2005).

own covenantal relations with humanity and the rest of creation. The distinguishing mark of *human* existence when compared with other creatures is thus the whole of human existence (and not some "part" of the individual). As the Genesis story unfolds, the vocation given humanity entails individuality within community and the human capacity for self-transcendence and morality — that is, the capacity to make decisions on the basis of self-deliberation, planning and action on the basis of that decision, and responsibility for those decisions and actions. The skeleton of what Francisco Ayala refers to as "ethical consciousness" (that is, the capacity to judge human actions as right or wrong),[7] is filled out in Scripture with reference to God's own character, God's "difference" (or holiness) in relation to the cosmos. In a signal text, for example, Leviticus 19 indexes holy behavior in terms of family and community respect (vv. 3, 32), religious loyalty (vv. 3b, 4-8, 12, 26-31), economic relationships (vv. 9-10), workers' rights (v. 13), social compassion (v. 14), judicial integrity (v. 15), neighborly attitudes and conduct (vv. 11, 16-18), distinctiveness (v. 19), sexual integrity (vv. 20-22, 29), exclusion of the idolatrous and occult (vv. 4, 26-31), racial equality (vv. 33-34), and commercial honesty (vv. 35-36).[8] Echoing Leviticus 19, Peter writes, "As he who called you is holy, be holy yourselves in all your conduct; for it is written, 'You shall be holy, for I am holy'" (1 Peter 1:15-16).

Genesis 1–2 does not locate the singularity of humanity in the human possession of a "soul," but rather in the human capacity to relate to Yahweh as covenant partner, and to join in companionship within the human family and in relation to the whole cosmos in ways that reflect the covenant love of God. Indeed, within the Old Testament, "soul" *(nepheš)* refers to life and vitality — not life in general, but as instantiated in human persons and animals; not a thing to have but a way to be.[9] To speak of loving God with all of one's "soul" (e.g., Deut. 6:5), then, is to elevate the intensity of involvement of the entirety of one's being. What, then, of Genesis 2:7 ("the Lord God formed the human being of the dust of the ground, breathed into his nostrils the

---

7. Francisco J. Ayala, "Biological Evolution and Human Nature," in *Human Nature*, ed. Malcolm Jeeves (Edinburgh: The Royal Society of Edinburgh, 2006), pp. 46-64.

8. This way of construing holiness is borrowed from Christopher J. H. Wright, "Old Testament Ethics: A Missiological Perspective," *Catalyst* 26, no. 2 (2000): 5-8.

9. For extended discussion, see Lawson G. Stone, "The Soul: Possession, Part, or Person? The Genesis of Human Nature in Genesis 2:7," in *What About the Soul? Neuroscience and Christian Anthropology*, ed. Joel B. Green (Nashville: Abingdon, 2004), pp. 47-61.

breath of life, and the human being became a living soul [*nepheš*]," my translation)? The term in question, *nepheš*, is used only a few verses earlier with reference to "every beast of the earth," "every bird of the air," and "everything that creeps on the earth" — that is, to everything "in which there is life *(nepheš)*" (1:30; my translation). This demonstrates that "soul" is not for the Genesis story a unique characteristic of the human person. Accordingly, one might better translate Genesis 2:7 with reference to the divine gift of *life:* "the human being became fully alive" (my translation). Genesis does not define humanity in essentialist terms but in relational, as Yahweh's partner, and with emphasis on the communal, intersexual character of personhood, the quality of care the human family is to exercise with regard to creation as God's representative, the importance of the human modeling of the personal character of God, and the unassailable vocation of humans to reflect among themselves God's own character.[10]

"To the Measure of the Full Stature of Christ" (Eph. 4:13)

Outside of Genesis 1-2 the phrase "image of God" plays little role in the Old Testament, though it is found in Jewish literature from the Second Temple period (e.g., Wis. 2:23-24; Sir. 17:1-13), including the letters of Paul. In 2 Corinthians 4:4, Paul refers to "the glory of Christ, who is the image of God," and in Colossians 1:15 he says of Christ, "He is the image of the invisible God, the firstborn of all creation." This Christology lies at the confluence of two streams of thought — (1) portraits of humanity in Genesis 1:26-27 as created in God's image and in Psalm 8:5 as "crowned . . . with glory and honor," and (2) Jewish speculation regarding Wisdom, described in Wisdom 7:25-26 as "a pure emanation of the glory of the Almighty . . . a reflection of eternal light, a spotless mirror of the working of God, and an image of his goodness." The apostle's thought in both contexts is similar, for in 2 Corinthians 4 he says the gospel unveils the very thing that Satan would hide from unbelievers — namely, "the knowledge of the glory of God in the face of Jesus Christ"

---

10. See further, Walter Brueggemann, *Theology of the Old Testament: Testimony, Dispute, Advocacy* (Minneapolis: Fortress, 1997), pp. 451-52; Colin E. Gunton, "Trinity, Ontology and Anthropology: Towards a Renewal of the Doctrine of the *Imago Dei*," in *Persons Divine and Human: King's College Essays on Theological Anthropology*, ed. Christoph Schwöbel and Colin E. Gunton (Edinburgh: T. & T. Clark, 1991), pp. 47-61.

(4:6); whereas in Colossians the work of Christ is manifest in the renewal of humanity in the image of the Creator (3:10).

Not surprisingly, then, the terms "image" and "glory" figure importantly, too, in Paul's depiction of humanity in its need of transformation. In the exodus journey, God's people "exchanged the glory of God for the image of an ox that eats grass. They forgot God, their Savior, who had done great things in Egypt, wondrous works in the land of Ham, and awesome deeds by the Red Sea" (Ps. 106:20-22). Expanding this portrait, Paul writes of the whole of humankind, "Claiming to be wise, they became fools; and they exchanged the glory of the immortal God for images resembling a mortal human being or birds or four-footed animals or reptiles" (Rom. 1:22-23). What is more, the psalmist observes, human beings become like the object of their worship: "Their idols are silver and gold, the work of human hands. They have mouths, but do not speak; eyes, but do not see. They have ears, but do not hear; noses, but do not smell. They have hands, but do not feel; feet, but do not walk; they make no sound in their throats. *Those who make them are like them; so are all who trust in them*" (Ps. 115:4-8; emphasis added). So too, for Paul, humanity has profaned God's glory — indeed, "all have sinned and fall short of the glory of God" (Rom. 3:23).

What then does it mean to speak of Christ as the image of God? Colin Gunton has aptly summarized: "first, that Jesus represents God to the creation in the way that the first human beings were called, but failed, to do; and second that he enables other human beings to achieve the directedness to God of which their fallenness had deprived them."[11] Not surprisingly then, Paul can elsewhere develop this affirmation of Christ as God's image in terms of its corollary, the conformation of human beings into the "image of Christ" (Rom. 8:29; 1 Cor. 15:49; 2 Cor. 3:18).

The renewal of the human being in the divine image is profoundly personal, and embraces the human person in his or her totality. This means that (trans)formation is fully embodied within a nest of relationships, a community. From Scripture we receive an all-encompassing perspective on human health in the cosmos and in relation to God, but also well-developed ways of identifying the sickness that spreads like cancer throughout the human family, even eating away at the world that humans call home. The term generally given this sickness in the Christian

---

11. Colin Gunton, *Christ and Creation* (Grand Rapids: Eerdmans, 1992), p. 100.

tradition is "sin," a multivalent term that points to the myriad ways in which humans — individually, collectively, and systemically — neglect, deny, and refuse simply to be human — that is, to embrace and live out their vocation as creatures made in the image of God. Accordingly, a Christian conception of human transformation does not allow the categorization of either the person or his or her salvation into "parts," as though inner and outer life could be separated. Angst among Christians in the past century over how to prioritize ministries of "evangelism" and "social witness" are simply wrongheaded, since the gospel, the "evangel" of "evangelism," cannot but concern itself with *human need in all its aspects*. Only an erroneous body-soul dualism could allow — indeed, require — "ministry" to become segregated by its relative concern for "spiritual" versus "material" matters. Nor does a Christian conception of human transformation allow us to think of the restoration of individuals, as it were, one at a time, but pushes our categories always to account for the human community and, beyond humanity, the cosmos. Persons are not saved in isolation from the world around them. Restoration to the likeness of God is the work of the community of God's people, the fellowship of Christ-followers set on maturation in Christ. From this vantage point, "image of God" points ultimately to the transformation of believers in resurrection, a transformation already at work in the creation of a new humanity through the dissolution of barriers dividing human beings from one another along gender, social, or ethnic lines (Col. 3:10-11; 1 Cor. 12:12-13; Gal. 3:28).

"Be Transformed by the Renewing of Your Minds" (Rom. 12:2)

Recent work in cognitive science has underscored the fallacy of Descartes' notion of the mind, free to engage in its own operations (quite apart from one's own body and from other minds), countering with its nonnegotiable emphasis on embodiment — that is, "the role of an agent's own body in its everyday, situated cognition."[12] From this we might infer, for example, the fallacy of imagining that intellect and affect are separable, the fallacy of imagining that mind and behavior are separable, the fallacy of imagining that human life can be understood

---

12. Raymond W. Gibbs Jr., *Embodiment and Cognitive Science* (Cambridge: Cambridge University Press, 2006), p. 1.

merely or primarily with respect to individuals, and the inescapable conclusion that human formation is a process. In important ways, these emphases correlate with New Testament perspectives on Christian conversion, so crucial to its depiction of the new humanity called forth in Christ. Because of their pronounced interest in conversion, let me focus on the two volumes in the New Testament attributed to Luke, the Gospel of Luke and the Acts of the Apostles, or Luke-Acts.

That the Lukan writings support a heightened interest in conversion is widely acknowledged. Indeed, the importance of conversion is signaled immediately in Luke's first chapter, with Gabriel's announcement to Zechariah that the son to be born to him, John, would be a prophet. Gabriel summarizes the effect of John's ministry as a call to repentance:

> *He will turn* many of the people of Israel to the Lord their God . . . he will go before him,
> *to turn* the hearts of fathers to their children, and
> *[to turn]* the disobedient to the wisdom of the righteous,
> to make ready a people prepared for the Lord.
> (Luke 1:16-17; my translation)

In these words we discover immediately that repentance in Luke-Acts will not be a theological abstraction, but rather is aimed at a transformation of day-to-day patterns of thinking, feeling, believing, and behaving. What begins with the angelic message in Luke 1 continues throughout the Lukan narrative, in which Jesus articulates his mission as calling sinners to repentance (Luke 5:32) and reports rejoicing at the repentance of even one of them (Luke 15:7, 10), in which the directed response to the good news is, "Repent, and be baptized . . ." (Acts 2:38), and in which Paul can summarize his entire ministry as declaring "first to those in Damascus, then in Jerusalem and throughout the countryside of Judea, and also to the Gentiles, that they should repent and turn to God and do deeds consistent with repentance" (Acts 26:20). Given its importance in Luke-Acts, how does Luke develop this motif?

A New "Conceptual Scheme"

The necessity of response to the gospel is set forth programmatically in the narration of the Pentecost address where Peter is interrupted by his audience: "What shall we do, brothers?" (Acts 2:37). Response is necessary because, according to Peter, the exaltation of Jesus and the consequent outpouring of the Holy Spirit have signaled a dramatic transformation in history. Within the speeches of Acts, Jewish people might hear the familiar stories borrowed from their Scriptures, but these stories have been cast in fresh ways. Israel's past (and present) is understood correctly and embraced fully only in relation to the redemptive purpose of God, but this divine purpose can be understood only as articulated by authorized interpretive agents — first, Jesus of Nazareth, and then his witnesses. Thus, for example, Paul's question to King Agrippa, "Do you believe the prophets?" (Acts 26:27), concerns not simply a commitment to the prophets, but to the prophets *as they have been expounded by Paul*. The coming of Jesus as Savior may signal the fresh offer of repentance and forgiveness of sins to Israel (Acts 5:31; 13:38-39), but the acceptance of this offer by Jewish people is dependent on their embracing this interpretation of God's salvific activity. Greek audiences, too, are asked to adopt a new way of viewing the world. Thus, at Athens, Paul distinguishes between how God worked in the past (17:30a; cf. 14:16) and how he will now operate (17:30b) — a distinction that calls for repentance. The "old story" thus receives fresh narration, itself the consequence of and an invitation to new patterns of dispositions and behavior.

What Luke describes can be understood in terms of a transformed "imagination" or "conceptual scheme" — at once *conceptual* (a way of seeing things), *conative* (a set of beliefs and values to which a group and its members are deeply attached), and *action-guiding* (we seek to live according to its terms).[13] To put it differently, life-events do not come with self-contained and immediately obvious interpretations; we have to conceptualize them, and we do so in terms of imaginative structures or conceptual schemes that we implicitly take to be true, normal, and good.[14]

---

13. For this description, I have borrowed from Owen Flanagan, *The Problem of the Soul: Two Visions of Mind and How to Reconcile Them* (New York: Basic, 2002), pp. 27-55.

14. Cf. Mark Johnson, *Moral Imagination: Implications of Cognitive Science for Ethics* (Chicago: University of Chicago Press, 1993), ch. 8. Paul gives witness to this hermeneutical reality when he writes, "From now on, therefore, we regard no one from a human point of view; even though we once knew Christ from a human point of view, we know him no longer in that way" (2 Cor 5:16). More broadly, see, e.g., Stephen P. Reyna, *Connections: Brain, Mind, and Culture in a Social Anthropology* (London: Routledge, 2002).

Humanity — Created, Restored, Transformed, Embodied

For Luke, embracing this new conceptual scheme is a fresh way of seeing things, an "opening of the mind" to understand what was previously incomprehensible (cf. Luke 24:30-32, 44-48), that takes as its starting-point the mission and message of Jesus, together with his death, resurrection, and ascension. In the same way that what was previously seen as a duck is now seen as a rabbit, so conversion signals not simply the introduction of new ideas into an old imaginative framework, but a transformed imaginative framework; within this framework, what was previously inconceivable is now matter-of-fact. This emphasis is set out programmatically in Luke 4:18-19, where Jesus' missionary program includes "proclaiming sight to the blind" — a statement that anticipates the recovery of sight instigated by physical healing, to be sure (Luke 18:35-43; Acts 9:18-19), but even more so portends the provision and reception of divine revelation, the passage from darkness to light, the movement from ignorance to insight — and so, entry into salvation and inclusion in God's family.[15]

Conversion and Socialization

If conversion is grounded in a fresh comprehension of the purpose of God as this is plotted in Scripture, then it is manifest in the community of God's people who are constituted by this biblical narrative, and whose practices embody this spirituality and leverage the ongoing conversion of its members. Conversion as an ongoing process of socialization needs particular emphasis here, both because it is often neglected in discourse about conversion and because it is so vital to the Lukan narrative. Without attempting to downplay those "moments" of conversion that Luke records, we may nonetheless draw attention to the nature of conversion as a social act. Seen from this vantage point, conversion entails autobiographical reconstruction. Conversion shatters one's past and reassembles it in accordance with the new life of the converted; former understandings of one's self and one's experiences are regarded as erroneous and are provided new meaning (cf. Luke 9:23). Of course, the prime example of this emphasis in the Lukan narrative is Paul, and especially his narration of his experience on the road to Damascus (Acts 26:4-29). More pervasive are those instances where

---

15. E.g., Luke 1:78-79; 2:9, 29-32; 3:6; 24:13-35; Acts 26:18.

one's reformed allegiances and dispositions are expressed in terms that reflect a creative imagination, especially with regard to revisionist conceptualizations of the character of the people of God — and thus, of Yahweh's purpose and Israel's history. Converts find explanations for phenomena in terms that are appropriate to the pattern of life they have embraced and that are often distinctive from the conceptual patterns held by others. Stephen, for example, as well as Paul, prove themselves to be masterful narrators of the history of Israel (e.g., Acts 7; 13:16-41). The whole of Israel's history and self-understanding is now reevaluated for presentation in light of the newly found understanding of God's purpose resident in Jesus' crucifixion and exaltation. In Acts, conversion as the process of embracing a new symbolic universe is on display in the Christian community and in the speeches of its spokespersons.

This symbolic world finds expression most fully in the context of one of the characteristic practices of the Christianity community. This is prayer, which provides the opportunity for the disclosure of God's salvific purpose, especially at pivotal points in the mission. Acts portrays prayer as a community-defining practice that directs the expansion of the community. This is because the habits of prayer counseled by Jesus serve as an ongoing catalyst for the conformation of the community around the unlimited mercy of God (cf. Luke 6:35-36; 11:1-13). Prayer of this sort allows for the infusion of a life-world centered on the gracious God, on dependence on God, on the imitation of God, and on the disclosure of God's purpose for humanity, all understood against an eschatological horizon in which the coming of God in sovereignty and redemption figures prominently.

Finally, conversion entails incorporation into a new community, including adopting the rituals and behaviors peculiar to or definitive of that new community. This is evident immediately in Acts 2:42-47, the first in a series of summaries that dot the landscape of the narrative of Acts — this one serving the dual function of exhibiting the communal dimension of the consequence of the outpouring of the Holy Spirit and demonstrating the quality of daily life characteristic of those who are baptized in the name of Jesus Christ. The generalizations about the community of Jesus' followers sketched here amplify the response urged by Peter in 2:38, "Repent and be baptized!" Baptism functions, on the one hand, as the medium by which repentance comes to expression and, on the other, as the sign that forgiveness has been granted. To put it differently, baptism serves a community-defining role — communicating on the part of the baptized an unswerving loyalty to the Lord and on the part of the church the full incorporation of the baptized into the community. Baptism is both response and gift. What is more, baptism in Acts has as its consequence, among other things, economic koinonia (e.g., 2:41-47) and the extension of hospitality (e.g., 10:47-48; 16:14-15, 28-34) — behaviors then, that must be included under the heading of "fruits worthy of repentance" (Luke 3:7-14).

A Community Formed and Forming

If repentance signals an essential reorientation of life, repentance is also something that persons "do." "Bear fruits worthy of repentance," John proclaims early in Luke's Gospel, before spelling out behavioral exemplars of repentance from the realm of socio-economic relations (Luke 3:7-14; cf. Acts 26:20). If we have learned in the last two or three centuries that "being" and "doing" are separable, we should not project such distinctions into the Scriptures, wherein the assumption that a person *is* one's behavior is more at home. We do what we are — that is, one's deepest commitments are inexorably exhibited in one's practices, so that attention focuses on "embodied life," disallowing the possibility that the "real" person might be relegated to one's interior life.[16]

What are these community-constituting practices? Though they scarcely exhaust the possibilities resident in the Lukan narrative, three are especially pervasive: economic koinonia, prayer, and witness.

Economic koinonia: Two summary statements, Acts 2:42-47 and 4:32-35, exhibit the communal dimension of the consequences of the outpouring of the Spirit at the same time that they demonstrate how the message of Jesus' resurrection manifests itself in the nature of the community. Luke's portrait of God's people thus places a premium on care of the needy, portrays the community of believers as an extended kin-group, and ties the life of this community into the formation of God's

---

16. See Robert A. Di Vito, "Old Testament Anthropology and the Construction of Personal Identity," *Catholic Biblical Quarterly* 61 (1999): 217-38; also "Here One Need Not Be One's Self: The Concept of 'Self' in the Old Testament," in *The Whole and Divided Self: The Bible and Theological Anthropology*, ed. David E. Aune and John McCarthy (New York: Crossroad, 1997), pp. 49-88; Klaus Berger, *Identity and Experience in the New Testament* (Minneapolis: Fortress, 2003).

people in exodus (cf. Deut. 15:1-18). Summaries, like these two texts in Acts, serve as interpretive "headings," so it is not surprising that Acts also narrates other instances of economic interest — for example, partnership between communities of believers (e.g., 11:27-29), Paul's claim that he was no lover of money (20:33-35), and especially the persistent correlation of embracing the Christian message with extension of hospitality (e.g., 10:44-48; 16:14-15, 30-34).

Prayer: Among the Gospel writers, Luke devotes an inordinate amount of attention to prayer, emphasizing especially the revelatory function of prayer. This emphasis begins as early as Jesus' baptism (Luke 3:21-22)[17] and continues into the book of Acts, where the community of God's people likewise experiences prayer as revelatory moment and as invitation to align oneself with the aim of God thus revealed.

For Luke, prayer is a practice that grows out of one's convictions and commitments. It is for him the conceptual scheme of the converted in practice. It is metonymic for one's character. Jesus uses prayer to speak to the issue of what sort of people, with what sort of commitments and character as well as behaviors, are fit for the kingdom of God. In the Third Gospel, prayer serves as a boundary marker, employed by the Pharisees, for example, to identify themselves over against others. In them we see that the habit of prayer is a catalyst for community formation. The question is: What sort of community? In Luke 5:27-39 and 18:9-14, prayer functions among Pharisees as an identity marker oriented toward maintaining clear lines of demarcation between groups — in these instances, as behaviors that separate Pharisees from toll collectors and sinners. Jesus' response is reminiscent of the prophetic criticism of pious acts when those acts are segregated from acts of justice and mercy (e.g., Isa. 58:3-9; Jer. 14:12; Zech. 7:5-6), which apparently include the humility necessary to extend hospitality and other signs of God's care to the marginal of society. Prayer is likewise for Christians in Acts a community-defining practice, leading to the conformation of the community around the gracious God.

Witness: The missionary portfolio Jesus gives to his followers in Acts 1:8 centers on practices of *witness:* "Rather, you will receive power when the Holy Spirit has come upon you, and you will be my witnesses in Jerusalem, in all Judea and Samaria, and to the end of the earth" (my translation). This mandate is especially interesting since it is self-

---

17. See also Luke 2:36-38; 9:18-27, 28-36; 10:21-22; 23:34, 46; 24:30-31.

evident that the significance of Jesus' words was not immediately obvious to his followers. The formation of disciples, as Luke develops it, is a process of conversion. It entails a reconstruction of one's self within a new web of relationships, a transfer of allegiances, and the embodiment of transformed dispositions and attitudes. The parade example of the interwoven nature of conversion and witness is the complex narration of the encounter between Peter and Cornelius and its aftermath in the Jerusalem church, in Acts 10:1–11:18. Cornelius is introduced first, with the result that we might gain the mistaken impression that this text centers on his conversion and that of his household. Instead, Luke's focus is on Peter and the Jerusalem church, and especially their ethnocentric practices. The significance of what transpires is accentuated by multiple evidences of the divine hand at work (e.g., 10:3-16; 10:44-47), which validate the practice of full fellowship between Jew and Gentile. Note that hospitality was at stake in the protestations first of Peter (Acts 10:28a) and then of the circumcised in the Jerusalem church (Acts 11:2-3). Cornelius is converted, to be sure, but so are Peter and those of the Jerusalem community — Cornelius, in the sense that he moves from his position as a God-fearer on the margins of the Jewish religion to full membership within the community of God's people for whom Jesus is Lord; Peter and the Jerusalem community to a fuller embodiment of their newly embraced life-world, expressed in the confession that Jesus is, indeed, "Lord of all" (Acts 10:34-36).

Much more could be said regarding conversion as a window into human formation as this is represented in Luke-Acts, but this is enough to validate the observation that the transformation proffered in Christ is deeply implicated in the concrete realities of daily existence. Conversion and spiritually more generally cannot be relegated to the ethereal for the simple reason that in human life "the spiritual" has no reality apart from "the material." Spiritual experience is embodied experience. Conversion for Luke-Acts is the transference of one's defining allegiances, exhibited and confirmed in practices appropriate to those new allegiances, and an ongoing transformation of one's theological and moral imagination that necessarily locates and immerses one in the multiethnic community of God's people. For Luke-Acts, there is no Christian conversion that is not fully embodied and nested in a community of Christ-followers, with change a divine gift facilitated through relational interaction and engagement in the practices by which the Christian community is constituted.

"When He Is Revealed, We Will Be Like Him" (1 John 3:2)

Writing to the Corinthians, the apostle Paul famously remarked, "If for this life only we have hoped in Christ, we are of all people most to be pitied" (1 Cor. 15:19). Indeed, resurrection faith helps to define Christianity — as the Apostles' Creed has it, "I believe . . . in the resurrection of the body, and life everlasting." In her examination of resurrection faith among Christians in the early and medieval periods, Caroline Walker Bynum demonstrated that Christian belief concerning the resurrection has stubbornly focused on the physicality of both resurrection and ultimate salvation,[18] this in spite of the obvious reality that our physical bodies decay upon death. Here is the problem: if the person does not have a body as something other than itself, then how are we to understand the nature of the afterlife? Does not the frailty of embodied existence vacate the doctrine of (bodily) resurrection of all sensibility?

If not through persistence of this body, how might continuity of personal identity, from death to life-after-death, be guaranteed? How can I be sure that the *me* that enjoys eternal life is really *me*? Here we raise the question of personal identity in general, and the possibility of the survival of personal identity in particular — an issue that has suggested to some that the hope of resurrection turns on a dualist anthropology: mortal body, immortal soul. Given the self-evident finality of death for the physical body, without recourse to a separate entity or personal "essence" (that is, a soul, which constitutes the real *me*) that survives death, how can we maintain a reasonable doctrine of the afterlife? If, instead of *possessing* a body, I *am* a body, then when my body dies do I not likewise cease to exist?[19]

The New Testament is virtually silent on the nature of personal continuity between this life and the next. Paul assures the Corinthians of the "that" of the resurrection, and he does so in somatic terms that

---

18. Caroline Walker Bynum, *The Resurrection of the Body in Western Christianity, 200-1336* (New York: Columbia University Press, 1995). She concludes that "a concern for material and structural continuity showed remarkable persistence even where it seemed almost to require philosophical incoherence, theological equivocation, or aesthetic offensiveness. . . . The materialism of [traditional Christian] eschatology expressed not body-soul dualism but rather a sense of self as psychosomatic unity" (p. 11).

19. For philosophical explorations of these questions, see Kevin Corcoran, ed., *Soul, Body, and Survival: Essays on the Metaphysics of Human Persons* (Ithaca, NY: Cornell University Press, 2001).

Humanity — Created, Restored, Transformed, Embodied

register both continuity and discontinuity, but in doing so he appeals to the mystery (μυστήριον, *mystērion* — a secret that transcends and baffles human ingenuity) of transformation:

> Listen, I will tell you a mystery! We will not all die, but we will all be changed, in a moment, in the twinkling of an eye, at the last trumpet. For the trumpet will sound, and the dead will be raised imperishable, and we will be changed. For this perishable body must put on imperishability, and this mortal body must put on immortality. (1 Cor. 15:51-53)

Paul himself helps to fill in the picture somewhat, but Luke's portrait of the continuity between the pre- and post-resurrection Jesus is also suggestive.

The Resurrected Jesus in Luke 24

The post-resurrection scenes of Luke 24 hold in tension two seemingly contradictory emphases: the (in)ability of people to recognize Jesus (see Luke 24:16, 31, 35) and Jesus' emphatic claim, "It is I myself," or "It is really me!" (my translation, 24:39). Jesus here demonstrates his corporeality without allowing his physicality to determine exhaustively the form of his existence.[20] On the one hand, we have evidence that Jesus' post-resurrection, bodily existence was extraordinary. In descriptions that call to mind the behavior of angels (e.g., Gen. 18:2; Dan. 8:15; 12:5; Acts 10:30), Luke reports that he disappeared and appeared suddenly (24:31, 36).[21] His disciples on the Emmaus road (24:15-16) and those gathered in Jerusalem (24:36-37) cannot identify him. Indeed, the latter regard him as a "spirit," a "ghostly apparition," the disembodied residue of a dead person. This analysis of things is flatly con-

---

20. More broadly, see Robert H. Gundry, "The Essential Physicality of Jesus' Resurrection according to the New Testament," in *Jesus of Nazareth: Lord and Christ: Essays on the Historical Jesus and New Testament Christology*, ed. Joel B. Green and Max Turner (Grand Rapids: Eerdmans, 1994), pp. 204-19.

21. On the connections of this material with angelophanies, see Crispin H. T. Fletcher-Louis, *Luke-Acts: Angels, Christology and Soteriology*, Wissenschaftliche Untersuchungen zum Neuen Testament 2:94 (Tübingen: Mohr Siebeck, 1997), pp. 62-70. Fletcher-Louis helpfully analyzes Luke's presentation of Jesus in these scenes as both more divine than angels and more human.

tradicted by Jesus, however, who immediately demonstrates that he is no ghost. On the other hand, Jesus goes to great lengths to establish his physicality. As Luke will later observe, Jesus thus begins to present himself "alive to them by many convincing proofs" (Acts 1:3). Jesus grounds the continuity of his identity ("It is really me!"), first, in his materiality, his physicality — in the constitution of flesh and density of bones: "Look at my hands and my feet; see that it is I myself. Touch me and see; for a ghost does not have flesh and bones as you see that I have" (24:39). Here is no phantom, no vision, no spirit-being. Jesus presses further, requesting something to eat, then consuming broiled fish in the presence of his disciples (24:41-43).[22] In Luke's report of Jesus' post-resurrection existence, we find no witness to resurrection as escape from bodily existence. Nor is it possible to confuse Jesus' postmortem existence with that of an angel. His, rather, is a transformed materiality, a bodily resurrection.

Luke's meal scene bears witness to Jesus' physicality, but also guarantees the postmortem persistence of Jesus' personal identity by reestablishing within the Lukan narrative Jesus' fellowship with his disciples at the table. Within the Third Gospel, meal scenes often provided Jesus with opportunity for disclosure of his mission (e.g., Luke 5:27-32; 14-15; 19:1-10) and, in the Emmaus episode, of his identity (24:30-31, 35). The eating scene Luke mentions here (see also Acts 1:4; 10:41) invites multiple layers of significance: restored fellowship with Jesus, Jesus' self-disclosure, material evidence of his resurrected status, and opportunity for teaching and discussion. He is not only capable of eating, but actually resumes the table fellowship that had characterized Jesus' ministry in Galilee and en route to Jerusalem. That is, the post-resurrection persistence of Jesus' identity is established also in terms of relationality and mission.

Luke thus navigates between two of the most popular views for imaging the afterlife — the one more barbaric, the other more sophisticated. First, he shows that Jesus' disciples did not mistake him for a cadaver brought back to life, a reanimated corpse. Luke distinguishes Jesus' resurrected body from the resuscitated bodies of the widow's son in Nain (7:11-17), Jairus's daughter (8:40-42, 49-56), Tabitha (Acts 9:36-

---

22. David Goodman observes that, from the second century BCE, it was axiomatic that angels did not eat ordinary, earthly food ("Do Angels Eat?" *Journal of Jewish Studies* 37 [1986]: 160-70); cf. Tob. 12:15, 19.

43), and Eutychus (20:7-12). Second, he certifies that Jesus' constitution is not that of an "immortal soul" freed from bodily existence. Jesus is present to his disciples, beyond the grave, as a fully embodied person. What is more, his affirmation concerning himself could not be more emphatic: "It is I myself!" "It is really me!" — intimating the profound continuity between these phases of his life: before crucifixion and after resurrection.

In the Lukan narrative, Jesus presents yet further evidence of personal continuity: "Then he said to them, 'These are my words that I spoke to you while I was still with you — that everything written about me in the law of Moses, the prophets, and the psalms must be fulfilled'" (Luke 24:44). Here is the move Jesus makes: he weaves a story; or, rather, he picks up the story that is already present, the scriptural story, within which, throughout his ministry, he has sought to inscribe himself. However else we might parse the character of personal identity, and continuity of identity, central to answering the question "Who?" is *the story of a life*. Within the Lukan narrative, the identity of Jesus is known by means of the story he tells of himself, and this story is continuous throughout the narrative, uninterrupted by death and burial.

This Lukan emphasis may seem strange to people of the West in the early twenty-first century, accustomed as we have become to notions of personhood that place a premium on self-actualization and self-legislation. As Jürgen Moltmann helpfully summarizes, our anthropology is "dominated by the will to give the conscious mind power over the instrument of the body," but this emphasis stands in stark contrast to concerns with embodiment, relationship, and narrative so at home in the world of Israel's Scriptures.[23] The Israelite has a sense of self above all in relation to the people of God, and this in relation to the covenant and promises of the God of Israel. Personal identity is found in the historical narrative within which people live, in relation to the divine vocation given that people.

As Luke presents it, Jesus' identity is worked out in terms of his relationship to God, his vocation within the purpose of God, and his place within the community of God's people — past, present, and fu-

---

23. Jürgen Moltmann, *God in Creation: A New Theology of Creation and the Spirit of God* (The Gifford Lectures 1984-85; San Francisco: Harper & Row, 1985), pp. 244-75 (citation from p. 245).

ture. And all of this converges in Luke 24. This is not death leading to the flight of the soul, freed from the encumbrance of a physical body, but the means by which the people of God would experience end-time restoration as God's people. Resurrection is not soul-flight, but the exclamation point and essential affirmation that Jesus has placed on display for all to see a life of service, even the service of life-giving death.

Paul on the *Sōma Pneumatikon*

I have already hinted that resurrection-belief constitutes an important battleground in the Paul-Corinth correspondence, and this controversy comes into focus above all in 1 Corinthians 15. Why Paul engages here in an extended discourse on the resurrection remains a matter of debate, though we should presume with most scholars today that Paul's theological concerns are motivated by issues intrinsic to the situation in Corinth and otherwise on display in his correspondence with them. Since Paul's primary stated objective in 1 Corinthians is to restore unity (1:10), the proposal made by Dale B. Martin concerning the nature of the Corinthian situation is especially attractive.[24] Following customary practice in the Roman world, persons of high status in Corinth, Martin suggests, would have extended hospitality to itinerant philosophers and thus have been exposed to more sophisticated notions about the afterlife. For them, Paul's talk of the raising of the dead would have been reminiscent of fables about the resuscitation of corpses, the stuff of popular myths. Taught to degrade the body, they would have found Paul's teaching about bodily resurrection incomprehensible, or barbaric. Indeed, for them, salvation would have constituted escape from the physical world, not an eschatological affirmation of bodily existence. Those of lower status, to whom Paul can refer as "those who have nothing" (11:22), on the other hand, would have been incapable of welcoming itinerant philosophers into their homes and, thus, would have lived apart from their influence. They would have had closer contact with superstitions and popular myths, including those relating to the resuscitation of corpses and the endowment of those corpses with immortality. Remembering the aim of this letter to catalyze unity, we can

---

24. Dale B. Martin, *The Corinthian Body* (New Haven: Yale University Press, 1995). This is true even if his understanding of the nature of the resurrection body is problematic.

Humanity — Created, Restored, Transformed, Embodied

see that Paul's challenge is to represent the resurrection-belief of early Christianity with enough sophistication to communicate effectively with those of high status while not alienating those of lower status. In short, it makes good sense that Paul is struggling with a Corinthian Christian community within which something of the diversity of Greco-Roman views surrounding the afterlife was present and that this lack of agreement was playing havoc both with the integrity of the church and with this central claim of the Christian gospel.

In 1 Corinthians 15, Paul defended belief in the future resurrection by (1) appealing to what had already become Christian tradition (vv. 1-11), (2) observing that a denial of the future resurrection was tantamount to denying the resurrection of Christ, and moving on to an affirmation of Christ's resurrection as "first fruits" of the future resurrection (vv. 12-34), and (3) sketching how one might plausibly conceive of the resurrection of the dead (vv. 35-58). Of particular interest is the last subsection, 15:35-38, where Paul turns from the "what" of the resurrection to the "how," and, among other things, affirms the following: (1) There is a profound continuity between present life in this world and life everlasting with God. For human beings, this continuity has to do with embodied existence. (2) Present human existence, however, is marked by frailty, deterioration, and weakness, and is therefore unsuited for eternal life. Therefore, in order for Christian believers to share in eternal life, their bodies must be transformed. Paul does not here think of "immortality of the soul." Neither does he proclaim a resuscitation of dead bodies that might serve as receptacles for souls that had escaped the body in death. Instead, he sets before his audience the promise of their transformation into glorified bodies (cf. Phil. 3:21). (3) Paul's ideas are, in part, rooted in images from the natural world and, in part, related to the resurrection of Jesus Christ. As it was with Christ's body, Paul insists, so it will be with ours: the same, yet not the same; transformed for the new conditions of life with God forever. (4) For Paul, this message underscores the significance of life in this world, which many Christians at Corinth had not taken seriously. We should not imagine that our bodies are unimportant, then, or that what we do to our bodies or with our bodies is somehow unrelated to eternal life.

Key to our thinking is the nature of the resurrection body, to which the NRSV unfortunately refers as "a spiritual body" in contrast to "a physical body" (15:44) — a translation that departs dramatically from the contrast the apostle actually registers. On the one hand, Paul underscores an essential continuity grounded in the import of the body (σῶμα, *sōma*) to human existence and identity in this life and in life-after-death. On the other, the distinction Paul draws is between the σῶμα ψυχικόν *(sōma psychikon)* and the σῶμα πνευματικόν *(sōma pneumatikon)*. The first expression is drawn from Genesis 2:7, which has it that Adam was created a living ψυχή *(psychē,* "life" or "vitality"); hence, the first Adam was a *psychikos* body. However, as is manifestly evident, this body was subject to death and decay on account of sin, and therefore was ill-suited to eternal life with God. What is needed, then, is the different form of existence given us by the last Adam, Christ, who does not simply receive life (as in the first Adam), but actually gives it. "Thus it is written, 'The first man, Adam, became a living being [ψυχὴν ζῶσαν, *psychēn zōsan;* citing Gen. 2:7]; the last Adam [Christ] became a life-giving spirit" (15:45). As a consequence, whereas the *sōma psychikon* is a body provided by God and well suited for this age, the *sōma pneumatikon,* also provided by God, is well suited for the age to come. Or, as Anthony Thiselton translates it, God has provided for this age "an ordinary human body," "a body for the human realm," but, in the resurrection, God will provide "a body for the realm of the Spirit."[25]

Characterizing the resurrection body in contrast to ordinary bodily existence in this world, Paul observes, "What is sown is perishable, what is raised is imperishable. It is sown in dishonor, it is raised in glory. It is sown in weakness, it is raised in power. It is sown a physical body, it is raised a spiritual body" (15:42-44). This helps further to distinguish the ordinary human body (perishable, inglorious, weak) from the resurrection body (imperishable, glorious, powerful) at the same time that it presses the question: What is the source of this new body? How is it constituted? Paul answers that the first Adam was dusty, the second Adam heavenly. In doing so, he makes use of the physical science of his world (15:47-49).[26] That is, ἐκ γῆς χοικός *(ek gēs choikos,* "from the dust of the earth") and ἐξ οὐρανοῦ *(ex ouranou,* "from heaven") refer to the nature of two kinds of body — the one made up of the stuff of the earth, dust, and thus well suited to earthly life; the other made up

---

25. Anthony C. Thiselton, *The First Epistle to the Corinthians: A Commentary on the Greek Text*, New International Greek Testament Commentary (Grand Rapids: Eerdmans, 2000), pp. 1276-81.

26. See Alan G. Padgett, "The Body in Resurrection: Science and Scripture on the 'Spiritual Body' (1 Cor 15:35-58)," *Word & World* 22 (2002): 155-63.

of heavenly stuff, and thus well suited to life in the heavens. Paul thinks of the afterlife in astral terms, with the resurrection body made up of the same matter of which the stars are made — that is, quintessence, that fifth and highest element of the universe, beyond air, earth, fire, and water.

Paul thus speaks to the nature of the resurrection body (free from decay and weakness) and the agency through whom the body is transformed (it is God's doing), while holding in tension his vision of both a transformed body and an organic continuity between our present, mortal existence and our future, transformed existence. Even if, as Paul avers, "flesh and blood cannot inherit the kingdom of God" (15:50), it remains the case that the world-to-come will be inhabited by embodied persons. What is more, for Paul resurrection simply is the transformation leading to a nonperishable existence. This transformation is not the release from the human body of a nonperishable soul, but the resurrection of the human person as "a body for the realm of the Spirit." That is, nothing in the created human being is intrinsically immortal.[27]

Conclusion

At what may be a surprising number of points, the theological witness of Scripture is congruent with portraits of the human person emerging from evolutionary psychology and the neurosciences. Points of tension remain, of course, and these beckon for ongoing, serious reflection — regarding original sin, for example, or human freedom and responsibility. What these brief remarks have underscored, however, is not so much the interaction of science and biblical theology but rather the significant points at which biblical theology parades its explanatory value and dispositions. For Scripture, human life — so profoundly characterized in terms of embodiment and individuation within community, at home in the cosmos, and called to holiness and integrity —

---

27. See further, Murray J. Harris, "Resurrection and Immortality in the Pauline Corpus," in *Life in the Face of Death: The Resurrection Message of the New Testament*, ed. Richard N. Longenecker (McMaster New Testament Studies; Grand Rapids: Eerdmans, 1998), pp. 147-70; Richard N. Longenecker, "Is There Development in Paul's Resurrection Thought?" in *Life in the Face of Death: The Resurrection Message of the New Testament*, ed. Richard N. Longenecker, McMaster New Testament Studies (Grand Rapids: Eerdmans, 1998), pp. 171-202.

can never be understood merely in biological terms, as important as those insights might be. Humanity finds its meaning in the creaturely vocation given by the God who made the human family in his own image, in the restoration of fallen to full humanity, and in the telos of being fully alive.

Imago Dei and Sexual Difference: Toward an Eschatological Anthropology

Janet Martin Soskice

> *In his own image God created man,*
> *And when from dust he fashioned Adam's face.*
> *The likeness of his only Son was formed:*
> *His Word incarnate, filled with truth and grace.*
>
> Traditional hymn

> *Nearly all the wisdom we possess, that is to say, true and sound wisdom, consists of two parts: the knowledge of God and of ourselves. But, while joined by many bonds, which one precedes and brings forth the other is not easy to discern.*
>
> John Calvin, *Institutes of the Christian Religion*, I.I.I

There is no shortage in Christian art of vivid portrayals of the human condition — Byzantine apses, Romanesque side-chapels, books of private devotion, faces of men and women redeemed and transformed. Sometimes, more darkly, we find men and women distressed and disordered — skewered and shoveled by devils into the pit.

"Man" (used as the collective here) is a protean race. It is not just that within our species we can find a pickpocket and a Plato, but individually each one of us can be small and great. This is true physically,

---

A version of this article appears in Janet Soskice, *The Kindness of God* (Oxford: Oxford University Press, 2007).

for we all begin as babies, but also spiritually, for each sinner has the capacity to become a saint.

Within Christian anthropology a better word than "protean" for this open-endedness is "eschatological": human beings are eschatological and teleological. The baby has its *telos* in the woman or the man, and the sinner has her *telos* in the saint. By contrast to the secular and social scientific discipline of the same name, "Christian" anthropology understands our human nature not only in terms of what we are, but of what we may be. We have the potential to become what we are not yet, or are not fully.[1]

Christian anthropology, a name preferable to "the Christian doctrine of man," is not a member of that list of sciences that includes entomology, rodentology, and ornithology. The extension to that list which covers our species is primatology. To include Christian anthropology in the list would be a category error. Christian anthropology is not a branch of the natural or the social sciences, although it may make use of all of them, but a division of *sacra doctrina*, or holy teaching, and its kindred disciplines are Christology, ecclesiology, pneumatology, and soteriology — the Christian understanding of the Christ, of the church, of the Spirit, of salvation.

Each of these *scientia* are predicated to some degree on revelation, but Christian anthropology needs very little to get started — sufficient to say that Christian anthropology depends upon saying that we are creatures. We are creatures in the strong sense — that is, we are created. But this implies a Creator and, in Christian, Jewish, and Muslim thought, a Creator understood to be good.

Christian anthropology is closely related to two other *scientia* — the first is "theology," a term we use generally to cover all manner of religious thought but which I use here to mean "the doctrine of God." Christian anthropology is close to theology not because we are God-like, but because we are created by God; and our destiny — the destiny of all reasoning creatures, according to Aquinas — is to share in the triune life of God. Augustine puts the same point in a different way — "Our hearts are restless until they rest in Thee." This is a creaturely *telos* as real for Augustine and Aquinas as that of the acorn becoming an

---

1. This is not a view only to be found in Christian anthropology. It is a central plank, for instance, in the views of Jean-Paul Sartre. See Stephen Wang, *Aquinas and Sartre* (Washington, D.C.: Catholic University Press, 2009).

oak, with the difference that human beings, uniquely among creatures, have the freedom to turn away from God, their true end.[2]

Human beings are growing, changing things — destined to become what they are not yet. But human beings are also, in Christian (and Jewish and Muslim) teaching, "made in the image of God" (Gen. 1:26-27). Theologians have puzzled for centuries over this mysterious claim. How can it be so? It cannot be by virtue of our physical bodies since God does not have a body. Might it be in virtue of rationality or mind? This is a favored settlement, reinforced in the West by a Cartesian hyper-Platonism that made the mind seem "spiritual" and the body only physical. Some Jewish writers have wanted to distance themselves from the idea that it is in virtue of reason that we are in the divine image. Michael Wyschogrod finds this too structuring; the human project is not to understand God but to obey God, and this means change. Animals have essences but human beings do not — they are always free to choose and constitute themselves. The essence of man, and by implication the way in which man images God, remains open to history and to possibility.[3]

Some Orthodox theologians suggest, to my mind convincingly, that to say "man is in the image of God" is to say that "man is mystery," because God is mystery.[4] On this reading, attractively, we do not know who or what we are — positively as well as negatively. "Know thyself" is, after all, a pagan injunction,[5] and St. Paul's psychological realism in

---

2. God is complete fullness of Being, abundant, outpouring life, whereas we are seeking, questing creatures. Put metaphysically, in God there are no accidents. Put positively from our point of view, we are designed to grow physiologically, morally, and spiritually.

3. Michael Wyschogrod, *The Body of Faith: God and the People of Israel* (Northvale, N.J.: Jason Aronson, 1996), p. 5: "Man is not a defined essence but an undertaking of possibilities who chooses himself as he constitutes his moral self."

4. Andrew Louth has used this to good effect in arguments about manipulation of embryos in reproductive technology.

5. Contrast this maxim of ancient philosophy with Augustine in the *Confessions*. As a brash and successful young rhetorician he *thinks* he knows himself. It is only when he embraces Christian faith that he has painfully to admit that he is, and remains, a mystery to himself. See also Cranmer's beautiful liturgical expression of the same:

> We have followed too much the devices and desires of our own hearts.
> We have offended against thy holy laws.
> We have left undone those things which we ought to have done;
> and we have done those things which we ought not to have done.

Romans 7:19 — "For I do not do the good I want, but the evil I do not want is what I do" — is instantly familiar.

Much has been made of the negative aspects of "not knowing who we are," but in Christian teaching this has positive meaning, too, and one that is at the heart of faith: "Beloved, we are God's children now: what we will be has not yet been revealed. What we do know is this: when he is revealed, we will be like him . . ." (1 John 3:2-3).

This brings us to the second of that list of theological subdivisions to which Christian "anthropology" is nearly related, "Christology," and to sexual difference.

Around the main door of Bologna's cathedral, the Basilica di San Petronio, run a series of carved stone tablets: on the left the creation of Adam and of Eve, the temptation of the serpent, and expulsion from the garden; on the right the manger, the visit of the shepherds, and of the magi. The whole magnificent series, executed by Jacopo della Quercia between 1425 and 1438, shows our human history: the first creation on the left of the portal, and our new creation in Christ on the right. It is to the artist's representation of the creation of Eve that I wish to draw attention.

Adam is asleep on the left, turned away from the center of the carving where God — clearly the triune God since he has a triangular halo — is drawing Eve out of Adam's side. It is a very statuesque "Eve." Although not yet risen to her full height, it is clear that when Eve does so she will be exactly the same height as God. Indeed she has the same distinctive aquiline nose as God, the same lips, and much the same hair. She has feminine and more youthful versions of God's eyes and God's mouth. She is fully in the image of God.

The artist has brought together two Genesis texts — Genesis 1:26-27 ("Then God said, 'Let us make humankind in our image, according to our likeness, and let them have dominion. . . .' So God created humankind in his image, in the image of God he created them; male and female he created them") and Genesis 2:18-23, where having created the earth, the plants, and *H'adam*, the earth creature, God sees that it is not good for *H'adam* to be alone. God then creates the animals and birds and, when *H'adam* fails to find one among them to be his partner, at last the "woman" from the man's side (*ishshah*, from *ish* in the Hebrew).

Jacopo della Quercia's carving captures the moment before Adam wakes to say "this at last is bone of my bone and flesh of my flesh." Adam sleeps soundly on while Eve and her Creator enjoy a quiet, dawn-of-creation *tête à tête,* and God delights in this, "his" newest creature.

Philosophical theologians, at least Catholic ones, do not characteristically treat the first books of Genesis as historical or scientific fact. Even St. Augustine in his *Literal Commentary on Genesis* conjectured that by six days the Genesis text could not mean six units of twenty-four hours, not least because the first "days" take place before the sun and the moon, whose movements describe days and nights, were created. Those who compiled Genesis did not mean to give an account of the first seconds of the universe. The origins that concerned them more had to do with relations — the relation of God to humankind, of God to Abraham and to the Israelites who descended from him, and so on. Genesis is thus consulted not as science but as a source for certain primitive Christian beliefs, "primitive" not because they are naïve, but because they are basic. Among these are that God created all that is; that "all that is" is good; that the human being is created in the image of God. None of these religious and metaphysical convictions conflict with anything science can tell us, nor could science demonstrate or falsify them. They play a regulative role in Christian thought and practice — for instance, the belief that each one is made "in the image of God" is substantially the basis for Christian respect for each human life, as we saw in earlier chapters.

The Genesis text also speaks about sexual difference. It is constitutive of human beings, and it is good. It is not good for *H'adam* to be alone.

Biblical critics now believe that the stories of humankind's creation in Genesis 1 and 2 arise from two different, and somewhat contradictory, sources that fed into the final text of the book. They do not nowadays spend much time trying to resolve the apparent contradictions. It was not so for the early Christian theologians, for whom any apparent inconsistencies had to be resolved.

One might have thought the Fathers with their biblical conservatism would have given priority to the narrative of Genesis 1 if only because it is first, but overwhelmingly they preferred to discuss the second creation narrative, where Eve is made from Adam's side. Genesis 1:27 on its own is certainly puzzling. What can it mean that God created man (*H'adam,* the Hebrew male collective) in his own image, male and female? Early theologians canvassed the idea of a primal androgyne which, or who, was subsequently supplanted by the later creation of two persons of different sexes, but this reading was generally dropped in favor of concentration on the second story, where *H'adam* (which seems in Genesis 2 to be the single male human) is made first, and Eve from his side.[6] This was the story of Genesis 2 read in a particular way — a way that fitted better the accepted order of things — man (the male) was alone first and God created Eve *for him* as a companion and a helper.

Unlike Genesis 1, where male and female together comprise the imago, Genesis 2 can be read as saying that Adam on his own was virtually sufficient. He could do everything, so it seems, except reproduce. Eve is made as a "helper," but "helper" was routinely understood by the early theologians as a subordinate — leaping over the fact that elsewhere in Genesis God himself is described as "helper" using the same Hebrew word.[7] Woman was routinely thought of as lesser, almost an afterthought. And how could it be any other way, given the position of women in the late antique Hellenistic culture now reading these ancient Jewish texts as their own, Christian texts?

What kind of helper? Augustine famously surmised that for help in the fields another man would have been more useful, and for conversation another man more interesting; and this, he concluded, leaves procreation as the one thing man cannot do by himself. Man is whole and complete on his own. The woman adds nothing new to the genius of the human race, otherwise complete in itself, except affording it the capacity to reproduce.[8]

---

6. See Wayne A. Meeks, "Image of the Androgyne: Some Uses of a Symbol in Earliest Christianity," *History of Religions* 13 (1974): 165-208.

7. Some exegetes have pointed out that reading "Eve" as God's afterthought goes against the general pattern of the Genesis creation narratives, in which the more perfect creatures are those made last — sea and dry land are followed by sun and moon, birds and beasts, man and — finally — woman.

8. This is not to say Augustine had a "low" view of women. On the contrary, for his time he emerges as a proto-feminist. He is trying to explain the sense in which she is "helper." His mother, Monica, is the "perfect Christian" of Augustine's *Confessions*. Gregory of Nyssa and others read Genesis as saying that, prior to the introduction of death into the world, Adam and Eve would not need to reproduce and would have been "sexless," acquiring genitalia like the "clothing of skins" only after the Fall. Augustine thought this nonsense. The prelapsarian Adam and Eve would have had genitalia and would have used them in procreation — but without lust. Women then are equal to men, without bringing anything new to the table.

Imago Dei and Sexual Difference

This picture of man (the male) as able to do everything except reproduce has informed theological anthropology down to the modern period. It is, in its way, a kind of egalitarianism in which women bring nothing other to the table but reproductive capacity, and "man" (here meaning "male") is the default position for humanity. Thus when we speak of "man" we include everyone, except when dealing with matters peculiar to females such as pregnancy, childbirth, and abortion. But this is not simply a matter of language. In Roman Catholic theological anthropology, for instance, sexual "monoculture" persisted in the text of the otherwise quite revolutionary document of the Second Vatican Council, *Gaudium et Spes,* and beyond.[9] Sexual difference, rightly or wrongly, is here largely a matter of indifference — women are to be treated just like "men" except where they have different problems, for instance, in questions of reproduction, or in women's freedom to work, or to marry without force, or to avoid exploitation, and so on.

This sexual monoculture is in one sense praiseworthy, for its rests on the conviction that women as well as men are fully in the image of God — a matter not uncontested in the early church. Early exegetes puzzled as to what to do with 1 Corinthians 11:7: "For a man ought not to have his head veiled, since he is the image and reflection of God: but woman is the reflection of man." Did this mean that women were not fully in the image of God, a reading that would put Paul at variance with Genesis 1? This verse furthermore had to be reconciled with Paul's teaching later in the same letter that the "first man [*anthropos*] was from the earth, a man of dust: the second man is from heaven. As was the man of dust, so are those who are of the dust: and as is the man of heaven, so are those who are of heaven. Just as we have borne the image of the man of dust, we will also bear the image of the man of heaven" (1 Cor. 15:47); and with Colossians 1:15, "He is the image of the invisible God, the firstborn of all creation: for in him all things in heaven and on earth were created . . . all things have been created through him and for him."[10]

The Christological texts weighed heavily with the Fathers. If Jesus Christ, unquestionably male, is the image of the invisible God and we

---

9. The Pastoral Constitution on the Church in the Modern World, promulgated in 1965.

10. See also Romans 8:29-30. In 1 Corinthians Paul here conflates Genesis 1 and Genesis 3, for mention of men and women made in the "image" comes only in the former, and the man of dust in the latter.

will all bear the image of the "man of heaven," then it seemed reasonable for some to conclude that women will be resurrected as men.[11] Augustine to his lasting credit said "no," and rejected at the same time the more orthodox view that the resurrected body will be "sexless." Those who hold the woman's sex to be a defect or something necessitated only by the Fall, he believes, are quite wrong. Women will be resurrected as women in heaven, although without inciting lust. In saying this Augustine sought to avoid the inference that woman, on her own, could not be in the image of God.

We find ourselves to this very day torn between two positions that are each compelling but seem at the same time incompatible. We must say that, Christologically speaking, women and men cannot be different, for "all will bear the image of the man of heaven." But we must also say that sexual difference is not, or should not be, a matter of theological indifference. Genesis 1 suggests that sexual difference has something to tell us, not just about human beings, but about God in whose image they are made, male and female. The unresolved question then is: Where, why, and how does sexual difference make a difference?[12]

One of the striking features of *Gaudium et Spes* is its Christocentric anthropology. It is a vision of the human being as everywhere related to Jesus Christ. The document was visionary in anticipating the changes taking place in the lives of women before feminism had made much of an impression in any of the Christian churches, but reading it now with a view to sexual difference is an interesting experience.[13]

---

11. See Kari Vogt, "'Becoming Male': One Aspect of Early Christian Anthropology," in *Women: Invisible in Church and Society*, ed. E. Schüssler Fiorenza and Mary Collins, *Concilium* 182, no. 6 (Edinburgh: T. & T. Clark, 1985). Reprinted in Janet Soskice and Diana Lipton, eds., *Feminism and Theology* (Cambridge: Cambridge University Press, 2003), pp. 49-62.

12. That it does on the ground and in actual matters of life and death is altogether evident from the findings of the United Nations, Aid agencies, and other NGOs over the last two decades. Poverty and its handmaiden, war, affect women, the elderly, and children disproportionately. Female morbidity figures outstrip male in all but the most affluent countries (see Amartya Sen's seminal work). The poorest of the poor are, overwhelmingly, women, and their status as "the poor" is not separable from the burdens they bear and the disadvantages they face *as women*. These facts don't need to be rehearsed here.

13. Especially in the new English translation of the text, which studiously avoids inclusive language and uses "man" generically throughout, except when women are being particularly discussed.

Imago Dei and Sexual Difference

Women, *per se,* are mentioned relatively rarely but come up where the document addresses the social tension between men and women (§8), their claim for equality (§9), the sexual traffic in women (§27), their lack of freedom, in some parts of the world, to choose their husbands (§29), the dignity of the conjugal pact (§47), and so on. The document says even less about men, *per se,* because when "man" is the default position it is hard to tell when males specifically are under discussion, and when human beings in general. Throughout the document "man" *(homo)* is meant to include everyone.[14] It drives home the points that man is made in the image of God, male and female, and that Christ is the true image.[15] The argument reaches a crescendo when we read:

> Only God, who created man in his own image and redeemed him from sin, provides the full answer to these questions through revelation in Christ his Son made man. Whoever follows Christ, the perfect man, himself becomes more of a man. (§41)

This is compelled by the biblical teachings, already called to mind in §21 of *Gaudium et Spes,* that Christ "became truly one of us, like us in everything except sin," and that the Christian, whether male or female, is to be "conformed to the image of the Son who is the first-born among many brethren" (Rom. 8:29; Col. 1:18). At the heart of this document, and at the heart of New Testament itself, is an anthropology in which

> [t]he mystery of man becomes clear only in the mystery of the incarnate Word. Adam, the first man *(primus homo),* was a type of the future, that is of Christ our Lord. Christ, the new Adam, in revealing the mystery of the Father and his love, makes man fully clear to himself, makes clear his high vocation. (§22)

---

14. So, for instance, the concluding sentence of the introduction reads, "In the light of Christ, the image of the invisible God, the first-born of all creation the Council means to address itself to everybody, to shed light on the mystery and man and cooperate in finding solutions to the problems of our time" (§10). It is biological males who are "the dark continent."

15. "All men have a rational soul and are created in God's image; they share the same nature and origin; redeemed by Christ, they have the same divine vocation an destiny; so it should be more and more recognized that they are essentially equal" (§28).

303

The unanswered question is: "Does Christ make woman fully clear to herself?" The Latin of the instruction uses the more inclusive *homo/homine,* but the patterning is upon Adam and Christ, both male. What can it mean for women to say that "Whoever follows Christ, the perfect man, himself becomes more of a man"? (§41 *Quicumque Christum sequitur, Hominem perfectum, et ipse magis homo fit.*) Do those aspects in which a woman is to become perfected or "more of a man" include only those aspects she shares with males, like her intellect and her life of virtue, or do they also include her mothering, her loving, her sense of her own embodiment, which must be different from that of a man? Is Christ the fulfillment of female "men," as well as male "men," and if so, how?[16]

In striking contrast to *Gaudium et Spes* is the letter "On the Collaboration of Men and Women in the Church and in the World," sent to the Catholic bishops in the summer of 2004. Whereas *Gaudium et Spes* almost elides sexual difference, the later letter speaks of sexual difference as "belonging ontologically to creation," an expression that is hard to construe but falls just short of saying that there is an "ontological difference" between men and women. That would indeed be an odd claim, for one can see an ontological difference between a stone and a human being, but it would be difficult to see an ontological difference between a man and a woman, unless one also said there could be an *ontological* difference between any two individuals. One could say this, but it would be somewhat vapid.

A more serious problem with this emphasis on "ontological difference" is not philosophical but theological. Too strong a stress risks putting the 2004 letter at odds, not only with *Gaudium et Spes,* but with Scripture itself if it suggests that a woman cannot say that "in every significant sense, Christ is like me except without sin." It is for this reason that we must insist that, Christologically speaking, men and women *cannot* be different.

But is sexual difference then without theological importance? Can we return to our tradition of sexual monoculture, of sexual "indifference"? I think not, and perhaps Jacopo della Quercia's creation of Eve can hint the way forward. Genesis 1:27, with its suggestion that male and

---

16. The biblical allusion seems to be to Ephesians 4:13, which reads "Till we all come in the unity of the faith, and of the knowledge of the Son of God, unto a perfect man, unto the measure of the stature of the fullness of Christ." (The *King James Version* retains "perfect man" in translation of *andra* in the Greek.)

female together comprise the imago dei, has yet to be fully explored by theologians.[17]

It's notable that Jacopo della Quercia's God, from his triangular halo, is clearly a triune God. God is three in one, unity in difference. Human beings in their createdness mirror this divine procession of love in being more than one, male and female. Christian theology must affirm that all human beings are *in* the imago dei and that women are different from men. This means that women were not *made for men* any more (or any less) than men were *made for women.* The as-yet unsung glory of Genesis 1:26-27 is that the fullness of divine life and creativity is reflected by a humankind that is male and female, encompassing if not an ontological then a primal difference.

In the midst of his *On Religion: Speeches to Its Cultured Despisers* Friedrich Schleiermacher provides, without explanation, this brief "midrash" on Genesis:

> Let me disclose to you a secret that lies concealed in one of the most ancient sources of poetry and religion. As long as the first man was alone with himself and nature, the deity did indeed rule over him; it addressed the man in various ways, but he did not understand it, for he did not answer it; his paradise was beautiful and the stars shone down on him from a beautiful heaven, but the sense for the world did not open within him; he did not even develop within his soul but his heart was moved by a longing for a world, and so he gathered before him the animal creation to see if one might perhaps be formed from it. Since the deity recognized that his (the deity's) world would be nothing so long as man was alone, it created for him a partner, and now, for the first time, the world rose before his eyes. In the flesh and bone of his bone he discovered humanity, and in humanity the world; from this moment on he became capable of hearing the voice of the deity and of answering it, and the most sacrilegious transgression of its laws from now on no longer precluded him from association with the eternal being.[18]

---

17. The idea that human beings are made in the *image of God* is only expressed in Genesis 1, where it is said they are made in God's image, male and female — the "Adam's rib" narrative of Genesis 2 says nothing of the "imago." Paul makes the conflation of Adam and the imago, and it may be that other Jewish writers of his time did the same.

18. Friedrich Schleiermacher, *On Religion: Speeches to Its Cultured Despisers,* trans. and ed. Richard Crouter (Cambridge: Cambridge University Press, 1996), pp. 119-20.

Schleiermacher never identifies the "flesh of Adam's flesh" as woman. His point is not that man needs woman, but that to be fully human, even to praise God, we need others who are different from ourselves. Schleiermacher realizes, as did Wittgenstein, that were Adam alone in the garden he would not only be unable to reproduce, he would be unable to speak. Speech is a preeminently social possession. And without speech there would be no praise, no prayer, no "world." We become ourselves through being with others.

God is Love. We learn love through the reciprocity of our human condition, through being in relation to others who are different from ourselves — mothers, fathers, brothers, husbands, and wives. Sexual difference is a primordial difference, a template for the fruitfulness that can come not when two are the same, but when they are different. For human creatures, as for sea and dry land, light and dark, fecundity is in the interval. And this is why sexual difference is not just instrumental to marriage or even to the family. It is good in itself.

We stand to learn a great deal in the years to come as women begin to do theology. Will they write the same things as men? It remains to be seen. But we will never know what man is until we can say, as Irenaeus obviously intended, "The glory of God is woman fully alive."

AFTERWORD

On How Complementary Perspectives Produce Enriched Portraits

Malcolm Jeeves

"With all deference to the sensibilities of religious people, the idea that man was created in the image of God can surely be put aside," proclaimed a lead article in the premier scientific journal *Nature*. In discussions of human nature, such headline-grabbing claims are all too familiar these days. The *Nature* article added: "Scientific theories of human nature may be discomforting or unsatisfying, but they are not illegitimate."[1] Some of the scientific theories of human nature presented in earlier chapters of this book may, at times, have been discomforting, and at times unsatisfying, but none were illegitimate. Rather, they add up to an attempt to "tell the story like it is."

The first quote from the *Nature* paper is not a scientific statement and reveals ignorance of what it means to be made in the image of God. The second, a statement about the current state of play regarding scientific theories of human nature, we can readily agree with. If the author of the *Nature* article had had the benefit of the historical perspective afforded by Fernández-Armesto's opening chapter, he would have known that, in fact, "most languages had no word for 'human' apart from whatever term designated the group [to which they belonged and members of which they recognized]" and that "the outsider would be called by some other name, usually roughly translatable as 'beast' or 'demon' or 'monster.'" As recently as 1967, the Australian government passed laws to reclassify Aborigines, no longer simply as part of the Australian "flora and fauna" but as humans. As Alison Brooks has reminded us, even in recent times "newly discovered peoples, such as the

---

1. "Evolution and the Brain," *Nature* 447 (June 14, 2007): 753.

'Hottentots' of southern Africa, were sometimes accorded less-than-human status."

Gaining Perspective When Defining Humanity

Fernández-Armesto makes clear that the idea of a common human identity that transcends barriers of culture and differences of appearance was first documented in the thought of Indian, Greek, Chinese, and southwest Asian sages in the first millennium BCE. By the Middle Ages, ethnographers and cartographers in Europe, following the lead of the elder Pliny, continued to use a broad category of the subhuman or the parahuman, what Pliny himself called "simulacra of humankind." Until confronted by black people, why should you believe that such existed? As Pliny commented: "Indeed is there anything that does not seem marvellous, when we first hear about it? How many things are judged impossible, until they are judged to be facts?"

But facts do not come with their interpretation conveniently attached. As Fernández-Armesto makes clear, as recently as a century and a half ago, "a veritable anthropological industry was dedicated to classifying 'negroes' as closer to gorillas than to true humans." It was perhaps a shock for Darwin to discover that "the racists who dominated the Anthropological Society of London in his day rejected the theory of evolution because they wanted to confine blacks to a separate and inferior creation." As in so many other areas, however, "in the long run, none of these beliefs withstood scientific scrutiny."

The Concept of Humanity Comes Under Scientific Scrutiny

One of the pervasive themes of this book has been the ways in which beliefs about humanity have or have not withstood scientific scrutiny. At the same time a balancing and equally important theme is the recognition that it is not from science alone that we derive or formulate our deepest beliefs and understandings of our nature. Physicist Freeman Dyson reminds us that "contemporary discussions of science and religion often have a narrow focus, as if science and religion were the only sources of knowledge and wisdom." He goes on to say that "if we look for insights into human nature to guide the future of religion, we find more such insights in the novels of Dostoevsky than in the journals of cognitive science. Literature," he adds, "is the great storehouse of human experience, linking together different cultures and different centuries, accessible to far more people than the technical language of science."[2] The rationale for seeking the views of both scientists and theologians is well summarized by John Polkinghorne, who sees "a theology bereft of the worldly curiosity of science as less than open to all of reality; while a science shorn of theological vision is incapable of attaining the deepest understanding."[3]

A Multi-Perspective Approach Is Needed

The multi-perspective approach of this book has been taken in the belief that portraits drawn from different perspectives may, in principle, enrich and give greater depth than any portrait available from one perspective alone. We listened in turn to those who can give an appropriate historical perspective to our current thinking, to those best equipped to ensure that we maintain an appropriate degree of semantic hygiene as we move from one category of description to another, to those who are students of art and aesthetics, to scientists from relevant disciplines, to an anthropologist, to a biblical scholar, and to a theologian.

The most relevant scientific disciplines are genetics, evolutionary biology, neuroscience, neuropsychology, and evolutionary psychology, as well as certain social sciences. The contributions from each of these were summarized in the third section of this book. In view of the very high profile of the sciences in contemporary thought, it is easy, unthinkingly, to assume that theirs is the only way of gaining reliable knowledge about ourselves and the world in which we live. There is a lively and ongoing debate within science itself about how best to balance the benefits of a reductionist approach to the phenomena we study, while recognizing that the contribution made, for example, by social science, cannot simply be reduced without remainder to biologi-

---

2. Freeman J. Dyson, "Complementarity, in Spiritual Information," in *Spiritual Information,* ed. Charles L. Harper Jr. (Philadelphia: Templeton Foundation Press, 2005), p. 53.

3. Daniel Muth, review of John Polkinghorne's *Science and Creation: The Search for Understanding* (London: SPCK, 1988; Philadelphia: Templeton Foundation Press, 2006) in *The Living Church,* November 26, 2006, p. 5.

cal science — and that the latter cannot simply be reduced to physical science. This need to recognize the proper place of reductionism is highlighted by several of the philosophers.

The Need for Vigilance in Maintaining Semantic Hygiene

Fernando Vidal launches our efforts at maintaining semantic hygiene by suggesting that we pause and scrutinize a widely shared way in which we refer to human nature. He asks: Is "human nature" a useful term? Are there better ones? To use the words "human nature" reminds us of the need to think about the sense in which we are using the word "nature." Humans are after all a part of nature, as nature is traditionally studied by scientists. This takes us back to Francis Bacon, who referred to the scientist's task as reading "the book of nature."

Vidal suggests we move the focus from *human nature* to *human personhood*. Remembering that humans are a part of nature underlines "the inescapable role of the body in the constitution of human personhood." But what does "human personhood" mean? It certainly resonates with many contemporary approaches within the sciences that study humans and, at the same time, places "the ideology of the cerebral subject in a historical perspective." Thus the focus now becomes not human nature but the human person, and that in turn raises questions about human identity.

Vidal argues that keeping in mind the central role of the body would remind us that within the context of mainline Christian thinking and doctrine, there is a need to constantly emphasize the key importance of the doctrine of the resurrection. The great creeds, for example, do not refer to the immortality of the soul but to the resurrection of the body.

By spelling out in detail the historical background to discussions of embodiment, Vidal raises questions about the current trend to replace "personhood" by "brainhood," thus exposing an incipient reductionism — that everything to be said and or that needs to be said about the human person can be covered by focusing on the brain as the generator of mind, behavior, and personality. Vidal thus sets the stage for the penetrating analysis by Jürgen Mittelstrass of the two different sets of approaches to the person: on the one hand, those of the various sciences and, on the other hand, the philosophical, the religious, and the humanist. Mittelstrass conclusively demonstrates the need to avoid slipping into simplistic reductionisms and at the same time the need to expose the naturalistic fallacy.

These same themes are taken up in another way by Evandro Agassi when he further underlines the ever present temptation to embrace reductionism. He illustrates this in his two catchphrases: "telling the truth" and "telling all the truth." He points out that if we are to "tell all the truth," we have to recognize the need to ask and answer three related questions: What is human? What is the world? What is the position of man in the world? Once again he notes how tacit assumptions of materialism in our worldview and reductionism in our metaphysics are easily smuggled into the accounts given of human nature.

Franco Chiereghin returns to the theme of the necessity for semantic hygiene when he points out that in any account of human nature we need to distinguish between what is necessary and what is sufficient. In a word, he points out how often the reductionist trap might snare us if we are not vigilant.

Focusing on the aesthetic appreciation of beauty, Chiereghin describes recent work in which data such as that recorded using fMRI shows that for every pronouncement of an aesthetic judgment there is a corresponding activation of a complex of specific cerebral areas operating interconnectedly, even though their quotients of activity are differentiated according to the type of experience. He points out that the relevance of this research cannot be denied, especially as regards the visual arts. Demonstrating how necessary it is to recognize the neural structures active in the aesthetic experience in order to understand how much the characteristics of the perceptive processes might influence and condition both the creation and enjoyment of beauty, he writes: "Nevertheless it is legitimate to ask: Is this side of research, in addition to being recognized as necessary, sufficient to explain the artistic phenomenon? Is this process of naturalization of aesthetic experience capable of exhausting the entire realm of the human experience of the beautiful? . . . It is precisely here," Chiereghin says, "that the Kantian teaching on the dialectic of teleological judgment continues to manifest its efficacy." He thus brings out the really important need to distinguish between *exhaustive* accounts of a phenomenon at one level from claims that they are the only and *exclusive* accounts necessary to do justice to what is being studied. Thus he writes: "In this way, though, we finish by taking for granted exactly what we are trying to explain: the movements induced by electrochemical reactions, through which our nervous system codifies environmental interactions (listening to music, looking at a painting, etc.), are then decodified, interpreted, and expressed in a judgment of taste."

Chiereghin further underlines this point by referring not to different levels of explanation but rather to two mutually irreducible perspectives. Thus he writes that " even the work of art finds itself collocated inside a characteristically dialectical situation, in which two mutually irreducible perspectives nonetheless perform a positive function for its comprehension: one tends toward the naturalistic reduction of the aesthetic experience; the other tends to take away the finalized level to the interpretation and to the discovery of the sense. . . . In other words, we place the problem as to whether in that which remains unknown to us in the passage from one perspective to the other there is not hidden a foundation for their unity, inside the nature of the work of art."

In December 2008, it was reported that the U.K.'s largest medical research charity was going to "plough £1 million into the search for the nerve mechanisms that explain beauty — and with it love, truth and happiness." The designated leader of the project is Professor Semir Zeki, who already has a distinguished reputation as a neuroscientist experienced "in using functional MRI brain scanning to study the 'neural correlates of subjective mental states' — in layman's terms what happens in the brain when we experience strong feelings." An interviewer asked Zeki, "What if this is all, to use the words of Keats, unweaving a rainbow — a momentous endeavour that in the end removes the mystery and awe from the things that make life worth living?"[4] Zeki responded that he "had pondered this possibility at length." He continued: "I don't see it like that, my sense of awe of Michelangelo's *pieta* isn't diminished by knowing that there is a part of my brain that responds to the human body and another part that responds to the face. There is still a feeling of wonder. What we gain is the knowledge of the characteristics of the human brain that give us our common humanity."

Zeki is here underlining yet again that at times more than one level of explanation is necessary to do full justice to a phenomenon. An exhaustive account of a phenomenon from one perspective cannot be an *exclusive* perspective that alone will give a full understanding of the

---

4. Simon Crompton, "Arts and Minds," *The Times*, November 10, 2007.

phenomenon. With this reminder, we turn to four different accounts, all from a scientific perspective, which begin to give clues to the emergence of human uniqueness.

Genetic Markers of Human Uniqueness

Graeme Finlay's chapter leaves us in no doubt that we are "of the earth, earthy," and that we are firmly rooted in the biological world. Our genes provide the substrate for all that we are. A question that was uppermost in the minds of some of those who sequenced the human genome of our closest relative, the chimpanzee, remains with us: What makes humans unique?

Finlay spells out in detail some of the salient findings from research on the chimpanzee genome. The huge databases of genetic variation within human populations that are currently being assembled should lead to new understandings of how genetic forces have shaped our biology.

The question of how DNA sequences produce phenotypes remains obscure. Central to the consideration of human uniqueness will probably be a better understanding of the activity of the brain. Work has accumulated identifying particular genes linked to neuronal development. Researchers have already identified twenty-eight genes that are expressed in the brain and that exist only in humans. But Finlay points out that while "the unique *potential* of the human brain must be specified by the human genome ... the *realization* of the brain's potential is not genetically determined. It is not true that 'genes make minds any more than a viola or a piccolo makes a sonata.'"

All this is exciting science and in due course will fill out the scientific picture of human distinctiveness. But genes do not work in isolation and they do not "make us human," as is clear if, through circumstances, we are isolated from human community during early life.

There are three key aspects to our adaptive history: the influence of biological evolution through genes, the evolution of neural circuits in the brain through experience, and the influence of cultural evolution. Where there is socio-emotional deprivation, as in a recent study of Romanian orphans, we find long-term effects on brain function. Sensory input from the attentions of loving caregivers is necessary for an infant to express its genetic potential and to form and maintain healthy relationships. The key role of community was further and repeatedly exemplified in David Myers's chapter.

Unique chromosomal rearrangement, such as deletions and inversions, may be shared by multiple species and so become powerful markers of phylogenetic relationships. In a word, they help fill out the evolutionary story. The fact that through mammalian history the genome that was to become ours was formed by natural and haphazard genetic processes may be seen by some as demeaning. Our genome carries scars arising in the DNA of primate ancestors that lived millions of years ago. In all of this, however, Graeme Finlay reminds us of the need to distinguish between the use of words within science and the use of the same words but with different meanings in nonscientific contexts. Thus while scientists study the randomness of genetic processes, some see this as totally incompatible with the idea of purpose. But chance events in the statistical sense of being probabilistic do not necessarily imply that the process is, therefore, the outcome of chance in the metaphysical sense of being unplanned. For example, even the exquisitely integrated system of cellular biochemistry arises from random molecular movements. Biological systems make use of randomness as a vital component of how they operate. Genetic mechanisms that operate during sexual reproduction represent institutionalized randomness. Randomness in fact is an aspect of design.

Our genes provide the substrate for what we are; our environments, physical and social, determine the potential for what we may become. How these environments influence our becoming is spelled out in the further scientific perspectives of neuropsychology and social psychology in later chapters.

The Evolutionary Story

It would be all too easy to be so dazzled by the evidence from genetics when it is used to identify powerful markers of phylogenetic relationships, and of how they point to our links with primate ancestors who lived millions of years ago, to forget that the idea that human beings share a common ancestor with other animals was around long before the advent of modern science. Sam Berry's chapter provides a succinct and illuminating account of the development of ideas about the possible links we have with other animals. The motivation of some of the distinguished scientists who fought against the idea of evolution gives a clue to the role of deeply held nonscientific views about human nature, such as the status of the human soul.

As Berry makes clear, Darwin himself was all too aware of some of the problems faced by a general application of his theory of evolution. One of these, as Berry notes, was the problem of how altruism could develop and spread if the bravest of men, willing to come forward in war and thus risk their lives, would on average perish in larger numbers than other men. Of this Darwin himself could write, "it hardly seems probable, that the number of men gifted with such virtues, or that the standard of their excellence, could be increased through natural selection, that is, by the survival of the fittest . . ." Berry demonstrates how this difficulty was resolved in principle by J. B. S. Haldane half a century later. An important aspect of the ultimate answer is that individuals have to be considered as members of groups; it is not sufficient to take them in isolation. This same theme comes up later in Berry's presentation, where he underlines how the efficiency and precision of communication between individual humans and groups distinguishes us from all other animals, noting the wide consensus that a key human characteristic is the complexity of language, a point that can be made without in any way denying or denigrating the sophistication and complexity of communication in many nonhuman groups.

In seeking a balanced and reasonable interpretation of the evidence he presents, Berry suggests that there are four conservative inferences that can be drawn from that evidence. These are the key importance and significant implications for human uniqueness of the slowness of human maturation, the existence of the supralaryngeal tract conferring an ability to make the finely differentiated sounds so important in speech, the importance of group size and migration, and the changing energy requirements that necessitated more energy-rich food — a trend that may have induced the change in *Homo sapiens* from vegetarianism to carnivory. The further interpretation of each of these influences must adhere closely to the facts. As Michael Ruse has pointed out, and Berry would agree, evolutionary just-so stories abound; they are easy to invent but usually lack the data for their refutation. Speculations become rife, and nowhere have they been so common, nor their protagonists more passionate, than around questions of human nature; hence the key importance of Berry's chapter for this whole book.

MALCOLM JEEVES

Clues from Neuropsychology and Evolutionary Psychology

My own chapter follows naturally from that of Sam Berry. While the focus of his chapter is evolutionary biology, the focus of mine is psychology; it deals primarily with psychology's links with both evolutionary biology and neuroscience. It is in these two areas that science most naturally raises questions about wider issues concerning human nature: for example, whether and in what way humans may be cognitively unique compared with their nonhuman primate cousins, and whether research underlining the intimate links between mind and brain call into question revered and long-held views about the supposed separate existence of an immaterial and immortal soul attached in some way to the physical body.

We saw that evolutionary psychology refers to the study of the evolution of behavior and of the mind using principles of natural selection. The presumption is that natural selection has favored genes that underlay both behavioral tendencies and information-processing systems that solved problems faced by our ancestors, thus contributing to their survival and the spread of their genes. Philosophers have long agonized over questions of what makes us human. Is there a difference in kind or merely a difference in degree between ourselves and other animals? For some, making comparisons between humans and animals is seen as demeaning or even offensive. But such comparisons are certainly not new. In the seventeenth century Pascal wrote, "It is dangerous to show a man too clearly how much he resembles the beast, without at the same time showing him his greatness. It is also dangerous to allow him too clear a vision of his greatness without his baseness. It is even more dangerous to leave him in ignorance of both."[5] Evolutionary psychology can help reduce that ignorance.

We saw in three specific and intensively researched areas of contemporary evolutionary psychology clear evidences for sophisticated cognitive and social aspects of behavior evident in nonhuman primates that in the past we might have thought would clearly separate us from them. Specifically, these were in mind-reading behavior, in aspects of social behavior where the capacity to read other minds was evidenced by deceptive behavior, and in the evidence for helping behavior that might seem to imply moral agency. In each case enthusiasm can lead to

5. Blaise Pascal, *Pensées* (1659).

overstating the case as far as the animals' abilities are concerned, and leaders in the research fields with no religious axe to grind warn about the dangers of what they call "rich" interpretations of behavior where more basic or "lean" ones are appropriate.

The capacity to show moral agency is particularly pertinent to our wider considerations since one leading theologian from the past, Jonathan Edwards, saw this as one defining feature of what it means to be made in the image of God. But to see this as a uniquely defining feature of human moral agency is called into question when, as Frans de Waal has put it, "aiding others at the cost or risk to oneself is widespread in the animal kingdom." He adds that "the fact that the human moral sense goes so far back in evolutionary history that other species show signs of it plants it firmly near the center of our much-maligned nature."[6] However, once again, because two behaviors are superficially similar does not necessarily mean that the underlying mechanisms and thinking patterns associated with them are identical. Self-giving, self-sacrificing behavior appears different in different animals. But that in itself tells us nothing about what underlies those behaviors. Self-giving behavior may occur with or without self-awareness. Neil Messer's recent distinction between the starkly scientific concept of "altruism" and the richly theological biblical concept of "love" is timely and helpful.

Foreshadowing some of the theological discussion in later chapters in which we find an emphasis on our human capacity to relate to others and to God as being a possible key component of what is meant by the image of God, we noted how significant developments at the interface of evolutionary psychology and neuropsychology already give clues to the possible neural basis of a capacity for relatedness. This evidence is most dramatic in those instances, as in some aspects of the autistic spectrum, where this capacity is diminished and where it is now possible to identify and to some extent to locate the likely neural malfunctioning. All of which reminds us yet again of the point made early on by Vidal when he underlined the centrality of the embodiment of personhood. Relatedness, a key component of personhood, is firmly embodied.

Vidal's point was further underlined as we noted how developments in neuropsychology repeatedly underline how mind (or what used to be

---

6. Frans de Waal, *Good Natured: The Origin of Right and Wrong in Humans and Other Animals* (Cambridge, MA: Harvard University Press, 1997), pp. 216f.

called soul) is firmly embodied in the brain and other bodily processes. This in turn raised questions about how to affirm our essential duality without embracing and seeking to defend a dualism of substances, in which an immaterial immortal soul is in some way fixed to a physical body. Looking ahead we may note that the New Testament scholar Joel Green presents a strong case against arguing for such dualism.

None of this scientific evidence forecloses the many unanswered questions about how, with so many similarities between ourselves and our nearest nonhuman primate cousins, we still find ourselves so different in our capacities for achievements of the mind — in science, literature, art, music, and so on. One possible clue raised by Richard Byrne has been the remarkable development of the neocortex in humans relative to the size of the rest of the brain. Others, such as Warren Brown, point to the new evidence of the vital role played by so-called spindle cells. As scientists and Christians, we can enthusiastically pursue these issues while remaining aware that, when we speak of human distinctiveness rather than human uniqueness, we are making a theological affirmation based on our unique calling, being made in the image of God, and not upon some anatomical, psychological, or other property, such as Richard Owen invoked in his debate one hundred and fifty years ago with Huxley when seeking to make a case for human uniqueness.

The Social Animal

Group processes in natural selection noted by Sam Berry and the current focus in evolutionary and neuropsychology on the capacity for mind reading both emphasize the importance of the social group. This is developed, underlined, and exemplified many times by David Myers in his chapter. Hundreds of empirical studies have emphasized the key role of the social group. These roles include the need to belong, with its consequential positive benefits, such as the basic one of survival, and conversely, evidence of negative effects where supportive relationships are absent. Once again there is accumulating evidence for the way in which negative effects also are firmly embodied. David Myers cites the example of what he calls "the ostracism effect," in which it is now evident that ostracism elicits heightened activity in a specific brain area, the anterior cingulate cortex, an area that is also activated in response to physical pain. Ostracism, it seems, is a real pain.

Any focus upon the effects of social groups must, however, be seen in its proper cultural context. There are cultural differences. While it remains true that we become who we are through our place in community, at the same time, in Western societies we also have a complementary emphasis on the benefits that we draw from our nonconformist individualism. As Myers put it: "We therefore do well to balance our 'me' and our 'we,' our needs for independence and for attachment, our individuality and our social identity."

The benefits of social support remain among the clearest findings, helping us to understand why actively religious people express relatively high levels of happiness. For active members, faith communities are social support networks. All of this is clearly evident in the many studies of marriage. Marriage may be a cause of both pain and pleasure, and has been linked to a variety of health measures. As Myers comments: "Seven massive investigations, each following thousands of people for several years, reveal that close relationships predict health." In his conclusions, and writing as a Christian, Myers says, "Contemporary psychological science strongly affirms ancient biblical wisdom: it is not good for humans to be alone. We humans have a basic need to belong, which historically has supported human survival and is manifest in our longing for belonging, our desire for approval and close relationships, and our experiences of the pain of ostracism. We flourish with greatest happiness and health when supported by close, enduring relationships. Children also tend to flourish when co-parented in stable, supportive families. We are indeed, as Aristotle recognized, social animals, made for relationship."

Archaeological Perspectives on the Origins of Humanness

Alison Brooks's contribution takes us back to a central theme of this book, namely, to the question, "What do we mean by human?" She reminds us that the discovery of hundreds of fossil human remains has enabled scientists to develop biological and morphological criteria for inclusion in the human lineage — for example, bipedalism, brain size, skull shape, tooth morphology, and so on. But even this way of looking at things leaves open the question of whether all of these ancestors were fully human. And that in turn leads to the further question of whether behavioral contrasts can provide the distinctions as to what makes us fully human. Part of the answer we have already seen in the evidence from evolutionary psychology, which, at times, further blurs the behavioral distinctiveness of humans. At other times, it underlines clear quantitative differences best seen as qualitative. Communication through language is an obvious example.

In order to study the evolution of human behavior, we must turn to the fossil and archaeological records. Brooks makes it clear that "one can recover traces of symbolic behavior, or morphological traces of changes in brain or vocal tract morphology, that suggests an ability for language. Ideologies or the capacity for abstract thought are not preserved, but one can recover traces of practices that seem to conform to ideas about spirituality — burial of the dead and cave art." She further points out that "signs of empathy may also be evident in the survival of individuals with crippling injuries or major deficits, who could not have survived long on their own."

Alison Brooks believes that the capabilities of modern humans must involve at least six different faculties. These are abstract thinking; planning depth; problem solving through behavioral, economic, and technological innovation; imagined communities; symbolic thinking; and theory of mind. She discusses possible answers to the question of when these abilities first appear. But the answer to this question is not as simple as it may sound, and she readily acknowledges that scholars such as Richard Klein argue that the earliest *Homo sapiens* in Europe were physically modern but behaviorally primitive, and that modern behavior came about suddenly, a "human revolution" tied to a rapidly spreading genetic mutation for language. Brooks herself argues otherwise: the capabilities for these behaviors, she says, began to be expressed and therefore existed before modern physical appearance, with the gradual assembly of the kinds of behavior that we see later. And this assembly was not unilineal but geographically and temporally spotty, with many reversals. The debates will continue. Brooks notes, in passing, that the oldest examples to date of known fossils attributed to *Homo sapiens* in the strict sense are from the Middle Awash in Ethiopia.

By focusing on three particular expressions of behavioral capabilities — technological innovation, long-distance exchange, and symbolic behavior — Brooks traces out the beginnings of an answer to the question of when we became fully human. As for symbolic behavior, she points out that "beads and other body ornaments are unequivocal evidence for symbolic behavior and for fully human status, as they have little utilitarian function." Giving the example of one individual at a burial site in Israel dated at 90,000 to 100,000 years ago, she points out that this individual was associated with seventy-one pieces of red ocher, and also with a perforated bivalve shell. She says this is "the earliest clear evidence for symbolic burial with grave goods and red ocher, practices that suggest a belief in the survival of a spirit after death."

She believes that the appearance of humanness is a gradual process and not a sudden event, pointing out that "[t]he more we know, the harder it is to draw a line between human and nonhuman or prehuman." She concludes that "[c]apacities for some of the most human qualities — creativity, empathy, reverence, spirituality, aesthetic appreciation, abstract thought, and problem solving (rationality) — were already evident soon after the emergence of our species."

Biblical and Philosophical Theology

Thus far in our endeavors to understand humanity we have looked for clues almost exclusively from the "great book of God's creation." As the opening paragraph of Joel Green's chapter makes clear, one of the fathers of neurology in the seventeenth century gave clear witness, within Christian tradition, of acknowledging two distinct sources of knowledge, the "book of God's Word" and the "book of God's works." It is therefore at this point that, while keeping in mind the salient features of the portraits of humanity emerging from the "book of God's works," we now turn to the salient features of the portraits of ourselves from God's Word.

Green makes clear his assumptions. We don't look to fit theological claims into any gaps left by the natural sciences; we don't regard theological statements as trumping or superseding statements made from sciences. Rather, we recognize that theological affirmations about the human person cannot ignore the findings of science; we recognize how problems easily emerge when theological studies masquerade as empirical science or when empirical science confuses its physical findings with metaphysical accounts. With these assumptions made clear, Green sets out the primary contours of a biblical anthropology. He makes his own starting-point the starting-point of Scripture, which describes the creation of humanity "in the image of God." The opening chapters of Genesis underline, on the one hand, the *continuity* of humanity with all other animals and the rest of creation, and, on the other hand, the *difference* between humanity and other animals.

The sense in which humanity is made in the image of God stands out in two key aspects. First, the call to exercise dominion and stewardship and, second, that human beings in themselves, and not merely in what they do, reflect the divine image. "Genesis 1-2 does not locate the singularity of humanity in the human possession of the 'soul,' but rather in the human capacity to relate to Yahweh as covenant partner, and to join in companionship within the human family and in relation to the whole cosmos in ways that reflect the covenant love of God."

Noting that the phrase "image of God" plays little role in the Old Testament outside of Genesis 1-2, Green emphasizes the way in which the focus of understanding "image of God" moves decisively in the New Testament to "Christ who is the image of God." Making reference to the statement by Colin Gunton, Green aptly sums up both of their views: "first, that Jesus represents God to the creation in the way that the first human beings were called, but failed, to do; and second that he enables other human beings to achieve the directedness to God of which their fallenness had deprived them."

In underlining the biblical emphasis on the unity of the person and the embodiment of mind, Green calls for "the nonnegotiable emphasis on embodiment." He then spells out a series of fallacies, the scientific grounds for which were spelled out in the earlier scientific chapters: "the fallacy of imagining that intellect and affect are separable, the fallacy of imagining that mind and behavior are separable, the fallacy of imagining that human life can be understood merely or primarily with respect to individuals, and the inescapable conclusion that human formation is a process."

Moving to a discussion of personal identity, Green echoes the relevance of the understanding earlier emphasized by Vidal. This in turn is tied to the need to recognize that there are no slick, easy answers and that the New Testament itself is virtually silent on the nature of personal continuity between this life and the next. For the Apostle Paul, it is a mystery, glimpses of which are given to us in his letters to the Corinthians. The continuity involves transformed materiality — a bodily resurrection. For Paul, identity is firmly grounded in relationality and mission. Identity above all is to be found in the story of a life. Thus, Green writes, "As Luke presents it, Jesus' identity is worked out in terms of his relationship to God, his vocation within the purpose of

On How Complementary Perspectives Produce Enriched Portraits

God, and his place within the community of God's people — past, present, and future." The calling for us as Christians is likewise to anchor our personal identity in our relationship to Jesus who is God incarnate, to situate our lives within the purposes of God, and to be active members of the community of God's people.

In all of this there is for Green an awareness of the congruence of the theological witness of Scripture to the nature of our humanity, and the salient features of the portraits emerging from the relevant sciences. This is not to pretend that points of tension do not remain; they do, and they will, but one day we shall know even as we are known.

Janet Soskice very helpfully continues the study of the imago dei, putting it under the microscope of trends in contemporary thinking and, in particular, the current focus on gender differences. Mindful of all that we have learned from the anthropologists' contribution in this book, Soskice makes the necessary distinction between Christian anthropology and secular anthropology. Christian anthropology is not another member of a list that would include entomology, rodentology, ornithology, and so on, an extension of which would lead not to anthropology but rather to primatology. As a philosopher, she again reminds us of the need to avoid category errors. Christian anthropology is not about social and natural sciences; rather, it is in the family of Christology, ecclesiology, pneumatology, and soteriology.

Soskice reiterates and underlines the puzzlement of theologians down the centuries over the mysterious claims that humans are in some fundamental sense made "in the image of God." She finds attractive the suggestion by Orthodox theologians "that to say 'man is made in the image of God' is to say that 'man is a mystery,' because God is a mystery." Catholic philosophical theologians, she reminds us, have no doubt that the messages of the early chapters of Genesis are primarily that "God created all that is; and 'all that is' is good; and that the human being is created in the image of God." And she notes that none of these religious and metaphysical convictions conflict with anything science can tell us, nor could science demonstrate or falsify them. Rather, "they play a regulative role in Christian thought and practice — for instance the belief that each one is made 'in the image of God' is substantially the basis for Christian respect for each human life," as we saw in earlier chapters.

Having made clear her presuppositions, Soskice addresses the puzzling question: "What can it mean that God created man (*H'adam*, the

Hebrew male collective) in his own image, male and female?" Early theologians, she writes, "canvassed the idea of a primal androgyne which, or who, was subsequently supplanted by the later creation of two persons of different sexes, but this reading was generally dropped in favor of concentration on the second story, where *H'adam* (which seems in Genesis 2 to be the single male human) is made first, and Eve from his side. This was the story of Genesis 2 read in a particular way — a way that fitted better the accepted order of things — man (the male) was alone first and God created Eve *for him* as a companion and a helper."

Having traced out attempts to resolve this puzzle, whether by the pronouncements of Vatican councils or the exegesis by biblical scholars, she concludes that "we find ourselves to this very day torn between two positions that are each compelling but seem at the same time incompatible. We must say that, Christologically speaking, women and men cannot be different, for 'all will bear the image of the man of heaven.' But we must also say that sexual difference is not, or should not be, a matter of theological indifference. Genesis 1 suggests that sexual difference has something to tell us, not just about human beings, but about God in whose image they are made, male and female. The unresolved question then is: Where, why, and how does sexual difference make a difference?"

But does to insist that, Christologically speaking, men and women cannot be different mean that sexual difference is then without theological importance? "Christian theology," says Soskice, "must affirm that all human beings are *in* the imago dei and that women are different from men. This means that women were not *made for men* any more (or any less) than men were *made for women*. . . . Sexual difference," she notes, "is a primordial difference, a template for the fruitfulness that can come not when two are the same, but when they are different. And this is why sexual difference is not just instrumental to marriage or even to the family. It is good in itself."

Back to the Beginning

We believe that science has taught us and will continue to reveal fascinating and illuminating new glimpses into our complex human nature. We do not believe, however, that the wisdom of the past is to be dis-

On How Complementary Perspectives Produce Enriched Portraits

carded. As we seek exhaustive accounts of our complex humanity at different levels of investigation from the micro to the macro, we recognize that no single account can claim to be the only and exclusive account. We emphasize the need not only to "tell the truth" but to "tell *all* the truth." We affirm that, with our shared theistic presuppositions, the already unbelievably awe-inspiring and complex portraits of humankind from art and literature, and those afforded by our various sciences, complement the theological portraits, which remind us that we are indeed "mysteriously and wonderfully made." The greatest wonder of all is that the One who made us and sustains us also emptied himself, took human embodiment, and showed us what it is to be truly human.

Index

Aborigines, 309
abortion, 28
Adam, 133, 149, 152, 174-75, 206, 292, 298, 300, 303, 306
adaptation, 83, 152, 164, 172
Adler, Alfred, 207
aesthetics, 313; aesthetic experience, 3, 82, 83; aesthetic judgment, 82, 83, 89, 93, 100, 102, 313; and architecture, 96; and interpretation, 103; and music, 96
African origin of humans, 243
afterlife, 288. *See also* eternal life; immortality of the soul
Agassiz, Louis, 16
Alexander, R. D., 157-58
Altheide, T. K., 113
altruism, 41, 157-59, 163, 198, 237, 272, 319; and "inclusive fitness," 157; reciprocal, 157
Alzheimer's disease, 44, 203
Anderson, Benedict, 237
animals: dance, 91-92; as part of moral community, 17; as thinking, 191
anthropocentrism, 66
Anthropological Society of London, 15, 310
anthropology: biblical, 6, 273, 323; Christian, 6, 46, 295, 296, 325; philosophical, 62; secular, 6, 325; theological, 301
apes, 18, 19, 20, 21, 22, 23, 24, 25, 27, 113, 120, 122, 124, 126, 139, 140, 141, 142, 143, 146, 147; as thinking, 191; tool use, 23-24, 234. *See also* bonobos; chimpanzees; gorillas; Old World monkey; orangutans; New World monkey; primates
Aquinas, St. Thomas, 33, 190, 296
architecture, 96. *See also* aesthetics
Aristotle, 18, 20, 33, 190, 207, 321
Arsuaga, José Luis, 26
art. *See* aesthetics
artifacts, 238-42, 243, 245; Neanderthal, 254-55; symbolic images, 250-53, 254; tools, 245, 247, 248, 249; weapons, 245-49
asah, 173
associative learning theory, 200
Atapuerca, 26
Augustine, St., 14, 190, 271, 296-97, 299, 300, 302
Australians, first, 254
Australopithecus, 164, 168, 229
Australopithecus afarensis, 232
autism, 199, 201, 319
awe, sense of, 314
Ayala, Francisco, 275

Index

baboons, 19, 23
Bacon, Francis, 213, 312
baptism, 282, 283
bara, 173
Barth, Karl, 198
Basilica di San Petronio, 298
Battel, Andrew, 19
Baumeister, Roy, 207
beads, 243
Beagle, 21
beasts, 152, 309
beauty, 82, 94, 100, 313; experience of, 87, 89, 90, 92, 93, 95, 101
Beethoven, Ludwig van, 88-89, 99
behavioral science, 131, 184, 250; and blameworthiness of individuals, 184
beliefs, 181, 194, 203
Bellah, Robert, 213
belonging, need for, 207-13
Benedict XVI (Pope), 30
Berry, R. J., 271
Bible: biblical anthropology, 6, 273, 323; biblical thought, 132; biblical understanding of creation, 132-38, 173-75; and humanity, 272-73; and humans as social creatures, 206; and human origins, 136, 137, 149-50, 152, 153, 174; interpretation of, 201, 202, 273
biocentrism, 66
bioengineering, 65
bioethics, 65, 67
biological evolution, 115
biologism, 62, 67, 69
bipartite, 190
bipedalism, 230
blacks, humanity of, 15, 16, 19
Blank, Robert, 45
Blumenbach, Johann Friedrich, 227, 234
Bodmer, W. F., 165
body, 2, 37, 176, 177; bodily resurrection, 290
Boethius, 33
Bolk, Louis, 165
Bonnet, Charles, 37-38, 49

bonobos, 19, 23, 24
Bowlby, John, 212
Bowler, Peter, 155-56
Boyle, Robert, 31-32, 47
brain, 4, 35, 37, 111, 113, 115, 133, 116, 123, 202; anterior cingulate cortex, 320; anterior hippocampi, 186; as blank slate, 185; blood flow in, 41; and body, intrinsic interdependence of, 188; and bottom-up study approaches, 187, 202-3; corpus callosum, 115; cortex, 115, 116, 161; Decade of the, 41, 43; face-responsive neurons, 182; fixity of, 179, 180; frontal lobe, 183; as hardwired, 185; hemispheric specialization, 39; hippocampus, 192; imaging, 41, 186; mind-brain-behavior balance, 187, 202-3; mirror neurons, 199; modular model of, 39; neocortex, 320; plasticity, 40, 180, 184-87; potential, 113, 315; research, 2; size, 169, 232; and specificity, 180, 182, 185, 186; split-brain, 39; states, 42; static model, 184; substance, 188; and top-down study approaches, 181, 185, 186, 187, 189, 203. *See also* brainhood; mind; mind-brain relation
brain death, 44-45
brainhood, 3, 35, 36, 37, 40, 42, 44, 46, 51, 52, 178, 312; and marketing brain fitness, 51
"breath of life," 173
Breydenbach, Bernhard, 20
Brown, Donald, 32
Brown, Peter, 47
Brown, Warren, 198, 320
Brunner, Emil, 198
Bruno, Giordano, 149
Buckland, William, 228
Buffon, George-Louis (Count), 150, 227
Burnett, James (Lord Monboddo), 20, 21, 234
Bynum, Caroline Walker, 286

INDEX

Byrne, Richard, 193, 194, 197, 198, 200, 203, 320

Cabot, Sebastian, 20
calling, 204
cannibalism, 242
carnivory, 168, 317
Carroll, Sean, 108
Cartesian dualism, 36, 72-73, 188
category: errors in, 62, 325
Cavalli-Sforza, L. L., 165
cave paintings, 243
cathedral of Syracuse, 99
"cerebralization" of personhood, 37
Chalmers, Thomas, 150
Chambers, Robert, 151-52
chance, 4, 135, 137, 138, 164, 316
Chardin, Teilhard de, 21
chimpanzee, 19, 22, 23, 24, 26, 91-92, 107, 108, 109, 110, 111, 112, 118, 122, 123, 124, 127, 139, 141, 143, 145, 146, 147, 148, 234
China, 18
Christian, Christianity: anthropology, 6, 46, 295, 296, 325; eschatology, 49; view of humankind, 53. *See also* conversion
Christology, 298
chromosome, 109, 117, 119, 121, 123, 124, 125, 139, 140, 142, 161
Cialdini, Robert, 208
Clayton, Nicola, 200
cognitive revolution, 182, 186
Cohen, Sheldon, 218
collectivism, 213
Collins, Francis S., 131-32, 133
commissurotomy, 39
common ancestor, 4, 124, 149, 316
common sense, 94
community, 16, 206-7, 212, 316; and communitarianism, 213
comparative psychology, 193
Congo, 15, 248, 249
consciousness, 34, 35, 37, 70, 115; conscious experience, 159

continuity, of humans with animals, 292, 323
conversion, 279, 281, 282, 285
Corp, N., 198
corporeality, 32, 49
covenant, 324
creation: biblical understanding of, 132-38; as eternal covenantal relationship, 135; human dominion over, 273, 324
creationism, 154
creativity, 85
criminal law, 184
criminology, 16
cryogenics, 51-52
culture, cultural, 61-64, 113, 115, 126, 127, 131, 163, 235, 310; context, 321; differences, 12, 321; essence, 61; evolution, 115; studies, 171; values, 171

Dahl, Roald, 51
Damasio, Antonio, 187
dance, 91
Darwin, Charles, 15, 21, 83, 150-58, 166, 169-70, 227, 229, 310, 317
Darwin, Erasmus, 151
Dawkins, Richard, 192
degeneracy, 16
deism, 151
Descartes, René, 33-34, 36, 72, 74, 132, 190, 278. *See also* Cartesian dualists
Descent of Man, The (Darwin), 21, 156, 227
design, 4, 136, 316
de Waal, Frans, 24, 158, 196, 319
Diamond, Jared, 160, 162
Diener, Ed, 221
Dissanakaye, E., 84
divine image. *See* image of God
divine revelation, 71
DNA, 17, 25, 107, 108, 109, 110, 111, 113, 117, 118, 121, 122, 123, 124, 125, 126, 127, 129, 131, 135, 138, 139, 140, 142, 143, 144, 145, 146, 147, 230. *See also* gene; genome
Dobzhansky, Theodosius, 134, 155

dominion, 324
Doye, J., 159
Draganski, B., 116
dualism, 36, 42, 71, 73, 76, 77, 176, 178, 188, 189, 190, 191, 278, 320; dualist anthropology, 286; dualistic philosophy, 36
duality, 188, 189, 190, 320; duality without dualism, 202
Dubois, Eugene, 229
Dumit, Joseph, 43
Dunn, James, 174
Dyson, Freeman, 310

Ecuador, 28
Edwards, Jonathan, 196, 201, 319
eliminative-materialist philosophy of mind, 40
embodiment, 133, 177, 181, 182, 187, 188, 199, 202, 203, 285, 286, 289, 293, 312, 319, 320, 324, 327
empathy, 41, 235, 236, 239, 242, 272, 322
empiricists, 172
endogenous retrovirus, 126, 127, 128
environment, 111, 113, 114, 115, 116, 124, 133, 136, 137
environmental ethics, 65
epilepsy, 39
episodic memory (for events), 183
eschatology, 205, 282
essence, 31, 33, 61
eternal life, 205, 291
ethics, 65, 67, 158; and anthropocentrism, 66; ecological, 66; normative, 67; and physiocentrism, 66; radical physiocentrism, 66; universal, 67. See also bioethics; ecological ethics; evolution: ethics; nervous system: neuroethics
Etzioni, Amitai, 213
Eve, 149, 298-300, 304, 326
evolution, 15, 21, 27, 29, 65, 67, 83, 85, 134, 152; co-evolution, 167; evolutionary ethics, 67; evolutionary idealism, 155; evolutionary psychology, 5, 176-77, 192-96, 272, 293; evolutionary relatedness, 126; evolutionists, 154; fossil record of human evolution, 228-34; group size and, 166, 317; human evolutionary history, 108-12, 115, 118, 123, 131, 134-38, 139-48, 149-75; migration and, 166; theory of, 210, 317
experience: aesthetic, 3, 82-104, 313, 314; early childhood, 114, 115, 185, 212; unity of, 73, 77, 80

faith communities, importance for happiness, 321
feral children, 114, 155, 228
Ferguson, Sinclair, 177, 198, 201
Ferret, Stéphane, 35
fetus, status of, 16; and "brain life," 45
fine arts, 96. See also aesthetics
Fisher, Christopher, 194-95
Fisher, R. A., 154
fMRI (functional magnetic resonance imaging), 82
Ford, E. B., 155
fossils, human, 5, 150, 152, 159-60, 164, 166, 170, 228-34, 235, 236, 240, 242-44, 321, 322
Frederick II of Hohenstaufen, 114
free will, 34, 74, 159, 176, 272
friendships, 214

Gage, Phineas, 183
Gambia, 19
Gaudium et Spes (Vatican II), 301-4
Gazzaniga, Michael, 37, 178
Gehlen, Arnold, 63
gender differences, 6, 295-306, 325. See also woman
gene, genetic, 3, 44, 107, 108, 109, 110, 111, 112, 113, 114, 115, 116, 117, 118, 119, 120, 121, 122, 123, 124, 125, 126, 127, 128, 129, 130, 131, 132, 133, 135, 136, 140, 141, 144, 145, 146, 147; constitution, 65; determinism, 85; disorders, 184; encoded, 131; expression, 112; history, 109; insertions, 108, 125, 126,

331

INDEX

129, 130, 137, 138, 143, 146; inversion, 124; "jumping," 126, 128-30, 136, 144-47; mutation, 119, 255; potential, 315; processes, as haphazard, 125; pseudogene, 121-22, 140, 141, 147; technology, 65; therapy, 171; transfer, 65; translocation, 108, 123, 124; variation, 110. *See also* DNA; genetics; genome; phylogenetic relationships
geneticists, 154
genetics, 12, 25, 26, 131, 154, 235, 245, 272
genome, 107, 108, 109, 111, 112, 113, 117, 118, 119, 121, 122, 124, 125, 126, 127, 128, 130, 136, 137, 138, 140, 142, 143, 145, 146, 147; genomic deletion, 108, 119, 121, 123, 130, 138, 141; genomic duplication, 108, 117, 118, 120, 121, 125, 138, 140, 143, 145, 146, 147; sequences, 109; transposons, 126, 145; unique to human, 118
God, 117, 131, 132, 133, 134, 135, 137, 138; Creator's love, 137; grace of, 133. *See also* image of God
Gintis, H., 158
Goodall, Jane, 23
gorillas, 15, 20, 108, 146, 165, 230, 310
Gosse, Philip, 152
Gould, Stephen Jay, 170
Goya, Francisco, 21
Gray, Asa, 134
Great Apes, 23; morphology of, 227
Green, Joel, 173
Gunton, Colin, 198, 277, 324

Haberman, D. L., 178
Haeckel, Ernst, 229
Haldane, J. B. S., 155, 157, 317
Hamilton, W. D., 157
happiness, 70, 213-16, 321
Hatfield, Gary, 52
Hay, David, 131
health, 216-20
heart, 177
Heidegger, Martin, 63

Hetherington, E. Mavis, 221
Hinde, Robert, 163
"hobbit," 26
Hody, Humphrey, 48-49
Holloway, Richard, 134
Holocaust, 220
Home, Henry, 149-50
hominids, 16, 25, 132. *See also* names of individual species
Homo divinus, 173
Homo erectus, 160, 164, 166, 168, 229
Homo floresiensis, 25, 26
Homo habilis, 160, 168
Homo sapiens, 160, 229, 243, 245, 255
Homo sapiens sensu strictu, 244
"Hottentots," 228
Hubel, David, 179, 181
human, humans: ability to imitate, 235; abstract thinking, 322, 237; African origin of, 243; brain size, 165, 169-70, 171; burial practices, 253; common humanity, 314; as composite being, 49; continuity with animals, 292, 323; culture, 77; diet, 239; dignity, 68; distinctiveness, 111, 113, 116, 131, 132, 133, 177, 202, 315, 320; early fishing techniques, 248; embryo, 45; hunter-gather groups, 168; identity, 3, 312; imagined communities, 237; maturation, 165, 317; moral sense, 197; nature, 36, 202; personhood, 273, 312; planning depth, 237, 244, 322; problem solving, 237; soul, 4, 152, 317; spirit, 73; spirituality, 131; traits, 111; transition from hunter-gatherer to farmer, 164; uniqueness, 2, 90, 191, 194-95, 196, 315, 320; use of fire, 239; world-openness, 62. *See also* brain; evolution: human evolutionary history; Human Genome Project; humanness
Human Genome Project, 107
human rights, 12, 26, 27, 68
humanness (or the human condition), 113, 114, 115, 132, 236

332

Index

hunter-gatherer, 164, 246
Hutton, James, 150
Huxley, Thomas, 153, 159, 192
hybridizations, 109

ideology, 69
Illes, Judy, 41
image of Christ, 277
image of God (imago dei), 5, 6, 133, 137, 138, 173, 175, 177, 190, 191, 196, 197, 198, 201, 202, 204, 273, 274, 276, 278, 297, 299, 303, 305, 309, 319, 320, 323, 324, 325
imagination, 94, 322
immortality, 2, 4, 33, 51, 52, 74, 289, 290, 312, 318
immune system, 120, 136, 218
Incarnation, 46
India, 18
individualism, 211, 321
Ingold, Timothy, 32
ingroup bias, 208
institutionalized randomness, 136
intellect, 94
Intelligent Design, 135
interbreeding, 109
intuition, 46, 97, 158
invertebrates, 158
Irenaeus, 306
Ituri, 15

Jacopo della Quercia, 298-99, 304-5
Jenny (orangutan), 21
Jesus, 132, 133, 138, 276, 277, 279-85, 324-25; on the Emmaus road, 287, 288; as imago dei, 204-5, 277, 301-2; Incarnation, 46; and prayer, 284; as resurrected, 287-91; suffering, 205
jewelry artifacts, 243
Jívaro, 28
Jobson, Richard, 19
Jonas, Hans, 66
judgment: determinant vs. reflective, 100, 102
"jumping gene," 126, 128-30, 136, 144-47

Kant, Immanuel, 67-68, 72, 76, 82, 87, 89-90, 92-103
Kanwisher, Nancy, 181, 185, 186
Karmiloff-Smith, A., 184-85
Kawabata, Hideaki, 82, 101, 102n.
Kendall, Robert, 187
Klein, Richard, 244, 322
koinonia, 283

Lamarck, Jean-Baptiste, 151, 227
La Mettrie, Julien Offray de, 75, 178
language, 114, 115, 133, 162, 200, 234, 236, 317; gesture as forerunner to, 200
La Peyrère, Isaac de, 149
Leaky, Louis, 24
Leary, Mark, 207, 209
Lembu, 15
Leonard, W. R., 168
Lepore, Stephen, 215
leukemia, 121, 126, 217
Lewis, C. S., 220
Linke, Detlef Bernhard, 50
Linnaeus, Carolus, 20, 21, 227
localization, 38, 179
Locke, John, 34-35, 37, 40, 48-50, 52
London taxi drivers, 186
long-term memory, 182
Lovejoy, Arthur, 32
Lucy *(A. afarensis)*, 26, 232, 233
Lucy (chimpanzee), 28
Lyell, Charles, 152

macaque, 107, 141, 142
machines, 73-75, 178; epistemological purport of, 74; ontological reduction of, 74
MacKay, Donald M., 159, 189
Magnus, Albertus, 14
Maguire, Eleanor, 186
Malik, Kenan, 177-78
manifest image of the world, 78
marriage, and health and happiness, 215-18, 221, 222-23, 321
Marsden, George, 201
Martin, Dale B., 290

INDEX

materialism, 73, 131, 135, 188, 313
Mauron, Alex, 43
McBrearty, Sally, 244
McGrath, Alister, 271
mechanism, 136; mechanistic model, 93; mechanistic principles of nature, 100
meditation, 41
memory, 182; semantic memory (for facts), 183
Mendel, Gregor, 154
mental illnesses, 43
Messer, Neil, 319
metaphysics, 71, 179, 313, 323
Michelangelo, 99
Miller, Patrick, 204
mind, 4, 33, 178, 202, 235; general-purpose mechanisms of, 185; mind-reading, 186, 193, 194, 318; special-purpose mechanisms of, 185; substance, 188; talk, 177; theory of, 191, 193, 194, 200, 238, 244, 322; vs. brain, 178, 188. *See also* mind-brain relation
mind-brain relation, 190; interdependence of, 176, 188, 189, 190; irreducible intrinsic interdependence of, 189, 202
miscegenation, 16
Moltmann, Jürgen, 196, 289
Monboddo, Lord, 20, 21
monism, 36, 176, 188
monkeys. *See* apes
monoamine oxidase, 184
Monod, Jacques, 164
monsters, 11, 13-15
Moore, Aubrey, 153
moral, morality, 275; moral agency, 177, 196, 197, 319; moral authority, 32; moral behavior, 177, 196; moral community, 11, 12, 17, 25, 26, 27, 28, 29; moral conduct, 67; moral law, 132, 163; moral sense, 196; moral structure, 137; moral value, 66; morally neutral, 197, 203
Morgan, Lloyd, 192

Morris, Leon, 174
Morris, Simon Conway, 164
Mozart, Amadeus Wolfgang, 99
MRIs, 41, 183, 186, 314
Munn, Norman, 193
music, 96; musical instruments, artifacts, 243. *See also* aesthetics
mystery, sense of, 314, 324

Nagel, Thomas, 42
Napier, John, 166
Native Americans, 19
natural selection, 5, 83, 110, 11, 112, 131, 154, 169, 203
Natural Theology (Paley), 151
naturalism, 64, 66; and aesthetic experience, 83, 101; naturalistic explanations, 178; naturalistic fallacy, 66, 313; naturalistic reduction, 101, 103, 314; naturalization, 313
nature, 64; "book of," 312; as God's viceregent, 31; human dominion over, 273, 324
Nazis, 28
Neanderthals, 25, 26, 109, 228, 235, 242, 246, 248, 250, 255; brain of, 242; extinction of, 253; traits of, 26
necessity, 137, 138
nervous system: neural circuits, 115, 116; neural correlates, 42; neural mechanism, 183; neural structures, 83; neurological enhancers, 50
"neuro fields": neuroaesthetics, 41, 101; neuroeconomics, 41; neuroeducation, 41; neuroethics, 42; neurophilosophy, 40; neuropsychoanalysis, 41; neuropsychology, adult, 184; neuroscience, 4, 272, 293; neurotheology, 41
neurology, 271
Newton, Isaac, 48, 150
New World monkey, 140, 146
Nietzsche, Friedrich, 62, 63, 68
Novas, Carlos, 43

Index

objectivity, 87, 171
O'Craven, K. M., 181, 186
O'Heeron, Robin, 219
Old World monkey, 122, 124, 126, 140
olfactory receptor, 119, 122, 140, 141
orangutan, 19, 20, 21, 23, 234
Origin of Species (Darwin), 151-52
ornaments, artifacts, 250
Orrorin tugenensis, 230, 232
ostracism, 209-12, 320, 321; ostracism effect, 320
Owen, Richard, 192, 320

paleoanthropology, 12, 25, 26
Parfit, Derek, 40, 46, 52
Pascal, Blaise, 192, 318
Passingham, Richard, 192
Paley, William, 151, 153
Paul (apostle), 47, 174, 276-77, 279-82, 284, 286-87, 290-93, 297, 301, 324
Payne, Roy, 216
Peacock, Thomas Love, 21
pedophilia, as brain tumor symptom, 183
Penfield, Wilder, 39
Pennebaker, James, 219-20
Pentecost, 279
Perls, Fritz, 212
Perrett, David, 182
person, personhood, 3, 16, 32, 35, 37, 178, 312; identity, 34; interrelatedness, 198; knowledge, 132; personal continuity, 289; physical attributes and, 35; physical continuity, 34; significance, 189
pheromones, 122, 123
phrenologists, 50
phylogenetic relationships, 124, 316; phylogenetic scale, 193
physicalism, 188
Pinker, Steven, 184
placebo effect, 203
Plessner, Helmut, 62-63, 64
Pliny, 13, 14, 310
Polkinghorne, John, 137, 311
polygenism, 150

positivism, 77
Povinelli, Daniel, 195
prayer, 284
pre-Adamites, 149
Premack, David, 194
Price, George McCready, 154
"Primal Testament," 136
primates, 27, 107, 108, 112, 116, 117, 118, 119, 120, 122, 124, 125, 127, 128, 130, 139, 140, 142, 145, 146, 147; primate evolution, 118-19; primatology, 12, 22, 26, 325
problem solving, 235, 237, 244, 322; and technological innovation, 238
progressionalism, 155
psychoneuroimmunology, 188
purpose, 4, 135, 155, 316
Putnam, Hilary, 40
pygmies, 15, 20

racists, 15, 310
Ramachandran, V. S., 199
randomness, 4, 129, 135, 136, 137, 316; institutionalized randomness, 136
rationality, 33, 156, 190
reality, 311; aspects of, 79
reason, 94, 177, 191
recognition, 11, 12, 13, 28, 29; recognition-instinct, 12
redemption, 138
reductionism, 4, 33, 34, 36, 42, 73, 74, 77, 188, 311, 312, 313; reductionist sense, 75; reductionist trap, 313
Rees, Sir Dai, 176, 204
reincarnation, 49
relationship, 108, 113, 115, 116, 121, 124, 135, 139, 140, 146, 177; relatedness, 198, 204, 274, 319; relational consciousness, 131
religion, 131; beliefs, 131; devotion, 156; experience, 41, 272; symbol, 237
repentance, 279, 280
res cogitans, 33, 72
res extensa, 72
resurrection body, 292, 293, 312; as glorious, 47

resurrection, 3, 36, 37, 46, 47, 48, 49, 50, 138, 286, 291, 312, 324
retrovirus, 126, 143; endogenous retrovirus (ERV), 126-28
Rizzolatti, Giacomo, 199
Robertson, M. A., 168
robotics, 12, 25, 26
Rogers, Carl, 212
Rose, Nicolas, 43
Rose, Steven, 176
Rothschild, Miriam, 167
Rousseau, Jean-Jacques, 20
Ruse, Michael, 171, 317
Russell, Bertrand, 27

Sahelanthropus, 230, 232
Sandawe, 245
Sartre, Jean-Paul, 216
Scheler, Max, 62-63
Schleiermacher, Friedrich, 305-6
science: scientific image of the world, 78; scientific psychology, 77; scientific truths, 80; scientism, 69, 77; as source of revelation, 272
Scientific Revolution, 47
Scripture. *See* Bible
scrub jays, 200
sculpture, artifacts, 243
Sedgwick, Adam, 152
self-consciousness, 34, 35, 197
self-disclosure, 214-15
self-esteem, 209
self-giving, 158, 196
self-transcendence, 275
Seligman, Martin, 211, 221
"semantic hygiene," 3, 311, 312
Seneca, 214
Seriman, Zaccaria, 20
sexual difference, 6, 295-306, 325. *See also* woman
Sheldon, Kennon, 208
short-term (working) memory, 182
sign language, 235
Singer, Peter, 12, 27, 29, 158
Skateholm, graveyard at, 17
skepticism, 40

skull ossification, 165
S. Maria degli Angeli, 99
Smith, Alexander McCall, 183-84, 203
social: animals as, 321; attention, 182; behavior, 318; group, 320; network, 245; support, 213-21
sociobiology, 1, 157, 158, 172
socio-emotional deprivation, 114, 315
soul, 2, 33, 37, 173, 176, 177, 190, 227, 275, 276; as immaterial, 4, 176, 177, 188, 318, 320; language for talking about, 177-78. *See also* immortality
Spanner, Douglas, 134
species, 11, 12, 15, 16, 17, 25, 27, 28, 29, 98, 110; subspecies, 15
speciesism, 27
Sperry, Roger, 39, 178-79, 189
spindle cells, 320
spirit, spirituality, 47, 49, 71, 75, 131, 133, 177, 181, 236, 256, 322; spiritual body, 291; spiritual dimension, 131, 202, 203; spiritual experience, 285
spiritualism, 49, 73, 170, 171
split-brain, 39
Stagl, Justin, 27
Steeves, H. P., 114
stem-cell research, 45, 171
Stevenson, Leslie, 178
stewardship, 18, 201, 204, 274, 324
subjectivity, 87, 95, 171
substance, 34, 188, 190
suffering, 137-38, 205, 209, 236
supralaryngeal pathway, 162, 166, 317
survival, 5, 84-85, 157, 164, 172, 193, 236, 239, 253, 317, 318, 322; belonging and, 207, 217, 223, 320-21; of spirit, 253, 286, 323
symbols, symbolism, 237; symbolic behavior, 5, 236, 244, 250, 322; symbolic thinking, 238, 244, 322
sympathy, 237

technology, 237, 244, 248, 322
teleology, 93, 100, 101, 135
Temerlin, Maurice, 28
Temple, Frederick, 153

Teniers, 21
theology, and science, 271-72
thinking, in animals, 191
Thiselton, Anthony, 292
Thorpe, W. H., 163
Tipler, Frank J., 50
Tocqueville, Alexis de, 212
Tomasello, Michael, 195, 200
tools, use of, 23-24, 234
totemism, 17
Tower of Badel, 150
traits, 38, 111
transcendentalists, 172
transposons, 126, 145
trauma, experience of, 219
Trockel, Rose-Marie, 22
Tulp, Nicolaes, 19
Tutu, Desmond, 209
Twenge, Jean, 210
Tyson, Edward, 19-20, 227

ultimate questions, 71
uniqueness, human, 90, 191, 194-95
unity, 314, 324; of experience, 73, 77, 80; of the person, 188

values, 30, 66-67, 156, 163, 171, 222-23, 280
van Huyssteen, J. Wentzel, 113, 117, 131
Van Till, Howard, 134
Varki, A., 113
Vatican councils, 2, 301, 326. *See also Gaudium et Spes*
Veatch, Robert, 45

vegetarianism, 168, 317
vision, 116, 119, 122, 140, 141; color vision, 119
visual arts, 313
vomeronasal organ, 122

Wallace, Alfred Russel, 169-71
Warfield, B. B., 153
Warr, Peter, 216
Watson, John W., 44
Watteau, Antoine, 21
Westerholm, Barbro, 204
White, Ellen, 154
Whiten, Andrew, 194
Wiesel, Torsten, 181
Wilkes, Kathleen, 44
Williams, Kipling, 210-11
Willis, Thomas, 271
Wilson, E. O., 157, 172
wisdom, 70, 207, 212, 223, 276, 279, 295, 310, 321, 326
witnessing, to Jesus, 284-85
Wolpert, Lewis, 131
woman, 298, 300-306
Woodruff, Guy, 194
Wrangham, R. W., 169
Wright, G. Ernest, 206
Wright, Sewall, 155
Wyschogrod, Michael, 296

Yovel, Galit, 185

Zeki, Semir, 82, 83, 101, 102n., 314
Zill, Nicholas, 222

www.ingramcontent.com/pod-product-compliance
Lightning Source LLC
Chambersburg PA
CBHW020638300426
44112CB00007B/163